Asia Bible Commentary Series

PSALMS 1–72

OPEN DOOR
Publications Pvt. Ltd

Asia Bible Commentary Series

PSALMS 1–72

Federico G. Villanueva

Contextualization Consultant
Joseph Too Shao

General Editor
Federico G. Villanueva

Old Testament Consulting Editors
Yohanna Katanacho, Tim Meadowcroft, Joseph Shao

New Testament Consulting Editors
Steve Chang, Andrew Spurgeon, Brian Wintle

Published in South Asia 2017 by
Open Door Publications Pvt. Ltd.
Sanjay Park, Rani Road, Udaipur
Rajasthan 313001 INDIA
www.odp.co.in

Published in partnership with Asia Theological Association - ATA
QCC PO Box 1454 – 1154, Manila, Philippines
www.atasia.com

ISBNs:
978-93-85885-07-5 Print
978-93-85885-15-0 Mobi
978-93-85885-16-7 ePub

British Library Cataloguing in Publication Data
A catalogue record for this book is available from the British Library
ISBN: 978-1-78368-191-4

Cover & Book Design: projectluz.com

To Rosemarie, with gratitude and love

CONTENTS

Commentary

Topics

SERIES PREFACE

In recent years, we have witnessed one of the greatest shifts in the history of world Christianity. It used to be that the majority of Christians lived in the West. But now the face of world Christianity has changed beyond recognition. Christians are now evenly distributed around the globe. This has implications for the interpretation of the Bible. In our case, we are faced with the task of interpreting the Bible from within our Asian contexts. This is in line with the growing realization that all theology is contextual. Our understanding of the Bible is influenced by our historical and social locations. Thus, even the questions that we bring to our reading of the Bible are shaped by our present realities. There is a need, therefore, to interpret the Bible for our own contexts.

The Asia Bible Commentary (ABC) series addresses this need. In line with the mission of the Asia Theological Association Publications, we have gathered Asian evangelical Bible scholars in Asia to write commentaries on each book of the Bible. The mission is to "produce resources for pastors, Christian leaders, cross-cultural workers, and students in Asia that are biblical, pastoral, contextual, missional, and prophetic." Although the Bible can be studied for different reasons, we believe that it is given primarily for the edification of the body of Christ (2 Tim 3:16–17). The ABC series is designed to help pastors in their sermon preparation, cell group leaders or lay leaders in their Bible study groups, Christian students in their study of the Bible, and Christians in general in their efforts to apply the Bible in their respective contexts.

Each commentary begins with an introduction that provides general information about the book's author and original context, summarizes the main message or theme of the book, and outlines its potential relevance to a particular Asian context. The introduction is followed by an exposition that combines exegesis and application. Here, we seek to speak to and empower Christians in Asia by using our own stories, parables, poems, and other cultural resources as we expound the Bible.

The Bible is actually Asian in that it comes from ancient West Asia and there are many similarities between the world of the Bible and traditional Asian cultures. But there are also many differences that we need to explore in some depth. That is why the commentaries also include articles or topics in which we bring specific issues in Asian church, social, and religious contexts into dialogue with relevant issues in the Bible. We do not seek to resolve every tension but rather to allow the text to illumine the context and vice versa, acknowledging that in the end we do not have all the answers to every mystery.

May the Holy Spirit who inspired the writers of the Bible bring light to the hearts and minds of all who use these materials, to the glory of God and to the building up of the churches!

Federico G. Villanueva

General Editor

ACKNOWLEDGEMENTS

The writing of this commentary started about five years ago. But the journey goes further back to my years as a pastor. It was in the context of worshiping communities that some of the core ideas in this commentary were conceived. Before I began writing, I was already preaching on the psalms and discussing the psalms of lament with cell groups and prayer meetings. My nine years of pastoral ministry at Life Gospel Church and the many opportunities to preach on Psalms in various local congregations have been a tremendous help in my writing. I am grateful to God for Life Gospel Church, St. Mary Magdalene Church (Bristol, UK), Jesus Cares Christian Fellowship (Bristol), Aikape Christian Church, Capital City Alliance Church, United Evangelical Church of the Philippines, and to my present church, Christian Alliance Fellowship East.

My years as a seminary student and later as a PhD student have also helped me. I thank my mentors: Dr. Rick Love, who not only became my mentor but also my friend; Dr. Russ Stapleton, who co-supervised my ThM thesis; Professor Gordon Wenham (Trinity College, Bristol), for supervising my PhD dissertation on the Psalms and encouraging me in my writing; and Professor John Day (Oxford University) for co-supervising my PhD.

It is said that one of the best ways to learn something is to teach it. Along with preaching, I have also had the privilege of teaching about the Psalms in seminaries and Bible colleges. I would like to thank my students at Alliance Graduate School; Asia Graduate School of Theology; International Graduate School of Leadership; Asian Theological Seminary; Faith, Hope, and Love Seminary; East Asia School of Theology, Singapore; Divine Word Seminary Tagaytay (SVD); and Loyola School of Theology (LST), Ateneo de Manila University. I hope that this commentary will remind them not only of the lectures I delivered but also of deep reflections that came out of our times of learning together.

I thank Dr. Jonathan Exiomo and my colleagues at Alliance Graduate School for allowing me to teach a course on "Psalms for Life and Ministry" and for their support and encouragement. I am blessed to be part of an institution that allows its scholars to devote time to writing. This is important, for while preaching assists us in forming our ideas, we need time and space to put them down in writing.

My writing would not have been possible without the prayers and generous support of a number of individuals and groups and institutions.

Accordingly, I would like to express my special appreciation to:

- Langham Partnership for giving me a grant so that I could devote time to writing, and for its postdoctoral program – the International Research Training Seminar (ITRS). The ITRS provided me not only the space to do my research, but more importantly, a community where my research skills could be further developed. I have richly benefited from and enjoyed the company of my fellow "Langhamites." I thank Ian Shaw, the coordinator of the ITRS, for his leadership and encouragement.
- Wheaton College, Wycliffe Hall in Oxford, and Trinity College Singapore for hosting me as a research fellow.
- Trinity College Bristol, for welcoming me as a research scholar in October 2012.
- My writing group, RootWord, with Dr. Rod Santos and Dr. Mona Bias, for times spent together in writing.
- St. Mary Magdalene Church, through Peter and Jenny Robottom, for their prayers and support.
- Asia Theological Association (ATA) through Dr. Bruce Nicholls.

I thank Dr. Bruce Nicholls for inviting me to write this commentary and the editorial board of the ABC (Old Testament) series – Dr. Joseph Shao, Dr. Andrew Spurgeon, and Dr. Tim Meadowcroft. I am blessed to have a wonderful team in the ATA Publications, with Bubbles Lactaoen who carefully checked the final draft of the manuscript, and Alex Lactaw, our Administrative Assistant. The valuable suggestions of Isobel Stevenson, Dr. Michael Malessa, and the efforts of our English editor, Rose Yu, have been of immense help in improving this book.

As I reflect back, I realize that actually the journey into the writing of this commentary goes back even further: to my father, Bishop Butch Villanueva, from whom I first heard the Bible preached; my mother, Melita Villanueva, who first taught me the stories of David; my brothers Pastor Demo and Pastor Jojo, for their prayers and encouragement; to my children, Emier and Faye, for their patience and love; and most especially to my wife, Rosemarie, who continues to journey with me through all the "lament and praise" not only in the writing of this book but in life itself. It is to her that I dedicate this book.

To God be the glory!

LIST OF ABBREVIATIONS

BOOKS OF THE BIBLE

Old Testament

Gen, Exod, Lev, Num, Deut, Josh, Judg, Ruth, 1–2 Sam, 1–2 Kgs, 1–2 Chr, Ezra, Neh, Esth, Job, Ps/Pss, Prov, Eccl, Song, Isa, Jer, Lam, Ezek, Dan, Hos, Joel, Amos, Obad, Jonah, Mic, Nah, Hab, Zeph, Hag, Zech, Mal

New Testament

Matt, Mark, Luke, John, Acts, Rom, 1–2 Cor, Gal, Eph, Phil, Col, 1–2 Thess, 1–2 Tim, Titus, Phlm, Heb, Jas, 1–2 Pet, 1–2–3 John, Jude, Rev

BIBLE TEXTS AND VERSIONS

Divisions of the canon

NT	New Testament
OT	Old Testament

Ancient texts and versions

Byz	Byzantine
LXX	Septuagint
MT	Masoretic Text
Syr.	Syriac
Vulg.	Vulgate

Modern versions

ESV	English Standard Version
GNB	Good News Bible
JB	Jerusalem Bible
KJV	King James Version
LB	Living Bible
NASB	New American Standard Bible
NEB	New English Version
NET	New English Translation
NIV	New International Version

NJB	New Jerusalem Bible
NJPS	*Tanakh: The Holy Scriptures: The New JPS Translation*
NKJV	New King James Version
NRSV	New Revised Standard Version
PHILLIPS	*The New Testament in Modern English,* J. B. Phillips
REB	Revised Standard Version
RV	Revised Version
RSV	Revised Standard Version
TEV	Today's English Version (= Good News Bible)

Journals, Reference Works, and Series

AB	Anchor Bible
ABC	Asia Bible Commentary
ABCS	Africa Bible Commentary Series
ABD	*Anchor Bible Dictionary*
BBR	*Bulletin for Biblical Research*
BDB	*The Brown-Driver-Briggs Hebrew and English Lexicon of the OT*
BerOl	Berit Olam
Bib	*Biblica*
BibInt	*Biblical Interpretation*
BKAT	Biblischer Kommentar Altes Testament
BST	Bible Speaks Today
CalTJ	*Calvin Theological Journal*
CBQ	*Catholic Biblical Quarterly*
EBC	Expositor's Bible Commentary
EvQ	*Evangelical Quarterly*
ExpTim	*Expository Times*
IB	Interpreter's Bible
ICC	International Critical Commentary
INT	Interpretation: A Bible Commentary for Teaching and Preaching
Int	*Interpretation*
ITC	International Theological Commentary
JSOT	*Journal for the Study of the Old Testament*
JSOTSup	Journal for the Study of Old Testament Supplement Series
NAC	New American Commentary

NCBC	New Century Bible Commentary
NIB	*The New Interpreter's Bible*
NIBC	New International Bible Commentary
NIDOTTE	New International Dictionary of Old Testament Theology and Exegesis
OTL	Old Testament Library
RevExp	*Review and Expositor*
SJOT	*Scandinavian Journal of the Old Testament*
TDOT	Theological Dictionary of the Old Testament
TynBul	*Tyndale Bulletin*
VT	*Vetus Testamentum*
VTSup	Vetus Testamentum Supplements
WBC	Word Biblical Commentary
ZAW	*Zeitschrift für die alttestamentliche Wissenschaft*

INTRODUCTION

We Filipinos have two treasures: our music and our faith.[1] Commenting on this in his welcome address to Pope Francis, Cardinal Tagle said: "Our melodies make our spirits soar above the tragedies of life. Our faith makes us stand up again and again after deadly fires, earthquakes, typhoons, and wars."[2] Thus the book of Psalms, which combines songs and prayer, is very important to us. It is read regularly in the masses attended by Filipino Catholics, who make up more than 80 percent of the population. Pope John XXIII specifically advised Filipinos to read the book of Psalms when representatives from the Philippines had an audience with him in 1959.[3]

Nor is it only Filipinos who love the Psalms. As Professor James L. Kugel of Harvard University remarks:

> No book of the Bible seems to summon up the concerns of spirituality in the biblical period more than the book of Psalms. Its prayers and songs of praise have long served as a model and focus of the spiritual concerns of later ages, and its words have been incorporated into, and indeed have shaped, liturgies in Judaism and Christianity for two millennia.[4]

A BOOK OF PRAISES AND LAMENT

Psalms is a book of songs. Its English title comes from the Greek word *psalmoi*, which means "songs" or "psalms."[5] This was the word that ancient Jewish translators chose to use for this book when they translated the Hebrew Bible into Greek. But in the original Hebrew, the book of Psalms is called *Sefer Tehillim*, which means "Book of Praises."

---

1. Horacio de la Costa made this remark about the Filipino people and it was cited by Cardinal Tagle in his welcome address to Pope Francis when the latter visited the Philippines in January 2015.
2. Luis Antonio G. Cardinal Tagle, "Welcome Address," Manila Cathedral, 16 January 2015. Online: http://www.saltandlighttv.org (accessed 26 March 2015).
3. Jose C. Abriol, "Mga Salmo," *Ang Banal na Biblia* (Manila, Philippines: St. Paul Publications, 1967), 926.
4. James L. Kugel, "Topics in the History of the Spirituality of the Psalms," in *Jewish Spirituality: From the Bible through the Middle Ages*, ed. Arthur Green (New York: Crossroad, 1986), 113.
5. The same word is also used to refer to the sound of musical instruments.

1

Although Psalms was called the Book of Praises, it includes more than just songs of praise. It also includes hymns, royal psalms, psalms of thanksgiving, individual laments, and communal laments.[6] In fact, there are more psalms of lament than psalms of praise! The lament is the most common among the different types of psalms. Although many of the lament psalms contain praise or move on to praise at the end, still the space given to lament in these psalms is remarkable.

The emphasis is similar in our songs. Most traditional Tagalog songs "depict a solemnity of pained somberness indicating a theme of struggle."[7] One reason for this is our own experience of suffering. On average, the Philippines experiences about seventy typhoons a year. Recently, the strongest typhoon in recorded history devastated the country, leaving thousands dead and communities destroyed.

In addition we have had a long history of colonialism, an experience we share with many other countries in Asia, and with the ancient Israelites. They too were subject to foreign powers for many years before and after their exile in 586 BC. Though the psalms were written over a long period of time, it was only after the exile that they were brought together into a book. Those who put the book together must have been greatly affected by the experience of exile (see, e.g. Psalm 137). That is why they gave such prominence to laments in the book of Psalms.[8] They knew that in the end God wins and so there is praise. But they knew through their own experience that the road to the land of praise leads through fields of lament.

SUPERSCRIPTIONS AND SUFFERING

Those who put the book of Psalms into its final form saw their own experiences of suffering reflected in David's life. This can be seen in the superscriptions, the short notes found before the first verse of each psalm. Usually, the

---

6. For more on the different types of psalms, see Hermann Gunkel, *The Psalms: A Form-Critical Introduction* (Philadelphia: Fortress, 1967).

7. Buenaventura S. Medina, *The Primal Passion: Tagalog Literature in the Nineteenth Century* (Manila, Philippines: Centro Escolar University, Research and Development Center, 1976), cited in Josefina D. Constantino, *The Asian Religious Sensibility and Christian (Carmelite) Spirituality* (Quezon City, Philippines: The University of the Philippines Press, 1983), 328.

8. For a study of the emphasis on lament in the Psalms, see Federico G. Villanueva, *The "Uncertainty of a Hearing": A Study of the Sudden Change of Mood in the Psalms of Lament*, Supplements to Vetus Testamentum (Leiden: Brill, 2008). Compare Claus Westermann, *Praise and Lament in the Psalms*, trans. Keith R. Crim and Richard N. Soulen (Atlanta: John Knox Press, 1981).

superscriptions simply identify to whom the psalm is attributed (e.g. "Of David").[9] But the superscriptions of thirteen psalms (3, 7, 18, 34, 51, 52, 54, 56, 57, 59, 60, 63, and 142) give brief historical background linking the psalm to an incident in the life of David. For example, the superscription to Psalm 3 reads, "A Psalm of David, when he fled from his son Absalom"; and that of Psalm 51 reads, "A psalm of David, when the prophet Nathan came to him after David had committed adultery with Bathsheba."

Why do the superscriptions refer to David's struggles rather than to his victories? The answer is because his struggles resonate more with people's experiences. Like David, we are plagued by many difficulties and we can see in him a model for dealing with our own troubles. As Old Testament (OT) scholar Brevard Childs puts it:

> The incidents chosen as evoking the psalms were not royal occasions or representative of the kingly office. Rather, David is pictured simply as a man, indeed chosen by God for the sake of Israel, but who displays all strengths and weaknesses of all human beings. He emerges as a person who experiences the full range of human emotions from fear and despair to courage and love, from complaint and plea to praise and thanksgiving . . . The psalms are transmitted as the sacred psalms of David, but they testify to all the common troubles and joys of ordinary human life in which all persons participate.[10]

This is the reason why many people today are drawn to the psalms. In their words we not only see our own struggles; they also lead us to the God who is able to accompany us in our difficulties.

---

9. We do not know whether all the psalms that have the name David in the superscription were actually written by David. The phrase translated "of David" could be translated to David," "by David, "for David," "about David," "belonging to David" or "belonging to David's collection of psalms." Some of the psalms labeled "Of David" contain verses referring to events that occurred long after he had died. For example, Psalm 51:18–19, which talks about the rebuilding of the walls of Jerusalem, could not have been written by David. It is possible that what we have here is a psalm originally written by David which had been re-used or applied by later generations. In thinking about these issues, it is important to bear in mind that authorship was not a big issue in ancient times as it is today. What is clear is that the editors of the book of Psalms saw in David the inspiration behind many of these psalms and were able to identify with the experiences of David.

10. Brevard S. Childs, *Introduction to the Old Testament as Scripture* (Philadelphia: Fortress, 1979), 521.

PRAYING THE PSALMS

All of us are confronted by uncertainties and situations that are way beyond what we can manage. And so we often cry to God for help. Thankfully, the Psalms is not just a book of songs; it is also a book of prayers. While "most of Scripture speaks *to* us, the Psalms speak *for* us."[11] In times when we do not know what to say because of the troubles that overwhelm us, we can take the words of the Psalms and make them our own. In doing this, we are following the example of Jesus, who himself prayed the psalms on the cross (Matt 27:46 quotes Ps 22:1; Luke 23:46 quotes Ps 31:5). Thus he also invites us to do the same.

Moreover, when his disciples asked Jesus to teach them how to pray, he did not give them a lecture on prayer. Instead, he gave them a prayer: the famous "Our Father" (Luke 11:1–4; see also Matt 6:9–13). It has been suggested that his answer to their question "is a precedent for turning to the specific prayers in the book of Psalms."[12]

Believers in the New Testament (NT) took heed of Jesus' invitation.[13] The Apostle Paul speaks of believers singing "psalms and hymns and spiritual songs" (Eph 5:19). The book of Revelation gives us a glimpse of the martyrs praying with words very similar to those found in the lament psalms: "How long, Sovereign Lord, holy and true, until you judge the inhabitants of the earth and avenge our blood?" (Rev 6:9–10; compare Ps 13:1–2).

Centuries later, St. Benedict (sixth century) introduced the practice of reciting specific psalms at six designated hours for prayer. This meant that each monk prayed the entire book of Psalms at least once a week! The Protestant reformers Martin Luther and John Calvin also had a high regard for the Psalms. Calvin referred to the book as the "anatomy of all the parts of the soul" because in it every emotion is represented before God. Luther considered the Psalms a mini-Bible because it contains the whole message of the Bible.

It was only from the eighteenth century onwards that the use of the Psalms in worship and prayer started to fade as people like Isaac Watts and Charles Wesley composed hymns. At first, Christians sang the hymns as well

---

11. Athanasius, cited in Ernest Lucas, *Exploring the Old Testament*. Vol. 3 (Downers Grove: IVP, 2003), 1.
12. James L. Mays, *Preaching and Teaching the Psalms,* eds. Patrick D. Miller and Gene M. Tucker (Louisville: Westminster John Knox Press, 2006), 3.
13. This and subsequent paragraphs are based on Gordon Wenham, *The Psalter Reclaimed: Praying and Praising with the Psalms* (Wheaton: Crossway, 2013), 37–55.

as the Psalms. But with the arrival of choruses and the so-called "praise and worship" movement, the Psalms were dropped from the worship of most Protestant groups. Such was not the case with the Catholic churches where the Psalms continue to be read.

The neglect of the Psalms in Protestant congregations has led to a distorted view of prayer. As Wenham comments: "I am not against hymns or modern worship songs. Some of them are really great, but if we sing only them, I think we get a very limited experience of worship, indeed a harmful imbalance in our praying and singing."[14] The Psalms provide us with important models for our prayers. Even though we have instructions or teachings on prayer in the NT, we seldom find an actual prayer. We need to go to the OT, especially to the book of Psalms, to find the actual prayers which can serve as our pattern for praying.[15] For instance, the NT instructs us to pray for kings and rulers (1 Tim 2:1–2). In Psalm 72 we have a prayer for a king (see comments in Ps 72). The NT teaches about confession of sins (1 John 1:9; Jas 5:16). But what does an actual prayer of confession look like? Psalm 51 and the other prayers of penitence (e.g. Ps 32) provide us with an excellent model. Thus, the NT teachings on prayer and the Psalms complement each other. Psalms also contains prayers for specific needs. There is a psalm for a sick person (Ps 38), for an elderly person (Ps 72), and for others. Indeed, there is a psalm for every season of life.[16]

LIVING THE PSALMS: THE PSALMS AS GOD'S WORD

What makes the book of Psalms unique is that it contains both the words of people to God (prayers) and God's word to his people. Because this book is part of Scripture, Christians believe it is also a message from God (2 Tim 3:16). The Psalms is a place where God and his people can converse. As we pray the words of the psalms, God is also revealed to us. The prayers and

---

14. Wenham, *The Psalter Reclaimed*, 40.

15. There are also a number of prayers scattered in the narrative sections of the Bible. According to Greenberg, "praying and prayers are mentioned, outside of the Psalms, about 140 times." Ninety-seven of these contain verbal formulation of the prayers (Moshe Greenberg, *Biblical Prose Prayer as a Window to the Popular Religion of Ancient Israel* [Berkeley: University of California Press, 1983], 7). For a list of the prayers, see p. 59, n. 3.

16. Walter Brueggemann, *The Message of the Psalms: A Theological Commentary* (Minneapolis: Augsburg, 1984).

songs preserved in the Psalms reflect the kind of God we serve, for the words that the faithful utter to God are like a mirror that reflects God himself.[17]

For example, the requirements set for entrance to God's holy hill in Psalm 15 indicate the kind of worshipers God wants, and thus tells us the kind of God we have. Since God is holy, those who come into his presence ought to live holy lives. The lament psalms, which contain some of the most disturbing words of prayer, reveal the character of God as one who is compassionate and merciful. Like a good counselor, he allows those who go through extreme difficulties to pour out their hearts to him, even uttering words ordinary humans would not allow. Cries of abandonment become the embrace of the loving Almighty. Likewise, the songs of praise highlight the God of power and might who has worked in and through the lives of his people. Thus the book of Psalms contains both prayer and theology.

The very structure of the book of Psalms signifies that those who put it together considered it God's word. These unknown editors took the individual psalms composed by various writers and arranged them in five "books," each of which ends with a doxology:[18]

Book 1	Psalms 1–41	(doxology – 41:13)
Book 2	Psalms 42–72	(doxology – 72:18–19)
Book 3	Psalms 73–89	(doxology – 89:52)
Book 4	Psalms 90–106	(doxology – 105:45)
Book 5	Psalms 107–150	(doxology – Psalm 150)

By dividing the psalms into five books, the compilers seem to have been attempting to link them with the five books of Moses (Genesis, Exodus, Leviticus, Numbers, and Deuteronomy). They were asserting that like these

---

17. Walther Zimmerli, *Old Testament Theology in Outline* (Edinburgh: T&T Clark, 1978), 141. See also Gerhard von Rad, *Old Testament Theology*, Vol. 1 (Edinburgh and London: Oliver and Boyd, 1962), 355–356. Von Rad considers the response of God's people to God found in the book of Psalms as "theologically a subject in itself. It shows us how these acts affected Israel, and how Israel on her side accepted and understood this existence in immediacy with Jahweh and in proximity to him, that is, the steps which, in this proximity to Jahweh, she took to justify or to be ashamed of herself, in her own eyes and before Jahweh" (von Rad, *Old Testament Theology*, 155–156).

18. Psalm 150 serves as the doxology for both Book 5 and the whole book of Psalms. We do not know why specific psalms are in specific books, but in recent decades some scholars have suggested possible purposes in the ordering of the Psalms. The most popular theory is that of Gerald Wilson, who argues that there is a story that runs from Book 1 to the final book. This story is the rise and fall of the Davidic kingship, which points to the kingship of the Lord. See Gerald Henry Wilson, *The Editing of the Hebrew Psalter* (Chico, California: Scholars Press, 1985).

books, the words of the Psalms are a message from God. It is thus no coincidence that the very first psalm (Ps 1) speaks about the "law of the LORD" and that this is also the topic of the longest psalm (Ps 119).[19] Thus the Psalms is not just a book of prayer and praises; like the Torah it also teaches us about God's law. It follows that the Psalms not only help us in our prayers; they also teach us how to live.

As God's word, the psalms are both effective and challenging. The very act of praying them orients individuals and communities and challenges them to realign their lives in accordance with the sentiments expressed. John Chrysostom, the fourth century archbishop of Constantinople, makes this point well when commenting on the refrain in Psalm 42:

> Do not think that you have come here simply to say the words, but when you make the response, consider that response to be a covenant. For when you say, 'Like the heart desires the watersprings, my soul desires you, O God,' you make a covenant with God. You have signed a contract without paper or ink, you have confessed with your voice that you love him more than all, that you prefer nothing to him, and that you burn with love for him.[20]

Here lies the challenge of the book of Psalms. We are called not just to pray its words but to actually live them out. This is very important in our Filipino-Asian context. For though we are very religious, our country is also very corrupt. We like to pray but we are not prepared to follow the Way. One reason for this is that we have not "deeply interiorized" the word. As the Carmelite nun Josefina D. Constantino writes: "The Word of God has come to people only in Gospels read or sermons preached during Sunday mass; but meditation as a way of listening to the Word speaking to the heart and to the conscience of man has been a very recent awakening in the Philippines."[21]

MEDITATING ON THE PSALMS

Although the book of Psalms contains teaching and preaching material, its teachings are embedded in poetry. We are drawn to its words of beauty. To meditate on and apply the book of Psalms we thus need to appreciate its

---

19. Some believe that at one point in the development of the Psalms, the book ended with Psalm 119.
20. Howard N. Wallace, *Words to God, Word from God: The Psalms in the Prayer and Preaching of the Church* (Burlington: Ashgate, 2004), 9.
21. Constantino, *The Asian Religious Sensibility*, 338.

nature as a work of poetry which can open our eyes to new ways of seeing our world.

As a means of communication, poetry is the most compact form of speech. According to Robert Alter, "poetry . . . is an instrument for conveying densely patterned meanings, and sometimes contradictory meanings, that are not readily conveyable through other kinds of discourse."[22] Thus it comes as no surprise that "poetry places greater demands on us than straightforward prose. It requires a more contemplative approach and requires more continuous interpretation than ordinary language."[23] Leland Ryken continues: "Biblical poetry is a meditative mode. The point in reading it is not to finish as quickly as possible but to let the fullness of the meanings filter into our consciousness."[24]

When we read the Psalms, we need to pause. We cannot be in a hurry. We need to read each psalm slowly and carefully. Ryken instructs us to never be "ashamed at staring at a poem . . . looking closely, long, and repeatedly at a poem until the patterns and meanings of the figures of speech start to reveal themselves."[25] Our goal is to be able to enter into the psalm.

Poetry is about experience: "Poetry takes all life as its province. Its primary concern is not with beauty, not with philosophical truth, not with persuasion, but with experience."[26] We need to be able to identify with the experiences depicted in the imagery and feel the emotions expressed. When we read a psalm, we must pay careful attention to the shifts in mood within that psalm.[27]

Filipinos have been referred to as the most emotional people in the world, and so they may have little difficulty in responding to the emotional aspects of the poetry of the psalms. But on a practical level, our appreciation of the poetry will be deeper if we have some knowledge on how Hebrew poetry works.[28]

---

22. Robert Alter, *The Art of Biblical Poetry* (New York: Basic, 1985), 113.
23. Leland Ryken, *Words of Delight: A Literary Introduction to the Bible* (2d ed.; Grand Rapids: Baker, 1992), 159.
24. Ryken, *Words of Delight*, 215.
25. Ibid.
26. Laurence Perrine, *Sound and Sense: An Introduction to Poetry* (New York: Harcourt Brace Jovanovich, 1977), 9.
27. Adele Berlin, "Introduction to Hebrew Poetry," in *NIB* (vol. 4; Nashville: Abingdon, 1996), 314.
28. It is beyond the scope of this commentary to provide a detailed discussion of the poetry of the Psalms. The reader is referred to the works of Robert Alter and Leland Ryken (see above).

The most common feature of biblical poetry is parallelism, which has traditionally been subdivided into synonymous, antithetical, and synthetic parallelism.[29] However, recent scholars have proposed that instead of limiting ourselves to these three categories, we should focus instead on analyzing how the second line develops the thought/idea in the first line.[30] Robert Alter puts it like this:

> The dominant pattern is a focusing, heightening, or specification of ideas, images, actions, themes, from one verse to the next. If something is broken in the first verset, it is smashed or shattered in the second verset . . . A general term in the first half of a line is typically followed by a specific instance of the general category in the second half . . . What this means to us as readers of biblical poetry is that instead of listening to an imagined drumbeat of repetitions, we need constantly to look for something new happening from one part of the line to the next.[31]

Here are some examples that illustrate what this looks like in practice:

> The voice of the LORD breaks the cedars,
> the LORD breaks in pieces the cedars of Lebanon. (Ps 29:5)

Notice that "the voice of the Lord" in the first line becomes "the Lord" himself in the second line. There is also a development from general ("cedars") to specific ("cedars of Lebanon").

Another example comes from Psalm 1:

> But whose delight is in the law of the LORD,
> and who meditates on his law day and night. (Ps 1:2)

The first line talks about the fact that the righteous person delights in the law of the Lord. But what does it mean to delight in God's law? The second line provides the answer: it is in meditating on the law day and night. Those who say they delight in the law of the Lord but never spend time meditating on it do not actually delight in God's law (see commentary of Psalm 1 below for further discussion).

---

29. Robert Lowth, *Lectures on the Sacred Poetry of the Hebrews,* trans. G. Gregory, a new edition with notes (Andover: Crocker & Brewster, 1829).
30. James L. Kugel, *The Idea of Biblical Poetry: Parallelism and Its History* (New Haven: Yale University Press, 1981).
31. Alter, *The Art of Biblical Poetry*, 615–616.

As we read and meditate on the psalms, we should remember that the beauty of poetry is that it is not specific, and thus allows for various possibilities of meanings and application.

> Biblical verse is elusive and open-ended; it adheres to some (known) poetic conventions, yet it also reflects much original and creative freedom of its own. Its diction is full of ambiguity of meaning. As with all poetry, but perhaps especially in this case, the concealing/revealing aspect of biblical verse means that any interpretation involves as much the power of imaginative insight as any so-called 'objective' analysis. On this account, contemporary meaning and a creative discourse between the text and the reader are not only possible but also desirable.[32]

READING THE PSALMS IN ASIA

Because they are poetry, the psalms allow and even encourage readings that take into consideration the context of the reader.[33] This realization fits well with the growing recognition that we all read the text of the Bible from our own contexts. Given our differences in culture, language, geographical locations, and the like, our reading will inevitably have different shades of emphasis. There is no such a thing as a universal reading where one interpretation applies to all. Our interpretation will reflect our own needs, worldviews, and realities.[34]

Since this commentary has been written within the Asian context, it is important to consider what it means to read the Psalms in such a context, and specifically within my own Filipino-Asian context. I cannot speak for the whole of Asia, because Asia is very diverse. Moreover, even the very concept of "Asia" itself is complex.[35] Nonetheless, there are common things

---

32. Susan E. Gillingham, *The Poems and Psalms of the Hebrew Bible* (Oxford, UK: Oxford University Press, 1994), 277. Compare Paul R. Raabe, "Deliberate Ambiguity in the Psalter," *Journal of Biblical Literature* 110, no. 2 (1991): 213–227.

33. In scholarship, this is sometimes phrased in terms of a shift in focus from the meaning behind the text (Author), to the meaning within the text (Text), to the meaning in front of the text (Reader). See Charles H. H. Scobie, "Biblical Theology and Preaching," in *Out of Egypt: Biblical Theology and Biblical Interpretation*, ed. Craig G. Bartholomew et al. (Grand Rapids: Zondervan, 2004), 454–455.

34. Philip Jenkins, "Reading the Bible in the Global South," *International Bulletin of Missionary Research* 30, no. 2 (2006): 67–73.

35. Daniel Franklin Pilario, "Spirituality and Postmodernity in Asia," in *Spirituality of Authentic Witnesses in Postmodern Asia*, ed. Spirituality Forum and Institute of Spirituality in

that bind us. One of these is that although many of us do not have many material resources, we are rich in life experiences. So let us look at these Asian resources we can draw on as we attempt to read the Psalms within our particular context.[36]

Our community

Asia is about people. The Asian people themselves are an important resource for interpretation. Samuel Rayan puts it well: "Asians themselves, their experience of life and their rich humanness are the main source of an Asian theology. The courage and the strength that have enabled Asians to survive, despite material destitution and great physical and mental suffering . . . the hope that sustains them and the hope that they sustain"[37] – this is one of our resources. We have a strong sense of community. The truth of John Donne's "no man is an island" runs deep in the heart of every Asian. We have a saying in Filipino, "*Sakit ng kalingkingan, dama ng buong katawan.*" ("The pain of the smallest finger is felt by the whole body"). That is why we continue to survive despite our difficulties. Because we know what it means to have nothing, we have a deep sense of compassion, especially for the vulnerable.

Our deep spirituality

Our sufferings and our poverty make us more open not only to others but also to God, as reflected in our rich spirituality. Aloysius Pieris has even said that poverty and spirituality are the twin realities that define Asia.[38] All the world's major religions were born in Asia. Constantino remarks: "The Asian is a person full of soul or of the sense of the sacred. It is as though he is forever plugged into the life of the universe, into the source of all life, and because life is sacred, into the source of life: the Sacred."[39] Visit Indonesia even for a day or two, and you will be transported to a different world. You will hear chants and calls to prayer throughout the day, from before sunrise until after sunset. Visit Thailand, and you will be amazed by people in saffron robes,

Asia, Spirituality Forum (Quezon City, Philippines: Institute of Spirituality in Asia, 2007), 24–52. See also R. S. Sugirtharajah, *The Bible and Asia: From the Pre-Christian Era to the Postcolonial Age* (Cambridge, Mass.: Harvard University Press, 2013), 1–3.
36. The following is adapted from my article, "Reading the Psalms with Asian Resources," *Journal of Asian Evangelical Theology* 17, no. 1 (2013): 35–50.
37. Samuel Rayan, "Reconceiving Theology in the Asian Context," in *Doing Theology in a Divided World*, eds. Virginia Fabella and Sergio Torres (Maryknoll, NY: Orbis, 1985), 132.
38. Aloysius Pieris, *An Asian Theology of Liberation* (Maryknoll, NY: Orbis, 1988).
39. Constantino, *The Asian Religious Sensibility*, 291.

from children to the elderly, both Buddhist priests and those training to be priests. Religion and daily life, spirituality and the material world, are one and the same. There is no such thing as a dichotomy between the secular and the sacred. In Asia, religion is a part of life from the cradle to the grave.

Our experience of suffering

Sadly, life for many Asians has been full of hardship because of poverty and the consequences of colonialism. Many Asian countries were once colonies. They still bear the scars of abuse, oppression, and dehumanization.[40] The Philippines was under the Spaniards for more than three hundred years. Before they came and conquered our land, Filipinos had a high view of themselves.[41] When the colonizers came, our dignity was trampled to the ground. We became like a bird imprisoned in a cage. One of our Filipino lament songs expresses the agony of being a colonized people: "*Ibon mang may layang lumipad, kulungin mo at umiiyak*" ("Even a bird which has the freedom to fly cries when it is caged"). For many years our people cried for liberty, for freedom. We finally got it, but not before America and Japan had their turn as colonizers. Now we have our freedom, and many of the present generation are not even aware of our history of colonization. But those hundreds of years of subjugation have left their mark on us. We are a broken people. Even now we remain a suffering nation.

Unfortunately, in many churches in Asia we usually hear only testimonies about victory or success. The same thing is true with our songs. In many Asian evangelical churches, most of our worship songs come from the West. Though some of these are good, they do not speak to our experiences as a suffering people. As a result, some find it difficult to identify with them.

As mentioned above, one reason the book of Psalms speaks so powerfully and deeply is because it came out of the people's experiences of suffering. We do not have to be ashamed of our own suffering, because this actually helps us understand the Psalms better. We are actually rich in resources for reading the Psalms. I suggest that we bring our deep sense of community, spirituality, and experiences of suffering with us as we approach the book of Psalms.

---

40. George M. Soares-Prabhu, "Two Mission Commands: An Interpretation of Matthew 28:16–20 in the Light of a Buddhist Text," *BibInt* 2, no. 3 (1994), 269; Rayan, "Reconceiving Theology in the Asian Context," 125–126.
41. Constantino, *The Asian Religious Sensibility*.

READING THE PSALMS WITH ASIAN RESOURCES

What reading of the book of Psalms will emerge when we bring our Asian resources with us?

Communal reading

First of all, I think that our reading will be more communal both in its overall approach to the book of Psalms and in its actual reading of a particular psalm.[42] This reading will tend to see the community rather than the individual. One of the biggest questions that occupied Western scholars studying the book of Psalms in the early part of the twentieth century was, Who is the "I" who speaks in the psalms?[43] They wanted to know whether the "I" is the king or another individual.

In contrast, I think Asians will ask a different question. Instead of the "I," they will think of the "we."[44] And this actually fits better with the way in which the "I" is perceived in the Psalms. The "I" is not someone who stands alone, separate from the others. The "I" is a representative of the community. Even when the "I" is speaking or praying, he is actually not praying alone; he is with the community or the community is with him. The individual suffers and rejoices with the community. Suffering alone in the privacy of one's own room is alien both to the community of Israel and to Asians.

In his book, *The Faith of the Psalmists*, Helmer Ringgren refers to the "religion of fellowship."[45] So central is fellowship for the Israelites that even in their prayer they anticipate the day when they can finally share with the "great congregation" what Yahweh has done. Blessings received are not only for private consumption; they are for the community to share. Ringgren writes, "God's gracious help is not a private matter; it concerns not only the individual but the whole community."[46] Similarly, Hans-Joachim Kraus

---

42. For an example of the communal reading of a psalm, see F. H. Welshman, "Psalm 91 in Relation to a Malawian Cultural Background," *Journal of Theology for Southern Africa* 8 (1974): 24–30. Though this reflects an African setting, Asians can easily identify with the practice of reading a psalm together.
43. John Herbert Eaton, "The Psalms and Israelite Worship," in *Tradition and Interpretation*, ed. George W. Anderson (Oxford: Oxford University Press, Clarendon Press, 1979), 255, provides a brief survey of the different positions regarding the "I."
44. In taking this position, I am not saying that there is no value in thinking in terms of the "I." The Western emphasis on the "I" can serve as a corrective to an overemphasis on community.
45. This is the title of one of the chapters in Helmer Ringgren's book, *The Faith of the Psalmists* (London: SCM Press, 1963).
46. Ringgren, *The Faith of the Psalmists*, 21.

observes, "There is no private piety in the book of Psalms. Every expression has its roots and its presuppositions, its basis of faith and its assurance of fulfillment in the community of Israel."[47] Gerhard von Rad asserts that the individual in the book of Psalms does not suffer alone:

> In the sphere of worship . . . the relationship of the individual to the type [lament] could positively not be abandoned, for in it and in it alone was his link with the community preserved. What the individual bemoaned was thus not exclusively his own distress. He never regarded it as his own alone, and he therefore expressed it in words and ideas taken from the liturgy. In so doing, he could enter the ranks of the invisible company of those who had had similar or comparable suffering and who had been heard, and in the words of such prayer others too might in turn 'find a lodging for the night of sorrow.'[48]

Because of the individualism that has formed such an important part of Western culture for the past two centuries, most Western academics struggle to come to terms with this aspect of the book of Psalms, certainly in regard to suffering. Walter Brueggemann admits, "We have learned [through the works of writers like Elisabeth Kübler-Ross] that letting go is fundamental to moving on. But we have yet to learn in any way about grief as a public practice."[49] This is where the poor in Asia have more resources; they know what it means to suffer together.[50] Without denying the ill effects of poverty,[51] John Dijkstra writes about the poor in Asia:

> They have faith in their fellow poor, a rare value in non-poor individuals who isolate themselves from one another . . . They strengthen their mutual dependence and use their gracious human values to serve their community beyond individualistic desires and needs. Those who want to live egotistically among the poor cannot last long in these communities . . . The poor are

---

47. Hans-Joachim Kraus, *Worship in Israel: A Cultic History of the Old Testament*, trans. Geoffrey Buswell (Atlanta: John Knox Press, 1965), 219.

48. Gerhard von Rad, *Old Testament Theology*, 399.

49. Walter Brueggemann, *Hopeful Imagination: Prophetic Voices in Exile* (Philadelphia: Fortress, 1986), 33.

50. I have actually witnessed communal lament in my own church in Manila. See Federico G. Villanueva, "Preaching Lament," in *Reclaiming the Old Testament for Christian Preaching*, ed. Grenville J. R. Kent et al. (Downers Grove: IVP Academic, 2010), 64–84.

51. The poor are sometimes forced to commit robbery and other acts against their neighbor because of need. In Filipino we call this *kapit sa patalim* (literally, "hold on to the knife").

more defenseless, vulnerable . . . are more cared for and served
. . . They enjoy together any good that comes to their fellow
poor . . . They know one another thoroughly . . . Their human
potentials are allowed to be used together for their common
good . . . The Asian poor have faith not only in their fellow poor
but also in their caring God and Lord.[52]

Because of our situation of need that can be quite extreme, the questions we
ask of the text tend to come from our actual experiences. Like the psalmist's
lament, they come from the depths. We do not have the time to speculate
about how many angels can dance on a pin. We cannot afford to ask questions of the text which do not resonate with our own experiences. Ivory-
tower speculation will have no place in our reading of the book of Psalms.

Spiritual reading

Springing from our deep sense of spirituality, an Asian reading of the psalms
will be concerned with how they can draw us closer to God. It will be a spiritual reading. By this I mean a type of reading that is appropriate to the Psalms'
dual nature as prayer to God and word of God, spoken by the believing
community but speaking to that community as well. As noted above, from
OT times to the present, the book of Psalms has been the prayer book of the
faithful.[53] It is also the word of God, so conceived by those who brought its
texts together and so presented by virtue of its place in the Christian canon.

Unfortunately, since the Enlightenment, the book of Psalms, like the rest
of the Bible, has often been read in a way that runs counter to its spiritual nature. With the historical-critical approach as the dominant method, the book
of Psalms has been treated like a frog on a laboratory bench. In the process,
as with the frog, we have learned a great deal about the psalms, but in the end
our study of their text, like our dissection of the frog, has reduced a living
thing to a corpse. The Enlightenment had little place for the supernatural and
the spiritual, only for the historical, here understood one-sidedly in terms
of human history.[54] George Soares-Prabhu is right: as long as the historical

---

52. "The Poor in Asia," *Information on Human Development*, 8/9 (September 1981): 8–9;
cited in Rayan, "Reconceiving Theology in the Asian Context," 132. See also, Benigno P.
Beltran, *Faith and Struggle on Smokey Mountain: Hope for a Planet in Peril* (Maryknoll, NY:
Orbis, 2013).
53. William L. Holladay, *The Psalms through Three Thousand Years* (Minneapolis: Fortress, 1993).
54. Anthony C. Thiselton, *Hermeneutics: An Introduction* (Grand Rapids: Eerdmans, 2009), 124.

method is the dominant mode for reading the Bible, there will be no Asian theology.[55] And let me add, an Asian reading of the book of Psalms will be impossible. I do not mean to suggest that we should discard the historical method. As Soares-Prabhu points out, the historical method can help us to fight dogmatism, as it has in the West.[56] But the historical method cannot be our main approach to reading the book of Psalms. What we need is a kind of reading that can be described as "spiritual" or "religious," in keeping both with the nature of the book of Psalms and with the deep Asian sense of spirituality.

One of our blessings as Asian Christians is that we are surrounded by people of other faiths who, like us, have their own sacred scriptures. These too are among our resources for doing theology and reading the book of Psalms.[57] We can learn much from the way those of other religions read their scriptures. In an important study, Paul Griffiths describes how early Buddhists and Christians interacted with those texts. Their reading was characterized by delight and a sense of reverence. They memorized what they read; their text was the memorized text. This contrasts sharply with the modern consumerist reading of such material:

> Consumers treat what they read only as objects for consumption, to be discarded when the end for which they are read has been achieved . . . Academic readers consume the works of others and produce their own; they are defined and given status by the body of literature they control and upon which they are accredited to give authoritative (expert) voice for proper reward; they cite and mention (rather than religiously read), and are in turn judged largely by the extent to which the works they produce . . . are cited and mentioned.[58]

Religious reading is totally different. First of all, "the work read is understood as a stable and vastly rich resource."[59] Religious readers consider the sacred text to be "a treasure-house, an ocean, a mine."[60] "For the religious reader, the work read is an object of overpowering delight and great beauty. It can

---

55. Soares-Prabhu, "Two Mission Commands," 265.
56. Ibid., 336.
57. Rayan, "Reconceiving Theology in the Asian Context," 135.
58. Paul J. Griffiths, *Religious Reading: The Place of Reading in the Practice of Religion* (Oxford: New York: Oxford University Press, 1999), 42.
59. Ibid., 41.
60. Ibid.

never be discarded because it can never be exhausted."[61] The book of Psalms expresses the same outlook:[62]

> Oh, how I love your law!
> It meditate on it all day long. (Ps 119:97)

"Religious readers therefore treat what they read with reverence."[63] Naturally, they consider the Scriptures to be authoritative. They recognize the three criteria of religious texts – comprehensiveness, unsurpassability, and centrality[64] – throughout the Scriptures. That is why approaches to the book of Psalms and to the Bible in general that tend to undermine its authority are actually alien to the Asian way of reading. This includes postcolonial interpretation, which "arguably tends to diminish the Bible."[65] Moonjang Lee argues that postcolonialism's suggestion that the Bible's authority be relativized will not be supported by Asians themselves, who have a high regard for their Scriptures.

> The attempt to relativize scriptural authority in the Asian hermeneutical discourse does not seem to be successful because traditional understanding of sacred books in Asia would safeguard the biblical authority within the Christian faith community. In this sense the Asian critique of scriptural authority fails to reflect the Asian religious ethos.[66]

Approaches that view the book of Psalms as the word of God and see it as an invaluable source for the life of the community of faith will be at home with the traditional Asian way of reading. Lee believes that "Asia's rich and diverse religious heritage could help the church recover, for example, the spiritual reading of Scripture found among the church fathers."[67] This kind of reading

---

61. Ibid., 42.
62. Gordon J. Wenham, "Prayer and Practice in the Psalms," in *Psalms and Prayers*, eds. Bob Becking and Eric Peels (Leiden: Brill, 2007), 283.
63. Griffiths, *Religious Reading*, 42.
64. Ibid., 6.
65. Thiselton, *Hermeneutics*, 277. Thiselton sees postcolonial hermeneutics as strongly reactionary to the Western reading of the Bible (Ibid., 272). I think it is time for us to move beyond such a reactionary stance and toward a view of the Bible that is more at home with the Asian way of reading.
66. Moonjang Lee, "Asian Biblical Interpretation," in *Dictionary for Theological Interpretation of the Bible*, ed. Kevin J. Vanhoozer (Grand Rapids: Baker, 2005), 69.
67. Moonjang Lee, "Asian Theology," in *Global Dictionary of Theology*, eds. William A. Dyrness and Veli-Matti Kärkkäinen (Downers Grove: IVP, 2008), 76.

is not only concerned with the historical background of the text but aims more for the transformation of the faithful. In other words, it is pastoral.

Pastoral reading

Reading the book of Psalms in Asia will be pastoral. In a study of biblical interpretation among the Chinese, John Yieh cites three "recurring hermeneutical assumptions":

> 1) The purpose of interpretation may be different (to save souls, to reform the society, or to save the nation), but the relevance of Scripture to the life of the reader is always treated with urgency. For Chinese Christians, Scripture is believed to be revelatory text, so biblical study is always existential, not simply academic.
> 2) The cultivation of personal character, moral and spiritual, is assumed to be the ultimate concern of biblical interpretation . . .
> 3) The perfection of personal character, it is further assumed, will eventually transform the entire society and strengthen the nation.[68]

The same thing is true with the Filipino way of reading. In the *Pasyon*[69] – a narrative of the sufferings of Jesus that is recited during Holy Week – we see this strong emphasis on application. Each of the *Pasyon*'s major sections contains a section called "Aral" (Lesson) in which the writer addresses the audience as to the proper response to what they have just heard. Throughout the *Pasyon* the author moves very naturally from exposition to application.

We do not separate "what the text meant" from "what it means." After all, doing theology in Asia has always been both a pastoral and a missiological task. According to Hwa Yung, "historically, Asian theological reflections have emerged in the context of mission."[70] He goes on to say that "Any authentic

---

68. John Y. H. Yieh, "Chinese Biblical Interpretation: History and Issues," in *Ways of Being, Ways of Reading: Asian American Biblical Interpretation,* eds. Mary F. Foskett and Jeffrey K. Kuan (St. Louis: Chalice, 2006), 30.

69. *Awit at salaysay ng pasiong mahal ni Hesukristong Panginoon natin: Sukat ipag-alab ng puso ng sinumang babasa : Pasiong Henesis/Nilinis sa kautusan ng Exmo. at Ilmo. Sr. D. Fr. Jose Segue, Arzobispo sa Maynila, ng M.-R. ex-Provincial Fr. Manuel Grijalvo sa orden ni S. Agustin, ama natin ; ipinalimbag ng isang devoto tungkol sa kapurihan ng Diyos at pakinabang ng Kristiano; sa kagandahang loob ni Amador W. Cruz, ay sinuri at isinaayos ang mga titik na Latin ng Pasiong mahal.* ([Sta. Cruz, Manila]: printed by Sto. Niño Catholic House, 2011).

70. Hwa Yung, *Mangoes or Bananas?: The Quest for an Authentic Asian Christian Theology* (Oxford, England: Regnum International, 1997), 18.

indigenous theology – indeed, any theology for that matter – must be missiological and pastoral in its fundamental conception."[71]

In line with this pastoral emphasis, an Asian reading will be concerned with the message of the book of Psalms for the community of faith as well as for the wider society. In this sense, we not only bring our resources to the text, we also open ourselves up to be addressed by the text. The book of Psalms, being part of the word of God, is "useful for teaching, rebuking, correcting and training in righteousness" (2 Tim 3:16).

Let me give an example of this in relation to one of the core messages of the Psalms – the lament. A serious problem in Asian churches today is a fixation on triumphalism. Our response to life is limited to one note, that of rejoicing, and we continue to sound that note even in the midst of a suffering Asia.[72] We are losing our capacity to mourn. As a result, many of our people are forced to deny what they are actually going through. They learn to hide their true feelings for fear of being rejected, because there is no space for their "not OK" experiences inside the church. It is here that I think the lament psalms can be of great benefit. The message of the lament psalms can be summarized in this way: "It's OK to be NOT OK."[73] There is room for our "NOT OK" experiences in the presence of God. Reading the book of Psalms pastorally enables us not only to hear the cries of David and the Israelites but also to see in their laments the God who has been faithful to us *"magmula pa sa ugat ng ating lahi"* (from the very beginning [literally, "root"] of our race).[74] *Dakila ka, O Diyos!* (You are great, O God!).

With that said, let us move on to an exposition of the rich message contained in the Psalms.

---

71. Ibid., 19.

72. Federico G. Villanueva, "The Rejoicing Church in a Suffering Asia: Participating in the 'pain of God' through the Lament Psalms," in *What Young Asian Theologians Are Thinking*, ed. Theng Huat Leow (Singapore: Trinity Theological College, 2014), 14–24.

73. Rico G. Villanueva, *It's OK To Be NOT OK: The Message of the Lament Psalms* (Manila, Philippines: OMF Literature, 2012).

74. The words *"magmula pa sa ugat ng ating lahi"* is taken from the song, *"Dakila ka, O Diyos"* composed by Arnel de Pano.

PSALM 1

Filipinos are generally a happy people. We have this ability to smile even when we fail. This is probably one of our ways of coping with our sufferings. I remember when typhoon *Ondoy* devastated Manila. Some of our people were even smiling when there was a camera taking photos of them.

Psalm 1 is about the happy person. It is an answer to the question, "Who is the happy person?" The word often translated in English as "blessed" in Psalm 1 comes from the Hebrew word *ashre* which means "happiness" or "fortunateness." Although "blessed" expresses the basic idea behind *ashre*, the word is better translated as "truly happy."[1] *Ashre,* being "happy," is more a result of being "blessed." The righteous are called the "truly happy" (1:1) because God blesses them (5:12). In Filipino *ashre* is better translated as *masaya* ("happy"), or more accurately *tunay na masaya* ("truly happy").

Indeed, if a book is judged by its opening, then the Psalms is a happy book. This does not mean, however, that Psalm 1 refers to all people who consider themselves "happy." Nor are we implying that those who are not happy or who do not feel happy are excluded. For our understanding of happiness may differ from that of the psalmist. Psalm 1 has its own definition of who the happy person is. It refers to someone who does not follow the ways of the wicked, but whose delight is in meditating on the law of the Lord. Being happy is not just a way of coping with life's failures and sufferings; it flows from one's commitment to live a righteous life and trust in the Lord through his word. The psalmist calls us to follow this kind of life by drawing a contrast between two kinds of ways: the way of the righteous and the way of the wicked. The former leads to life; the latter, to destruction (cf. Matt 7:13–14). In Psalm 1, the psalmist sets out to define who the happy person is in terms of what they do not do (v. 1), followed by what they do (v. 2). Central in the psalm is the law of the Lord and the meditation on it.

---

1. This is reflected in the difference between "blessed" and "happy" in Hebrew. Brown explains: "In spite of some semantic overlap . . . *ashre* and *baruk* ('blessed') are not synonymous." The former "stresses a state of happiness," while the latter "speaks more of being . . . favored as the recipient of blessing from the Lord, and thus, 'blessed' " (Michael Brown, "*barak*," in *NIDOTTE* 1:763).

1:1 WHAT THE HAPPY PERSON DOES NOT DO:
THE PROGRESSION OF EVIL

Psalm 1 describes the happy person in terms of what he does not do and what he does. First let us look at what the happy person does not do (v. 1). He does not:

— walk in step with the wicked;
— stand in the way that sinners take;
— sit in the company of mockers.

Notice the progression from walking to standing to sitting.[2] It's like what can be commonly seen in some streets of Manila, *inuman* (literally, "drinking," but the word refers broadly to a gathering of men who drink alcohol). When you pass by them, they ask you to have *tagay* (drink). Soon, you are no longer just walking or passing by but are standing watching the group. Finally, you find yourself sitting with them and joining in their drinking.

The road to evil is slow but sure . . . if one is not careful. It's similar to the way I remember my grandfather catching his chickens in the afternoon. He would scatter grains of rice one after another, leading to an open cage where there were many grains. The chickens would peck one grain of rice at a time, unaware of where this chain of rice was leading them. Once all the chickens were in the cage, my grandfather would close the door and shut them in.

That is why the proper attitude to evil and wickedness is to follow the advice of the Apostle Paul: "Flee!" (2 Tim 2:22). This explains the emphasis on the word "not" in verse 1. In the original Hebrew, the word translated "not" is repeated three times:

— does *not* walk in step with the wicked;
— does *not* stand in the way that sinners take;
— does *not* sit in the company of mockers.

The repetition of the negative ("not") brings a tone of the law into it. Although Psalm 1 does not explicitly refer to the Law of Moses, we hear echoes of the Ten Commandments in the repetition of "not": "You shall *not* . . . worship them . . . You shall *not* steal" (Exod 20:5, 15).[3] There is a strong warning here. Psalm 1:1 urges us to make a resolve to say "no" to the counsel or advice of

---

2. Here we see what Alexander called the "successive stages of deterioration" in the three descriptions. See Joseph A. Alexander, *Commentary on Psalms* (Grand Rapids: Kregel Publications, 1991; originally published in 1864), 18.
3. The division of the Psalms into five books further supports this view.

the wicked; to make a firm decision in advance not to take the road that leads to destruction.

But saying "no" is not enough; we need to have something to hold on to. That is the focus of the positive statement in verse 2. The happy person says "no" to wickedness and says "yes" to God. The direction of the heart is towards God. It's all about desire.

What is the desire of your heart? What brings you joy? What is your delight?

1:2–3 WHAT THE HAPPY PERSON DOES: THE IMPORTANCE OF MEDITATION OF GOD'S WORD

Psalm 1 tells us where the heart of the happy person lies: his delight, his joy is "in the law of the LORD" (v. 2). The word "law" is a translation of the Hebrew word *torah*. It is used here more broadly in the sense of "instruction" or "God's will." For Christians, this can be applied broadly to the Bible, the word of God. But it is not just instructions in general, or in our case, the Bible. Some people do read the Bible but live far from God. The law is linked closely with the Lord; it is "*his* law," "the law *of the LORD.*" We delight in the law of the Lord because we want to know him more. As Eaton puts it: "This way of tora-study and devotion is prized as a way of meeting and knowing the Lord, a way of living from the breath of his lips, in the light of his face. The longing, the fainting for God's ordinances . . . all is a variation of the thirst for the living God."[4]

How does the psalmist express this longing for God? What does he do?

Earlier, the psalmist talked about what the happy person does not do. Here he talks about what he does. Yet it is interesting to note, as Alter observes, that when the psalmist begins to tell us what the happy person does, "he initially is given no verb."[5] Verse 2 literally reads, "his delight in the law of the LORD." You just need to supply the verb "to be" (is). This contrasts sharply with verse 1 which has three verbs: walk, stand, and sit. In the next line, when the psalmist does employ a verb, he uses "a verb of contemplative activity"[6] – the happy person is one "who meditates on his law day and night" (v. 2).

---

4. John Herbert Eaton, *The Psalms: A Historical and Spiritual Commentary with an Introduction and New Translation* (London/NY: T&T Clark, 2003), 38.
5. Alter, *The Art of Biblical Poetry*, 115.
6. Ibid.

In Hebrew, the word "meditate" (*hagah*) is associated with vocal activity. It could refer to speaking (37:30; 71:24), uttering praise (35:28), singing (63:5–7) or even to inarticulate sounds like sighing (90:9).[7] But though the word is linked with activities related to speech, the word *hagah* "is not a common word for speaking. Hebrew has other words for this, like *amar*, *dibber*, or *qara*."[8] LeFebvre explains that when *hagah* "is used rather than another speech-verb, it highlights that the speaker's wholehearted sentiments are being revealed."[9] Specifically, in Psalm 1, the word "meditate" is used as "an expression of innermost delight in *Torah*."[10]

The act of meditation referred to in Psalm 1 is not necessarily quiet; it could involve the reciting of the memorized text[11] or the reading of the text, or even the singing of it. But it is something that is done in a posture of delight and serenity as reflected in the following description: "That person is like a tree planted by streams of water" (v. 3). Robert Alter observes that the image describing the happy person is introduced "not with an active verb but with a past participle that denotes the opposite of movement – 'planted.'"[12] The "righteous man stands still – indeed, his righteousness may depend on his ability to stand still and reflect upon true things."[13] The beginning of meditation lies in learning to rest in the Lord. As we let go of our anxieties and feverish striving, we open our hands to receive the gifts God graciously provides for our journey. We realize, as we look back through our lives, how God had been there long before we entered the scene. It is he who "planted" us.

But this does not mean that we don't have to do anything. As one Filipino proverb says, *Nasa Diyos ang awa; nasa tao ang gawa* ("To God belongs mercy, but we also need to do our part"). The meditation on the law of the Lord should not be taken to justify what some of our people do: hang around idly without doing anything (*istambay* = just standing doing nothing). No. The happy person is not like *Juan Tamad* ("John the lazy"). As verse 3 tells us,

---

7. A. Negoiță, "*haghah*" in *TDOT* 3:321–322; cf. Michael LeFebvre, "Torah-Meditation and the Psalms: The Invitation of Psalm 1," in *Interpreting the Psalms: Issues and Approaches*, eds. David Firth and Philip S. Johnston (Downers Grove: IVP, 2005), 218.
8. Negoiță, "Meditation in the OT," in *TDOT* 3:323.
9. LeFebvre, "Torah-Meditation and the Psalms," 219.
10. Ibid.
11. During the psalmist's time, it would be very rare to have a written text, so it is likely that his hearers had memorized the text.
12. Alter, *The Art of Biblical Poetry*, 115.
13. Ibid., 116.

"whatever they do prospers." This is because their actions flow out of their times of meditation of God's word.

Conversely, Psalm 1 challenges today's preoccupation with being busy, becoming successful and feverishly striving for that which is spectacular and big. As a writer on spirituality, Richard Foster, remarks: "The desperate need today is not for a greater number of intelligent people, or gifted people, but for deep people."[14]

But how do we develop depth? The image of the tree "planted by streams of water" reminds us it takes time to develop depth. And that is why the psalmist says he spends "day and night" meditating on "his law." "Day and night" is a poetic device (merism) which emphasizes continuity and consistency. There has to be a deliberate attempt on our part to spend time in meditation. The two lines in verse 2 form a parallelism: "whose delight is in the law of the LORD, and who meditates on his law day and night." In this parallelism, the second line defines for us what it means to delight in God's law (i.e. to meditate on it). For how can we say we delight in God's law if we never spend time reading or contemplating it? One of our problems is that we are religious but our religiosity does not flow into actual change. A major part of the reason for this is that many Filipinos do not spend time meditating on the word of God. They just attend mass. As Josefina Constantino notes:

> The Word of God has come to people only in Gospels read or sermons preached during Sunday Mass; but meditation as a way of listening to the Word speaking to the heart and to the conscience of man has been a very recent awakening in the Philippines and everywhere for that matter.[15]

1:4–5 WHAT THE WICKED PERSON IS LIKE

One noticeable difference between the happy person and the wicked one is that the former is established ("planted") whereas the latter is not. The wicked are "like chaff that the wind blows away" (v. 4). They keep on changing. Now you see them, now you don't. They are like those so-called "butterfly

---

14. Richard J. Foster, *Celebration of Discipline: The Path to Spiritual Growth* (San Francisco: Harper & Row, 1988), 1.
15. Constantino, *The Asian Religious Sensibility*, 338. She is speaking from a Catholic background, but the same thing can be said about Protestants in general.

Christians" who move from church to church. More radically, the text tells us they will be blown away and perish.

Because they are not established, they "will not stand in the judgment" (v. 5). What does "stand in the judgment" mean? Does this refer to the final judgment? In the Hebrew text, the connection to the "Day of Judgment is far from clear."[16] Further, in the OT, the resurrection of the wicked is found only in Daniel 12:2. Yet it is interesting that in subsequent ancient writings, Psalm 1:5 has been interpreted with reference to the final judgment (see Targum).[17] Although the doctrine of the afterlife is not yet developed in the OT, it is possible to see here glimpses of its growth. In the NT the doctrine of the final judgment becomes clearer (see 2 Cor 5:10; Matt 25:32–33). Ultimately, the wicked will not stand before the great throne of judgment.

But Psalm 1 does not only refer to the future. It also pertains to the present. Verse 5b speaks of the "assembly of the righteous," where sinners will not be allowed to "stand."[18] What does this mean? This may refer to the congregation of the righteous in this life who stand in the presence of the Lord. As Psalm 24 declares, only those whose life is characterized by holiness will be allowed to "stand in his holy place" (24:3-4). We cannot just enter into God's holy presence; there are "qualifications" (see comments on Psalms 15 and 24). Only the righteous will be allowed to dwell on God's holy hill. The wicked will not be admitted (cf. 5:4). Psalm 1:5b gives us a preview of what will transpire at the end of time.

---

16. Timothy Edwards, *Exegesis in the Targum of the Psalms: The Old, the New, and the Rewritten* (Piscataway, NJ: Gorgias Press, 2007), 91.

17. The Targum translates Ps 1:5a as follows: "Therefore the wicked do not stand in the *great day of* judgment." English translation taken from David M. Stec, *The Targum of Psalms* (Collegeville, MN: Liturgical Press, 2004), 29. A passage in the Mishnah (*Sanhedrin* 10:3) also interprets Ps 1:5 as a reference to end time judgment (Edwards, *Exegesis in the Targum of Psalms*, 92–95).

18. The word "stand" comes from the verb *qum* which means "arise." Although most modern versions render the word *qum* in v. 5 as "stand," it is to be distinguished from the word "stand" (*amad*) in v. 1. Han-Joachim Kraus, *Psalms 1–59* (Minneapolis, MN: Augsburg, 1988), 119–120, sees the connection between the word *qum* and Psalm 24, a psalm about entrance into the sanctuary. He points out that the Hebrew construction *qum* ("arise") plus the preposition *be* in 1:5 also occurs in Ps 24:3. Psalm 24 along with Psalm 15 teaches us that not everyone will be allowed entrance into the congregation of the Lord. We may apply this to church worship gatherings.

1:6 THE BLESSEDNESS OF THE RIGHTEOUS
AND THE PITIABLE END OF THE WICKED

The psalm concludes with a summary statement on the status of the happy person, now described in verse 6 as "righteous," and that of the wicked: "for the LORD watches over the way of the righteous, but the way of the wicked leads to destruction." This verse forms an A-B-B'-C structure which contrasts the secure standing of the righteous and the destructive ending of the wicked:

> For the LORD watches (A)   - - - - - - - - - - - - - the way of the righteous (B)
> But the way of the wicked (B') ⤫ - - leads to destruction (C)

Both lines mention the word "way" (*derek*). But there is a difference: in the case of the righteous there is one who is "watching." Actually, the Hebrew word translated as "*watches*" is the word *yada*, which means "to know." The Lord *knows* the way of the righteous. We learn from the teachings of Jesus about two roads: the broad road that leads to destruction and the narrow road that leads to life (Matt 7:13). The latter is difficult and the way through it is hard. But the great consolation is this: the Lord is there watching, taking care of his people. By contrast, there is no one taking care of the way of the sinners. The Lord is not even mentioned in the description of the way of the sinners (see structure above). It simply says, "the way of the wicked leads to destruction." Their situation is pitiable indeed.

So at the very beginning of the book of Psalms an option is presented to us: the way of the righteous and the way of sinners. The psalmist has made a strong case for choosing the way of the righteous. It is a way that succeeds and is prosperous because it is the way the Lord "knows," i.e. "attends to" or "cherishes" (NJPS). By contrast, the way of the sinners is slippery and shaky. It has no stability, like the chaff which the wind blows away.

A survey by the US research firm Gallup identified the Philippines as the "most emotional country in the world."[20] This may lead to the view that though many of our people are poor, they are still happy. As we often hear, "It's more fun in the Philippines." On the other hand, being happy is not a guarantee we are on the right track. How do we define happiness? Psalm

---

19. Verse 6 forms what I would call an "imperfect chiastic structure." While the word "way" is repeated in B and B', A and C are not parallel, thus the dotted line.
20. Online: http://www.gmanetwork.com/news/story/283217/lifestyle/people/it-s-more-emotional-in-the-philippines-says-us-pollster (accessed 30 November 2012).

1 teaches us that happiness is an outflow of one's relationship with God. Happiness is not the main goal. Rather, it is doing God's will. Happiness only comes as a result of delighting in God and living according to his word.

As the following psalms will make clear, a happy life does not mean an absence of trouble or lament. In fact, many of the psalms are laments (see for example, Psalm 3). Thomas Merton rightly observes:

> [the] Psalms themselves later on have to face the unpleasant question presented by the fact that the just man does not, in fact, always prosper. His leaf does fall off and he does not bear fruit, while the storehouses of the wicked are full, their sheep fruitful, their oxen fat."[21]

---

21. Thomas Merton, *Bread in the Wilderness* (New York: New Directions Books, 1953), 27.

PSALM 2

Psalm 1 can be likened to a road map, and Psalm 2 is the first exposure to the actual places found on that map. A map gives you some idea about a place but it does not give you an actual picture of it. You need to go there yourself to see it. And when you do, you realize the place is not as simple as the map presents it. This is the case in my own experience of Manila!

When we read Psalm 1 we get the impression that everything is nice and tidy, with no hassles. Psalm 1 presents two kinds of people: the righteous and the wicked. The righteous person is established and certain, likened to a tree planted by streams of water that always bears fruit in its season. But the very first word in Psalm 2, "Why?" disturbs this serenity. Psalm 2 begins, shouting as it were, "Why do the nations conspire and the peoples plot in vain?" The interrogative "Why?" can be extended to verse 2: Why do "the kings of the earth rise up and the rulers band together against the Lord and against his anointed?" (v. 2). The peaceful and quiet streams surrounding the tree in Psalm 1 are suddenly disturbed.

We do not know the exact events behind Psalm 2. Scholars call this a "royal psalm," a category which pertains to situations in the life of a king from the line of David (see "Royal Psalms," pp. 34–35). There are a number of these in the psalms (e.g. Pss 45 and 110). Psalm 2, in particular, relates to the coronation of a king. It is a time of leadership transition. At such times the potential for rebellion and chaos is high. These are uncertain times. And the reading of Psalm 2 should reflect this situation. We are not to read the first verses of Psalm 2 quietly; the psalm is dramatic in its impact. We hear the tone of anxiety and even panic in the face of uncertainty. But as promised in Psalm 1 – "the Lord watches over the way of the righteous" (v. 6) – God assures his people that he is in control. God speaks from his throne in the heavens (2:6). He is in control.

The psalm has an important message. In the midst of uncertainties in our nations or in our personal lives, we can trust that God remains in control. At the same time Psalm 2 reminds us that the life of faith consists of challenges. We do not do our meditation only in the quietness of our room; we do it also in the midst of wicked people. Serenity is experienced in the midst of the noise. The wicked in Psalm 1 take the form of the "nations" or "peoples" in Psalm 2.[1] And like the righteous, those peoples also meditate. In fact, the word for "meditate" (*hagah*) reappears in Psalm 2. But there is a difference: whereas the righteous person meditates on the law of the Lord (1:2), the peoples "plot" (*hagah*) in vain (2:1).[2] Their meditation is disruptive and rebellious. It's not easy being righteous. It never was.

2:1–3 LAMENT

The opening verses (vv. 1–3) can be read either as expressions of confidence or as expressions of lament. Read together with the rest of Psalm 2, these verses are more of a taunt to the nations and rulers who are rebelling against the Lord and his anointed. The psalmist is confident that however much noise the nations make, it is simply that – noise. On the other hand, if we read Psalm 2 together with Psalm 1, the case is no longer as simple as it looks. As scholars have shown, the two psalms are connected. First, while almost all of the psalms in Book 1 (Pss 3–41) have a superscription, Psalm 2 does not have one.[3] The repetition of the important phrase "Blessed" at the beginning of Psalm 1 (v. 1) and at the end of Psalm 2 (v. 12) brings the two psalms together. The phrase serves as a marker. Moreover, there are close verbal links between the two. We already mentioned the repetition of the word "meditate" (see above). Two other significant words repeated are "way" and "perish." Like the wicked in Psalm 1:6 whose "way" (*derek*) "leads to destruction" (*abad*), so the "way" (*derek*) of the kings/judges will "lead to destruction" (*abad*), if they do not heed the warning (v. 12).[4]

If the two psalms are closely connected, then we need to read them together. The problem is that Psalm 1 has just declared that the righteous person is secure. The wicked, on the other hand, are on sinking sand, likened to a "chaff that the wind drives away" (1:4). The way of the wicked perishes while the Lord "watches over the way of the righteous" (1:6). It comes as a shock, then, for the psalmist to find that such is not the case, or at least not yet. If the wicked cannot stand in the judgment, nor sinners in the assembly

---

1. The links with Psalm 1 lead to the identification of the "nations"/"peoples" and their "kings"/"rulers" with the wicked in Psalm 1. "Therefore, it is not surprising that their destiny, if they persist in opposing God, is described the same way as in Psalm 1" (J. Clinton McCann, Jr., "The Book of Psalms," in *NIB*, ed. Leander E. Keck [Vol. 4; Nashville: Abingdon, 1996], 689).
2. The word "meditate" and "plot" come from the same Hebrew word.
3. Psalms 10 and 33 also do not have a superscription because like Psalm 1, these two psalms are closely linked to the psalms that precede them.
4. For other connections between the two psalms, see Robert Alan Cole, "An Integrated Reading of Psalms 1 and 2," *JSOT* 26, no. 4 (2002): 75–88.

of the righteous, then why do the nations make so much noise? Or as Cole puts it: "If a judgment is certain in which Yahweh distinguishes between the way of the wicked and that of the righteous (1:4–6), why then are the nations allowed to conspire and revolt against Yahweh and his anointed (2:1–2)?"[5]

In verse 2 we have a description of what the nations, through their leaders, do. And in verse 3 we hear their speech: "Let us break their chains and throw off their shackles." This speaks of rebellion. They no longer want anything to do with their "masters" or those above them. But what may be disturbing for the psalmist is that the kings and rulers are allowed to "band together against the LORD and against his anointed" (v. 2b). So Rabbi Isaac may be correct in seeing the first verses as addressed to God in a form of lament (for an explanation of lament, see "What Is Lament?" p. 57). He comments that "when a man says to his friend: 'Why dost thou this or that?' his friend gets angry." But the good thing is that when "the righteous say to the Holy One, Why do the heathen rage? . . . God does not get angry, and the righteous are not punished."[6] Psalm 2 actually resembles the general structure of a lament:

> Lament (vv. 1–3);
> Divine response ("oracle") (vv. 4–6);
> Praise (vv. 7–9);
> > Certainty of a hearing (vv. 7–8);
> > Expression of trust (v. 9);
> Exhortation (vv. 10–12).

The last part (exhortation) is more at home with thanksgiving psalms. But the overall flow of the psalm – as shown above – is closer to the lament.

2:4–6 "A VIEW FROM THE THRONE ABOVE": THE DIVINE RESPONSE

In verse 4 we have a view from heaven. This contrasts with the "kings of the earth" (v. 2). "The One enthroned in heaven laughs; the LORD scoffs at them" (v. 4). There is a progression here from simply laughing without mentioning the object of his laughter, to the identification of the object – "them" (those

---

5. Cole, "An Integrated Reading," 77. Cole does not explicitly say whether vv. 1–3 are directed to God.
6. William G. Braude, *The Midrash on Psalms* (New Haven: Yale University Press, 1959), 36. John Goldingay, *Psalms*, Vol. 1 (Grand Rapids: Baker, 2006), 97–98, rightly observes that R. Isaac sees Ps 2:1–3 as "addressed to God, in the manner of a lament," though he does not agree that this is a lament.

in vv. 2–3) – and then the word "scoff" which is stronger than "laugh." But he does not just laugh and scoff at them. He "rebukes them in his anger and terrifies them in his wrath" (v. 5). This verse has the following chiastic structure:

He rebukes them
   in his anger
   in his wrath
He terrifies them.

In verse 6 we hear the speech of the Lord: "I have installed my king." That is, in contrast to the words or claims of the kings, the Lord has decided on his own course of action. He remains in control. Not only is he in the heavens, but he has also "installed" his king.

2:7–9 THE ANOINTED ONE PROCLAIMS THE DECREE OF THE LORD

Verses 7–9 represent the speech of the anointed king, quoting the divine decree. This is probably part of the language of installation of a king. Here the king is considered as a son of God (v. 7). Verse 8 talks about God giving him the nations as an inheritance, the ends of the earth as property, should the king wish for them. How will this king rule? Verse 9 tells us he will rule with an iron hand. He will break the nations with an iron rod, shatter them like a potter's vessel.

2:10–12 EXHORTATION

Because God has spoken and acted in installing his king, there is no more reason to rebel. The "Therefore" (v. 10) is climactic. The kings are exhorted to be wise and the judges of the earth are to take warning. The judges here are the representatives of the people, in place of the rulers in verse 2. There are actually two main groups of people here: the peoples/nations and the kings/rulers/judges. The latter's role is crucial because it is they who speak for the people, and, in such a society, make decisions for the people. Therefore it is they who are being addressed. This speaks of the crucial role of leadership.

The series of imperatives is continued in verse 11: "Serve the LORD with fear and celebrate his rule with trembling." It is not clear what "celebrate with trembling" means. "Kiss his son, or he will be angry and your way will lead to your destructions, for his wrath can flare up in a moment" (v. 12). Who is being referred to here with the words "angry" and "his wrath" in verse 12? Is it the king or God? Earlier, it was God who was angry and full of wrath (v. 5). The "son" here is the anointed king, so it is more likely that he is the subject of the verb here, though we can also say it speaks of God's anger too, since it is he who has decreed the Son's kingship.

In the light of the above, what really matters is whether we take refuge in God: "Blessed are all who take refuge in him" (v. 12c). Psalm 1 defines the happy person as one who seeks to live a righteous life. Psalm 2 presents a more realistic view of the life of the righteous and underlines the importance of taking refuge in God. There is also a shift from "the man" in Psalm 1 to the community ("all who take refuge in him") in Psalm 2. In the path of righteousness one does not walk alone.

ROYAL PSALMS AND THE ASIAN CONTEXT

Psalms 2, 18, 20, 21, 45, 72, 89, 101, 110, 132, and 144 are known as "royal psalms" because they pertain to the life of the king.[1] For instance, Psalms 2 and 110 are associated with the king's coronation; Psalm 101 contains a vow the king makes at the time of his enthronement; Psalm 45 was written for a royal wedding; Psalm 20 is a prayer for the king before he goes to war; and Psalm 18 is a king's prayer of thanksgiving after victory has been granted to him. In its present canonical context, Psalm 21 may also be considered a prayer of thanksgiving in answer to the people's prayer for the king's victory.

But as Psalm 89 reminds us, kings are not always victorious. That psalm begins with a prayer of thanksgiving and a recollection of the promise to David about his everlasting reign (Ps 89:1–37), but it ends with an impassioned lament over the defeat of a king and the consequence of that defeat for the people. The psalmist utters a great cry: "But you have rejected . . . you have been very angry with your anointed one" (v. 38). The king had failed because he had not lived up to the ideals of the kingship as set forth in the law of the Lord.

The anointed king was called to trust in the Lord and obey the law of the Lord (the Torah). As the old hymn puts it, he was to "trust and obey." The first two psalms in the book of Psalms affirm these ideals. In Psalm 1, the person who is considered "happy" or "blessed" is the one who does not walk the path of wickedness but delights in meditating on the law of the Lord (1:1–2). At the end of Psalm 2, the "happy" people are those who "take refuge" in the Lord (v. 12). Thus the king is not to trust in his weaponry or in the number of his chariots but in the Lord (33:16–17). As part of his obedience to the Lord, the king makes a vow to "lead a blameless life" (101:2).

In another royal psalm – Psalm 72 – the king is presented as one who shows concern and fights for the cause of the poor and needy: "May he judge your people with righteousness, and your poor with justice . . . May he defend the cause of the poor of the people, give deliverance to the needy, and crush the oppressor" (vv. 2, 4, NRSV). He does not rule for the benefit of his wealthy associates but for the benefit of the needy.

British people understand what it means to be ruled by a king, and so do some Asians in countries like Thailand. But people from countries like the Philippines have not had that experience, and so we find it difficult to appreciate the royal psalms. We are more used to *barangays*, small groups of

---

1. See Gunkel, *The Psalms*, 24.

families living together under a local chief, who does not have absolute power as a king does. He is more of an administrator than a ruler.[2]

But, ironically, the name of our country (Philippines) is derived from that of a king, King Philip of Spain. It was the Spaniards who gave us our first experience of being "under a king." But this experience was not the same as that of Israel. We were never part of Spain, and as an entire people never identified the king of Spain as our leader. We were colonized by Spain, and so we know more of what it means to be subjugated and overpowered than of what it means to conquer and rule. We can identify more easily with those who are a king's vassals, that is, those who are forced to obey him are not inherently part of his kingdom.

What makes it even more difficult to identify with the royal psalms is that no king or ruler has ever actually lived up to the picture of the ideal king presented in these psalms. All kings have failed. This may be the reason why the psalmists kept on looking for that one king who would exemplify the ideals of the true Davidic king.

Ultimately, when human kings fail, the Lord is there. He is the true king, the righteous and just ruler. As Christians, we see in Jesus the ultimate fulfillment of the true king in the psalms.

---

2. Renato Constantino and Letizia R. Constantino, *A History of the Philippines: From the Spanish Colonization to the Second World War* (New York: Monthly Review Press, 1975), 27–28.

PSALM 3

Psalm 3 serves as a continuation of Psalm 2. In Psalm 2 the psalmist was crying out, "Why?" (2:1). Here the psalmist cries out, "How many are my foes!" (3:1). And it gets personal. For Absalom, David's own son, has rebelled against his father. As a result, David is on the run. The superscription reads: "A Psalm of David. When he fled from his son Absalom."[1] In Psalm 3 Absalom takes the place of the nations/peoples in Psalm 2. Here it is the king's own son who has risen against him. "The uprising of nations (2:1–3) is replaced in the superscription by one led by his own son. So he [David] takes refuge in God (cf. 2:12)."[2]

Psalm 3 further develops the reality of the life of faith. As McCann writes: "Psalm 3 dramatically introduces the situation and the faith that is evident in all the prayers: 'The righteous person may have many troubles, but the LORD delivers him from them all'" (34:19).[3]

3:1–2 "O LORD, HOW MANY ARE MY FOES!"

The psalmist feels overwhelmed, as indicated by the threefold repetition of the word "many" in vv. 1–2:

> LORD, how many are my foes!
> How many rise up against me!
> Many are saying of me,
> "God will not deliver him."

In a culture that values community, this is a difficult situation. It is tragic when people reject you and say, "God will not deliver him." Yet in this situation there is one to whom the psalmist can cry out – God, whom he calls out to at the start of his prayer: "LORD." The word "LORD" is the very first word in the whole psalm. The psalmist mentions the "LORD" before he mentions all his troubles. I think this is important. The statements of trust begin not with "I" but with "you." No matter how overwhelming the situation, the Lord is there. We can always cry out to him. Taking refuge in the Lord means

---

1. This is the first superscription in the Psalms. See "The Significance of the Superscriptions," p. 258.
2. Geoffrey W. Grogan, *Psalms* (Grand Rapids: Eerdmans, 2008), 46.
3. McCann, "The Book of Psalms," 693.

acknowledging the Lord in all our circumstances, even in the overwhelming ones . . . even when people tell us there is no more hope.

3:3–6 "TO THE LORD I CRY ALOUD"

At such a time, we need to hold on to God as firmly as we are able. One way to do this is by affirming who God is for us: "But you, Lord, are a shield around me, my glory, the One who lifts my head high" (v. 3). There are times when we really need to assert who God is for us, to declare with all our might who God is in our hearts. But this declaration is more than just a positive-thinking type of confession. The adversative ("But") at the beginning of verse 3 is a strong one; it counters the statement of the enemies in verse 2b. Even though so many were rising up against him, the psalmist was able to draw from his own experience of God. In verses 5–6, he continues to declare his trust in the Lord: "I lie down and sleep; I wake again, because the Lord sustains me. I will not fear though tens of thousands assail me on every side."

We may ask, how can the psalmist sleep when he should be lying awake? He has so many enemies. He feels overwhelmed. How can he sleep? How can he even lie down? And yet here is the psalmist, able to sleep. What is his secret?

His secret is revealed in verse 4: "I call out to the Lord, and he answers me from his holy mountain." These words appear between the psalmist's statements of assurance and confidence in verses 3 and 5–6. It seems he is telling us, "The reason I am able to sleep and be confident even in my situation is because I know how to call out to the Lord."

3:7–8 CONTINUING STRUGGLE AND DECLARATION OF TRUST

Curiously, right after his declarations of confidence in verse 6, we find the psalmist crying out for help again in verse 7a: "Arise, Lord! Deliver me, my God!" This warns us against reading too much confidence into the text, which can lead to what is called "hyper-faith." Trust and confidence in the Lord this side of eternity is never perfect. It does not mean that when you pray and cry to the Lord you will never feel overwhelmed again. Our advantage lies not within ourselves; it remains in God. The good thing for the psalmist is that whenever he is confronted with a difficult situation, he can always recall what God has done in the past and how the Lord delivered him from his troubles. This serves as the basis for his confidence. As he prays to the Lord in the face of a new challenge, he knows God will be there for him as he had been in the past. Thus, after the petition, "Arise, O Lord!" in verse 7a, the psalmist says: "Strike all my enemies on the jaw; break the teeth of the wicked" (v. 7b). Here the NIV has translated the verse as an imperative: "Strike." That is one possible translation. The Hebrew can also be translated as either a present tense ("you strike"; NRSV) or as a perfect verb ("You have smitten"; NASB). Here is a case where the verbal form can be ambiguous. The verb may be read as past tense. The psalmist recalls what the Lord has done in the past, which serves as the motivation for his present petitions (cf. Ps 4:1). It could also be read as a petition (imperative).[4]

With the confidence that stems from past experiences of God's deliverance, the psalm ends with a recognition that deliverance belongs to the Lord (v. 8). Earlier the enemies had said to the psalmist, "God will not deliver him" (v. 2). Here the psalmist declares: there is help in the Lord. He affirms the source of his help, which comes even when other people tell him it is hopeless. Indeed, there is hope for those who "take refuge in him."

Psalm 3 is a powerful psalm of trust in the midst of troubles. It is one with which we can identify, for we too often find ourselves in trouble and need a place we can go to. The good news is that God himself can be this place. As one of the most popular Filipino Christian songs says:

Kakalong sa iyo	In your embrace I will come
Magsusumbong ako	Tell you what's in my heart
Magtatanong	Express my questions
maghihintay ng kasagutan N'yo	wait for your answer
Magtitiwala na pangako'y	Trust that your promise you will fulfill
tutupdin . . .	
Sa paraiso N'yo	In your paradise
Ako ay dadalhin	There you will bring me

There is always a place for us in the presence of God. As a shield around us, the Lord sustains and saves us (vv. 3, 5, 8).

---

4. The difficulty with rendering the verb as an imperative is how to make sense of the preposition *ki* if we translate the verbs as petitions.

PSALM 4

Psalm 4 is closely connected with Psalm 3. Both continue the theme of trust in the midst of oppositions, and in the Psalter the phrase "many are saying" occurs only in these two psalms (3:2, 4:6).[1] Both psalms also repeat the words "lie down and sleep" (3:5; 4:8). But whereas Psalm 4 speaks about lying down in safety, Psalm 3 moves on to say "I wake again" (3:5). This has led many to think that Psalm 3 was to be used for evening prayers and Psalm 4 for morning prayers. We recall Psalm 1:2: "on his law they meditate day and night." As we meditate on the law of the Lord day and night (1:2), so we also pray day and night.

But Psalm 4 goes beyond Psalm 3 to emphasize the connection between praying and righteous living. Those who trust in the Lord are called "faithful" (4:3). The psalmist refers to the "sacrifices of the righteous" (v. 4). The emphasis on the word "righteous," which we find at the very beginning of the chapter, further brings out the message that prayer and righteous living go together. This theme will be further developed in Psalm 5.

Psalm 4 may be structured as follows:

"Answer me" (v. 1);
Complaint against enemies (v. 2);
  Declaration of confidence (v. 3);
  Exhortation (vv. 4–5);
Complaint against enemies (v. 6);
Answer to prayer (vv. 7–8).

4:1 "ANSWER ME"

Psalm 4 begins with a petition for God to hear: "Answer me when I call . . . You have given me relief when I was in distress" (Ps 4:1, ESV).[2] Many of us can identify with these words. Most of us have had situations when life was just heavy and difficult. But after we prayed, the Lord made a way for us and brought us to a place of security. The words "you have given me relief" is lit-

---

1. Richard J. Clifford, *Psalms 1–72* (Nashville: Abingdon, 2002), 51. The NIV translates the phrase in 4:6 differently as "many are asking" but in Hebrew the phrase is exactly the same in both 3:2 and 4:6.
2. The NIV translates the perfect verb in v. 1b as an imperative ("Give me relief from my distress"). I follow the ESV here. I think the latter makes more sense with the context.

erally "you have provided a wide room." When we are distressed, we feel as if we are being strangled (*sinasakal*). We can't breathe (*naghahabol ng hininga*). It was only by God's grace in answer to our prayer that we are able to breathe again, find relief, and go on with life. Afterwards we find ourselves in distress again. So we come to God again, praying as we did before: "Answer me when I call . . . have mercy on me and hear my prayer" (v. 1). As in Psalm 3 there is an alternation between lament and expression of trust. There is never a moment when we do not need God. The good news is that the same God who had been there for us in our times of distress is also with us right now when we are confronted with new challenges.

But lest we think that God is just there for us, always at the end of the line waiting for a call from us, the psalmist's invocation reminds us we also have a responsibility. The psalmist refers to God as "my righteous God" (v. 1). This phrase can have two senses. The first one has God as the focus: the righteous God or the God who is faithful in acting on behalf of his people on the basis of his covenant. The structure of verse 1 supports this:

Answer me when I call to you,	a
my righteous God.	b
You have given me relief when I was in distress,	b'
Be gracious to me, and hear my prayer!	a'

As can be observed, the phrase, "righteous God" occurs in the inner structure which highlights what God has done in the past. It parallels the statement "You have given me relief when I was in distress." Thus, the phrase could be translated as "God who secures my salvation"[3] or the "God who vindicates me,"[4] both focusing on God and what he does.

The second sense of the title "my righteous God" focuses on a person's righteousness (see also Ps 7). The Hebrew of verse 1 literally reads, "my God of my righteousness." The phrase, "my righteousness" highlights how a person lives. As will be seen in verse 3, the psalmist identifies himself closely with the "faithful." The word "righteous/righteousness" shows up again in verse 5 when the psalmist exhorts those who oppose him to offer "sacrifices of the righteous."

---

3. Eaton, *The Psalms*, 71.
4. Clifford, *Psalms 1–72*, 52.

Here the word "righteous" does not mean perfect. It needs "to be understood in terms of the relationship between God and his people.[5] To be righteous means to do what is required in the relationship, not necessarily to be perfect, although there is an element of attaining a certain standard (see Pss 15 and 24).

Thus, the phrase, "righteous God" refers both to God's righteousness and to the righteousness of the psalmist. Because God is righteous, those who come to him are expected to live a life worthy of him. This is a much needed reminder. For as Charles Ringma writes:

> One of the flaws of Christianity of the modern world, particularly in the West, is that Christians have the idea God is there just for them. There is little idea that things should be the other way round. God is the center and we should live our lives for the glory and purposes of God.[6]

4:2 COMPLAINT AGAINST ENEMIES

In verse 2 the psalmist complains about his enemies: "How long will you people turn my glory into shame?" It is possible that his enemies were challenging his righteousness and he had to defend himself against them. The central issue is the experience of "honor and shame." In a closely-knit culture like Israel where the community is central, the issue of honor is crucial. To have one's honor trampled on is tantamount to having the very source of one's life cut off. So the situation is grave. The psalmist asserts his own righteousness (cf. v. 1) which apparently is being challenged.

This is not the first time the psalmist complains about his opponents. In the preceding psalm, he complains about the "many" who rise up against him (3:1). In Psalm 2 it is the nations and the peoples whom the psalmist was complaining about: "Why do the nations conspire?" (2:1).[7] Here it's the "people" (literally, "sons of men" [4:2]). It is increasingly becoming evident that the person who tries to live righteously will be plagued by opposition!

---

5. Gerhard von Rad, *Old Testament Theology*, 371.
6. Charles R. Ringma, *Hear the Ancient Wisdom* (London: SPCK, 2013).
7. Interestingly, the word *riq* occurs in both contexts (Ps 2:1 – Why do the peoples plot vain [*riq*]? Ps 4:2 – "you love vain" [*riq*]).

4:3 DECLARATION OF CONFIDENCE

And yet by calling God "righteous" (v. 1), the psalmist acknowledges that God is the basis of his righteousness. That is why he can turn to his opponents and confidently declare to them, "Know that the LORD has set apart his faithful servant for himself" (v. 3). This is similar to the confident assertion of Psalm 2 that, despite all the rumblings and plotting of the nations and peoples, kings, and rulers, the Lord has set his king on Zion (2:6). A closer resemblance is found in Psalm 6:8 where the psalmist tells his enemies: "Away from me, all you who do evil, for the LORD has heard my weeping." This manner of addressing one's enemies is common in prayers. Prayers find their vitality in the context of opposition. The experience of the early church in Acts 4:23–31 testifies to this. Their prayers arose from the context of persecution. Interestingly, they quote from Psalm 2, a psalm that shows links to Psalm 4.

4:4–5 EXHORTATION

Earlier, the psalmist exhorted the peoples and their rulers in Psalm 2:10–11. Here the psalmist does the same for the people. The "people" here may be the same as the wicked people. The difference is that unlike in Psalm 1:6, the wicked people do not just perish; they are given a chance or warning (cf. 2:10) and instructed: "Tremble and do not sin; when you are on your beds, search your hearts and be silent" (4:4).

It is not clear what specific situation the psalmist is addressing when he gives his advice in these verses. The first one is often translated as "Be angry and do not sin" in light of the translation in the ancient Greek translation of the Old Testament, known as the Septuagint [LXX] (cf. Eph 4:26). But in Hebrew the word has the meaning "quake" or "tremble."[8] It is uncertain which reading represents the original Hebrew word. What is clear is the psalmist's concern that the people do not sin. One of the ways of avoiding sin is that, rather than speaking, one should "search your hearts and be silent" (4b).[9] As James 3:2 says, "We all stumble in many ways. Anyone who is never at fault in what they say is perfect, able to keep their whole body in check." Further advice about avoiding sin is given in Psalm 4:5: "Offer the sacrifices

8. Hence, the NRSV rendering, "When you are disturbed."
9. The word "search" in Hebrew literally means "say." It is a way of speaking to oneself, of pondering or of heart searching. The word "say" is repeated in v. 6 in connection with the second complaint of the psalmist (see below).

of the righteous and trust in the LORD." The advice in verse 5 is connected with the emphasis earlier on "righteousness" in verse 1. Our sacrifices should be evident in the kinds of lives we live. The emphasis on trusting in the Lord in verse 5 also teaches us that righteous living is an expression of our trust in God.

4:6 COMPLAINT AGAINST ENEMIES

Unfortunately, it seems the people are not listening. For instead of searching their hearts and being quiet, they continue to speak: "Who will bring us prosperity?" (v. 6). The "prosperity" (literally, "good") here may refer to the abundant "grain and wine" which the psalmist mentions later in verse 7. It is not wrong to wish for prosperity. For as the Scripture says, "Every good and perfect gift is from above" (Jas 1:17). What is wrong is when we seek these for the wrong motives . . . when we pray yet live wicked lives (see Jas 4:1–4). Interestingly, the second half of verse 6, "Let the light of your face shine on us" alludes to the Aaronic blessing (see Num 6:24–26). Even sinners know how to utter the right words of prayer. The question is, do they really mean them?

4:7–8 ANSWER TO PRAYER

To pray without paying heed to the call for righteousness misses the real point of prayer. For the blessing does not only come in terms of material provisions. The joy that comes from God's generosity consists of *shalom*: "You have put gladness in my heart more than when their grain and wine abound" (v. 7, NRSV). Here the psalmist is drawing a contrast with the words of the wicked in verse 6. Notice the contrast between the "Many are asking, "Who will bring us prosperity?" (v. 6) and "You have put gladness in *my* heart more than when *their* grain and wine abound" (v. 7). You may have a lot of money but it is the Lord who gives joy of heart, which is more than the material things of life. *Shalom* has to do with wholeness and well-being. This was the blessing which the enemies were hoping to secure but they failed for they did not take heed of the advice.

Those who trust in the Lord and live righteous lives not only have gladness in their hearts, they are also able to "dwell in safety" (v. 8). The word "safety" (v. 8) in Hebrew comes from the same root as "trust" (v. 5b). It is only as we trust in the Lord that we are able to rest.

SPLIT-LEVEL CHRISTIANITY AND THE PSALMS

In the Philippines, 95 percent of our people consider themselves Christians. We hold the record for the highest number of people ever to attend a papal visit (about 6 million people). We value the religious acts of going to church, praying and so on. Yet we neglect issues of justice. Presently our country is the only Christian nation in Southeast Asia. But we are also one of the most corrupt countries in the world. In our government offices we have images of the child Jesus (Sto. Niño) on the table, but there are many "under the table" deals.[1]

We have a serious problem with what Jaime Bulatao calls "split-level Christianity." This can be illustrated in a number of ways. A policeman who goes to mass in the morning finds nothing wrong with asking *kotong* ("bribery money") later the same day. Church members recite prayers and then go back to their old ways. We are like students who behave well when the teacher is around but misbehave as soon as the teacher's back is turned!

One of the major reasons for this split in our thinking is the lack of good role models. Christianity was introduced to us along with colonialism, and so the message of the gospel was diluted, marred by its very opposite – hypocrisy and inauthenticity. Some who were bringing the message of Christ were also oppressing us. Those who ought to have been bringing the message of Christ were the same ones who were oppressing us. They ought to have been the ones introducing us to a life of righteousness. But they hindered those seeking the way to righteousness by living a life that was the exact opposite of what they were teaching. Thus, we inherited a kind of spirituality that is shiny and clean on the outside but smells rotten, for at its core there is a corpse. We say we trust in the Lord, yet in reality we trust in our own strength and in our *padrino* ("godfather"). We go to mass or attend church only to find ourselves doing the very opposite of the things we hear being preached.

Our own national hero, Jose Rizal has this to say about Filipino religiosity:

> To them a just and good Christian is one who frequents the church, who attends the most processions, who lights the most candles, and gives luxurious dresses to the images, without taking into account whether the money used in these works (pious, yes, but not at all necessary) has been acquired at the cost of the hunger and tears of many unfortunate men . . . To do good to one's fellowmen, to make a sacrifice for the happiness of others, to tell the truth even to one's detriment, to look upon all as brothers are acts that go unnoticed, either because

---

1. "Under the table" is a term used for practices of bribery.

true virtue is modest and simple or because it is unknown to men . . . And so it happens to the idea of sin. To mix or eat meat on days of abstinence, to break a fast or something of the kind, is generally considered a sin graver still than to lie which hurts and injures, than backbiting or the insult to misfortune and poverty. You can hurt even unjustly the self-love of an unfortunate man; you can rob the orphan and the widow, or take away the honor of a man who has no other patrimony; you can call him the most injurious and basest names; you can make him pay with bitter tears his sad fate and your enviable situation; in short, even maltreat him, slap him, and kill his mortal life. You can do all this and even more, and no one will say that you are a bad Christian so long as you hear mass, you confess, you take communion, and attend all processions, praying all day and fasting on fast days marked on the calendar.[2]

We can indeed be religious but not righteous. But the Holy Scriptures remind us that religiosity and righteousness are not the same (see Psalms 4 and 5). We can be very prayerful, but unless our lives are characterized by righteous living, all our religious acts are mere externalities, without substance or worth. The beginning of righteousness is an experience of God's abundant grace. And the proper response to God's abundant grace is a life that overflows in righteous acts for others.

---

2. Dr. Jose Rizal, "The Religiosity of the Filipino People" (http://www.thefilipinomind. com/2005/10/religiosity-of-filipino-people-dr.html; accessed October 13, 2015).

PSALM 5

One can be religious without being righteous. But not before God. With God, prayers and all kinds of religiosity are nothing without righteousness. Prayer and righteous living go together. The two are parallel in Psalm 5. As the psalmist asks God to listen to his cry and sighing (vv. 1–3), so he declares, "For you are not a God who is pleased with wickedness; with you, evil people are not welcome" (v. 4). The Lord hates "all who do wrong" (v. 5); he detests "the bloodthirsty and deceitful" (v. 6). The psalm does not provide a definition for righteousness; we know what it is through its opposite. Violence, deceit (v. 6), and lies (v. 9) are the things God hates (vv. 5–6). Yet what is instructive is the way God's character is revealed through prayer. In the very words the psalmist is uttering to God, God is reflected as in a mirror.[1] At the same time, the psalmist realizes that the words he is praying are not just prayers. By praying them, he is committing himself to ordering his life according to the character of God revealed in his prayer.[2] The psalmist knows that prayer without righteousness is worthless, and so he prays, "Lead me, LORD, in your righteousness" (v. 8).

The psalmist is aware of threats and danger coming from wicked people, and so he adds, "because of my enemies" (v. 8). References to enemies, or people who oppose the righteous, abound in the Psalms. We were introduced to them in Psalm 1. In Psalm 2 they were represented by the nations/peoples and their kings and rulers. In Psalm 3, they were the "many" who were rising against the psalmist. And in Psalm 4, they were the people who loved vain words and sought after lies (v. 2). Though the psalmist has complained about them, this is the first time that he asks God to deal with them: "Declare them guilty, O God! Let their intrigues be their downfall" (5:10).

There will be many imprecatory prayers like this one in the Psalms (see article, "The Imprecatory Psalms," pp. 274–276). What is significant here is the link this prayer has with righteousness. And I think it is from this perspective that the petition in Psalm 5 should be understood. The concern for righteousness will lead God's people to hate those whom God hates (see

---

1. Walther Zimmerli, *Old Testament Theology in Outline*, 141, writes that God is revealed in the Scriptures not only in the words it has to say about God but also in the response of the people: "And it is also true that in the 'response' God expects from those he addresses God himself can be recognized as in a mirror." Cf. von Rad, *Old Testament Theology*, 355–356.
2. See Gordon J. Wenham, *Psalms as Torah: Reading Biblical Song Ethically* (Grand Rapids: Baker, 2012), 57–76.

139:21). This may sound shocking for some in the light of Jesus' command to love our enemies. But we should not forget that the love of God and the justice of God go together.

Structurally, the psalm may be outlined as follows:

Petition (vv. 1–2a);
Motivation (v. 2b);
Petition (v. 3);
Motivation (vv. 4–6);
Main Petition (vv. 7–8);
Motivation for the main petition (v. 9);
Petition (vv. 10–11):
for the wicked (v. 10): Declare them guilty;
for the righteous (v. 11): Let them be glad and rejoice;
Refrain: For you bless the righteous (v. 12).

The ending of this psalm is similar to that of Psalm 1.

5:1–3 "TO YOU I PRAY"

Psalms 3 and 4 appear to be respectively morning and evening prayers (see comments on 3:5 and 4:8).[3] Now Psalm 5:3 mentions "in the morning" twice (the first explicit mention of "morning" in the Psalms) suggesting that Psalm 5 is also a morning prayer. Some scholars believe that these three psalms were grouped together "to teach the importance of regular prayer."[4]

If this is true, then it is interesting to see what "regular" morning prayer looks like in the light of these psalms. Both morning prayers mention enemies (3:1; 5:8) and in both we find the psalmist crying out to God (3:4; 5:2).[5] We normally want to begin our morning "positively"; we don't want to think about our problems right away. But here we find exactly the opposite. At the start of the day the psalmist is already pleading for God to "consider my lament" (v. 1). In the morning we already hear him lamenting and crying out for help (v. 2).

---

3. The words "lie down and sleep" occur in both psalms (3:5; 4:8). But Psalm 3 goes on to say, "I wake again," suggesting that it may be a morning prayer.
4. Grogan, *Psalms*, 49.
5. These two psalms do contain a note of confidence in God, yet they do not deny the darkness the psalmist has endured.

Some Christians teach that we should start the day positively with rejoicing and praising. That is a good practice. But there are times when we feel like crying even in the morning.[6] The good thing is that even our crying also counts as prayer. Our prayers need not be perfectly formulated to be acceptable to God.

The psalmist begins by calling God "LORD" (v. 1) and then addresses him as "my King and my God" (v. 2). Note the progression in intimacy. It is often during our times of distress that we have more opportunity to be close to our Lord. Note, too, the repetition of the first personal pronoun "my." There is also a sense of urgency, as indicated by the words, "In the morning, LORD, you hear my voice" (v. 3a). He is not content just to say, "Listen to my words" (v. 1); he seems to be saying, "You can actually hear me." At the beginning of the day, he is already pleading his case before the Lord: "in the morning I lay my requests before you and wait expectantly" (v. 3b).[7]

5:4–8 THE KIND OF GOD WE PRAY TO

In verse 2, the psalmist seems to offer some sort of a "motivation" for God to hear him by saying "for to you I pray." Some may ask, is there anyone else to whom he could be praying? But that is not the issue here. Biblical faith is monotheistic. There is only one God. The emphasis is on the word "you" – the kind of God he is praying to. In verses 4–6 the psalmist describes the character of this God to whom he is praying.

He declares, "For you are not a God who is pleased with wickedness" (v. 4). In Psalm 15 the psalmist asks, "Who may dwell in your sacred tent?" (v. 1) and then comes up with a list of characteristics of the people who will be allowed to dwell in God's holy tent (15:2–3):

- The one whose walk is blameless

---

6. Most new commentaries either do not comment or comment very little at all on "crying". Kraus, *Psalms 1–59*, 154, cites in a footnote the following comment by Calvin, but does not discuss it: "Again, the word *cry*, which signifies a loud and sonorous utterance of the voice, serves to mark the earnestness of his desire. David did not cry out as it were into the ears of one who was deaf; but the vehemence of his grief, and his inward anguish, burst forth into his cry." John Calvin, *Commentary on the Book of Psalms*, trans. James Anderson (Grand Rapids: Eerdmans, 1949).

7. Literally, the statement, "I lay my requests" is simply "I prepare to you." The verb does not have a direct object; the NIV supplies the direct object "requests," as the practice of some scholars. Some, like Terrien, see the verb as reflexive: "I prepare myself toward thee" (Samuel Terrien, *The Psalms: Strophic Structure and Theological Commentary* [Grand Rapids: Eerdmans, 2003], 105).

- Who does what is righteous
- Who speaks the truth from their heart;
- Whose tongue utters no slander,
- Who does no wrong to a neighbor,
- And casts no slur on others . . .

Psalm 5 explains why only these people will enter into God's presence. "with you, evil people are not welcome" (v. 4). The kind of life we live should be in accordance with the kind of God we worship.

One of the things God hates the most is being "boastful." Verse 5 tells us that "the arrogant cannot stand in your presence" (v. 5a). In the next line the boastful are described as those "who do wrong" (v. 5b).[8] Pride is the root of evil. There is no place for boasting in the presence of the Lord. The only thing we can boast of is that we know the Lord (Jer 9:24). Boastful people "will not stand" before the Lord, in the same way that "the wicked will not stand in the judgment, nor sinners in the assembly of the righteous" (1:5). The only thing that awaits them is destruction: "You destroy those who tell lies" (5:6).[9] Psalm 5 goes even further to indicate not only God's action against the wicked but also his attitude towards them: "The bloodthirsty and deceitful, you, LORD, detest" (v. 6b). It is not a coincidence that when the psalmist talks about violent people, he uses the strongest word of contempt possible. The Lord does not just hate them; he abhors them![10]

At first it seems that the focus of verse 7 is now on the psalmist because of its opening words: "But I." He is actually drawing a contrast between himself and the wicked. He speaks about entering the "house" of the Lord. Earlier he asserted that the wicked cannot "sojourn with you" (v. 4); that is, the wicked cannot enter into the presence of the Lord. In contrast to this, the psalmist declares, "But I . . . can come into your house" (v. 7). Interestingly, just when we thought he would talk about his own righteousness, he gives all the credit to God. He acknowledges that it is "by your great love" that he can enter into God's presence.[11] Verses 7 and 8 are full of the second person pronoun referring to God. It's all about "your great love," "your holy temple" (v. 7),

---

8. Psalm 15:2 refers to those "who do what is right" (*poel tsedeq*) whereas Ps 5:5 speaks of those "who do wrong" (*poel awen*). Ps 5:5 is in the plural form; Ps 15:2 is in the singular form. But the verb for "do" is the same.

9. Again this reminds us of Psalm 1. The word "destroy" is translated from the Hebrew word *abad,* the last word used in Psalm 1: "but the way of the wicked leads to destruction."

10. In Genesis 6 violence is one of the reasons why the Lord sent the flood to destroy humanity (Gen 6:11, 13).

11. Peter C. Craigie, *Psalms 1–50* (Waco, Texas: Word Books, 1983), 87.

"your righteousness," "your way" (v. 8). It's not about "my way" but "your way." This posture contrasts with that of the boastful (v. 5). The psalmist for his part, once allowed to enter into the house of the Lord, says, "in reverence I bow down toward your holy temple" (v. 7). Literally, "in reverence" reads, "in the fear of you." Here we have an emphasis on God's grace and God's greatness (cf. 62:11–12). Those who experience these will be enabled to live according to his righteousness. But again the psalmist realizes the road towards righteousness will not be easy "because of my enemies" (v. 8). And so he prays that God will make his way straight before him. The mention of the enemy marks another turning point in the psalm.

5:9–10 WHAT THE ENEMIES ARE LIKE

The psalmist is aware of the danger confronting him because of his enemies. In verse 9 he describes the wicked and how dangerous they are. This adds an element of urgency to his prayer. The NIV translation, "Not a word from their mouth can be trusted" is literally "there is nothing established in their[12] mouth." This reminds us of the depiction of the wicked in Psalm 1 as chaff that the wind blows away, in contrast to the righteous who are "planted by streams of water" and thus "established." You cannot rely on the wicked. What is more, "their heart is filled with malice; their throat[13] is an open grave; with their tongues they tell lies" (v. 9). The Apostle Paul cites this verse in Romans 3:10–13. The psalmist prays that God will "Declare them guilty . . . Banish them for their many sins" (v. 10). This may sound too judgmental for some and shocking to others. But we have to understand what the enemies did. The psalm seems to draw a connection between the "great love" of the Lord (v. 7) and the "many sins" of the enemies (v. 10). Both are described using the same phrase: "in your great (*berob*) love" (v. 7) and literally, "in their many (*berob*) sins" (v. 10). The proper response to God's abundant love is gratitude and humility. But the enemies have neither humbled themselves nor repented. Instead, "they have rebelled against you" (v. 10). At its root, ingratitude is an act of rebellion.

---

12. The Hebrew is actually third person singular, but most translations follow the ancient Greek translation of the Old Testament, known as the Septuagint, which has the third person plural.
13. The word "throats" means "inward part" and is parallel to "heart" (Clifford, *Psalms 1–72*, 58).

5:11–12 PRAYER FOR THE RIGHTEOUS

Those who will be allowed to sojourn on the holy hill are people who despise the wicked but honor those who fear the Lord (15:4). So after offering an imprecatory prayer against the wicked, the psalmist now prays that God will "spread your protection" over the righteous (5:11b) and that all who take refuge in God will rejoice: "let them ever sing for joy" (v. 11a). As Wenham writes, "The fundamental characteristic of the righteous is that they depend on God."[14] In Psalm 5 the phrase "all who take refuge in him" (2:12) takes on this added meaning: they not only express their trust in the Lord through prayer, but they also live righteous lives.[15] Indeed, they are called "righteous" in 5:12. For the first time the word "bless" (*barak*) occurs in the Psalms. We often hear Psalm 1 translated as "blessed is the one," when actually the translation there is "happy." At the end of Psalm 2, those who take refuge in the Lord are called happy. At the end of Psalm 5, the psalmist says, "Surely, LORD, you bless the righteous." Here the act of trusting in God is expressed through a life of righteousness. The two go together. (For more on this, see "Split-level Christianity," pp. 44–45).

---

14. Wenham, *Psalms as Torah*, 150.
15. This continues the theme in Psalm 4.

PSALM 6

"All night long I flood my bed with weeping and drench my couch with tears" (6:6). These words are attributed to David – yes, the macho man, David. Unfortunately, in some churches today where the emphasis is on rejoicing and victory, it's hard to find a place where one can cry. This makes Psalm 6, and many other psalms like it, special.[1] They create space for our tears. They make room for our sighing and laments. They tell us it's all right to cry. The psalmist was not ashamed to admit his situation: "I am faint . . . my bones are in agony" (v. 2). He feels as if he is about to die (v. 5) and he is tired of moaning, having flooded his bed with tears (v. 6). Partly he blames his situation on his enemies (v. 7).

We do not know the exact cause of his suffering, but at that time the dominant belief was that suffering meant you had done something wrong. So it was not uncommon to find enemies taking advantage of the situation and coming in to taunt and persecute someone who was suffering. This naturally aggravated the person's suffering.

And so the psalmist pleads for God's mercy, desperately looking for God's answer. God hears him, and "accepts" his prayer (v. 9). The word "accept" is important here. This means that this manner of praying is acceptable to God. It's okay to cry.[2] As a result of God's answer, he is able to turn to his enemies and rebuke them: "Away from me, all you who do evil, for the LORD has heard my weeping" (v. 8).

Structurally, the psalm begins with a plea not to be treated severely (v. 1). Verses 2–3 and 6–7 are parallel; both describe the suffering of the psalmist. In between the descriptions we find the central petition, "Turn, LORD" (vv. 4–5). The last part (vv. 8–10) corresponds to this petition, where the psalmist turns to his enemies and tells them to "depart (literally, "turn") from me."

6:1–3 "HAVE MERCY ON ME, LORD"

Psalm 6 is one of the seven psalms that are traditionally known as penitential psalms. (The others are Pss 32, 38, 51, 102, 130, and 143.) Of the other penitential psalms, Psalm 6 is closest to Psalm 38. Their opening words are

---

1. E.g. "My tears have been my food day and night" (Ps 42:3); "list my tears on your scroll" (Ps 56:8).
2. Villanueva, *It's OK To Be NOT OK*.

basically the same: "LORD, do not rebuke me in your anger, or discipline me in your wrath" (6:1; 38:1).[3] But Psalm 6 differs from the other penitential psalms in that it contains no explicit admission of sin.[4] But this does not necessarily mean the psalmist has not been repenting his sins. Nowhere is he asserting his own righteousness, something he is capable of doing as can be seen in Psalm 7. The emphasis is rather on "mercy" (v. 2). He is not questioning the "rebuke" or "discipline" (v. 1) he is receiving. He only pleads that it not be too much. As Calvin explains, "He does not take God to task as if he had been an enemy, treating him with cruelty without any just cause; but yielding to him the right of rebuking and chastening, he desires and prays only that bounds may be set to the punishment inflicted on him."[5] Just like Jeremiah, the psalmist is asking, "Discipline me, LORD, but only in due measure—not in your anger, or you will reduce me to nothing" (Jer 10:24).

The psalmist is in a terrible situation. He is languishing and his "bones are in agony" (Ps 6:2). St. Augustine understands "bones" here as "the support of my soul, or strength." If we think of the bones as the structure holding the whole body together, then the language of "bones in agony" refers to a situation where the whole being of the person is crumbling, like a wall about to fall (cf. 62:3). This person no longer has any strength left.[6] And this situation has been going on for a long time now. Hence the cry, "How long?"[7] (6:3). This makes the suffering even more unbearable. As Hengstenberg comments, "In troubles of this kind, delay is the most severe and insupportable pain."[8]

In such a situation the psalmist comes to God (vv. 1–3). His prayer reveals to us the character of God as one who is merciful and gracious. He allows his people to pour out their hearts to him when they feel their suffering

---

3. The only very minor difference is that in the original Hebrew, Ps 38:1 does not have the second negative *al*.

4. Of the seven penitential prayers, the only other psalm which does not contain this element is Psalm 102. See also the prayers of confession in Ezra 9:6–15; Neh 1:5–11; 9:6–37; Dan 9:4–19. For a detailed analysis of these prayers highlighting the element of admission of sins, see Federico G. Villanueva, "Confession of Sins or Petition for Forgiveness: A Comparative Study of the Penitential Prayers in Ezra 9, Nehemiah 1, 9, and Daniel 9," (ThM thesis, Asia Graduate School of Theology, Manila, 2002).

5. Calvin, *Commentary on the Book of Psalms*, 66.

6. St. Augustine, *Expositions on the Book of Psalms* (Oxford: John H. Parker, 1847–1857), 36.

7. The question "how long?" is introduced by the adversative "but," which in other cases may signal a turn to a more confident mood (e.g. Ps 3:3 – "But you, O LORD, are a shield around me"). But here the adversative only pulls the psalmist even further down as he cries out, "But you, O LORD, how long?"

8. Ernst W. Hengstenberg, *Commentary on the Psalms* (3rd ed.; Edinburgh: T&T Clark, 1851), 99.

is already beyond what they can bear. They can actually come to the Lord and say, "God, it's just too much already." They acknowledge that God's actions are just and fair. They also know that he is merciful. He is not a cruel judge who cannot be questioned once he has assigned punishment. With God, we can be assured we will be heard, for he is merciful.

6:4–5 "RETURN, O LORD"

Still reflecting on the merciful character of God, the psalmist prays, "Turn, LORD" (v. 4). The word "turn" comes from the Hebrew word *shub* which can also be translated "return." It is used elsewhere to call people to repentance (Jer 3:13; Hos 14:1). Obviously, the psalmist is not asking God to "repent." Rather, he is praying that God "return" to him because he can already hear the words "return to dust" as echoed in Psalm 90:3, "You turn people back to dust, saying, 'Return to dust, you mortals'" (cf. Job 34:15; Gen 3:19; Eccl 3:20). He feels near to death and near the place called *Sheol*, the "underworld abode of the dead."[9] In such a place, the psalmist asks, "Who can give you praise?" (v. 5). This is a rhetorical question, to which the expected answer is "no one."

The doctrine of the afterlife is not yet as fully developed as it is in the NT. This may explain the urgency in his prayer, although even with a fully developed doctrine of resurrection, a suffering believer may also find himself or herself in a similar position. Prolonged or excessive suffering brings us to a place where we find there is only one to whom we can go. And on the basis of his mercy we cry: "save me because of your unfailing love" (v. 4).

6:6–7 "TO YOU, O LORD, I CRY"

As we have seen in the previous psalms, crying is common. In Psalm 5 we heard the "sound of my cry" (5:2, NRSV). Here he talks about flooding his bed with tears and drenching his couch with weeping (v. 6). People cried loudly in ancient times. Joseph Roberts writes: "Silent grief is not much known in the East. Hence, when the people speak of lamentation, they say, Have I not heard the voice of his mourning?"[10]

---

9. Clifford, *Psalms 1–72*, 62.
10. Joseph Roberts, *Oriental Illustrations of the Sacred Scriptures, Collected from the Customs, Manners, Rites, Superstitions, Traditions, Parabolical, Idiomatical, and Proverbial Forms of Speech, Climate, Works of Art, and Literature, of the Hindoos* (2d ed., London: Printed for Thomas Tegg, 1844), 305; cited in Hengstenberg, 102.

This is also true in more traditional cultures. Ancient Filipinos are known for their mourning when bereaved. They mourn before, during and after the funeral.[11] But this is becoming rare in modern times, according to James Wilce. He observes that traditional mourning has become "increasingly rare" over the last century. He says "people laugh at, or express religious disapproval of, crying out loud. Quiet crying is becoming more common, particularly among urban classes and upwardly mobile rural people. They express a kind of shame about 'traditions' like loud crying."[12] Even modern Bible commentators think the description in verses 6–7 may "sound bizarre to modern observers"[13] and seem "laughable to us."[14]

But for suffering people, weeping is not "bizarre" and is never "laughable." It is normal for them. Together with the psalmist they can cry, "How long?" The good news is that when we cry to God, when we weep on our beds, he is listening. He even keeps a record of our tears (see 56:8).

My former senior pastor was once asked by a church member why his face was always radiant. He responded: *"Dahil ibinabad sa luha"* ("Because it has been drenched in tears"). It is our tears through the night that transform our faces into radiance.

6:8–10 "THE LORD ACCEPTS MY PRAYER"

In the very next verse we hear the psalmist speaking with a new voice, the voice of confidence. He mentioned his enemies at the end of verse 7, and now he turns to them and tells them: "Away from me, all you who do evil, for the LORD has heard my weeping" (v. 8). Notice that he uses the word "weeping," which recalls verses 6–7, showing that this is an important element in the psalm. There is a clear transition here. First, there is a shift from addressing the Lord directly to addressing his enemies. Second, there is a change of mood. From his pitiful condition, the psalmist testifies that the Lord has heard his supplication, and "the LORD accepts my prayer" (v. 9). The prayer that was full of tears was acceptable to God. With assurance he declares that "all my enemies will . . . turn back" (v. 10). The word for "turn back" is the

---

11. Pablo Fernandez, O. P., *History of the Church in the Philippines (1521–1898)* (Manila, Philippines: National Bookstore, 1979), 8–9.
12. James M. Wilce, *Crying Shame: Metaculture, Modernity, and the Exaggerated Death of Lament* (Oxford: Wiley-Blackwell, 2009), 3.
13. Terrien, *The Psalms*, 114.
14. Goldingay, *Psalms*, Vol. 1, 138.

word used by the psalmist when he asked God to "turn" (v. 4). Because God has turned to him, his enemies will "turn back."

Crying, lamenting and grieving is part of our culture as indicated in our poetry (e.g. *kundiman*, Florante at Laura), literature (*Pasyon*), and grieving practices (*dung-aw*, "crying for the dead"). But with the influence of modern Western culture we are losing this tradition. In some of our churches we rarely hear songs of lament. Even when we are suffering we continue to sing victory songs. In our funeral services some groups are singing happy songs – a stumbling block to most Filipinos who have a deep sense of sympathy (we call it *pakikiramay* or being at one with those who suffer). That is why Psalm 6 is an important psalm for us, to recapture this tradition of crying. There are times when our situation calls for weeping, not dancing. And we should not feel guilty or think it is unacceptable to God to do so. The examples of Psalm 6 and of our Lord himself teach us that we can cry to God. Remember, "Jesus wept" too (John 11:35).

WHAT IS LAMENT?

People complain about almost anything – traffic, the cost of living, government, and so. But a lament is very different from simply complaining. We lament when something has gone terribly wrong – as when a loved one has died or some natural disaster has struck. None of our usual methods of coping work and the situation persists or even worsens. Like the writers of the lament psalms, we find ourselves crying out, "How long?" (Ps 13). It feels unfair. "Why?" is the characteristic cry of those who lament (Ps 22). Why me? Why my child? Why? Why? Why?

When we are in a situation like this, we long to be somewhere else. Like the psalmist we sigh, "Oh, that I had the wings of a dove! I would fly away and be at rest. I would flee far away and stay in the desert; I would hurry to my place of shelter, far from the tempest and storm" (Ps 55:6–8). We feel alone, "like a bird alone on a roof" (102:7). We flood our bed with tears (6:6). We are overwhelmed and feel we are about to be engulfed by the raging waters (69:2). We struggle with finding our way. We feel lost. We are angry with the world (62:3), with others (55:12–15), and even with God. We feel hurt that he has left us (42:9).

In spite of our situation, we refuse to give up. We struggle and fight. We try to face our fears, confront our issues, and deal with our situation *in the presence of the Lord*. Though we wish to "fly away" and be gone, we choose to stay and face our pain. From the depths, we "cry aloud to the Lord" (142:1). With groans washed in tears we utter our prayer to him, whom we believe remains present though unseen and unfelt. We pour out our hearts to him, as one does to a friend or a loved one. Lament is a prayer of the most intimate kind.

Lament occurs in the context of a relationship because we do not just pour out our hearts to anybody. We lament to God because he is our God, our Father, and our friend. He made a covenant with his people, first in the OT and later through the blood of Jesus Christ. As Jesus told his disciples, "I no longer call your servants . . . Instead, I have called you friends" (John 15:15). The ability to lament is an indication of intimacy with God. That is why, David cries out, "*my* God, *my* God, why have you forsaken me?" (Ps 22:1).

Asians generally have a deep respect for superiors and for those who are older than us. So to some of us, the lament psalms may seem disrespectful. But it is not a sign of disrespect to tell God what we truly feel. It is better to be honest with him than to nurse feelings of anger or bitterness. As we say in Filipino, "*Ang nagsasabi ng tapat, nagsasama ng maluwat*" (Being honest makes for better relationships).

One indication that we are free to lament to God is the fact that a third of the psalms are psalms of lament. There are more lament psalms than thanksgiving or praise psalms.

A typical lament psalm like Psalm 13 has the following elements (see Psalm 13):

Invocation

Complaint

Petition

Sudden change of mood

Expression of trust or vow of thanksgiving

The most common movement is from lament to praise. But not all laments follow the same sequence. Some lament psalms begin with thanksgiving and move on to lament (e.g. Pss 9–10; Ps 40). Others contain a movement from lament to praise and then end in lament (Ps 12). There are three lament psalms that do not contain any movement to thanksgiving or praise – Psalms 39, 70, and 88. These are called "pure laments."

The variety of movements and types of laments reflects the reality of life. Although we do experience deliverance and answers to our prayers, there are times when we receive the opposite of what we are praying for. Instead of experiencing healing and victory, we find that our condition worsens and there is defeat. But what is encouraging is that even the latter has a place in God's sovereign grace. There is a place for all kinds of laments in the presence of the Lord. So long as we are honest to God about what we truly feel and express our feelings in the context of a growing intimate relationship with God, our lament is acceptable to him.

PSALM 7

A member of our church was fired from his job for no reason at all except that, according to his boss, he did not know how to "dance with the music." In other words, he did not say "yes" to everything the boss said, even when it was not right. That was the problem: he did not cooperate. Instead, he exposed the corruption in their office. So his boss fired him. What should this Christian do? He had done nothing wrong.

Some Christians, especially those who have known oppression and colonialism, may respond passively and not fight for their rights. Psalm 7 presents a challenge to this outlook. It tells us it is okay to fight for our rights. Like the psalmist, we can say, "Vindicate me, LORD, according to my righteousness, according to my integrity" (Ps 7:8). There is room in the presence of God for presenting our case. If we know we have done nothing wrong, then we can come to God and plead for his justice. And if it is okay to do this in the presence of God, then by implication it is also okay to do this before people.

For many of us, this type of prayer is not an easy one to appreciate. We do not normally assert our righteousness. Isn't this a form of *pagbubuhat ng sariling bangko* ("carrying one's own chair" [a form of boasting])? Doesn't the psalmist lack humility? Yet before rejecting the psalm right away, we should read it closely and in its entirety.

We should also note that this psalm challenges us about how we live and about our view of God. Do we have the confidence that we have done nothing wrong in relation to the accusations against us? Is there no blood on our hands? It's not easy to read or pray this psalm if we are not living right before the Lord. And do we truly think of God as righteous, the one who searches the innermost being of people (v. 9) and who judges people with equity? If so, how does it affect how we act and how we pray?

The psalmist pleads his case before God with desperation and a sense of urgency. He boldly tells God that if he did anything wrong, then his enemy should trample his life to the ground (v. 5). He asks God to take action against those who furiously attack him (vv. 6–9). He places his trust in God (vv. 10–11), but recognizes that if God does not do something (v. 12a) then he is in trouble, for the wicked are bent on mischief (vv. 12–14). But that did not happen, for God acted (vv. 15–16), and so the psalm ends with a vow of thanksgiving (v. 17).

7:1–5 "LORD MY GOD, I TAKE REFUGE IN YOU"

In the Psalms, the idea of taking refuge in the Lord is first mentioned in Psalm 2:12. It means putting one's whole trust in the Lord. In Psalm 5 we saw that taking refuge in the Lord is closely connected with living a righteous life. In the present psalm this emphasis on righteousness now applies in a situation of extreme desperation. The psalmist is being falsely accused by his enemies. He has nowhere to go but God.

In the OT a person who was being pursued by his enemies but had done nothing wrong could go to the Temple and plead his case before the Lord.[1] This is the background for the psalmist's statement in verse 1. The psalmist is in a desperate situation. If the Lord does not act, he will be "eaten alive" by his enemies. The image used is that of a lion tearing apart his prey (v. 2). So he presents his case to the Lord, the righteous judge.

How does one present a case before the Lord? The psalmist utters words equivalent to an oath: "If I have done this . . . then let my enemy pursue and overtake me; let him trample my life to the ground" (vv. 3–5). He says that if he has done something wrong, he is prepared to accept any consequence from his enemies, even if this would mean his destruction. Some of us may find these words too bold, even boastful. We cannot even imagine praying like this. But we are dealing here with a difficult case. As Terrien explains, "In exceptional circumstances, with an appeal to the just judge, one easily understands that the supplicant would defend with vigor his integrity and even his rights."[2] Of course, in normal situations, we would not pray in this way. At the same time, however, "the psalm assumes that people who belong to God should be able to claim that they have been living faithful lives."[3]

7:6–9 "RETURN . . . ESTABLISH THE RIGHTEOUS"

There is a great sense of urgency in the prayer of the psalmist. He wants God to act right away, and so he calls on him to "arise" and to "awake" (v. 6). We have a song in Filipino entitled, *Natutulog ba ang Diyos?* ("Is God sleeping?"). Of course we know that God never sleeps, unlike the gods of the nations (1 Kgs 18:27). But sometimes when you are in a desperate situation you want God to do something right away so that even a little delay might lead you to

---

1. Kraus, *Psalms 1–59*, 169, cites 1 Kgs 8:3 1ff. as background for the possible setting of this psalm.
2. Terrien, *The Psalms*, 123.
3. Goldingay, *Psalms*, 145.

suspect that God may be sleeping (Mark 4:38). The psalmist asks God to act not just swiftly but also in a way that matches the "rage of my enemies" (v. 6).

In verses 7–8 we enter a courtroom where God himself is the judge. The psalmist prays that God will take his rightful place as a judge. Verse 7b literally reads, "on it to the heights return." I think the word "return" is important here. It occurs again in verses 12 and 16. Like most modern versions, the NIV reads the Hebrew as deriving from a different root, *yashab* ("to sit"). Thus, the translation, "sit enthroned." But in the Hebrew and in the ancient Greek translation known as the Septuagint, the word is *shub* ("return"). So we should maintain it (see the ESV). The psalmist not only feels that God has to be awakened, but also that God should "return" to his rightful place as a "righteous" judge (v. 9). Unlike human judges, God knows the deepest recesses of our being; he knows what is in our hearts: "you, the righteous God, who probes minds and hearts" (v. 9). This was one of the prophet Jeremiah's favorite description of God, for Jeremiah knew what is was to be falsely accused (Jer 11:20; 17:10; 20:12; cf. also Rev 2:23).[4] For those who cannot find justice, God becomes the ultimate Judge.

In verse 9, the psalmist prays: "let the evil of the wicked come to an end, but establish the righteous" (v. 9, NRSV). The grammatical construction of the prayer is similar to the statement about the wicked and the righteous in Psalm 1:6: "for the Lord watches over the way of the righteous, but the way of the wicked leads to destruction." The Lord is directly involved in the life of the righteous as reflected in the petition, "establish the righteous." By contrast, the wicked are left to perish on their own.

7:10–14 "IF GOD DOES NOT RELENT"

When you are falsely accused, arrows are aimed at you from all directions. This probably explains why the psalmist refers to God as "my shield" (v. 10a). God is not only a refuge, he is also a shield. But God is a shield only for those who are "upright in heart" (v. 10b). For those who are not upright, the "righteous judge" is a "God who displays his wrath every day" (v. 11).

Verses 12–14 are ambiguous. The Hebrew text simply reads, "If he does not relent, he will sharpen his sword" (v. 12). It is not clear whether the "he" is God or the wicked. Some translations like the NRSV interpret the first "he" as referring to the wicked and the second as referring to God, yielding the

---

4. Alexander F. Kirkpatrick, *The Book of Psalms* (Cambridge, UK: University Press, 1895), 33.

reading: "If one does not repent, God will whet his sword" (cf. ESV). This translation has God offering the wicked a chance to repent, an idea which is present elsewhere in the Psalms. As Alter writes, "Although Psalms repeatedly divides the world into the doomed wicked and the righteous who will flourish, it also allows for the possibility that those bent on evil may turn back."[5] For instance, in Psalm 2 the psalmist warns the kings and rulers to act in a particular manner so that they will not be destroyed (vv. 10–11). Likewise, in Psalm 4, the psalmist offers advice even to the very people who persecute him (vv. 4–5). Sadly, the wicked do not repent in spite of the warnings: "See how they conceive evil, and are pregnant with mischief" (v. 14, NRSV). Notice the progression of evil here (cf. also 1:1), from conceiving of evil to becoming pregnant with mischief to giving birth to lies.

Another possibility is that the first "he" in verse 12 refers to God and the second "he" to the wicked. After all, the previous verse began "God is a righteous judge." If God was the subject of that sentence, it would be natural for him to be the subject in verse 12. Moreover, in verse 7 the psalmist begged God to "return" (see above). The same verb is often translated "relent/repent" in verse 12, but it is possible that the psalmist is linking the two verses and implying that if God does not "return," the psalmist will suffer unjust consequences at the hands of the wicked. If God does not "return" (or answer), there will be no one to hinder the wicked from destroying the psalmist. The construction is also similar to the earlier petition beginning "If I have done this . . ." (vv. 3–4) with the character of the enemy as depicted in verse 2. He is bent on destroying the psalmist. The image of someone preparing the bow and arrow is used elsewhere to refer to the wicked (v. 11:2). Verse 14 also fits in well with this interpretation.

Whichever interpretation is correct, the good news for the psalmist is that God did return. We observe what happens to the enemies in the following verses.

7:15–17 "THE TROUBLE THEY CAUSE RECOILS ON THEM"

There is a dramatic turnaround in verses 15–16. The psalmist's enemies dug a deep pit to trap him in, but they were the ones to fall into the hole they had made (v. 15). What is surprising is that the psalmist does not use any strong expressions to introduce this defeat. He just mentions it without marking

---

5. Robert Alter, *The Book of Psalms* (New York: Norton, 2007), 20. But he did not give examples in the Psalms.

it as a climax to his prayer. It's the same with the portrayal of the miracle of the feeding of the five thousand in the NT. The narrator just presents it as if nothing spectacular had occurred.

Maybe that is the way God works. When he does something, it looks so simple, as if it is nothing out of the ordinary. But you know something has taken place that will alter the whole story. God has "returned" (cf. v. 12) and as a result the "the trouble they cause recoils [literally "returns"] on them" (v. 16).[6]

This deliverance naturally leads to thanksgiving. The psalmist vows to "give thanks to the LORD because of his righteousness, and sing the praises of the name of the LORD Most High" (v. 17). Notice that the psalmist ends with a declaration of God's righteousness ("his righteousness"), not "my righteousness." That's how it is when we have experienced God's gracious power in our lives.

---

6. The verb in both vv. 12 and 16 which is translated "return" is exactly the same in form – *yashub*.

PSALM 8

Psalm 8 is the first hymn of praise in the Psalms. It is also the first text in the Bible to reach the moon when Apollo 11 landed on July 20, 1969. Most of the preceding psalms are laments. In Psalm 3 we hear the psalmist crying, "LORD, how many are my foes!" (v. 1). In Psalm 4 we heard him complaining, "How long will you people turn my glory into shame?" (v. 2). In Psalm 6, we felt his agonizing cry, "How long, LORD, how long?" (v. 3b). Notice the word "how" is repeated three times. The word comes from the same Hebrew word (*mah*) in Psalm 3:1, 4:2, and 8:1. So we still hear the same word in Psalm 8. But the sound is different. It is the sound of wonder, of amazement, of exultation: "LORD, our Lord, *how* majestic is your name in all the earth!" (v. 1). How we have waited for this one! Those reading the Psalms from the beginning might have wondered whether they would ever see or hear a hymn of praise, as lament after lament keeps coming. The good news is that it's not all laments. There are also hymns of praise.

The arrangement of the first cluster of psalms is very interesting. Psalm 8 is preceded by laments (Pss 3–7) and followed by another set of laments (Pss 9–14). It seems as if the one who arranged these psalms did so on purpose.[1] The arrangement matches our experience, in which our praise is surrounded by laments, and our laments include praise.

The praise in Psalm 8 arises out of the psalmist's contemplation of the greatness of God, which has made a deep impact on his heart. What has led to his sense of wonder and amazement is the realization that this great God, though high and exalted in the heavens, has condescended "so far as graciously to take upon him the care of the human race."[2] As Hengstenberg notes, "The greatness of the Lord in his creation of the world is only celebrated for the purpose of presenting in a more striking light his condescending goodness towards weak man."[3] The structure of the psalm reflects this emphasis. The refrain at the beginning and end of the psalm (vv. 1, 9) finds its central point in the question of verse 4: "What is mankind that you are mindful of

---

1. Zenger sees Psalms 3–14 as forming a cluster. See Erich Zenger, "Was wird anders bei kanonischer Psalmenauslegung?" in *Gott, eine Offenbarung*, eds. Friedrich Vinzenz Reiterer and Notker Füglister (Würzburg: Echter, 1991), 397–413.
2. Calvin, *Commentary on the Book of Psalms*, 99–100.
3. Hengstenberg, *Commentary on the Psalms*, 125; cf. also Calvin, *Commentary on the Book of Psalms*, 99–100.

them?"[4] The psalm alternates between an emphasis on the greatness of God (vv. 1, 3) and the fact that he still pays attention to human beings (vv. 2, 4).

8:1–2 "HOW MAJESTIC IS YOUR NAME IN ALL THE EARTH!"

The psalm begins with the address, "LORD, *our* Lord." This is not just an intellectual or objective statement. The psalmist is talking about something he has experienced with this God. This God is "*our* Lord." There is also a strong sense of community. God is not only "my Lord;" he is "*our* Lord." In times of lament, when others have turned their backs on us and we feel so alone, we call him "my God" (cf. 7:1; 22:1). But it seems that in praise we are more drawn to the community. We are bursting with joy and amazement and we want others to share this with us. We want to call our brothers and sisters and say, "Glorify the LORD with me" (Ps 34:3). In Psalm 8 it seems the psalmist is so caught up in praising God that he does not address the community at all.[5] The whole psalm is directed to God.

The psalmist praises the greatness of God's name, which is exalted "in all the earth" (8:1). Names in the Bible are significant, for they represent who a person is and what he does. So God's name represents all that he is for the psalmist, as far as he has experienced and known him. The second part of verse 1 continues the theme of the first line. This time God's glory is not only "in all the earth" but also "in the heavens."

The transition to verse 2 is surprising to say the least. The psalmist has just been talking about the height and breadth of God's glory, and then without any warning he suddenly mentions "children and infants" (v. 2). We are reminded of the story about Jesus bringing in a little child and having him stand in the midst of the disciples (Matt 18:1–5). The disciples had been talking about who should be the greatest in the kingdom of heaven. They must have been shocked when Jesus called a child and had this child stand in their midst. Children "were the powerless ones on the bottom rung of Hebrew and other ancient societies."[6] The word-pair "babes and infants," according to Lund, "is a set phrase for the most helpless of the people."[7]

---

4. Øystein Lund, "From the Mouth of Babes and Infants You Have Established Strength," *SJOT* 11 (1997): 96–97, has some interesting observations on the structure of the psalm. He notes how similar the refrain and the question in v. 4 are.
5. Usually, in the genre called hymns to which Psalm 8 belongs, there is an address to the congregation (e.g. Psalms 100, 117).
6. Joseph A. Grassi, "Child, Children," *ABD* 1: 905.
7. Lund, "From the Mouth of Babes," 85.

It occurs seven times in 1 Samuel 15:3, 22:19, Jeremiah 44:7, Psalm 8:3, Lamentations 2:11, 4:4, and Joel 2:16[8] in "contexts of destruction and horror."[9] Thus "Psalm 8 applies the expression to create an association with the weakest groups of people, those who are elsewhere only mentioned in connection with extermination."[10] In the same way that Jesus set a child before his disciples, so here the psalmist declares, "Out of the mouth of babes and infants, you have established strength" (Ps 8:2, ESV). The weakest and the lowest become strong and great because the great God has "established strength" "out of their mouths."

The meaning of the phrase, "out of their mouths," has proven a challenge to scholars.[11] The ancient Greek translation of the OT known as the Septuagint (LXX) translates the Hebrew word for "strength" as "praise" (cf. NIV), which works better with "out of their mouths."[12] There is a tradition which links Psalm 8 with the song in Exodus 15, saying that at the crossing of the Red Sea, even the children praised God. For example, according to the apocryphal book known as the Wisdom of Solomon, when Israel crossed the Red Sea, Wisdom "opened the mouth of the dumb, and made the tongues of babes speak clearly" (Wis 10:21).[13]

Whether we adopt the reading "strength" or "praise," the verse highlights God's condescension in reaching out to humanity. If it is true that the kind of God we have is known by the kind of worshipers he has, then it is instructive that God is associated with the lowest in society as the psalmist knows it. This moves him to an even deeper sense of awe at God's greatness, which is expressed in the next verses.

But briefly before that, the psalmist mentions "your enemies." He also refers to an "enemy" and "avenger" (Ps 8:2). It is not clear who these are. It has been suggested that this is a reference to the ancient Mesopotamian creation story, Enuma-elish, which depicts creation in terms of conflict and opposition and chaos.[14] In contrast to this, God's creation came about in an orderly fashion, coming into being by the power of the Almighty God.

---

8. Ibid.

9. Terrien, *The Psalms*, 128; cf. also Goldingay, *Psalms*, vol. 1, 156.

10. Lund, "From the Mouth of Babes," 86, mentions this figurative interpretation, although he himself favors a more literal interpretation.

11. Ibid.,78–79.

12. Matt 21:16 follows the Septuagint (LXX).

13. William D. Davies and Dale C. Allison, *Matthew: A Shorter Commentary* (London/New York: T&T Clark, 2004), 352. Cf. Martin McNamara, *Palestinian Judaism and the New Testament* (Dublin: Veritas, 1983), 250–251.

14. The connection with Genesis 1 in the latter part of Psalm 8 also points in this direction.

8:3–4 "WHAT IS MANKIND THAT YOU ARE MINDFUL OF THEM?"

In verse 3 we are back to an emphasis on the greatness of God. The psalmist no longer speaks in terms of "our God" and instead speaks as an individual, using the word "I." We are privileged to share in his personal experience. He looks up to the heavens and sees the "moon and the stars." The "heavens" are described as "the work of your fingers." They are like "the art of a sculptor whose fingers, even more than his hands, fashion and mold the intricate designs of the Milky Way."[15]

We are invited to stop and see the work of the universe's Artist. Having surveyed and pondered the vastness of the heavens, the light from millions of stars singing their praises to their Master, the psalmist is led to wonder, "What is mankind that you are mindful of them, human beings that you care for them?" (v. 4). He is full of awe at how a God so great would even pay attention to human beings. And yet the marvel of all marvels is that God does indeed pay attention to us. What's more, he cares for us!

8:5–9 GOD HONORS HUMAN BEINGS

God has made human beings a "little lower than angels" (v. 5). The word "angles" here comes from *elohim*, a plural form that can be translated "gods." When used to refer to God, it is translated as singular. Yet it is also possible that the word may refer to heavenly beings or angels. The Septuagint seems to have this view as it translates the word as "angels."[16] The language used to refer to humans is the language of royalty.[17] God crowns us with "glory and honor" (v. 5).

Further, God has given humans dominion over the works of his hands – the sheep, the cattle, the birds of the air, and the fish of the sea (vv. 7–9). This should not lead us to exploit creation. Instead, our privileged position should lead us to worship and praise our maker. Worship should then lead us to become responsible "rulers" of the earth, for in the Psalms creation worships the Lord. The psalmist even calls upon the trees to sing for joy (96:12; see also Isa 55:12).

---

15. Terrien, *The Psalms*, 129.
16. The Hebrew version of the Old Testament known as the Masoretic Text reads, "you caused him to lack a little than gods," while the Septuagint reads, "you made him a little lower than angels."
17. McCann, "The Book of Psalms," 711–712.

8:10 "HOW MAJESTIC IS YOUR NAME IN ALL THE EARTH!"

The final refrain is unusual in that it exactly repeats verse 1: "O LORD, our Lord, how majestic is your name in all the earth" (v. 9, ESV). Alter writes:

> It closes a perfect circle that celebrates the harmony of God's creation. The "all" component to the "all the earth," which at first might have seemed like part of a formulaic phrase, takes on cumulative force at the very end of the poem. God's majesty is manifest in all things, and the creature fashioned in his image has been given dominion over all things. The integrated harmony of the created world as the poet perceives it and the integrated harmony of the poem make a perfect match.[18]

What makes the psalm even more striking is in its portrayal of the God who is perfect in power and majesty yet reaches down to the weak and vulnerable, empowers them, and crowns them with glory. For many of us in Asia who have experienced colonization, there is a tendency to look down on ourselves. The foreign is always viewed as better than the local. "Stateside" is always better. We struggle with low self-esteem. Part of this has to do with how we were treated by our colonizers. In our case, the Spaniards made us feel as if we were second-class citizens in our own land. Even our national hero Jose Rizal was caned and imprisoned for failing to salute an officer. The Americans too regarded us as "little children" needing help. But Psalm 8 tells us that though we may not be important in the eyes of the world, in God's eyes we are special. The God who is greater and more powerful than the leaders of the richest nations of the earth has taken the time to reach down to us. We are indeed very special!

---

18. Alter, *The Book of Psalms*, 24.

PSALMS 9–10

At the end of Psalm 7 the psalmist made a vow to give thanks to the Lord (v. 17). Psalm 9–10 can be read as a fulfillment of that vow.[1] Its opening words pick up the same theme from Psalm 7: "I will give thanks to you, LORD, with all my heart" (9:1). These words also capture the theme of Psalm 9–10, for it is a psalm of thanksgiving.

But what does it mean to thank the Lord? For some the answer is obvious – thanking the Lord. But in Psalm 9–10 an important element is added to the thanksgiving – lament. The second half of the psalm is a lament. That may be why Psalms 9 and 10 appear to be two separate psalms in our Bible, although they are actually a single psalm.[2] We know this is the case because they were composed using the Hebrew alphabet. Verses 1–2 of Psalm 9 begin with the first letter of the Hebrew alphabet, verses 4–5 with the second letter, and so on. By the time we reach Psalm 10, we are at the letter *lamed* – the equivalent of the English letter "l"[3] and the alphabetic pattern continues until Psalm 10 ends with the last letter of the Hebrew alphabet (vv. 17–18). If we stopped reading at the end of Psalm 9, the psalm would be incomplete.

By combining thanksgiving and lament, Psalm 9–10 radically changes our usual understanding of thanksgiving. Thanksgiving includes lament. Without lament our thanksgiving is incomplete. And the movement from thanksgiving (Ps 9) to lament (Ps 10) reminds us of the reality of the life of faith, which includes tragedy. From this perspective, the opening words of the psalm take on new meaning. By beginning with the words, "I will give thanks to the LORD with my whole heart," the psalmist incorporates all of life's experiences – the joyful and the sad, the tragic and the victorious. Everything is brought into the presence of God. The very form of the psalm reinforces this sense of completeness.[4] When we thank the Lord, we cannot ignore the sufferings of our world.

---

1. Patrick D. Miller, "The Beginning of the Psalter," in *The Shape and Shaping of the Psalter*, ed. J. Clinton McCann (Sheffield, UK: JSOT Press, 1993), 90.
2. In Hebrew and in the ancient Greek translation known as the Septuagint, the two psalms are counted as one.
3. The acrostic is not perfect, since some letters are missing, but the formation of Psalm 9–10 as a single psalm is clear.
4. What is the function of an acrostic? Commenting on Psalm 119 – the longest acrostic in the Bible – Wenham explains that it is "an aid for memorization . . . But it also helps to underline the message of a poem. By going through the whole alphabet systematically, it conveys the

9:1–2 "I WILL GIVE THANKS"

As noted above, verse 1 expresses the overall theme of the psalm – "I will give thanks to you, LORD, with all my heart." Twice in this verse the word "all" (*kol*) is used: "*all* my heart" and "*all* your wonderful deeds" (v. 1). Thanksgiving involves the act of "telling" or declaring the wonderful things that God has done. When the heart is full of thanksgiving it is impossible to be quiet (cf. 30:11–12). For with thanksgiving comes rejoicing: "I will be glad and rejoice in you" (v. 2). The words are similar to the Apostle Paul's famous "Rejoice in the Lord" (Phil 4:4). Although the psalmist recognizes the wonderful things God has done, God himself remains the object of his joy.

9:3–6 WHAT GOD HAS DONE

When God is the object of one's joy, recalling what God has done becomes an occasion for further exulting in God. In verses 3–6 the psalmist recalls what God has done to his enemies. "Enemies" occur at the beginning and end of this section (vv. 3 and 6). The enemies here are not what we might call "personal enemies." The enemies are the "wicked" (v. 5) who oppress the weak and the poor (see v. 9; 10:2, 8–10). God's destruction of these enemies should be seen in the context of the next section, which highlights the righteousness and equity of God's judgment.

9:7–11 SING PRAISES TO THE LORD

In contrast to the wicked whose memory God has blotted out forever (vv. 5–6), "the LORD reigns forever" (v. 7). The good news is that the righteous judge, whose rule is characterized by righteousness and equity (v. 8), reigns "forever." Nations and cities fall but God remains in control.

God is said to be a "refuge for the oppressed" (v. 9). "Oppressed" is the first of five words used to refer to the poor in this psalm. The word is important as it sheds some light on the previous verses. Seen in the light of verse 9, the enemies in the previous section are those who oppress the weak. The word "oppressed" also establishes further support for the link between Psalms 9 and 10 for it recurs at the end of Psalm 10 (v. 18). In verse 9 the word

---

idea of totality or completeness" (Wenham, *Psalms as Torah*, 82). This can be applied to Psalm 9–10. By using an acrostic the psalmist underlines what it means to thank God with one's "whole heart."

"oppressed" is also linked with the key phrase, "in times of trouble," which reappears in 10:1.

The psalmist asserts that "those who know your name trust in you" (9:10). With this conviction the psalmist exhorts the people to "Sing the praises of the Lord" (v. 11). The psalmist has already declared that he will "sing praise" to God's name (v. 2b), and here he calls on the people to do the same.

A motivation statement follows the call to worship: "For he who avenges blood remembers" (v. 12). Literally, the Hebrew reads, "For he who seeks (darash) blood." The word "seek" (darash) occurs later in 10:13 in the context of a lament.

The reference to the "cry of the afflicted"[5] (9:12b) signals the shift to the petition that follows.

9:13–14 "BE GRACIOUS TO ME"

We might expect thanksgiving to contain only words of praise and rejoicing. But in verse 13 we are reminded of the dynamic nature of thanksgiving. Thanksgiving is as much a process as it is an act of faith. Right after the psalmist has encouraged the people to sing praises to the Lord, he suddenly changes gear and moves back to what we may imagine to be the situation before the thanksgiving: "Lord, see how my enemies persecute me!" (v. 13). This poses a problem only when thanksgiving is viewed as a one-way movement which consists of a single element. But in the Psalms thanksgiving and lament are inseparable. For a similar movement from thanksgiving to petition, see 27:6–7.

9:15–20 "RISE UP, O LORD!"

Verses 15–20 recall what God has done to the psalmist's enemies (cf. vv. 3–6). The difference is that here the subject of the verbs is the nations, not God. Whereas earlier it was the Lord who had "destroyed the wicked," "blotted out their name" (v. 5), and uprooted the cities (v. 6); here the destructions is described simply in terms of what has happened to them: "The nations have fallen into the pit they have dug . . . the wicked are ensnared by the work of their hands" (vv. 15–16; cf. v. 17).

We see a similar pattern of change when we compare verses 10, 13 and 18:

---

5. For a good discussion of the word "afflicted," see Kirkpatrick, *The Book of Psalms*, 47–48.

"You, LORD, have never forsaken those who seek you" (10b).

"He does not ignore the cries of the afflicted" (12b).

"The needy shall not always be forgotten" (18a, ESV).

There is a development in the three verses above. In verse 10b, God is referred to in the second person ("You"). In verse 12b, God is referred to in the third person ("He"). In both lines God is the subject of the sentence. But in verse 18a, the sentence is in the passive voice and God is no longer the subject, but is simply the implied actor. The statement also implies that the needy are presently being forgotten. As a result the psalmist cries out in the next verse, "Arise, LORD! Do not let the mortals triumph . . . Strike them with terror, LORD" (vv. 19–20).

This section may be likened to the usual Filipino way of communication, which is indirect. We do not normally say what we really want to say right away. We move slowly, encircling the target as it were. Sometimes we do not reach the main point; we simply hope the other person will get it. The psalmist, after slowly building his case, is able to pour out his heart to God. He becomes more direct with God.

10:1–11 "WHY, LORD, DO YOU STAND FAR OFF?"

Nothing in the previous verses prepares us for the transition here. The mood is totally different, though as we have seen, the psalmist had been slowly moving towards this point at the end of Psalm 9. As the psalm turns to the letter "*l*" of the Hebrew alphabet, the psalmist suddenly mentions the word *lamah* ("why?") – the characteristic cry of lament.[6] We first encountered this word in Psalm 2:1 ("*Why* do the nations conspire?"). The words are similar to the famous lament of Psalm 22 ("My God, my God, *why* have you forsaken me?"). Earlier, the psalmist used the phrase "in times of trouble" (9:9b) in the context of thanksgiving and assurance. Here the phrase is repeated but in a question: "Why do you hide yourself *in times of trouble*?" (10:1b). The movement is anticlimactic, if not tragic.

How are we to explain this transition?

---

6. Gunkel (*The Psalms*) thinks that the turn to lament is because of the use of the Hebrew acrostic. But if the psalmist does not really want to move on to lament, he could easily think of other words beginning with *lamed*. Gunkel's method prevents him from seeing the possibility for a sudden change of mood from thanksgiving to lament.

We usually want to maintain the mood of thanksgiving and rejoicing and do not want to move on to lament. But by moving from thanksgiving to lament, Psalm 9–10 teaches us that the life of faith consists not just in a movement from defeat to victory, struggle to resolution. There is also room for movement in the opposite direction.[7] This is an important corrective for the overemphasis on victory in some churches. It teaches us that there is also a place for the tragic in the life of faith. In the presence of God there is both joy and anguish, thanksgiving and lament. There are times when our thanksgiving will need to be mingled with tears of lament in order for it to remain genuine. In a broken world where injustice and wickedness are a rampant reality, thanksgiving will inevitably be mixed with lament. The lament purifies our thanksgiving and strengthens it.

The psalm also shows us how prayer can make the things of this world clearer. In prayer we should be able to see more clearly the realities of our world. As we turn our eyes upon Jesus the things on earth do not "grow strangely dim." Gordon Smith remarks that the song "Turn your eyes upon Jesus," particularly the line that says, "And the things of earth will grow strangely dim" is theologically incorrect. It is actually the other way around. As we turn our eyes upon Jesus the reality of our world becomes clearer.[8] For in the prayer of thanksgiving and lament we gain the courage to face our world in all its ugliness and brokenness.

In the next verses the psalmist brings into the presence of God the brokenness of this world. The wicked is free to do whatever he wants: "He boasts about the cravings of his heart" (v. 3). He is not afraid of God: "In his pride the wicked man does not seek him; in all his thoughts there is no room for God" (v. 4). This does not mean that the wicked are atheists, for the Bible never questions the existence of God. But in a sense the wicked in Psalm 10 are worse than atheists, for although they believe there is a God, they show no regard for him. They even curse and mock God (vv. 3–4). They feel that nothing and no one – neither their enemies nor God himself – can hinder them (vv. 5, 11). This is because whatever they do goes unchecked. Though they are wicked, they are like the happy person in Psalm 1, always successful. Apparently, there is no God to punish them, and no God to make them realize they are "only mortal" (9:20). As a result the poor get persecuted (10:2), the innocent get murdered (v. 8), and the helpless fall by their might (v. 10).

7. See Villanueva, *The "Uncertainty of a Hearing,"* 254–256.
8. Gordon Smith made the remark in one of his classes at Alliance Graduate School (formerly Alliance Biblical Seminary) where I was a student.

When I read verses 8–10 I cannot help but think of the Maguindanao massacre in which fifty-seven innocent people were brutally murdered.[9] The murder was premeditated and the place where they would be buried already prepared. Some were buried alive. Those who have gone through such experiences know how the psalmist feels.

10:12–18 "ARISE, LORD!"

How does one respond to such a situation? The psalmist pours out his heart to God. He prays that God will bring the wicked to destruction: "Let them be caught in the schemes they have devised" (v. 2, ESV). He pleads with God to "arise . . . lift up your hand . . . Do not forget the helpless" (v. 12b). Earlier, in 9:12b the psalmist declared God had not forgotten the cry of the afflicted (cf. 9:18a). In the face of his laments he tries to hang on to this hope that God will indeed not forget. But he is also honest about what he feels, for God seems to be doing nothing. And so he asks, "Why does the wicked man revile God? Why does he say to himself, 'He won't call me to account'?" (v. 13).

But even if the psalmist asks God why, he does not give up. His continuing lament is actually a sign of hope. That is the power of the laments. In their words we find a heart filled with concern and compassion for a broken world that will never give up even if it means pouring out one's lament before God. The psalmist continues to cling to his hope in God. "But you, God, see the trouble of the afflicted; you consider their grief and take it in hand" (14a). In a moving description of the fate of the poor and oppressed, the psalmist says, "The victims commit themselves to you" (v. 14b). Literally the Hebrew reads, "On you the helpless abandon (*azab*) himself." The word "abandon" recalls 9:10 – "for you, O LORD, have not forsaken (*azab*) those who seek you." The helpless, the afflicted, and the poor have no one else to turn to. They have only God. Thus, in a more direct manner, the psalmist utters an imprecatory prayer and asks God to "break the arm of the wicked man" (v. 15). (For discussion on this kind of prayer, see topic on "The Imprecatory Psalms," pp. 274–276.) He continues to acknowledge that God reigns (v. 16), and expresses hope that "you, LORD, hear the desire of the afflicted . . . you listen to their cry, defending the fatherless and the oppressed" (vv. 17–18).

---

9. This massacre took place in 2009. Thirty of those killed were reporters.

THANKSGIVING AND LAMENT

We sometimes hear statements like this in church: "We are now in the presence of God, so let us forget about our problems." This reflects a view which tends to limit worship to only praise and thanksgiving. Psalm 9–10 urges us not to forget our problems but to bring them into the presence of God. Thanksgiving ought not to be limited to praise; even our problems and the needs of our world form part of it. For the psalmist even these are part of his thanksgiving – his "whole heart."

Thanksgiving is coming to God "just as we are." It means opening up our hearts to him. The psalmist sees no problem with continuing his thanksgiving through the lament in Psalm 10. Lament is an important part of thanksgiving, for unless we are honest with God about what we truly feel, our thanksgiving will be hindered, if not meaningless. Instead of hiding his feelings about God, the psalmist tells him, "Why, O LORD, do you stand far off? Why do you hide yourself in times of trouble?" (10:1). Psalm 9–10 teaches us it is only when we are honest to God that we are able to thank him with all our heart. Thanksgiving and lament go together. Thanksgiving without lament is empty. Lament without thanksgiving is impossible to bear.

In Psalm 9–10 we are given a model of what thanksgiving looks like. Giving thanks to the Lord includes all of life. Thanksgiving is not separated from daily life. Our present realities form part of our thanksgiving. That is why the psalmist mentions the reality confronting him even in his thanksgiving. The different words he employs describe the struggles and difficulties of his people. The psalm abounds with words about the poor[1] – *dak* ("oppressed") occurs at the beginning and end of the psalm (9:9; 10:18); *yatom* ("orphan") appears with "oppressed" at the end (10:18, cf. v. 14); *ebyon* ("poor"; 9:18); *khelkah* ("helpless"; 10:8, 10, 14), a word that occurs only in this psalm in the whole OT; and *ani,* the most common term used to refer to the poor, occurring seven times in Psalm 9–10 (9:12, 18; 10:2, 9 [2x], 12, 17). If prayer and righteous living go together as we learned from Psalm 5, Psalm 9–10 teaches us that thanksgiving includes the suffering of our world. And we have not properly thanked the Lord until we are one with those who are suffering.

---

1. William J. Dumbrell, "anah," *NIDOTTE* 3: 459.

PSALM 11

One of the striking things about the Psalms is how much opposition the godly person experiences. In Psalm 1 we are already introduced to groups of people in opposition to each other – the one who meditates on the law of the Lord and the wicked (1:1; cf. 11:2).[1] By Psalm 3 the psalmist is already crying out, "LORD, how many are my foes!" (v. 1; cf. 4:2; 6:8; 7:5). No doubt about it, there will be an abundance of people who tell us "God will not deliver him" (3:2). In Psalm 11 there are people who say to the psalmist, "Flee like a bird to your mountain" (11:1). "Like a bird" speaks of swiftness, as in "right now." "To your mountain" suggests "you don't belong here!"

Even though we want to maintain harmony in our relationships, the reality is that there will always be people who seek to oppose us. The great fourth century theologian Athanasius was exiled four times under four different emperors during his forty-five years of ministry as bishop.[2] Sometimes the opposition can be fierce and dangerous. Imagine walking in a dark place when suddenly someone shoots at you. That's the image here (v. 2). You don't know where the arrows are coming from. You feel afraid. And you ask yourself, "When the foundations are being destroyed, what can the righteous do?" (v. 3).

"What can the righteous do?" The answer is given in verse 1: "In the LORD I take refuge." From the previous psalms we have learned what taking refuge in the Lord means. It means putting one's trust in God alone (Ps 2:12); crying out to God in prayer (3:4; 5:2b); and doing what is right (Pss 4 and 5). And here in Psalm 11, taking refuge in the Lord takes on a new emphasis. It means remembering that God is still on his throne (v. 4). From the heavens he looks at everyone, both the wicked and the righteous, testing them (v. 5). The question is, when he looks at our hearts, will he find righteousness? He had better, for only the righteous can see his face (v. 7).

11:1–3 "IN THE LORD I TAKE REFUGE"

The psalm begins with an expression of trust: "In the LORD I take refuge" (v. 1). Yet immediately after uttering these words, indeed even as the words have barely escaped his lips, we hear his enemies telling him (v. 2), "Flee like a bird

---

1. The Hebrew word for "wicked" *reshaim* occurs in both passages.
2. Albert Haase, *Athanasius: The Life of Antony of Egypt* (Downers Grove: IVP, 2012), 14.

to your mountain."[3] Expressions of trust are often uttered in the midst of opposing voices. Those voices tend to be dominant while the expression of trust is like a lone voice in the wilderness. When the psalmist asserts in Psalm 3:3, "But you, LORD are a shield around me," he does so in the midst of a crowd who are telling him, "God will not deliver him" (3:2).

It requires a lot of courage (*lakas ng loob*) to trust in God. It takes a lot of faith. For the other option is tempting. It is so easy just to go to the mountains (*mamundok na lang*) especially when the foundations of society are crumbling. Some Filipinos, for instance, flee abroad because they can no longer find hope in our country. Justice is impossibly slow. The rich are becoming richer while the poor are becoming poorer. We often hear people complain that they do not see the effects of the economic development the government is reporting about. Unfortunately, economic growth rarely trickles down to those at the bottom of the ladder. So some of our *kababayan* ("people") opt to go abroad. Others literally go to the mountains as "rebels" (*namundok na*).

However, the psalmist finds the idea of flight unacceptable.[4] In fact, he disdains it. The word *ek* ("how?") expresses an element of reproach.[5] "How can you say to me . . .?" (v. 1). He continues to hold on to God. Retreat for him would signify a lack of faith, so is not an option. We do not mean to say here that we should never retreat or seek refuge elsewhere by going abroad in order to work when to do otherwise would mean hunger for our own family. To be fair, the reason many of our *kababayan* go abroad is because of our situation in the Philippines. But some leave the country because they have lost hope that anything good will ever come out of our situation.

The message of the psalm is for people like them. If everyone goes away, who will be left to continue the fight for righteousness in our own land? It is easier just to escape, especially when we are confronted with a very difficult situation. The enemies in Psalm 11 are not easy to deal with. They hide in

---

3. The Hebrew version of the Jewish Old Testament known as the Masoretic Text (MT) does not seem to make sense. Literally it reads, "flee (plural) your mountain bird." The majority of translations follow the reading in the ancient Greek translation of the Old Testament, known as the Septuagint (LXX), which has "flee to the mountains as a bird (sparrow)."

4. The common view is that the psalmist is being advised by others to flee to the mountains because of his situation (Alexander, *Commentary on Psalms*, 60; Kirkpatrick, *The Book of Psalms*, 58; Artur Weiser, *The Psalms: A Commentary* [trans. Herbert Hartwell, London: SCM Press, 1962], 154–155). This is possible though the text is not certain. It could be that the palmist is quoting the words of his enemies (see also Ps 3:2).

5. William L. Holladay, *A Concise Hebrew and Aramaic Lexicon of the Old Testament* (Grand Rapids: Eerdmans, 1971), 12.

the darkness, aiming and shooting their arrows in the dark while the righteous stand vulnerable. Thus, the question, "When the foundations are being destroyed, what can the righteous do?" (v. 3). The situation seems hopeless.

11:4–7 THE LORD IS ON HIS THRONE

But the situation is hopeless only from a human point of view. In Psalm 121:1 the psalmist asks, "I lift up my eyes to the mountains – where does my help come from?" And he answers, "My help comes from the LORD, the Maker of heaven and earth" (v. 2). Similarly, in Psalm 11, right after the psalmist asks, "What can the righteous do?" given the hopeless situation, the answer comes: "The LORD is in his holy temple; the LORD is on his heavenly throne" (v. 4). The good news is that even in the midst of our situation, God is still on his throne. He is in control. He is the ultimate judge who tests the righteous and the wicked (v. 5). God has a bias – he hates "those who love violence" (11:5b; cf. 5:6b – "the LORD abhors the bloodthirsty").

Psalm 11:6 can be read as an expression of confidence: "On the wicked he will rain fiery coals."[6] It can also be translated as a petition or wish: "Let him rain coals on the wicked" (v. 6, ESV). The image reminds us of what God did to Sodom and Gomorrah. Verse 6 may be understood as a petition urging God to judge the wicked as he did in earlier times.

Both senses of the verse should be maintained. On the one hand there is confidence that God will act righteously. Given the present reality of the psalmist, on the other hand, there is also the struggle to keep on taking refuge in God. This struggle will find its fuller expression in the next psalm, Psalm 12.

But at least for the time being, it is confidence that pervades the psalmist. He has confidence in God, for "the LORD is righteous, he loves justice; the upright will see his face" (v. 7). The word "see" is used in verse 4b to refer to the Lord whose eyes "observes"[7] – the one who gazes on humankind. In that context, God is examining all of humankind, both the righteous and the

---

6. Literally the Hebrew reads, "Let him rain snares" (*pakh*, "bird snare"; cf. LXX). But it is possible that the word is *pkhmy*, "coals of fire" (NRSV). The *yod* and the *mem* might have been mistakenly switched.

7. It is interesting that in this verse the LXX adds "the poor" as the object of the verb *khzh* ("behold") – "his eyes look upon the poor." This may have been a mistake because the word for poor and behold in Hebrew are similar – *'ny* and *'ynyw*, respectively (Kirkpatrick, *The Book of Psalms*, 59, n. 1). This change is interesting for it gives us a glimpse of the world of the translators. We tend to see or read our situation into the text.

wicked. Those who wish to "see" the Lord ought to live righteous lives. As Jesus said, "Blessed are the pure in heart, for they will see God" (Matt 5:8).

The challenge is how to remain "pure in heart" in the midst of difficulties. We know what it means to have the "foundations destroyed," both literally and figuratively. We are familiar with earthquakes. From 1950 to 1975 alone, the Philippines had a reported 2126 earthquakes. It is said that our country has the highest number of natural hazards in the world.[8] Sylvia Palugod rightly remarks: "If there was anything he [the Filipino] could be certain of, it was that he was very vulnerable."[9] She explains:

> Life for the indigenous Filipino, as simple as it may appear to be, was anything but cozy. There were many dangers about — from feral creatures, elemental forces, other men, and the spirits. Despite his best plans and best efforts, there were many things he was helpless to prevent or solve.[10]

This is probably the reason why we are easily drawn to God. We cast ourselves on him, knowing there is no one else who can truly help us. So the idea of "taking refuge in the Lord" is attractive to us. The challenge is to include righteousness within our religious consciousness (see "Split-level Christianity," pp. 44–45).

---

8. Greg Bankoff, *Cultures of Disaster: Society and Natural Hazard in the Philippines* (London and New York: RoutledgeCurson, 2003), 31–32.
9. Sylvia Palugod, *Filipino Religious Consciousness* (Track 2 Report, ISACC Conversion to Protestant Christianity Research, 1999), 65–66.
10. Ibid.

PSALM 12

What do we do after we have cried for help and been given an answer, but come to realize the situation remains the same or has even become worse? Such is the overall picture depicted in Psalm 12. The psalm begins with a cry for help: "Help, LORD, for no one is faithful anymore" (v. 1). Somewhere in the middle of the psalm, we find God responding to the cry of the psalmist. We have an actual quote of God's answer in verse 5: "Because the poor are plundered and the needy groan, I will now arise, says the LORD; 'I will protect them from those who malign them.'" We couldn't ask for a better answer than that! How we wish that whenever we pray we would hear the Lord answering us with words as clear as those in Psalm 12:5. Naturally the psalmist was filled with praise for the reliability of the word of God (v. 6). He expresses assurance that indeed "You, LORD, will keep the needy safe and will protect us forever from the wicked" (v. 7).

It would have been great to end on this note. But Psalm 12 continues in verse 8 with a rather anticlimactic comment: "On every side the wicked prowl, as vileness is exalted among humankind" (NRSV). Having cried at the beginning that the godly are no more, one would expect the psalmist to end with something like, "The wicked are no more," or "The godly are here once more." But no, the wicked are still around. In fact they are as free as ever, prowling like dogs. So we have in this psalm a movement from lament to praise, then back to lament and then ending just like that . . . in lament. It is a somber psalm, even a tragic one, yet I believe it has an important message for us today. For don't we sometimes find ourselves in a similar situation? We pray to God. The answer comes. But the answer appears to be another form of question, leading to another prayer. The great news is that there is a place for this kind of experience in the Bible, and it is even given to us in the form of a prayer.

12:1–2 "HELP, LORD"

The psalm begins with a cry for help: "Help, LORD, for no one is faithful anymore; those who are loyal have vanished from the human race" (v. 1; cf. 3:1). Some people might say, "So what? So what if there are no more godly people around? What's the big deal?" To this the psalmist would respond: "It is a big deal when there are no more godly people around." As the next verses will show, if there are no more godly people around, we'll be left only with people who lie to each other: "Everyone lies to their neighbor; they flatter with their lips but harbor deception in their hearts" (v. 2). You can no longer trust anyone, for everyone is a liar. As a song says, "Honesty, is such a lonely word; everyone is so untrue." Especially with the Internet these days, it's becoming harder and harder, or nearly impossible, to know whom to trust. Everyone tries to portray the best about themselves – the best stories, the most beautiful pictures, as we see on Facebook. This is an example of what the psalmist calls a "double heart." They say one thing but mean another. A double heart is a heart without integrity.

12:3–4 "CUT OFF ALL FLATTERING LIPS"

In verse 3, the psalmist asks God to "silence all flattering lips" (literally, "cut off all flattering lips"). Why only the lips? The lips here, together with the tongue, are a form of synecdoche, a way of speaking of the whole through its representative parts. The lips represent the wicked people. So the psalmist is actually asking God to destroy the wicked. In this sense verse 3 is an imprecatory prayer, similar to what we find in 10:15. According to Wenham, of all the sins that are mentioned in the Psalms it is the sins of the tongue that are most prominent.[1] The NT agrees with this way of presenting the wicked (see James 3). When we sin with our tongues, it won't be long before we destroy others.

The tongue makes great boasts: "By our tongues we will prevail; our own lips will defend us – who is lord over us?" (v. 4). This tells us what kind of people the speakers are: they are boastful, followers of no one, not even God. And when people become powerful and independent from one another and from God, they take advantage of those who are weak (v. 4). So to the question, "What's the big deal if the godly are no more?" the answer is, it is a very big deal! When the godly are no more, there will be people who will be trampled down. It is possible that the psalmist who is crying out here, or the group he represents, has been a victim of the powerful. This explains the sense of urgency in the prayer. The poor want help because they are already being trampled upon.

---

1. Gordon J. Wenham, "The Ethics of the Psalms," in *Interpreting the Psalm: Issues and Approaches*, eds. Philip Johnston and David G. Firth (Downers Grove: IVP, 2005), 186.

12:5 GOD'S RESPONSE: "I WILL NOW ARISE"

God responds: "Because the poor are plundered and the needy groan, I will now arise," says the LORD; "I will protect them from those who malign them" (v. 5). If the speech of the wicked tells us something about their character, the divine speech tells us something about the character of God. The speech of the wicked reveals their self-centeredness; God's speech shows his other-centeredness. God's answer is motivated by the needs of the poor and the groans of the needy. It does not arise from his own needs but because of the needs of others. This reminds us of the words of Jesus: "This is my body which is *for you*." God cares about the oppression of the poor and the needy.

The statement "I will now arise" is significant. The psalmist has been asking God to "arise" (see 3:7; 7:6; 9:19; 10:12). But this is the first time that God actually says "I will now arise." The psalmist can only say "Amen" to the response of the Lord.

12:6–8 THE PSALMIST'S RESPONSE

Verses 6–7 represent the psalmist's response to the divine oracle. He praises the reliability of the words of the Lord. They are true, in contrast to the words of the wicked that are characterized by lying, flattery, and double-heartedness. He even compares the promises of the Lord to "gold refined seven times" (v. 6). So with confidence and assurance, the psalmist declares: "You, LORD, will keep the needy safe and will protect us forever from the wicked" (v. 7).

What a perfect ending this would have made! But the psalm still has one more verse.

Some scholars find the last verse of the psalm anticlimactic. So they propose to amend the Hebrew text or suggest other ways of reading it than the plain sense of the sentence.[2] The plain sense of the verse is expressed simply as follows: "On every side the wicked prowl, as vileness is exalted among humankind" (v. 8). In the light of God's response in verse 5 this sounds like a disappointing ending. The psalmist had cried out to God for help (vv. 1–2). God had already responded. And the psalmist, encouraged by the divine response, has just declared his confidence in what God will do (vv. 6–7). So

---

2. For example Friederich Baethgen, *Die Psalmen* (HKAT; Göttingen: Vandenhoeck & Ruprecht, 1904), 34, reads v. 8 as a continuation of v. 7. He renders it as a concessive clause (cf. Hermann Gunkel, *Die Psalmen*, [HKAT; Göttingen: Vandenhoeck & Ruprecht, 1926], 44). But as it stands, v. 8 is better read as an independent statement (see Villanueva, *The "Uncertainty of a Hearing,"* 142–143).

to find him making another statement which basically recalls the situation reflected in his earlier cry may be disturbing.

In our society the wicked continue to prowl (12:8). The statement, "vileness is exalted among humankind" is a day-to-day reality in our country. The situation remains the same and has not changed. As we have noted in our comments on Psalm 11, many of our countrymen are forced to go abroad in order to support their families. Meanwhile, those of us who are left in the country continue to struggle against the temptation to give up because of our situation.

In spite of the rather anti-climactic ending of Psalm 12, what makes this psalm particularly encouraging is its capacity to hold the tensions of life together in the presence of God. Psalm 12 teaches us that the way to face our challenges is to bring them to God. For it is only when we have experienced God that we can face the realities of life. The psalmist is able to confront the evil and hopelessness in his world because he knows God is there.

PSALM 13

"I am a Christian. I should be happy all the time." This is a common expectation among many Christians. Somebody has even said that joylessness is a sin! And yet we know that the Christian life is not happy all the time. God is indeed good all the time. But we are certainly not happy all the time, even though one of the most common Filipino songs says the Christian life is happy all the time (*Ang buhay ng Kristiyano ay laging masayang tunay*). In fact, even some of the people closest to God testify to having gone through what is called the "dark night of the soul."[1] At some point in our lives we will go through the dark night. We may feel we are already there. How do we survive the dark night?

This is where lament psalms like Psalm 13 can be of great help. They serve as our companions as we go through our own "valley of the shadow of death." First, they help us to understand what the dark night is.[2] When we are in the dark night, we feel as if the darkness will never end. Thus the words, "How long?" are repeated four times in the psalm (vv. 1–2). People who go through the dark night feel abandoned by God: "Will you forget me forever? How long will you hide your face from me?" (v. 1). Their experience is similar to those who are depressed: "how long must I wrestle with my thoughts and day after day have sorrow in my heart?" (v. 2).

Second, the lament psalms tell us we are not alone. Reading the lament psalms makes us realize we are in the company of those who have gone through the dark night themselves and have survived.

Third, because the lament psalms are prayers, they provide us with words we can utter to God during our times of darkness when we just don't know what to say. Finally, they remind us that the darkness is not forever. There is an end to it, as the last part of Psalm 13 shows us: "I will sing the LORD's praise, for he has been good to me " (v. 6).

---

1. The phrase "dark night of the soul" was popularized by St. John of the Cross who wrote a book with the same title.
2. Federico G. Villanueva, "The 'Dark Night of the Soul,' the Lament Psalms, and Juan De La Cruz," in *Walking with God: Christian Spirituality in the Asian Context*, ed. Charles Ringma et al. (Manila, Philippines: ATS/OMF Literature, 2014), 127–137. St. John of the Cross was right on target when he appealed to the lament psalms among others to explain the experience of the dark night of the soul.

Psalm 13 has been called the model of the genre called individual lament psalms. All the key elements of an individual lament are presented in a straightforward manner:

Invocation: "O LORD" (v. 1);
Lament (v. 2);
Petition (vv. 3–4);
Declaration of trust (v. 5);
Vow of praise (v. 6).

13:1–2 INVOCATION AND LAMENT

Anyone reading the opening words of Psalm 13 ought to do so in a manner that does justice to the agony reflected in them. The words "How long?" are repeated four times in the psalm (vv. 1–2). This four-fold repetition indicates that the psalmist has been suffering for a long time. Today, with the internet around, two minutes is a long time. Because of our fast-paced world, we are becoming more and more impatient. We even sometimes pray: "Lord, give me patience. And I want it right now!" But when people in ancient times say, "How long?" they are probably talking in years, not just minutes. The psalmist has been praying for a long time, but no answer has come. Prolonged illness and years of depression are examples of this kind of suffering. Those who are in such situations know what it means to cry in the middle of the night, "How long?" The cry of the psalmist articulates what suffering Christians feel: "Will you forget me forever . . . will you hide your face from me?" This verse intensifies as it moves from one line to the next, from the word "forget" to the word "hide." From a human point of view, forgetting is more accidental. We would say, "Oh sorry, I forgot." But "hiding" is more deliberate. The psalmist feels God has abandoned him (cf. 22:1).

Some Christians think we ought never to question God even when we are suffering terribly. They tell us that we ought to declare our faith in God all the more, and even praise him. But while this response may be commendable, it is not always applicable. In some situations, it is also unrealistic. It is better to be honest with God about what we truly feel than to hide it. He knows our hearts anyway. And the fact that God has allowed these words to be preserved in the Scriptures tells us it is okay to express our questions to God when we can't hold on any longer.[3] If it is just a simple problem or some

---

3. See Villanueva, *It's OK To Be NOT OK.*

kind of suffering for a season, it may be possible to bear it. But we are talking about prolonged suffering here: How long must I wrestle with my thoughts and day after day have sorrow in my heart? (v. 2ab) How long will my enemy triumph over me? There is not even a moment when the psalmist is not in pain, no moment when his heart is not filled with sorrow.

Adding to his torment are his enemies (v. 2c). With the mention of the enemy, we have all three subjects of lament present: God, self and enemy. The psalmist laments:

a.   God's absence: "How long, LORD? Will you forget me forever?" (v. 1).

b.   His personal situation: ": How long must I wrestle with my thoughts and day after day have sorrow in my heart?" (v. 2ab).

c.   His enemies: "How long will my enemy triumph over me?" (v. 2c).

The three are interrelated. In ancient times, as is also true in some Asian cultures, suffering and sickness were viewed as a consequence of a person's sins. Enemies take advantage of such occasions to bring trouble on the suffering person. So in addition to his sickness, a suffering person may have to deal with his enemies. And if the situation persists even after much prayer, it can lead to a sense of abandonment by God. The suffering in the lament reflects psychological, sociological, and theological dimensions. This explains the sense of urgency in the next verses.

13:3–4 PETITION: "CONSIDER AND ANSWER ME"

The psalmist asks God for help: "Look on me and answer, LORD my God. Give light to my eyes, or I will sleep in death," (v. 3). The psalmist is saying, "Look on me . . . O LORD. See how much I have been suffering for a long time." It's another way of saying, "Have mercy on me."

The second part of the verse reflects urgency. If the Lord does not answer, "I will sleep in death" (v. 3). The Hebrew word *yashen* (sleep) has been used in the context of being able to lie down and sleep (see 3:5) because of the rest and protection that God provides. But here the word is used to refer to death.

A second reason why God should answer is mentioned in verse 4: and my enemy will say, "I have overcome him," and my foes will rejoice when I fall. Here we are confronted again with the theme of the enemy (cf. 3:1; 6:10). There is always someone giving a hard time to the psalmist. He is worried that his enemies will rejoice because he is "shaken." Earlier, in Psalm 11, the psalmist asked, "When the foundations are being destroyed, what can the righteous do?" (11:3). And the answer was that God was still in control:

"the LORD is on his heavenly throne" (11:4). Similarly, in the last section of Psalm 13 we see a declaration of trust in God despite the psalmist's situation.

13:5–6 DECLARATION OF TRUST AND VOW OF THANKSGIVING

The psalmist affirms his trust in God's "unfailing love" (13:5). And this brings him assurance of and joy in God's salvation: "my heart rejoices in your salvation" (v. 5). The word "rejoice" is repeated here. Earlier the psalmist was worried that his enemies would rejoice over his downfall (v. 4b); here he is rejoicing because of God's salvation. And in the very next verse he is already offering a vow of thanksgiving: "I will sing the LORD's praise" (v. 6).

How quickly the psalm has turned to rejoicing! Just three verses earlier the psalmist was crying, "How long, O LORD?" Now he is already singing. How is that possible? How does one turn from lament to praise so suddenly? This question has puzzled scholars for at least a hundred years.

One of the common explanations is psychological. Heiler suggests that as one pours out one's soul to the Lord a "wonderful metamorphosis" takes place, leading to a change of mood.[4]

An even more popular explanation is that while the speaker was pouring out his heart in the temple, a priest delivered an oracle promising salvation.[5] The knowledge that his prayer has been granted explains the change of mood in verse 6. But there is the problem that there is no evidence within this psalm or other lament psalms of such an event actually taking place.

So, in the end, we do not really know what caused the change. What we know is that the psalmist poured out his lament to the Lord and as he did so, there was a change. Maybe the act of lament itself was the grace which caused the change. Through the gift of lament, the psalmist has been reminded that indeed the Lord is good. In allowing his child to pour out his heart, God has opened the door for restoration. The psalm ends fittingly with the words: "he has dealt bountifully with me."

---

4. Friedrich Heiler, *Prayer, A Study in the History and Psychology of Religion*, ed. and trans. Samuel McComb (New York: Oxford University Press, 1932), 260.
5. Joachim Begrich, "Das priesterliche Heilsorakel," *ZAW* 52 (1934): 81–92.

DEPRESSION AND THE LAMENT PSALMS

According to the World Health Organization, depression will be the second leading cause of disease by 2020.[1] Even in the Philippines where we say, "It's more fun," depression is a growing phenomenon.[2] The problem is that we do not want to acknowledge it. We always want to appear okay. Trained to be always happy, we tend to deny what we truly feel inside. And so we isolate ourselves from others. We cry alone . . . until it's too late and our jobs fail, our marriage breaks up, and our health disintegrates.

It is here that the lament psalms can be of great assistance. They tell us it is okay to admit we are depressed and down. The psalmists were certainly not ashamed to admit it. The word translated "downcast" in Psalm 42:5 comes from a Hebrew word that also means "depressed." The psalmist is free to admit, "my soul is downcast within me" (v. 6). Psalm 13 describes the experience of one who is in depression: "How long must I wrestle with my thoughts and day after day have sorrow in my heart?" (v. 2). Prolonged sorrow is one of the manifestations of depression.

We often think that those who are close to God will not be depressed. But the writers of Psalms 13 and 42 are people who are close to God. Psalm 13 is attributed to David, while Psalm 42 is believed to have been written by the "Sons of Korah," who were part of the worship team in the temple. The fact that God has allowed these psalms to be preserved in the Scriptures tells us that God acknowledges that his people will also experience depression.

God gave us the lament psalms so that those of us who go through depression can have the affirmation that what we are experiencing is not something abnormal for God's people. It is normal for Christians who live in a broken world to find themselves in depression. But the lament psalms not only affirm depression, they also provide a means of dealing with it. It is not that they offer all the answers. Rather, they provide great help by welcoming those who are depressed into the presence of the Lord, to just cry out to him, confess their struggles, and tell him about their unending loneliness. And when they cannot even find the words to express their feelings, the words of the lament psalms become a gift from God. In them God has given us not only his words but also words we can utter to him when we just do not know what to say.

Even God's people can be depressed. But they do not remain in that state. They fight, they struggle. The words of the lament psalms enables the

1. www.calgaryherald.com/healthypeople.gov/2020/mental-health-and-mental-illness-disorders (accessed 6 March 2015).
2. Randy David, "A Little Book on Depression," *Philippine Daily Inquirer*, opinion column, 23 December 2010.

depressed person to move forward, to fight and not give up. The mere act of lamenting is a sign of hope and of bold faith. When we lament we are not giving up. We lament because we believe there is one who is listening to us. And even when we no longer feel his presence, we continue to cling on to him: "My God, my God, why have you forsaken me?" (Ps 22:1). Even when we feel God has abandoned us, we continue to call him "my God." We never give up.

PSALM 14

In 2012 in a historic judgment the Chief Justice of the Supreme Court in the Philippines was found guilty of not filing his Statement of Assets and Liabilities Net Worth (SALN) and was impeached. For five months the prosecution and the defense panel laid out their arguments. Then on the concluding day of the trial twenty-three senators stood to pronounce and explain their verdict. Only three of them voted to have him found "not guilty." One of them vehemently argued her case: "Are we so righteous here that we have the courage to judge the chief justice?" She seemed to be saying that since none of us is righteous, we have no right to judge.

She was right in saying no one is righteous. In the first opening verses of Psalm 14, God himself states that "there is no one who does good" (v. 1). That is the verdict God himself makes as he looks at all of humanity (vv. 2–3). Yet in the second half of the psalm we find people who are referred to as the "company of the righteous" (v. 5), called by God as "my people" (v. 4). How can this be? Theologically, we may surmise that though everyone is a sinner, God has made a way for some to be called his people. As to how this is accomplished, we need to go to the NT teaching concerning salvation and the grace of God (see Eph 2:8–9).

But the fact that all have sinned should not stop us from doing what is right. As Melba Maggay commented:

> The fact that there are no good guys and bad guys here should not make us obscure the fact that there is a good side and a bad side, and when the choice presents itself, we should not be by-standers. This is why we often miss our historical cues as church people. God means us to be engaged, even in a fallen world. We are all sinners, it is true, but good is done in the world whenever God's people . . . stand up for what is right, even if none of the actors are lily-white. There are always moral ambiguities in any human project, the enterprises of the church not excluded.[1]

---

1. Personal correspondence (31 May 2012).

14:1–3 WHAT HAPPENS WHEN "THERE IS NO GOD"

In Psalm 12, the psalmist cries for help, "no one is faithful anymore" (v.1). Here the fool says, "There is no God" (14:1). As in Psalm 1, humanity is divided into the foolish and the wise, representing the wicked and the righteous, respectively. The statement by the fool should not lead us to think that we are dealing here with an atheist. The general view in the Bible is that there is a God. The very first verse in the Bible does not prove the existence of God; it simply accepts it as fact. The view is similar to that held by most Asians, who generally believe in a deity or some kind of powerful being. Filipinos, in particular, readily accept a belief in God. In Psalm 14, what is being denied is not the existence of God but the place of God in one's heart: "The fool says *in his heart*." The fool has no regard for God or fear of him (Ps 10:4). The following two statements in verse 1 are parallel:

v. 1a	A "The fool says in his heart,	B 'There is no God.'" ('*en elohîm*)
v. 1b	A' "They are corrupt, they do abominable deeds;	B' there is no one who does good." ('*en oseh-tob*)

The parallelism defines who the "fools" are. It refers to those who are "corrupt," people who "do abominable deeds." The psalm reminds us that when "there is no God," "there is no one who does good." The answer to bad religion is not "no religion."[2]

Who is this God? Verse 2 names him as Yahweh, the God who made himself known to Abraham, Isaac and Jacob, and to the people of Israel. The language of verse 2 reminds us of two stories in the book of Genesis: the tower of Babel (Gen 11) and Sodom and Gomorrah (Gen 18–19).[3] In the former, God is said to have come down to see the city that "mortals had built" (Gen 11:5). The word "mortals" comes from a Hebrew phrase that literally means "the sons of man." This is the same phrase used in Genesis 14, where the LORD is said to look on "the sons of man."[4] In Psalm 14 God looks directly at humanity. He looks from heaven "to see if there are any who understand, any who seek God" (14:2). The primary concern is not to see

---

2. I borrowed this phrase from a title of an article I read. Unfortunately, I did not write down the reference.
3. Kirkpatrick, *The Book of Psalms*, 66–67.
4. Translated as "humankind" in NRSV.

how many wicked people there are, but whether there are still people who are righteous. The concern is similar to that in the story in Genesis 18. Abraham asks God whether he would destroy Sodom and Gomorrah if righteous people were found there. God said no. That is why it is important for any city or country to have people who seek God, who live righteous lives. They are the "salt of the earth" (Matt 5:13). Unfortunately, as in the case of Sodom and Gomorrah, when God looked to see if there were any righteous people, he found none: "there is no one who does good, not even one" (v. 3).

14:4–7 "GOD IS PRESENT IN THE COMPANY OF THE RIGHTEOUS"

The difference in Psalm 14 is that God has not yet acted in judgment against the wicked. But the psalmist believes they will be judged – those who "devour my people as though eating bread" (v. 4) will be "overwhelmed with dread" (v. 5). This is because "God is present in the company of the righteous" (v. 5).

The mentioning of the "company of the righteous" raises a question. If there is no one who does good (vv. 2–3; Rom 3:10–12), then how come there are those who are called "righteous"? They are also referred to as "my people" (v. 4). There seems to be a contradiction here.

One way to answer this question is to say that everyone has indeed turned away from God, and no one is perfect. But then there are those who have been chosen and called the people of God, not because of anything good they have done but solely because of the mercy of God (see Deut 7:6–8). There are those who, though they are sinners, have chosen to put their trust in the Lord; they have God as "their refuge" (14:6). It is they who have hope, even in a world where no one does good.

They continue to hope that one day deliverance will come from Zion: "Oh, that salvation for Israel would come out of Zion!" (v. 7a). What does this mean? In the next line this is clarified: "When the LORD restores his people" (v. 7b). It is the LORD who restores his people, not the place or any person. And when he does, "Jacob will rejoice; Israel will be glad" (v. 7c, NRSV). As Christians, we see this fulfilled spiritually when Christ came to save sinners from their sins.

PSALM 15

The author of Psalm 15 regards the sanctuary as a holy place. This view was common in ancient times. Entry into sanctuaries was regulated, and sometimes written warnings were posted at the entrances to shrines.[1] Thus Psalm 15 may originally have functioned as a liturgy for entrance into the sanctuary.[2] The opening question about who may abide in God's holy place (v. 1) is followed by a series of statements describing such a person (vv. 2–5a). The psalm ends with a declaration (v. 5b).

In a world where worship services are no longer solely held in church buildings or sanctuaries but also in public places like malls, theaters, basketball courts, and even pubs, we may find it hard to grasp the sense of holiness that the author of Psalm 15 is speaking of.

Think about how you would feel if you went to church and found someone standing at the door, asking those who were entering: "Who is worthy to enter the church?" After that, this person would recite a list of characteristics of those who are qualified to enter. You might be surprised or even embarrassed. As a devout Christian you might protest, "Why is this necessary? Didn't Jesus already open the way for us through his death on the cross? Aren't we going back to a gospel based on works when we do this?"

But Psalm 15 provides a necessary balance to the NT emphasis on salvation by grace, which teaches that through Christ we have access to God's presence. Though this teaching is correct, it can lead to "cheap grace" if we do not balance it with the necessary qualities for righteous living. This is the contribution of Psalm 15. It reminds us that entrance into the presence of God is not a minor matter. We do not just barge into the place of worship. Like Moses, we should come into the place of worship conscious of the holiness of the one we are approaching (Exod 3).

The psalm also underlines an important truth – it is the Lord who determines who is worthy to dwell in his sanctuary. That is why the opening question is directed to the Lord, not to the people or to the priest: "LORD, who may dwell in your sacred tent?" (Ps 15:1).

God's response is given in verses 2–5a. We learn from these verses that what matters is not our social standing or economic status but our character and the way we deal with others. The qualifications also do not involve the

---

1. Clifford, *Psalms 1–72*, 92.
2. For background, see Kraus, *Psalms 1–59*, 227.

things we do inside the church but our activities *outside* the church – lending money without interest, not accepting bribes, relating well with our neighbors, etc. This tells us that going to church and living right go together. The proper preparation for entering into the presence of God is outside the church or temple; it's out there, right where we are – in our offices, schools, homes, and streets. How we behave outside will determine whether we are worthy to come inside the place where God dwells. For bishops, priests or pastors who already work inside the church, the expectation is even higher (1 Tim 3:1–7; Titus 1:5–9).

Worshipers ought to live authentically in the society. They should effect change in the society by their sanctified lives (vv. 1–2), saintly lips (v. 3), and sacrificial love (vv. 4–5).

15:1 "LORD, WHO MAY DWELL IN YOUR SACRED TENT?"

We might have expected that the opening question in this entrance liturgy would be addressed to the people. But as noted above, the question in verse 1 is addressed to the Lord. This brings the issue of entrance into the sanctuary to a higher plane. In the final analysis it's not about us, but about God. It's not what we say or think about ourselves, but what God says and thinks about us that determine whether we are worthy to enter into God's presence.

The opening question is similar to Psalm 24:3, which also asks: "Who may ascend the mountain of the LORD? Who may stand in his holy place?" But there are two differences. First, in Psalm 24 the question is not explicitly addressed to the Lord. Second, the concern in Psalm 15 is not just how one may "ascend" the hill of the Lord (24:3) but how one may "dwell" there (15:1). In Psalm 15 it is more permanent. We do not just visit the place where God dwells; we live there.[3] Or at least we desire to stay there as long as we can. This same desire is expressed in Psalm 84:10: "Better is one day in your courts than a thousand elsewhere; I would rather be a doorkeeper in the house of my God than dwell in the tents of the wicked."

But how will we be allowed to live there? We know from NT teaching that it is ultimately through Christ that we can have access to the presence of God. Yet the NT also teaches the importance of living a life worthy of being

---

3. The two lines in v. 1 are parallel, with the second line developing the thought expressed in the first line. The verb *gur* (sojourn) in the first line speaks of a temporary visit to God's holy place, while the verb *shakan* ("dwell") in the second line speaks of a more permanent place there. Similarly, a "tent" is a temporary dwelling while God's "holy hill" is permanent.

called God's people (1 Pet 2:9; 1 Cor 3:16). It is from this perspective that we may read the following section.

15:2–5A CHARACTERISTICS OF THOSE WHO MAY DWELL ON GOD'S HOLY HILL

In verses 2–5a we have some kind of a list describing those who may dwell on God's holy hill. The list is not meant to be exhaustive, as the presence of another "list" in Psalm 24 indicates. It describes how worshipers should live in general (v. 2), coupled with specific references to the proper use of one's tongue (v. 2b), good relationships with others (v. 3), right values (v. 4), and the proper handling of one's material resources (v. 5a). Let us briefly look at each of these.

First, the worshipers are described as "whose walk is blameless" (v. 2). The word "walk" refers to the manner in which a person lives (cf. Eph 5:15). In Psalm 1 the righteous person is described as one "who does not walk in step with the wicked" (v. 1). What Psalm 1 expresses negatively, Psalm 15 describes positively: they "walk blamelessly." What does "walking blamelessly" mean? The answer is in the parallel statement in verse 2: It is "doing what is right." Earlier, God is described as "righteous" (4:1). Thus, doing what is right is acting in accordance with the God who is righteous. If we wish to live with God, we ought to be like him. This flows naturally from the description of the place where God dwells in Psalm 15:1 as "your sacred."

Second, the worshipers are those who "speak the truth from their heart" (v. 2). From doing what is right, the psalm moves to speaking the truth. There is a close connection between doing and speaking. We have integrity when what we say matches what we do. Communication experts tell us that non-verbal elements of communication carry more weight than the words we utter.

There is a redundancy in the way verse 2b is formulated; it is not just about speaking the truth, it is about doing so "from their heart." This is the opposite of the "double heart" of Psalm 12:2. When they speak, God's people do so sincerely. They mean what they say.

We need to be aware of the importance and power of our tongues, as the book of Proverbs reminds us (Prov 18:21; 10:31; 21:23; see also Jas 3:1–10). It is worth remembering that of "all the sins in the Decalogue it is surely that of the ninth commandment which receives the fullest treatment: 'You shall not give false testimony against your neighbor' (Exod 20:16; cf. Ps 12:3–4)."[4]

The use of the tongue is always connected with relationships. So the third description is a natural consequence of the second: Acceptable worshipers "utter no slander" and "do no wrong to a neighbor" (v. 3). The focus here is on relationship with others. The worshipers are those who relate well with their neighbors. They do not utter slander against them. Literally the Hebrew reads, "he does not foot with his tongue." It is important to emphasize that how we relate with others and our ability to nourish our relationships forms a crucial part of our spirituality.

A church member once came to me and said all he wanted in the church was worship; he didn't care about fellowship. I'm afraid that is not possible. Without good relationships with others we cannot enter into worship, for how can we relate to the God we do not see when we cannot even love our neighbor whom we do see (1 John 4:20)?

Third, they hate what is evil and love what is good (v. 4; see also 1 Cor 13:6). They are not pleased with the wicked, who are despicable in their eyes. But they have high regard for those who fear the Lord. This way of valuing people reflects the kind of life they live – a righteous life cannot live with evil (see Ps 5:4).

Fourth, they keep their promises at all costs: they "keep an oath even when it hurts" (v. 4). We often make promises but later find it hard to fulfill them. So we break them instead. I remember making a promise to my sending institution to return after completing my PhD studies in the UK. It was easy to make the promise. But after more than three years of living abroad, I realized that keeping it was not easy. We were already beginning to establish ourselves where we were. My wife had a job. My children were receiving opportunities they would never have in our own country. So I dreaded the day when we would pack up and go to Heathrow airport in London. But I'm glad we returned. It's more important to keep one's promise, even when it hurts, than to break it. Character is more important than financial and social gains.

Lastly, those who will be allowed to dwell on God's sacred tent do not use their material resources to take advantage of others. They lend "money to the poor without interest" (v. 5a). One of the Mosaic laws states: "If you lend money to one of my people among you who is needy, do not treat it like a business deal; charge no interest" (Exod 22:25). Those who enter into God's

---

4. Wenham, "The Ethics of the Psalms," 186.

holy presence are those who are generous, especially to the poor and needy. They are not greedy, nor do they "accept a bribe against the innocent" (v. 5b). It is worth noting that the last item in the list of qualifications has to do with money. How we handle our money is part of our spirituality and worship.

15:5B DECLARATION

The list of requirements for those who will dwell on the holy hill of the Lord is followed by a declaration: "Whoever does these things will never be shaken" (v. 5c). We are reminded of where our true security lies. We will never be shaken because we will be dwelling in the presence of the Lord.

PSALM 16

"Too busy not to pray."[1] This phrase describes the experience of many Christians today. The need to survive, the rising expectations in the workplace, the effect of consumerism with its ever-increasing clamor for what is new and exciting – all these make life in the 21st century fragmented. It is not that we do not have time to pray. But we cannot concentrate when we do pray. Our minds are distracted, our hearts confused. But a life of continuing awareness of the presence of God remains the goal of the life of faith. The question is, how do we actually achieve this?

Psalm 16 can be our guide. From this psalm we learn what Brother Lawrence calls "the practice of the presence of God." This refers to the deliberate act of becoming "ever mindful of the LORD's presence" (16:8, NJPS) in whatever we are doing, be it washing the dishes or preparing a sermon. "Practicing the presence of the Lord" begins with the acknowledgement, "You are my Lord" and that apart from him we have no good thing (v. 2). It is making God the very center of our being so that the things on earth receive new meaning because they flow out of our intimate communion with him. This happens when we make God our "portion and inheritance" (v. 5), when our goal becomes, in the words of Kierkegaard, "to will one thing."[2]

Structurally, the psalm begins with a petition. The psalmist asks God for protection on the basis of his trust in him (v. 1). This is followed by two related declarations: "You are my Lord" and "apart from you I have no good thing" (v. 2). The following verses (vv. 3–4) bring out the implications of verses 1–2. Verses 5–6 declare God to be "my portion" and inheritance. The second half of the psalm (vv. 7–11) gives the psalmist's responses to the blessings he experiences. The central theme of Psalm 16 is found in verse 8: "I keep my eyes always on the LORD." The psalmist's experience of guidance (v. 7), joy, security, and overflowing blessings (vv. 9–11) springs from this.

16:1–6 "YOU ARE MY LORD"

Some scholars are puzzled about the genre of the psalm because its opening words sound like a lament but then the rest of it shines with confidence in

---

1. Bill Hybels wrote a book with this title.
2. Søren Kierkegaard, *Purity of Heart Is to Will One Thing: Spiritual Preparation for the Office of Confession* (New York: Harper, 1956).

God. The psalm begins with the petition, "Keep me safe, my God" (v. 1). But the two are not separate. Confidence or trust in God arises out of lament (see the topic on "Thanksgiving and Lament" on p. 75). It is in the context of lament that the opportunity to trust in God best presents itself. So following the petition is the motivation: "for in you I take refuge" (v. 1b). When life is full of storms, we learn how to take refuge in God. That is also the time when we make a firm commitment to God. Thus the psalmist declares, "You are my Lord" (v. 2a).[3] We do not wait for things to be perfect before we fully surrender our life to God. It is often in times of need that we realize that apart from God we have no good thing (v. 2b).[4]

In verse 2 the psalmist declares, "You are my Lord." It takes a deeper commitment to make this statement. It requires the working of God's Spirit as well as our own commitment. As the Apostle Paul says, "Therefore I want you to know that no one who is speaking by the Spirit of God says, "Jesus be cursed," and no one can say, "Jesus is Lord," except by the Holy Spirit." (1 Cor 12:3). To confess "You are my Lord" means to say "yes" to God, and to say "yes" to God means saying "no" to other gods. We cannot serve two (or more) masters. The psalmist makes this clear in Psalm 16:4b where he asserts he will not participate in the worship of other gods: "I will not pour out libations of blood." The pouring out of "libations of blood" is part of the worship ritual for other gods, whose "names" the psalmist vows never to mention.

What is not clear is how we understand the preceding verses. The Hebrew of verses 3–4a is uncertain.[5] Part of the question is the identity of the "holy people" and the "noble ones" (v. 3). There are two possibilities. The words could be understood as a reference to other gods. The words *qedoshim* ("holy ones") and *addirim* ("nobles") are used with reference to divine beings in Psalm 89:7 and 1 Samuel 4:8, respectively.[6] The context of verse 4, which

---

3. Here we follow the reading in the ancient Greek translation of the Old Testament, known as the Septuagint (LXX), "I say" instead of the form found in the Hebrew of the Jewish Old Testament known as the Masoretic Text (MT) which has "you say". The former works better with the context, and the majority of translations follow the LXX (e.g. RSV, NASB, ESV).

4. Literally, the MT reads, "my good, not on you," if we read *bal* with its usual meaning "not" in poetry. The LXX has: "you do not have a need of my goodness." But what does this mean? How does this fit in the context? The MT textual notes suggest reading it as *bal-bil adeykha* "not apart from you." Together with *tobati* the phrase may be taken to mean, "apart from you I have no good thing." Most modern versions follow this (ESV – "I have no good apart from you"; cf. NASB, NIV, NRSV, RSV). But see NJPS, "my benefactor; there is none above you."

5. Literally, v. 4a reads "they will increase their sorrow, another one, they hasten to" (cf. Robert G. Bratcher and William D. Reyburn, *A Translator's Handbook on the Book of Psalms* [New York: UBS, 1991], 141).

6. Clifford, *Psalms 1–72*, 96.

mentions "other gods," supports this.[7] The other alternative is to understand these words as a reference to the righteous, as is reflected in the NIV: "I say of the holy people who are in the land, 'They are the noble ones in whom is all my delight'" (v. 3). The parallel attitude towards the wicked and the righteous in the preceding psalm supports this. In Psalm 15 the wicked are despised while those who fear the Lord are honored (v. 4).

Psalm 16:5–6 elaborate on the psalmist's earlier declaration in verse 2 that apart from God he has no good thing. Here he declares that the Lord is "my portion and my cup" (v. 5). The cup could refer to victory coming from the Lord (cf. 116:13). The word "portion" is used elsewhere in the OT with reference to the Levites, who of all the twelve tribes of Israel, are the only ones who did not have any inheritance. This is because, as the Lord tells them through Aaron: "I am your share and your inheritance among the Israelites" (Num 18:2). This idea is beautifully expressed in Psalm 73:26: "My flesh and my heart may fail but God is the strength of my heart and my portion forever."

What is remarkable is that here the word "portion" is being applied to David. Being a king, David can claim many lands. Still, he maintains that it is the Lord who is his portion. And because of this he can say, "The boundary lines have fallen for me in pleasant places; surely I have a delightful inheritance" (16:6). Not because he has everything. Not because everything is just perfect. But because he has made the Lord the center of his being. "For where your treasure is, there your heart will be also" (Matt 6:21).

16:7–11 "I HAVE SET THE LORD ALWAYS BEFORE ME"

The psalmist goes on to praise the Lord (v. 7). Interestingly, he praises the Lord *not* because of the "delightful inheritance" (v. 6) he received but because the LORD "counsels" him (v. 7a). How does the Lord counsel us? God speaks to us *through our heart*, when in the quietness of the night we set out to listen to what he is saying: "even at night my heart instructs me" (v. 7b). This does not mean God speaks to us only during the night; rather, it suggests that we can sometimes listen better in the silence associated with the hours of the night.

---

7. The translation in the NJPS reflects this reading: "As to the holy and mighty ones that are in the land, my whole desire concerning them is that those who espouse another god may have many sorrows!" (vv. 3–4a).

To develop the ability to listen to him in our hearts, we need to "practice his presence" at all times so that we can say with the psalmist: "I keep my eyes always on the LORD" (v. 8). In his book, *The Practice of the Presence of God*, Brother Lawrence tells us how to apply this principle in our daily lives. One of the things he suggests is to turn every task, no matter how mundane or ordinary, into an occasion to commune with the Lord.[8] One of our problems today is that we are so preoccupied with so many things that we no longer have the time to listen to the Lord. Our attention is too divided. We do not have what Kierkegaard calls "one desire."

That is why we are easily shaken. But the psalmist is not: "With him at my right hand, I will not be shaken" (v. 8). He is protected, for "the place at the right of a person was where his defender in a trial would stand (see Ps 109:31)."[9] In the Philippines we use the expression *kanang kamay* ("right hand") to refer a position of power or honor. Applied to the text, this means giving the Lord the best place in our life. When we do that we are not shaken because the Lord is with us. When we practice the presence of the Lord, there is rejoicing and a sense of security: "Therefore my heart is glad and my tongue rejoices; my body also will rest secure" (v. 9). As St. Augustine aptly writes: "My soul is restless until it finds rest in you."

The psalmist provides another reason for his joy and sense of security: "Because you will not abandon me to the realm of the dead, nor will you let your faithful one see decay." (v. 10). In the OT, where the doctrine of eternal life and resurrection is not yet developed, continuing life on earth is viewed as a special favor.

In verse 10 the psalmist used a negative when he said, "Because you will not abandon me to the realm of the dead." But in verse 11 he stresses the positive, "You make known to me the path of life." The "path of life" refers to continuing existence, to being alive. Those who have gone through serious illness appreciate all the more the "path of life." But what makes life a joy to live is the presence of the Lord: "In your presence there is fullness of joy; in your right hand are pleasures forevermore" (v. 11, NRSV). It is the Lord who fills our hearts with joy.

But this joy comes when we are "in his presence," as we keep our "eyes always on the LORD" (v. 8). Verses 11 and 8 are connected, as confirmed by

---

8. See Jean Pierre de Caussade, *The Sacrament of the Present Moment* (San Francisco: Harper & Row, 1982).

9. Bratcher and Reyburn, *A Translator's Handbook*, 145.

the repetition of the words "right hand." As the psalmist has the Lord at his right hand (v. 8), so eternal pleasures flow from "your right hand" (v. 11).

Psalm 16 speaks to us in Asia, for this region is home to major religions that are rich in the practice of meditation. So Asians, with their deep traditions of spirituality, can easily identify with the words of this psalm. As Josefina Constantino writes: "The Asian is a person full of soul or of the sense of the sacred. It is as though he is forever plugged to the life of the universe, to the source of all life, and because life is sacred, to the source of life: the Sacred."[10]

But we also face challenges. The growing secularization and materialism in our society threaten to erode the core of our spirituality. Our challenge is to hear the words of Jesus in a fresh and new way: "Whoever wants to be my disciple must deny themselves and take up their cross daily and follow me." (Luke 9:23). May we hear the words of Jesus: "Come with me by yourselves to a quiet place and get some rest" (Mark 6:31). O, how we need this!

---

10. Constantino, *The Asian Religious Sensibility*, 291.

PSALM 17

Psalm 17 is a difficult psalm for many Christians because of the psalmist's claim to be righteous. Can we use our righteousness as the basis for our petitions? Many Christians today would rather not mention their righteousness. We would prefer to admit we are not worthy before the Lord and move on from there to bring to God our petitions.

We may find it easier to appreciate this psalm if we think of the psalmist's position as someone who is enduring oppression at the hands of the wicked. He needs some vindication (v. 2). He feels oppressed by his enemies who are bent on destroying him (vv. 10–12). And so he prays an imprecatory prayer against those whose ways are wicked using language similar to the imprecatory prayer found in Psalm 10:15 – "Break the arm of the wicked." See "The Imprecatory Psalms," pp. 274–276.

As I have noted in Psalm 10, we have to understand these imprecatory prayers in the light of who these people were and what they did. The similarity in language between Psalms 10 and 17 leads us to connect the two. The contribution of Psalm 17 is that it reminds us we cannot pray imprecatory prayers if we are not living righteous lives. How can we pray "Bring them down!" when we ourselves are not living right? This psalm challenges us to live a righteous life. We may not have the courage to pray this kind of prayer. But the challenge to live this kind of life remains.

But the prayer goes beyond concern for justice and deliverance. Picking up on the theme that inspired the composition of Psalm 16, the psalm ends with a longing to be "satisfied with seeing your likeness" (17:15).[1]

Psalm 17 contains so many links with Psalm 16 that the two psalms were possibly composed as a pair.[2] The close links between them remind us that a life of spirituality consists of a life of struggle, not only within us but also with external forces. The righteous person always cries out, "Lord, how many are my foes!" (3:1). Even a life of constant communion with God does not exempt us from human attacks. But our communion with God sustains us to continue living for him.

---

1. Kirkpatrick, *The Book of Psalms*, 79, notes: "The ground of appeal in 17 is that integrity of devotion which inspires 16; in both Psalms communion with Jehovah is set forth as the highest joy."
2. Alexander, *Commentary on Psalms*, 78. He likens Psalms 16 and 17 to the other paired psalms – Psalms 1 and 2, Psalms 3 and 4, and Psalms 9 and 10. See also Kirkpatrick, *The Book of Psalms*, 79.

Structurally, the psalm is united by the repetition of the words *tsedeq* ("righteousness") (v. 1) and *khazah* ("see") (v. 2) in the final verse (v. 15). The effect of this repetition is to highlight the emphasis on righteousness. The flow of the psalm may be outlined as follows:

> Introductory plea: the psalmist's righteousness (vv. 1–5);
> Petition on the basis of the psalmist's righteousness (vv. 6–9);
> Imprecation (vv. 10–14);
>> What the wicked do (vv. 10–12)
>> Imprecatory prayer (vv. 13–14)
> Longing for communion with God (v. 15).

17:1–5 "HEAR ME, LORD, MY PLEA IS JUST"

The opening verse forms a chiastic structure, beginning and ending with an emphasis on righteousness:

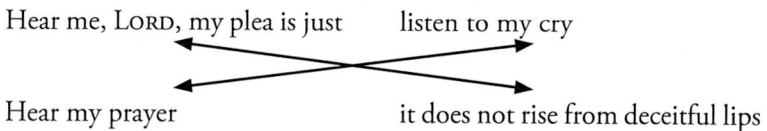

Hear me, LORD, my plea is just   listen to my cry

Hear my prayer   it does not rise from deceitful lips

The word translated as "just" is from the Hebrew word, *tsedeq*. In the structure above, this word is defined in terms of lips free of deceit. The "lips" is a synecdoche representing the whole person. So having "lips free of deceit," the psalmist prays for his vindication to come from the Lord (v. 2a). Ultimately it is the Lord who sees whether our heart is pure or not: "may your eyes see what is right" (v. 2b).

The psalmist becomes bolder about his righteousness. Even if God tries his heart, he says; even if God visits him by night (night is also mentioned in 16:7); even if God tests him as one does gold that is purified through fire, the psalmist is confident he will be found innocent (v. 3). He has lived a life of integrity, avoiding the "ways of the violent" (v. 4) and walking in accordance with God's will. He declares: "My steps have held to your paths; my feet have not stumbled" (v. 5).[3] The last word comes from the Hebrew word *mot* ("be moved/shaken") – the same word used in Psalms 15:5 and 16:8. In all cases

---

3. There is a contrast between the "ways of the violent" and the "paths" of the Lord. The psalmist avoids the former but holds fast to the latter. The psalmist declares: "My steps have held to your paths; my feet have not slipped." There are lots of words on feet, steps, ways in the psalm: *'orah* ("way," v. 4), *ashur* ("step," v. 5), *magal* ("path," v. 5), *paam* ("feet," v. 5).

the word is preceded by a negative: "I will not be shaken" (16:8). Moreover, on all three occasions, it is the effort that derives from human striving that causes the psalmist not to be moved. In Psalm 15, it is those who live a life worthy of a worshiper who will not be moved. In Psalm 16, it is because the psalmist has kept the Lord always before him that he was able to say, "I will not be shaken" (v. 8). Likewise, here, it is the psalmist's actions, mentioned in the preceding verses, which enable him not to "stumble."

17:6–12 PRAYER TO THE "SAVIOR OF THOSE WHO SEEK REFUGE" IN HIM

The above should not lead us to say, "It's all because of our own good works." Our own actions matter in our approach to God. But they are not everything. It is ultimately the Lord that determines who is worthy to come before him (see comments on Ps 15:1). Nor are our efforts enough to deliver us when we are confronted with life's trials. Life is such that without God we become vulnerable. We need a savior. That is why the psalmist cries out to God. The term used to refer to God in verse 6 is 'el ("God"), the same title used in Psalm 16:1. In verse 7, he is called upon as the "savior of those who seek refuge" (NRSV) In the Psalms, righteousness and trust in God belong together (see Ps 5 above). The righteous know how to take refuge in God. They trust not in their own righteousness to deliver them; they trust in God.

The next verses give us a glimpse of the urgency of the psalmist's situation. Wicked people are bent on destroying him, people who are ruthless[4] and arrogant (v. 10). Even now they surround him (v. 11; cf. v. 9). The enemy is likened to "a lion hungry for prey" (v. 12). Their eyes are set on him, to cast him down (v. 11). That is why the psalmist prays: "Keep me as the apple of your eye" (v. 8). Earlier, the psalmist resolved to keep the Lord always before him (16:8). The Lord is the focus of his attention. In the same way, and even more fervently, he prays for protection. Literally the "apple" of the eye is the pupil, the most sensitive part of the eye which requires utmost care. The prayer signifies the psalmist's vulnerable state. His enemies are also likened to a "fierce lion crouching in cover" (literally in "hiding") (v. 12). So he asks the Lord to hide him "in the shadow of your wings" (17:8b).

---

4. Verse 10 reads: "They close up their callous hearts." Literally, the Hebrew version of the Jewish Old Testament known as the Masoretic Text reads, "they close their fats (*khelbamo*)." The *BHS* suggests that the two words *kheleb libbamo* ("fat of their heart") have been accidentally copied as one word.

17:13–14 "OVERTHROW THEM!"

These verses represent the climax of the petitions of the previous sections. The focus is on the enemies. The psalmist describes them as "violent" (v. 4), "wicked" (v. 9), ruthless and arrogant (v. 10), and like a lion/young lion (v. 12). In verses 9, 11, he reports on what the wicked have been doing to him. In the Filipino language we can describe what the psalmist is doing here as *pagsusumbong sa Diyos*. There is no exact English equivalent for this expression. Basically it is telling God what others have been doing to you. Usually, these "others" are more powerful than you. More significantly, the "telling" or "reporting" (*pagsusumbong*) is made to someone who is considered not only powerful (and thus able to redress the situation), but one who is close to you and can be trusted. *Pagsusumbong* speaks of intimacy and trust, like that shown by children who tell their father or older brother about something that their friends have done to them. There is a strong element of trust. The psalmist feels that with God he is secure. He can tell him what is really in his heart. So after the *pagsusumbong*, the psalmist tells God what he wants God to do to his enemies.

Specifically he prays, "Rise up" (*qum*) (v. 13). This is a common prayer request in the Psalms (see e.g. 3:7; 10:12). Next he asks God to "confront" and "bring them down." Verse 14 is problematic.[5] Particularly challenging is the second part of the verse. Does 14b have a good or bad sense? Is it talking about something that is beneficial or something bad that the psalmist wishes would happen to his enemies? The Bible translations are divided. For example, the ESV takes the former view, the NIV, the latter:[6]

> "You fill their womb with treasure; they are satisfied with children, and they leave their abundance to their infants." (v. 14, ESV)

> "May what you have stored up for the wicked fill their bellies;
> may their children gorge themselves on it,
> and may there be leftovers for their little ones." (v. 14b, NIV)

In view of the preceding context, I think NIV represents the better alternative. Verse 14 is a continuation of the imprecatory prayer of verse 13. The psalmist asks that God pour out upon his enemies whatever God has prepared for them, and more. He wants this to be extended to their children. As Toombs

---

5. See Bratcher and Reyburn (*A Translator's Handbook*) for various alternatives.
6. One of the key differences between the two is how one reads the word "treasure": Is it a noun – *tsapin* ("treasure") – or a verb – *tsapan* ("what was stored up")?

writes, the verse is a request which says, "Let the family of the wicked suffer to the third generation."[7]

What are we to make of this kind of prayer?[8] Is the psalmist sinning before God when he utters it? The fact that this prayer and others like it (see 137:8–9) were recorded in the Bible tells us at least not to judge them too readily as wicked or wrong. As they stand, they are testimony to the kinds of people who wrote the Psalms. They were not people who never got angry, people who never struggled. They were people who were honest about what they really felt. But the good thing was that they did not take the law into their own hands. Instead, they came to God and told him just how they felt. We know God is not foolish enough to do exactly what we ask. He is a just God. The value of the imprecatory psalms lies in their potential for intimacy with God as well as for growth in humility on our part.

It is not surprising that this psalm ends on a note of intimacy with God: "As for me, I will be vindicated and will see your face; when I awake, I will be satisfied with seeing your likeness." (v. 15). The psalm ends by going back to the emphasis on righteousness (v. 1). But it also moves beyond this, to speak about a deep longing for God, for the face of God, for beholding God's likeness. This is similar to Moses' experience in the desert (Exod 33) and the experience of the psalmist in Psalm 16:8–11.

The previous verses talk a lot about the wicked being "satisfied" by God with the things he has in store for them in terms of punishment. By contrast, the psalmist will be satisfied "with seeing your likeness" when he awakes.

---

7. Cited in Bratcher and Reyburn, *A Translator's Handbook*, 158.
8. For a more detailed explanation of the imprecatory psalms, see Villanueva, *It's OK To Be NOT OK*, 172–204. See also Erich Zenger, *A God of Vengeance?: Understanding the Psalms of Divine Wrath* (Louisville: Westminster John Knox Press, 1996).

PSALM 18

Who is God for *you*? How would *you* describe him? What images would *you* use? The images we use to describe God tell us something about our own experiences of him. In Psalm 18 the psalmist piles up metaphor upon metaphor of God. He refers to him as "my rock, my fortress and my deliverer . . . my shield and the horn of my salvation, my stronghold" (v. 2). These metaphors are not some generic attributes of God. They arise from the psalmist's personal experience and encounter with him. For the psalmist, the images signify his experiences of trouble, danger, opposition (see vv. 4–5, 17–18) and how God intervened and answered him when he called upon the Lord (vv. 3, 6). That is why we can observe that all the images are personal: "*my* rock, *my* fortress and *my* deliverer . . . *my* shield . . . *my* stronghold." It makes a lot of difference when we ourselves have experienced what we are confessing.

Of all the metaphors used in Psalm 18, the most common is "rock," which is repeated four times (vv. 2 [2x], 31, 46).[1] This metaphor depicts firmness, toughness, certainty, and assurance. In Psalm 18 even the foundations of the mountains are trembling (v. 7, cf. v. 15). The psalmist finds himself in "deep waters" (16). In these situations God becomes to the psalmist a "rock," providing him with a firm place to stand. In our world today where there are a lot of uncertainties, the image of God as a "rock" communicates as powerfully to us as it did for the psalmist.

But for this to become a reality for us today, we need to experience God himself as our "rock." This happens when we learn what it means to "take refuge in the Lord" – a key phrase in Psalm 18. It occurs in the middle of the metaphors used to describe God in verse 2 (see below) and is repeated in verse 30. From the previous psalms we have learned what taking refuge in God means. It means trusting in the Lord (2:12) and pouring out one's heart to him. It also means living a righteous life (5:11–12). In the Psalms, "obedience and trust are not separated but thought of as a single feature of human conduct in relation to God."[2] We cannot seek to take refuge in the Lord if we are not willing to be like him. The Lord himself is righteous (v. 25); so should those be who seek to take refuge in him (vv. 20, 24).

---

1. James Luther Mays, *Psalms* (Louisville: John Knox Press, 1994), 91, writes: "The metaphor 'my rock' . . . is the most frequent in Psalms . . . The metaphorical sense seems to lie in the firm and strong character of rock as support."
2. Ibid., 93.

Structurally, the psalm may be outlined as follows:

Superscription;
Ascriptions (vv. 1–2)
The psalmist's experience (vv. 3–6)
Answer in the form of a theophany (vv. 7–15)
Two reasons why the Lord delivered the psalmist (vv. 16–19)
The importance of righteousness (vv. 20–30):
    In the experience of the psalmist (vv. 20–24)
    As a character of God himself (vv. 25–30)
Refrain: God my Rock (v. 31; cf. v. 2)
God gives victory (vv. 32–45)
    Arms me with strength (vv. 32–34)
    Makes me great by reaching down to me (v. 35; cf. v. 16)
    Victory (vv. 36–45)
Refrain: God my Rock (vv. 46–48)
Praise (vv. 49–50)

Psalm 18 is also found in 2 Samuel 22. It is one of thirteen psalms that contain historical background concerning the life of David in their superscriptions (see also Introduction). What makes Psalm 18 unique is its emphasis on victory. The superscription says that David "sang to the LORD the words of this song when the LORD delivered him from the hand of all his enemies, and from the hand of Saul." By contrast, the other superscriptions are about difficult situations in the life of David, including Absalom's rebellion in Psalm 3 and David's adultery in Psalm 51. Unlike many modern churches today where the emphasis is on victory, most of the superscriptions highlight David's difficult experiences. One possible explanation for this is that those who put the Psalms together had been through difficult experiences themselves (see Introduction). As a people they had experienced exile. So it is understandable that they were able to identify more with the difficult experiences of David. Psalm 18 stands out in this regard as a reminder that life is not all about defeats and suffering; there are also times of victory.

18:1–6 "I LOVE YOU, LORD"

The opening words of the psalm, "I love you, LORD," capture the overall mood of the psalm. It expresses the feeling of one who has been deeply touched by God. Another psalm which begins with similar words is Psalm 116: "I love the LORD."[3] In both psalms the words, "the cords of death encompassed me" appear (18:4; 116:3). The "storyline" is the same. The psalmist finds himself in deep trouble (18:4–5; 116:3). Out of his trouble he cries out to God (18:6a; 116:4) and God hears him (18:6b; 116:1–2). In response, the psalmist praises God.

The common pattern should not lead us to think that the psalmist is just following a script or that there is no emotion involved here. We need some form to express our experiences – whether praise or lament – which is why some kind of a pattern like that found in these psalms is helpful. They enable us to express our thanksgiving without going "out of bounds." The same thing is true with expressions of lament.

But while there are similarities, each psalm is also unique. Where Psalm 18 differs from Psalm 116 is in the former's numerous descriptions of God and, as will be seen below, in the employment of a theophany (vv. 7–15). The psalmist describes God as "my strength" (v. 1b) and one "who is worthy to be praised" (v. 3a). Between these two expressions, he adds a number of metaphors that describe how he sees God:

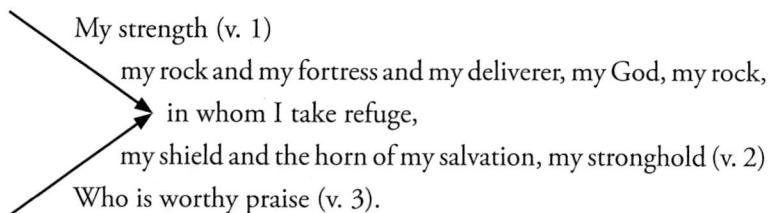

> My strength (v. 1)
> 　　my rock and my fortress and my deliverer, my God, my rock,
> 　　　in whom I take refuge,
> 　　my shield and the horn of my salvation, my stronghold (v. 2)
> Who is worthy praise (v. 3).

In addition to calling God "my deliverer" and "my God," the psalmist describes God as his 1) rock (*sela*), 2) fortress, 3) rock (*tsur*), 4) shield, 5) horn of salvation, 6) stronghold. These words should be read in the context of the superscription, which connects these titles to an actual event in the life of David. Titles and metaphors describing God in the Bible arise out of the people's experience of him. They have meaning only in connection with these experiences.

---

3. The verb "I love" in Psalm 18 comes from the rare word which is linked more to the meaning "to be compassionate." But as ancient versions and modern versions have rightly rendered it, it means "I love" in this context (Bratcher and Reyburn, *A Translator's Handbook*, 160). In Psalm 116 the word "I love" is the usual verb *ahab*.

As we can see above, between the metaphors there is the statement, "in whom I take refuge." The theme of God as "refuge" is a recurring one in the Psalms. It is often used in contexts of trouble (e.g. 2:12; 5:11; 16:1; 17:7). Those who take refuge in the Lord know that they will never be put to shame (cf. 9:10). In Psalm 18, this theme is repeated in verse 30 to include "all who take refuge in him" (for a similar shift from singular to plural in reference to taking refuge in the Lord, see 16:1 and 17:7, respectively). It is as we constantly take refuge in the Lord in all our troubles that we come to know him more.

18:7–15 THEOPHANY

In verses 7–15 the psalmist describes God's response through the use of theophany.[4] A theophany is a distinct literary genre which makes use of meteorological and geological phenomena as a way of depicting God's manifestations.[5] In the OT, volcanic phenomena were manifestations of Yahweh's appearance.[6] The same phenomenon can be observed in the NT.[7] When God is present, the foundations shake. We recall the story of Elijah on the holy mountain where he encountered God. There are some similarities with the use of elements of creation – a great wind, mountains splitting, rocks breaking, earthquake, and fire (1 Kgs 19:11–12). But we are told that God was not in these forces. Instead, God spoke in a "gentle whisper" (1 Kgs 19:12). Apparently, God was speaking in a rather unexpected way to Elijah.

In Psalm 18 it is the other way around. God is far from silent. We are struck by the awesomeness of the images presented. The "foundations of the mountains" (v. 7) tremble and the "foundations of the earth" (v. 15) are laid bare. Indeed, what envelops this section is the shaking of the foundations. In verse 7 alone three words are used to describe the reeling, rocking, and quaking of the foundations of the mountains. There is smoke coming from God's nostrils, fire from his mouth and glowing coals too (v. 8). We see "hailstones

---

4. For ancient Near East background of the images used here, see Othmar Keel, *The Symbolism of the Biblical World: Ancient Near Eastern Iconography and the Book of Psalms* (Winona Lake, IN: Eisenbrauns, 1997), 212–224.

5. Mays, *Psalms*, 92.

6. Keel, *Symbolism of the Biblical World*, 218, notes that "Mesopotamian theophany accounts are marked throughout by storm phenomena such as tempest, lightning, fire, thunder, and rain."

7. For NT examples of similar phenomenon, see Matt 28:2 and Acts 4:31. In the former, an earthquake occurred when an angel of the Lord came down and rolled the stone on Jesus' tomb. In the latter, the place where the believers were staying was "shaken" after they prayed.

and bolts of lightning" breaking through the clouds (v. 12) and God thundering in the heavens (v. 13), his lightning flashing forth (v. 14). Here we have elements of nature used as a means of describing God's actions.

The purpose of the theophany is to communicate that God is present. We see God parting the heavens and coming down (v. 9). We would imagine that when he comes down he would already be on earth. But no, upon coming down he flies on the wings of the wind (v. 10), with dark clouds under his feet (v. 9b). God is so high that even when he goes down, he's still up there in the clouds!

18:16–24 "THE LORD WAS MY SUPPORT"

The remarkable thing is that this God, even though he is so high, can come down in answer to the prayer of his servant, in answer to the cry of his people. In verse 16, the psalmist says, "He reached down from on high and took hold of me." That is impressive. For one who is so high to come down to the level of the lowly touches the heart of the lowly like no other. It is an echo of Psalm 8 where the psalmist asked, "What is mankind that you are mindful of them?" (v. 4). And yet it's true! This God does show concern and care for human beings like us.

God knows when we are in a disadvantaged situation (or as we say in Filipino, "*Alam ng Diyos kung agrabiyado tayo*") . . . when our enemies are "too strong" for us (v. 17) . . . when they attack us at our weakest point ("They confronted me in the day of my disaster," v. 18). At times like these God is there to rescue us. The psalmist declares, "But the LORD was my support" (v. 18b). The word "support" suggests the image of one who is helping us from below so as to prevent us from falling. The noun form of the word "support" comes from the verb *shaan* which means "to lean on, to rely on" (see Isa 50:10).[8] God did not only go down; he also made himself lower just so he could support us. In his study of the ancient Near East background for the theophany in Psalm 18, Shnider points out that the parallel materials show God as the one who supports the warrior king David. He writes: "It is as though God . . . is standing next to the warrior helping him fight his enemies."[9]

---

8. Bratcher and Reyburn, *A Translator's Handbook*, 172.
9. Steven Shnider, "Psalm xviii: Theophany, Epiphany Empowerment," *VT* 56, no. 3 (2006): 396.

But God does not help us just because we are vulnerable and weak. He also looks at our life. The psalmist claims, "He rescued me because he delighted in me" (v. 19b). The next section (vv. 20–24), bracketed by the words "according to my righteousness" (vv. 20, 24), explains why the Lord delights in him. The phrase does not mean the psalmist is perfect. It should be understood in the context of the covenant relationship between God and his king.

For his part the king asserts he has fulfilled his responsibilities. Verses 21–22 follow the same pattern of moving from positive ("I have") to negative ("I have not") statements:

"For I have kept the ways of the LORD; I am not guilty of turning from my God . . ." (v. 21)
"All his laws are before me; I have not turned away from his decrees . . ." (v. 22)

18:25–30 "TO THE BLAMELESS YOU SHOW YOURSELF BLAMELESS"

The claim in verse 23 introduces us to a similar emphasis in the following section: "I have been blameless before him and have kept myself from sin." Taking up the word "blameless" (v. 23), the theme of righteousness is further affirmed by the emphasis on the "blamelessness" of God. As in the previous section, the present section (vv. 25–30) is enveloped by an emphasis on righteousness. The word "blameless" occurs in verses 25b and 30a.

There is a shift from third person ("the LORD") to second person ("you") address in verse 25. The last time the psalmist addressed God in the second person was in verse 15. Except for verses 1 and 15, almost all the verses up to verse 24 are in the third person. But in verse 25, the psalmist turns to God and declares: "To the faithful you show yourself faithful; to the blameless you show yourself blameless" (v. 25). The word "faithful" is from the word *khasid*. It refers to the devout. To such a person, God shows himself to be also faithful.

The word "blameless" (*tamim*) should not be understood as meaning "without sin," but as a characteristic reflecting wholeness and integrity. The blameless is the one whose words are faithful like God (v. 30).

Verse 26 continues the theme of verse 25, adding the opposites of "faithful" and "blameless": "to the devious you show yourself shrewd" (v. 26). These two verses emphasize that God's dealings are in accordance with how we live. The next verse provides a specific example of how this is worked out – God saves the humble but brings down those who are boastful (v. 27). The word "humble" here comes from the word for those who are afflicted, "the poor" (*ani*). Those who are often trampled down because of their lowly situation learn to be more humble, though of course, this is not always the case.

When you always experience being put down by others, by those who are boastful (v. 27), when you are confronted with so many enemies – an entire troop – and faced with a wall (v. 29), it is easy to be discouraged. But the psalmist says that during those times when the light of his lamp is almost gone, during the times of his darkness, the Lord is there to provide light (v. 28). Again we see God's support for the psalmist (cf. v. 18). Indeed, the Lord is "blameless." He is faithful: "The LORD's word is flawless; he shields all who take refuge in him" (v. 30). The word "refuge" recalls the beginning of the psalm (v. 2). Here the psalmist applies what he has experienced to all who take refuge in the Lord.

The metaphor of God as a "shield" is interesting, for being a 'shield-bearer' was a subordinate position. Thus, to "summon Yahweh as one's shield-bearer presupposes that intimacy which permits one to ask a friend to perform a lowly service without in any way offending him."[10] This further supports the idea that God stoops down to reach his servant and also to be his support.

18:31–35 GOD IS OUR ROCK

The next section (vv. 31–35) begins with a refrain (v. 31). The word "rock" recalls verse 2. Recalling the theme of God as blameless, the psalmist applies it to the way the Lord has prepared and trained him to ensure victory over his enemies. As "[God's] way is perfect (*tamim*)" (v. 30), so God "made my way blameless (*tamim*)" (v. 32, ESV).[11] But whereas the former refers more to God's moral character, the latter points to a more practical skill – that of training for battle. Thus the next verses talk about God's training the psalmist for battle (vv. 33–34).

Verse 33 focuses on the feet of the psalmist which God has made "like the feet of a deer." He can easily escape when danger comes (33b). Verse 34 focuses on hands which God trains for war, strengthening them so that they can bend even a bow of bronze. The first part of verse 35 speaks of protection: "You make your saving help my shield." Verse 35b speaks of God's power, "your right hand." Yet as we have seen earlier in the psalm, even though God

---

10. Keel, *Symbolism of the Biblical World*, 222.
11. Notice that in both verses the words "way" and "blameless/perfect" occur.

is high and exalted, up there and powerful, he reaches down to the psalmist. And here he supports the psalmist. What power and what gentleness! The psalmist declares: "your help has made me great." The word "help" comes from the Hebrew word which means "humility." The psalmist acknowledges that God's act of stooping down just to reach him was what "made me great" (v. 35; cf. 2 Cor 8:9).

18:36–50 GOD GIVES VICTORY

Verse 36 continues on the theme of protection and recalls verse 33 with its mention of "feet": "You provide a broad path for my feet, so that my ankles do not give way." He was able to pursue his enemies and destroy them (vv. 37–38, 42). "I beat them as fine as windblown dust" (v. 42) may be compared to Psalm 1:4 where the wicked are like "chaff that the wind blows away"). The psalmist acknowledges it is all because of the Lord that he has experienced victory over his enemies: "You armed me with strength for battle" (v. 39; see also vv. 33–34). God caused his enemies to retreat (v. 40). Even when they cried to the Lord he did not answer them (v. 41), unlike his response to the psalmist (v. 6).

Does God play favorites? We have to assume in the light of the context that the enemies were not righteous. Thus God dealt with them accordingly (see vv. 25–27). God not only gave the psalmist victory but also exalted him over other peoples, including foreigners (vv. 43–45).

This leads to the final section (vv. 46–50) which commences with another refrain, "The Lord lives! Praise be to my Rock" (v. 46). Again, the word "rock" is repeated (see also vv. 2, 31). Because of what the Lord has done, the psalmist declares, "I will praise you" (vv. 49–50).

How does a psalm about victory over one's enemies, including peoples from other nations, speak to those who have been under foreign powers for a long time? It is not easy to identify with the triumphant. Filipinos, in particular, have a deep sympathy for those who have been defeated. This is probably because of our own experience of suffering under foreign rulers. So the overall emphasis on victory in this psalm may not resonate with us.

What I think will resonate with our experience is the portrayal of a God who, though powerful and exalted, has stooped down to reach us. The vision of one who is powerful but at the same time willing to support the weak touches our hearts like no other. *Pakikiramay* ("being one with those who suffer") is central in our culture. This explains why Filipinos were deeply moved when Pope Francis went to Tacloban to visit the survivors of typhoon Yolanda (Haiyan).

But someone greater than Pope Francis has already shown us the character of the God we encounter in Psalm 18 – Jesus,

> Who, being in very nature God, did not consider equality with God something to be used to his own advantage; rather, he made himself nothing by taking the very nature of a servant, being made in human likeness And being found in appearance as a man, he humbled himself by becoming obedient to death— even death on a cross! (Phil 2:6–8)

Why did he come down? It was for our sake. As the Apostle Paul writes: "Though he was rich, yet for your sake he became poor, so that you through his poverty might become rich" (2 Cor 8:9).

PSALM 19

Our world is characterized by too many words; *bumabaha sa salita* ("It's flooding with words"). There is too much noise. As a result, people have grown tired of words. How can we speak or write in such a way that our words will matter?

Psalm 19, the psalm which C. S. Lewis considers "the greatest poem in the Psalter and one of the greatest lyrics in the world,"[1] shows us how. For like us, creation too is full of words: "The heavens declare the glory of God; the skies proclaim the work of his hands" (19:1). Like us, creation is constantly speaking. The verbs "declare" and "proclaim" in verse 1 are Hebrew participles that indicate continuous, ongoing action. The heavens are continually declaring and proclaiming. In fact, there are five words used in the Hebrew for the "word/s" in Psalm 19: "speech" (*omer*, v. 2), "words" (*debarim*, v. 3), "sound" (*qol*, v. 3), "voice" (*qav*; literally, "line," v. 4a), and "word" (*milla*, v. 4).

But there is a big difference between our words and creation's words. For one thing, creation is not speaking about itself. Rather, it is declaring "the glory of God." Words become empty when they are used for selfish ends. They become meaningful only when they are used to minister to others for the glory of God. Jesus, the living Word, said, "For I have come down from heaven not to do my will but to do the will of him who sent me." (John 6:38).

Psalm 19 consists of three sections dealing with the creation (vv. 1–6), the Torah (vv. 7–11), and prayer (vv. 12–14). The focus on the Torah ("law") reminds us that the words that really matter are not our own words, but the word that comes from God. That is the word that revives the soul, makes people wise, gives joy to the heart and enlightens the eyes (vv. 7–8). It is only when our words are founded on the living word that they become life-giving, sustaining, and empowering.

19:1–6 CREATION DECLARES THE GLORY OF GOD

Psalm 19 resembles Psalm 8. The latter proclaims that God has set his "glory in the heavens" (v. 1b). Psalm 19 develops this idea and declares that the heavens themselves "declare the glory of God; the skies proclaim the work of his hands" (v. 1). As noted above, in Hebrew the words, "declare" and

---

1. C. S. Lewis, *Reflections on the Psalms* (London: Geoffrey Bles, 1958), 63.

"proclaim" are participles that convey continuity and ongoing action. God's creation is constantly making known God's glory. Creation is full of "words." "Day after day they pour forth speech; night after night they reveal knowledge" (v. 2). The heavens are overflowing with speech. "Their voice goes out into all the earth" (v. 4).

Paradoxically, although the heavens continue to "speak," "they have no speech, they use no words; no sound is heard from them" (v. 3).[2] This statement appears in the middle of assertions that the heavens are full of speech that reaches the ends of the earth (vv. 2, 4), as shown in the following diagram:

"Day to day they pour forth speech" (v. 2).
"They have no speech, they use no words" (v. 3).
"Their voice goes out into all the earth" (v. 4).

What does this tell us? Creation, though full of words, does not need words to communicate. The heavens have their own way of speaking. Creation speaks out of silence; that is why it is deep. We have a saying in Filipino: *Ang balon kapag tahimik, malalim; kapag maingay, mababaw* ("A deep well is quiet; a shallow one noisy").

Nahum M. Sarna comments, "The heavens . . . recount God's glory in their own special way, in a language that is neither perceptible to the ear nor understandable to human beings on earth."[3] But while we agree that the heavens have their "own special way" of speaking, we disagree with Sarna on his second point. We think human beings can still perceive and understand what creation is saying. In fact, as verse 1 tells us, the psalmist himself understands that the "heavens declare the glory of God." But this requires a certain kind of seeing or comprehending. It is posture that is meditative; it demands a lifestyle that is not in a hurry but lingers. It is a kind of living that knows how to stop just to listen to creation. It is a kind of listening that is open to all things – not just to spiritual things but to all of creation. Indeed, it is the kind of vision that sees in all things the fingerprints of God (see 8:3).

The psalmist's description of the sun demonstrates the kind of seeing we are talking about. First he views the sun's rising and setting as the work of

---

2. The ancient Greek translation of the Old Testament, known as the Septuagint (LXX) adds a relative pronoun, *on* ("which"), maybe as a way of making sense of the apparent contradiction in vv. 2–4. Some modern versions follow the LXX. But we think the Hebrew version of the Jewish Old Testament known as the Masoretic Text (MT) preserves the original reading. There is no contradiction, only a paradox.
3. Nahum M. Sarna, *On the Book of Psalms: Exploring the Prayers of Ancient Israel* (New York: Schocken Books, 1993), 80.

God: God has "pitched a tent for the sun" (v. 4c).[4] Second, using imagery common in the ancient Near East,[5] the psalmist likens the sun to a bridegroom emerging from his wedding canopy and to a "champion rejoicing to run his course" (v. 5). We have never heard of anything close to the way the sun is described here. The images are "poetic expressions of how the heavens tell God's glory day after day."[6] The sun is full of excitement; there is so much life, as it fulfills its role of declaring God's glory. Verse 6 brings out the extent of the sun's reach: "It rises at one end of the heavens and makes its circuit to the other; nothing is deprived of its warmth." Earlier the psalmist declared that the heavens' voice goes "to the ends of the world" (v. 4). The word "end" is repeated twice in verse 6 to speak about the sun's journey from one end of the heavens to the other end. This highlights the comprehensiveness of the sun's reach. "Nothing," the psalmist asserts, "is deprived of its heat" (v. 6).

19:7–11 "THE LAW IS PERFECT"

Psalm 19 creatively brings together the themes of creation and the "law of the Lord." Although some may find the juxtaposition rather unnatural,[7] in the ancient Near East, creation and law were closely related.[8] Like creation, comprehensive in its "telling of the glory of God," so the "law of the LORD is perfect" (v. 7). In Hebrew the word "perfect" can also be translated as "whole" or "entire." Further, like creation which is actively proclaiming God's glory, the "law" is actively at work, "refreshing the soul" and "giving joy to the heart" (vv. 7–9).

From creation the psalm moves to an emphasis on the law. There are three psalms that focus on the subject of the "law of the Lord": Psalms 1, 19, and 119. The concept of the law (Torah), as used in the Psalms, is broad. It concerns the law as found in the Pentateuch, but it also embraces "the whole

---

4. This sentence dethrones once and for all the sun as a deity. In the ancient Near East, the sun often represented a god that people worshiped. But in the biblical view, the sun is simply God's creation, not a god (Gen 1:14–18).
5. For ancient Near East background, see Sarna, *On the Book of Psalms*, 80.
6. Alter, *The Book of Psalms*, 61.
7. Unable to see the connection between creation and the law of the Lord, some scholars have viewed the psalm as consisting of two compositions that have been brought together.
8. Sarna, *On the Book of Psalms*, 76, 82, notes: "Whatever the name under which the sun god was venerated, it was everywhere taken to be the guardian of law and justice. The hymns devoted to that deity portray him as both the god of light and the god of justice, the two motifs intermingling and succeeding one another smoothly and naturally. By analogy, the apparent lack of logical thought sequence in Psalm 19 may be a reflex of a well-established liturgical pattern in the ancient Near East."

revelation of God"[9] which includes nature. The "law of the Lord" is about knowing the will of the Lord. Wenham writes: "The psalmist's one preoccupation is to know . . . the will of God better and put it into practice, so as to enjoy complete communion with God, day and night, as long as he lives."[10]

So the law here, though similar in some ways to our understanding of law today, is also different. It involves a relationship with a person – God. This relationship is founded on God's initiative, revealed in the OT in the Sinai covenant (Exodus 19), and ultimately in the coming of our Lord Jesus Christ. Viewed from this perspective we can understand how the law can be a "delight" (Ps 1:2) and how it can be considered as more valuable than gold and "sweeter than honey" (19:10).

Psalm 19 uses five synonyms for the law: decrees, precepts, commandments, fear (of the Lord), and ordinances (vv. 7–9). All five, including "law" are said to be "of the LORD." The focus is not on the law per se but on the fact that it is."the law *of the* LORD" (see comments in Ps 1:2). Interestingly, the word translated "LORD," Yahweh, is repeated seven times in Psalm 19: six times in verses 7–9 and once in the prayer at the end (v. 14). This covenant name for God reminds us of the relationship between God and his people.

We noted above that Psalm 19 is similar to Psalm 8. But in the last part of Psalm 19, we notice a departure from Psalm 8. While Psalm 8 focuses on man's perfection and dominion over creation,[11] Psalm 19 highlights human beings' imperfection and need of correction. Sarna notes, "It is not the inconsequence or greatness of human beings that interests our psalmist, but the recognition of their inherent imperfection and their need of divine help in striving for self-improvement" (vv. 12–15).[12] This probably explains the sudden shift from delight in the law of the Lord to an awareness of the frailty of the human heart. Humans need to be warned: "By them [the laws of the Lord] your servant is warned" (v. 11a). And even though the psalmist recognizes that "in keeping them there is great reward" (v. 11b), he is also quick to admit, "But who can discern their own errors?" (v. 12a).

---

9. Wenham, *Psalms as Torah*, 84.
10. Ibid., citing Jean-Luc Vesco, *Le psautier de David: traduit et commenté* (Paris: Cerf, 2006).
11. Kirkpatrick, *The Book of Psalms*, 36, comments on Psalm 8: "The Psalmist looks away from the Fall with its heritage of woe, from the sin and failure and rebellion of mankind, to man's nature and position and destiny in the original purpose of God."
12. Sarna, *On the Book of Psalms*, 75.

19:12–14 "MAY THE MEDITATION OF MY
HEART BE ACCEPTABLE TO YOU"

With a deep sense of awareness of human weakness, the psalmist prays, "Forgive my hidden faults" (v. 12b). In the end the psalmist turns to heart-searching, moving from reflection on creation (vv. 1–6) to meditation on the "law of the LORD" (vv. 7–11), and finally to prayer (vv. 12–14). The words "hidden faults" come from the same root as the word "hidden" in verse 6. In the same way that nothing is hidden from the sun's heat, so the psalmist acknowledges nothing is hidden from the Lord.

The psalmist applies the same comprehensiveness, the same searching light as the sun, to his heart. He wants the Lord to shed his light in the darkest recesses of his being. He longs to be blameless before the Lord and so he confesses even his hidden sins. The psalmist's acute ability to listen to creation makes him sensitive to the more tricky movements of his heart. The deceptiveness of sin is difficult to discern (v. 12a).

We might expect the psalmist to be more advanced in his journey towards holiness and no longer struggling with sin. But it is often the case that those closest to God are more conscious of their sins. They are more acutely aware of their need for the light of the "law of the Lord," which like the sun brings to light our dark sides. The psalmist has no other desire than to do the will of God in order to please him (v. 14).

Psalm 19 reminds us of the need to listen in our interpretation of the word. Even in hermeneutics the discipline of listening is crucial. As Gadamer writes: "Hermeneutics is above all a practice . . . In it what one has to exercise above all is the ear, the sensitivity for perceiving prior determinations, anticipations, and imprints that reside in concepts."[13] But above all, the reason we want to develop this kind of listening is that we want to please the Lord: "May these words of my mouth and this meditation of my heart be pleasing in your sight, LORD, my Rock and my Redeemer" (v. 14).

---

13. Hans-Georg Gadamer, "Reflections on My Philosophical Journey," in *The Philosophy of Hans-Georg Gadamer*, ed. Lewis Edwin Hahn (Chicago: Open Court, 1997), 17, cited in Anthony C. Thiselton, *Hermeneutics: An Introduction* (Grand Rapids: Eerdmans, 2009), 225.

CREATION AND MEDITATION

There is a close link between creation and meditation as we have seen in Psalm 19. The first part of the psalm is about creation (vv. 1–6) while the second part is a declaration of the beauty of the law (vv. 7–11), the object of the psalmist's meditation. Pope Francis captures this close relationship very well in his reflection on ecology: "An integral ecology includes taking time to recover a serene harmony with creation, reflecting on our lifestyle and our ideals, and contemplating the Creator who lives among us and surrounds us" (*Laudato si'* 225).

The words "serene harmony" are crucial.[1] The psalmist models for us what having a "serene harmony" with creation means. It is the capacity to see beyond the appearance of things into the reality of creation. We have serene harmony with creation when we treat creation with awe and reverence, when we take the time to stop and listen to what creation is saying to us. That capacity to stand in wonder of creation which we see in the psalmist's description of the sun is what we need to recover in our time.

"Serene harmony" requires a posture of openness, of listening. Though Psalm 19 speaks a lot about speaking and words, the thread that holds the psalm together is the theme of *openness* – openness to listen, to see, and to hear what God is trying to tell us and making known to us through creation and his word.

A certain kind of listening is required to be able to hear what creation is revealing. Creation is full of words: "Day after day they pour forth speech" (v. 2a). And yet, paradoxically, verse 3 tells us, "they use no words; no sound is heard." To hear what creation is telling us, we need to be open. This openness to creation, this particular kind of listening, is also what is called for by the "law of the Lord." To hear what God has to say, we need to develop the ability to see God in the events of everyday life, including ordinary events like the rising and setting of the sun. Such listening enables us to discern the hidden things of our hearts.

It is important to evaluate our lifestyle because if we are too busy we naturally elbow out the people around us. The problem with us is that we are always on the rush. Our cities are full of lights so we can no longer see the light from the moon by night. We fill our lives with so much noise that we can no longer hear what God is telling us through his creation. Especially with the Internet and social media, there is no room left for that still, small voice. We see everyone and everything from a consumerist point of view, including

---

1. Fr. Albert Alejo brought this to my attention during a Faculty Recollection at Loyola School of Theology.

creation. We no longer have time for our children or our spouse. We step on other people's head just to reach the top.

When we do that to people, it will not be a surprise when we do the same to creation. As they say, *"Ang basura ng lipunan ay nanggagaling sa basura ng puso"* (The garbage of society comes from the garbage of the heart). We treat creation as something to be used and abused; we no longer have respect for it. Instead, we use it for our own selfish benefit, without regard for the effects on creation and the next generation. We have given Genesis 1:28 a wrong interpretation. We have literally taken dominion of the earth and used it for our own purposes.

PSALM 20

Psalm 20 is the first psalm that comes close to what we call intercessory prayer. While intercessory prayer may be common in the NT, there are few examples of it in the Psalms, where personal prayers are more common (e.g. "Deliver me, my God" in 3:7; see also 4:1; 5:1). We do have prayers for others, but these are mostly imprecatory prayers (7:9; 10:15; 12:3; 17:13), that is, they are prayers to God against other people, usually the psalmist's enemies. This makes Psalm 20 the first prayer offered for others which is positive in its content. It is actually a prayer on behalf of the king, but we may also include it in the broader category of intercessory prayer (see comment on v. 9 below).

Psalm 20 is a prayer of the people for their king. In the NT we are exhorted to pray for "kings and all those in authority" (1 Tim 2:1–2). But the instruction is general and may include all kinds of requests and petitions. The value of the prayers in the Psalms is that here we are provided with an actual prayer which gives us some idea of how we may construct our own prayers. More importantly, in the prayer itself is reflected the theology which inspired the prayer. Psalm 20 is a prayer for a specific concern, that of victory for the king. It is a solemn prayer, coming from those who have no power but who know where true power and deliverance come from. People who have a lot of power may find it hard to pray. They may feel no need to pray, since they have plenty of resources. But those who acknowledge their limitations know they can rely only on God for help.

The situation envisaged in the psalm is one of trouble. It talks about times "when you are in distress" (v. 1), of times when "help" is much needed (v. 2). Some scholars think this psalm is part of a liturgy on the eve of battle, though the language is far from specific and can be applied more generally to any situation of need. What we know is that in a time of need the people join together in praying for success and victory for their king. The people's lives are closely linked with that of their king. Be it peril or deliverance, what happens to him will affect their lives. And so they come to God, the one who they believe can intervene in any situation.

In countries where corrupt leaders are the norm, applying this psalm is a challenge. How can we pray for victory for our leaders when they are corrupt? In a world marked by increasing violence, we would rather pray for peace than for victory for our leader. So what we need to do when we read this psalm is not to associate the king with a specific modern leader but rather to focus on the theology reflected in this prayer.

One important lesson we can learn is the importance of dependence on God. Our country may be small and poor. But if we have God, if we trust in him, we have hope. That is the strength of Filipinos, their being religious and prayerful. However, this does not negate the need for *pagsusumikap* ("self-determination"). Often because of our strong belief in fate, we do not exert ourselves to somehow alleviate our condition. But the emphasis on trusting in God "does not mean that human resources of power are to be renounced."[1] It should not lead us to the negative aspect of *bahala na*,[2] where everything is left to God or to chance. We also need to try our best. As we say, "*Nasa Diyos ang awa; nasa tao ang gawa*" ("To God belongs mercy, but we also need to do our part").

Let us pray for the leaders of our country, that they will have strength with God's help (vv. 1–3), success with God's blessing (vv. 4–5), and submission to God's will (vv. 6–9).

20:1–5 PRAYER FOR THE KING

The main concern in the psalm is that God answer the prayer of the people for their king. This is reflected in the way the psalm is structured. The verb "to answer" appears at the beginning and end (vv. 1, 9), forming an inclusio. It also occurs after a major shift in verse 6. The petition for God to answer their prayer reflects their belief in a God who hears the prayers of his people. As David called on the Lord in his distress (*tsar*) (18:6), so now the people pray for the king: "The Lord answer you in the day of trouble (*tsarah*)" (20:1). As David declared that God was his "stronghold" (*misgab*) (18:2), so they pray God will "protect" (*sagab*)[3] (20:1) their king.

Verse 2 stresses where help comes from. It comes from God's sanctuary,[4] the temple, which is also called the house of prayer (Isa 56:7; Matt 21:3). The word "sanctuary" recalls the preceding psalms. "If Psalm 15 shows the conditions of fellowship with God at his sanctuary, and if Psalms 16–19 explore

---

1. Weiser, 209.
2. There is also a positive element in the expression *bahala na*. For a very good discussion on *bahala na*, see Jose M. de Mesa, *In Solidarity with the Culture* (Quezon City, Philippines: Maryhill School of Theology, 1987), 147–177.
3. Literally, this verb means "to make high, inaccessible" (Holladay, *Concise Hebrew and Aramaic Lexicon*, 349), similar to the idea expressed in the noun form, "stronghold."
4. Literally, "holy" (place) (see also Pss 28:2; 60:6).

the godly character, these psalms (20–21) show God sending help from the sanctuary to a godly king."[5]

Closely associated with the sanctuary are sacrifices and offerings. There are different kinds of offerings in the OT.[6] Two words associated with offerings are mentioned in verse 3 – *minkha* ("gift," "offering") and *olah* ("burnt offering"). The former is the more general word. However, burnt offerings are used for a wide variety of purposes (entreaty, thanksgiving, appeasement, etc.). The structure of verses 4–5 suggests that the purpose of the offerings mentioned in this psalm is request victory for the king:

> Prayer that God fulfill all the king's plans (v. 4);
> Rejoicing together at the king's victory (v. 5ab);
> Prayer that God fulfill all the king's petitions (v. 5c).

Here we see a fulfillment of the Apostle Paul's command to "rejoice with those who rejoice" (Rom 12:15). The people wish success and victory for their king. They hope that he will succeed so that they can share in his joy: "May we shout for joy over your victory" (Ps 20:5). Note that it is not just rejoicing but *shouting* for joy. The image of setting up banners refers to some kind of a victory party.

20:6–9 ASSURANCE OF BEING HEARD

There is a sudden shift from prayer to a strong sense of confidence that God has already heard their prayer. There is also a change of voice from the first person plural ("we") to first person singular: "Now this I know: The LORD gives victory to his anointed"[7] (v. 6). The shift does not necessarily mean a change of speaker. It could be a literary device employed to focus attention on the element of assurance. Having expressed their prayers for the king, the people have gained confidence that the Lord will answer. Earlier, the answer is described as coming from the "sanctuary" and "Zion" (v. 2). Here it comes from God's "heavenly sanctuary" (v. 6). The temple is important, but ultimately help comes from the Lord.

---

5. Grogan, *Psalms*, 69.
6. Burnt offerings, cereal offerings, peace offerings, sin offerings, and guilt offerings (see Leviticus 1–5),
7. This is my own translation (compare the ancient Greek translation of the OT, known as the Septuagint [LXX]). The Hebrew is in the perfect tense, which could be rendered in the past tense, though Hebrew tenses especially in poetry can be flexible. Still, I think the perfect tense preserves that sense of certainty. See also Mark 11:24.

Help that comes from the Lord is described as "mighty victories by his right hand" (v. 6, NRSV).[8] The plural form of the first phrase ("strengths of salvation") highlights the awesomeness of God's power, greater than even the best weapon available. In the psalmist's time, chariots and horses represented the most powerful military resources available. This explains why people boasted in them: "Some trust in chariots and some in horses" (v. 7a). In contrast to this, the people assert, "But we trust in the name of the LORD our God" (v. 7). Those who know the Lord trust in him instead (9:10). The chariots and horses will be "brought to their knees and fall," but the people will "rise and stand firm" (v. 8).

The last verse reverts to intercessory prayer. Compared with the earlier prayer, which is more of a strong wish (vv. 1–5), this last prayer is more direct: "LORD, give victory to the king" (v. 9).[9] This stands in tension with the statement in verse 6. Although the latter expressed assurance that help had already come, verse 9 shows that help had not yet come. In a way, many of us live in this tension. So the last line is apt: "Answer us when we call!"

---

8. Literally, "with strengths of salvation of his right hand."
9. Like most modern translations do, this translation from the NRSV follows the LXX, which takes the "king" LORD as belonging in the first clause (cf. Franz Delitzsch, "Psalms," in *Commentary on the Old Testament*, Vol. 5 Repr., eds. Carl F. Keil and F. Delitzsch [Grand Rapids: Eerdmans, 1980] 5:299). For an alternative translation that follows the Hebrew version of the Jewish Old Testament known as the Masoretic Text, see NJPS: "O LORD, grant victory! May the King answer us when we call" (see also Mays, *Psalms*, 102; Alexander, *Commentary on Psalms*, 102).

PSALM 21

Psalms 20 and 21 currently form a pair. Psalm 20 represents the prayer of the people for their king; Psalm 21, the thanksgiving of the king for the request granted. One notices a shift from a posture of waiting to one of rejoicing and celebration. The people wished they could "shout for joy over your victory" (*bishuateka*) (20:5). Now the "king rejoices" and greatly exults "in your help" (*bishuateka*) (21:1). Note that the word translated as "over your victory" (20:5) and "in your strength" (21:1) comes from the same word in Hebrew. The people prayed that God would grant the desires of the king's heart (20:4). Psalm 21:2 reports: "You have granted him his heart's desire."

We can no longer be sure about the original setting of both psalms.[1] But from a theological perspective the two psalms affirm that God answers the prayer of his people. Since they reflect the differing situations of need and answer, respectively, they also instruct us on how to respond to God in similar situations.

One thing that binds the two psalms together is the response of trust. In Psalm 20, when the temptation is to trust in chariots and horses, the people chose to trust in the Lord. In Psalm 21, when victory is already achieved, the response remains the same. It is not in the strength of the king or the people that the king rejoices, but "in your strength," that is, God's strength (v. 1). Indeed, this theme of God's strength runs through the whole of Psalm 21, occurring at the beginning and end of it (vv. 1 and 13). The people are convinced that the reason for the king's blessings and success is that he "trusts in the LORD" (v. 7). Thus in victory or in trouble, we continue to trust in God. There is never an occasion when we can say we have no need of him.

Structurally, the psalm may be divided into two main sections: verses 1–6 and verses 8–13, with verse 7 as the center. The first section is bound together by the note of rejoicing (vv. 1, 6). Most of the verbs used are also in the perfect tense (relating to the past). This differs from the second section where the verbs relating to God's actions are all in the future tense. This makes the element of trust central in the psalm (v. 7).

---

1. Some scholars hold that Psalm 20 is a liturgy used on the eve of battle while Psalm 21 is used *after* the battle has been won. But the lack of specific details in Psalm 21 prohibits one from making a conclusion on this matter. Others propose other settings for Psalm 21 (e.g. the king's coronation, birth, etc.). But again we cannot be certain about these.

21:1–6 REJOICING IN GOD'S BLESSINGS

Because the king did not trust in chariots or horses (20:7) but in the Lord (21:7), he now rejoices in the Lord's strength (21:1). The mood of rejoicing fills this psalm. As noted above, the first section begins and ends with a comment on the king's rejoicing (vv. 1, 6).

The king has many reasons to rejoice. He has experienced the generosity of God. The verb *natan* ("to give") is repeated. God has given him the desires of his heart (v. 2). Specifically the king asked for "life" and God gave it to him (v. 4). The psalm may be likened to God's answer to Solomon's prayer. When the Lord asked Solomon what he wanted, his answer was only one thing ("a discerning heart to govern your people"; 1 Kgs 3:9) and yet God gave him more than he asked for (1 Kgs 3:11–13). Likewise in this psalm, the king asked for life and God granted him life and more. He has been richly blessed. The word "blessings" is repeated, in both cases in the plural and with a positive addition – "rich blessings" (v. 3) and "unending blessings" (v. 6). The blessings include long life (v. 4), glory, splendor and majesty (v. 5), and the "joy of your presence" (v. 6). It is interesting that the blessings are described as "unending" before the last blessing is mentioned, that of the "joy of your presence." For the psalmist there is no greater joy than to be in God's presence (27:4).

21:7–13 "THE KING TRUSTS IN THE LORD"

Verses 1–6 begin and end with the note of joy. There is joy because of what God has done. Verse 7 is important in this regard because it provides the human side of the presence of joy. It is because the "king trusts in the LORD" (v. 7) that he is able to rejoice in him. Had he trusted in his chariots and horses, he would not have been rejoicing in the Lord. He would have been rejoicing in his *own* strength and power. But had he done this, he would have been unlikely to rejoice at all, for no one succeeds on their own, though some may think they can. It is only "through the unfailing love of the Most High" that we "will not be shaken" (v. 7).

Verses 8–12 continue the theme of the previous section. It is not because of the king but because of the Lord:

- "*Your* hand . . . *your* right hand" (v. 8). There is a parallelism here. The verb "find out," translated as "lay hold" and "seize," occurs in both lines. But there is heightening from "your hand" to "right hand."

- "When *you* appear for battle, *you* will burn them up as in a blazing furnace" (v. 9). Whereas the presence or the appearing of the Lord brings joy and blessings for the king, it has the opposite effect on the king's enemies. The image of fire in this verse speaks of destruction. In his wrath the "LORD will swallow them up . . . and his fire will consume them."

- The destruction extends to the next generation: "*You* will destroy their descendants" (v. 10). This verse speaks of wiping out the memory of enemies by destroying even their descendants.

The only verse that does not explicitly mention the Lord is verse 11. But the message remains the same. On their own, no one will succeed, even with horses and chariots. How much more when "they plot evil against you"? Certainly, "they cannot succeed" (v. 11).

- "*You* will make them turn their backs" (v. 12). The second line reads: "You [God] will aim at their faces with your bows" (v. 12, NRSV). Taken together the two actions are interesting. Imagine enemies fleeing, which means their backs are turned from you. Yet even while they turn, arrows are being aimed at their faces. They are surrounded; whichever way they turn, God is there. That is the strength and power of God.

And so the psalmist ends with an exaltation of God for his strength (v. 13). The second part of verse 13 declares: "We will sing and praise your might." This last line establishes the connection with the previous psalm. In Psalm 20 it was the people who prayed for their king, who hoped one day to shout for joy when he won. Yet in Psalm 21, when the king is victorious, the people are nowhere mentioned. We wonder where they have gone. Psalm 21 says nothing at all about the people rejoicing because of their king's victory . . . until we reach the end of the psalm where we find the words "*We* will sing and praise your might" (v. 13). We may infer from this that the people are one with the king in his rejoicing.

The theology of Psalm 21, along with Psalm 20 which emphasizes the truth that God hears the prayer of his people, is an encouragement to us. Let us not give up in our prayers for our leaders. At the same time, Psalms 20–21 should be read in the broader context of Psalms 15–19 which bring out the important element of righteousness. We can only pray for victory for our leaders and expect answers from God if we and our leaders are living right.

PSALM 22

Psalm 22 is one of the most well-known psalms for Jesus quoted from it when he cried at the cross, "My God, my God, why have you forsaken me?" (v. 1; cf. Matt 27:46). This is important for it validates the cry of lament. By praying the opening words of Psalm 22, Jesus affirms it is okay to lament. Lament is not just an OT thing; it is also part of the NT.

But Psalm 22 is not all lament; the second half of the psalm is praise (vv. 22–31). Through its juxtaposition of lament and praise, Psalm 22 portrays both the cross and the resurrection in a way that holds them together. Lament does move on to praise. But lament is not deleted as the psalm moves to praise. The element of tension is preserved. We are a people of the resurrection and a people of the cross at one and the same time.

The significant thing about this psalm is that it gives substantial space for lament. This is important because many people in our churches and communities do not know how to lament. Some who do lament rush on to praise as quickly as they can. In testimonies in the church, for instance, people will share their problems, but then quickly move on to the resolution of whatever trouble they were facing: "I have been in trouble, but . . ." Unfortunately, because we have not really explored the depths, our praises are shallow. Because we have not properly dealt with our questions, we do not really receive the answer. Our praises are forced. For how can our praises be real when we are not honest with God about what we really feel?

It is here that Psalm 22 can be of great help to us. It shows us the way forward, while at the same time reminding us there is a process. In Psalm 22 this process involves confronting our sense of abandonment by God (vv. 1–2), facing our internal contradictions (vv. 4–8), and naming our pain and suffering (vv. 12–18). It also includes crying out to God (v. 2) and pleading for help (vv. 19–21). It is only after the psalmist has expressed his lament that the door of praise is opened, as can be seen in the second section of the psalm (vv. 22–31). This does not mean, however, that the lament is forgotten once the psalm has moved to praise. The way the psalm is put together, there is a movement to praise without eliminating the tension between lament and praise.[1]

---

1. Villanueva, The "Uncertainty of a Hearing," 94–99.

22:1–21 "MY GOD, MY GOD, WHY HAVE YOU FORSAKEN ME?"

The opening words of Psalm 22 recall Psalm 10:1, where the psalmist cries: "Why (*lamah*), LORD, do you stand far (*rakhoq*) off?" The words "why?" and "far" reappear in Psalm 22: "My God, my God, why (*lamah*) have you forsaken me? Why are you so far (*rakhoq*) from saving me?" (22:1). Psalm 10 too is preceded by a psalm of thanksgiving (Ps 9). The transition to lament in Psalm 10 is sudden and unexpected. Similarly, Psalm 22 is preceded by two psalms which teach that God answers prayer. A reading of the three psalms together creates a sense of contrast or contradiction similar to that we experience with Psalms 9 and 10.

McCann observes that three key words from Psalms 20–21 reappear in Psalm 22, namely "salvation" (*yeshuah*), "answer" (*anah*), and "trust" (*batakh*).[2] In Psalm 20 the people prayed for their king, "the LORD answer (*anah*) you in the day of trouble" (v. 1). In Psalm 21 we find that "the king rejoices," for his heart's desire has been granted (vv. 1–2). In contrast to this, the psalmist complains, "My God, I cry out by day, but you do not answer (*anah*)" (22:2). "Thus, the canonical sequence emphasizes the sharp contrast; there is no help and answer for the psalmist" in Psalm 22.[3]

The sense of contradiction builds up in verses 3–10. The psalmist compares himself with his ancestors. His ancestors "trusted" (*batakh*) in God, and God delivered (*palat*) them (v. 4). The same thing is true in Psalms 20 and 21. The people prayed for their king (20:1–5), and their prayer was answered (21:1–6), because "the king trusts (*batakh*) in the LORD" (21:7). But in Psalm 22 things did not work like this. The psalmist also trusted in the Lord: "from my mother's womb you have been my God" (22:10). But unlike his ancestors, he did not experience deliverance.

The psalmist describes his situation in the most pitiable terms: "But I am a worm, and not human" (v. 6). This is far from the David who, in Psalm 18, can confidently say, "As for God, his way is perfect: The LORD's word is flawless; he shields all who take refuge in him." (v. 30). In Psalm 22 David is crushed in spirit, depressed, barely human. People scorn him (vv. 6–7). They mockingly tell him: "He trusts in the LORD . . . let the LORD rescue (*palat*) him . . . since he delights in him!" (v. 8). The words "he delights in him"

---

2. McCann, "The Book of Psalms," 762.
3. Ibid.

(*khapets bo*) further recall Psalm 18.[4] Here David claims the Lord delivered him because "he delighted in me" (*khapets bi*) (18:19b). The similarity between the two passages further brings out the element of contradiction. His enemies took advantage of his situation, taunting and despising him. The Gospel of Matthew portrays the suffering of Jesus in similar ways:

- "Those who passed by hurled insults at him, shaking their heads" (Matt 27:39; cf. 22:7).
- "In the same way the chief priests, the teachers of the law and the elders mocked him. 'He saved others' they said, 'but he can't save himself.'" (Matt 27:41–42; cf. 22:8).

Because of his experience the psalmist feels God is far from him. The word "far" (*rakhoq*) occurs three times in the psalm (vv. 1, 11, and 19), bringing out a strong sense of God's absence. In verse 1 he laments, "Why are you so far from saving me?" In verse 11 he cries out to God: "Do not be far from me, for trouble is near." He repeats the same petition in verse 19. The psalmist does not deny his feelings of divine abandonment, but neither does he give up. Even though he feels God is far from him, he continues to cling to him. Even when he cries, "Why are you so far?" he still calls him "my God" (v. 1). As Westermann beautifully puts it: "It is the bitter complaint of one who despairs, who has no one else to whom he can turn. He clings to God against God . . . Doubt about God, even the kind of despair that can no longer understand God, receives in the lament a language that binds it to God, even as it accuses him."[5]

Christians today, however, tend to deny feelings of divine abandonment. We do not usually articulate them. We think it is not okay to express our questions to God, and so we keep them within us. Meanwhile our heart goes farther and farther from God. This psalm teaches us it is better to be honest with God about what we feel than to keep it within ourselves and in the process slip farther from him. One way of doing this is to admit our feelings of divine abandonment, express our sense of contradiction, and accept our situation by naming it. This is what the psalmist did.

In between his prayers that God not be far from him (vv. 11 and 19), we have a series of depictions of the psalmist's suffering as he tries to give it all a

---

4. Psalm 18 is considered a royal psalm, and is close to Psalms 20–21, two royal psalms. It is also closely related to Psalm 22.
5. Claus Westermann, "The Role of the Lament in the Theology of the Old Testament," *Int* 28 (January 1974): 32.

name. This is important, for without being able to name our suffering there will be no progress towards restoration. Naming our suffering is part of the process of owning our situation, which is the first step towards healing. It is also one of the most difficult parts. This explains why the whole description is enveloped by the petition, "Do not be far away!"

The image of bulls encircling him, opening their mouths wide (vv. 12–13; cf. v. 16 which speaks of dogs) depicts his feeling of dread. In verse 14 he feels his life is ebbing away, like water being poured out. The reference to his bones being out of joint (v. 17) suggests that the very structure of his being is falling apart. He no longer has any strength left, nor courage to continue. Like wax, his heart has melted (v. 14; cf. v. 15). He can already smell death. Verse 18 "depicts the final stages of a person about to die or already considered dead."[6] Kraus quotes a song from ancient Mesopotamia: "The coffin lay open, and people already helped themselves to my valuables; before I was even dead, the mourning was already done."[7]

In verses 20–21 the petitions intensify. These two verses form a parallelism. Both have an ellipsis in the second line:[8]

> v. 20 – Deliver my soul from the sword,
> my precious life from the power of the dog!
>
> v. 21 – Save me from the mouth of the lion,
> my afflicted soul from the horns of the wild oxen! (RSV)

The two petitions, "deliver" and "save," are parallel. Both verses contain an ellipsis, and the verb should be read into the second line. Through the ellipsis, the attention is focused on the two direct objects, "my life" (literally, "my only one") (v. 20) and "my afflicted soul" (v. 21). With this reading the first part of the psalm ends without any resolution. This makes the transition to the next verse and the second section sudden. The mood changes entirely from lament to praise.

This sudden change has led many to prefer an alternate reading of the words translated "my afflicted soul." Those words are based on the *nyty* found in the ancient Greek translation of the OT, known as the Septuagint (LXX). However, in the Hebrew version of the OT known as the Masoretic Text (MT), the word is *nytny*, which can be translated "he answered me." In that case, verse 21 would read "Save me from the lion's mouth; From the horns of

---

6. Villanueva, *The "Uncertainty of a Hearing,"* 78.
7. Kraus, *Psalms 1–59*, 298.
8. The verb is omitted in the second line in both verses.

the wild oxen You answer me" (NASB). Those who prefer that version say that it ties this section together by linking up with the word "answer" in verse 2.

But the problem with that translation is that it disturbs the parallelism we would expect between the two halves of verse 21. And we are also left puzzled by the reference to God's answer coming "from the horns of the wild oxen." So it seems to me, and to many Bible translators, that the LXX reading is better.[9]

22:22–31 "FROM YOU COMES MY PRAISE"

Where the preceding section is a lament, the second section of the psalm is focused on praise. The transition to praise is very sudden. The last words in verse 21 are "my poor soul." They are part of the petition asking God for deliverance. How can the lament so suddenly turn into praise? The common explanation is that in between these verses a word from the Lord is given to the person who has been lamenting. The problem is that there is nothing in the text to indicate that anything has happened between verses 21 and 22. Maybe the lament itself is the answer. As the psalmist pours out his heart to God through the lament, a change transpires within him, enabling him to move on to praise.[10]

He declares, "I will declare (*safar*) your name to my people; in the assembly I will praise (*halal*) you" (v. 22). The word "declare" comes from the same word as "count" (*safar*) (v. 17, NRSV: "I can count all my bones"). From "counting his bones" he is now "counting his blessings." There is also a change from isolation ("I am a worm and not human," v. 6) to community ("my people," "the assembly").

When God does something for an individual, it is meant to be shared with the community. Thus he calls upon those "who fear the LORD" to praise the Lord (v. 23). The word praise (*halal*) is repeated from verse 22.

As is typical in hymns of praise, the reason for praise follows the call to worship: "For he has not despised or scorned the suffering of the afflicted" (v. 24; see also 100:4–5). The phrase "suffering of the afflicted" alludes to the

---

9. For an in-depth discussion of this textual issue, see Villanueva, *The "Uncertainty of a Hearing,"* 81–89.

10. See Heiler's psychological explanation for the sudden change of mood (Heiler, *Prayer: A Study in the History and Psychology of Religion*).

last word in verse 21, "my afflicted soul."[11] This further supports the LXX translation and links the two sections of the psalm (see v. 22).

More significantly, the reference to affliction affirms the lament. Lament is not something God despises or abhors. It is accepted by him. The second part of the verse further shows the movement from lament to praise: "he has not hidden his face from him but has listened to his cry for help"[12] (v. 24). This is a response to the earlier lament that God was far from him (v. 2).

Another link between the two sections of the psalm is found in verse 25: "From you comes the theme of my praise (*tehillah*)." Earlier, the psalmist declares in the context of lament: "You are holy, enthroned on the praises (*tehillah*)[13] of Israel" (v. 3, NRSV; cf. v. 23 which also mentions "Israel"). The links between the two sections demonstrate the close connection between lament and praise.

In the final verses of the psalm (vv. 26–31) praise extends beyond the bounds of the psalmist's personal experience. The "poor" (singular in verse 24), becomes plural, *anawim* in verse 26. In this context, the *anawim* are those "who fear the LORD" (v. 23) and those who seek him (v. 26). They are not just afflicted. They may be poor but they continue to hope in the Lord and live reverently before him. These people will "eat and be satisfied" and "will praise" the LORD."[14]

In verse 27 "all the ends of the earth" and "all the families of the nations" join in the company of those who worship the Lord. Even those who have died (v. 29)[15] and those yet to be born "will be told (*safar*) about the Lord" (v. 30). Here the word *safar* forms an inclusio with the beginning of the second section (v. 22; cf. v. 17).

If there is a feeling that the lament has gone beyond bounds, here praise "explodes the limits," to use a phrase by Ellen Davis.[16]

---

11. The two words are very similar in Hebrew both in terms of meaning and in their consonants.
12. In the MT the pronominal suffix is third person singular, "He did not hide his face from *him* when *he* cried he heard him." This makes the connection with v. 21 closer. The answer is directly linked to the preceding lament.
13. Here the noun is in the plural form.
14. Cf. Deut 8:10 for a passage which links eating and being satisfied with praising or blessing the Lord.
15. This is based on the reading of "all who go down to the dust," which is parallel to "all who sleep in the earth" in the first line.
16. Ellen F. Davis, "Exploding the Limits: Form and Function in Psalm 22," *JSOT* 53 (1992): 93–105.

LAMENT AS *PAGTATAMPO SA DIYOS* (HURT FEELINGS AGAINST GOD)

It is not easy to apply Psalm 22, especially the lament part, in our contexts. Because of our strong belief in the concept of fate, we do not question God. Even in extremely difficult experiences such as the tragic loss of a loved one, we are simply resigned to God's will. If this is God's will, then let it be so.

But for some of us, particularly children who have lost loved ones as a result of natural disasters or wars, there can be a deep dissonance between what they believe and their experience. This can lead to questioning God. After Typhoon Yolanda devastated the city of Tacloban, some of those who came to help encouraged survivors to use art to express their feelings. One boy drew two pictures of a church. In the first picture, the church was full of people. In the second picture, the church was almost empty. Asked to explain his drawings, the boy said that in future very few people would go to church since they had cried out to the Lord for help and he had not answered.[1]

How should we respond to such a statement? It is important that we do not condemn such words and questioning as evidence of unbelief. From our cultural context, we may understand them in terms of the Filipino concept of *pagtatampo* ("a sense of hurt"). There is no exact equivalent of this word in English. It is the feeling of being hurt by the failure of someone close to you to do what was expected of them.

Pagtatampo is associated only with intimate relationships. It applies in the relationship between a mother and daughter, between lovers, between husband and wife, between close friends. We would never use it with strangers or mere acquaintances. For example we would never say, "*nagtatampo ako kay mayor*" (I have feelings of hurt against the mayor), unless you are close to the mayor.

If we interpret the experience of the psalmist in Psalm 22 in terms of *pagtatampo*, we recognize that he is so intimate with God that he addresses God as "my God." He has known God from his earliest days: "from my mother's womb you have been my God" (v. 10). It would thus be natural for the psalmist to expect an answer from God in his time of great need. But just as in the case of the many who cried out to God for help as Typhoon Yolanda swept away their loved ones, there was no answer. The psalmist did not experience God's deliverance (v. 2).

---

1. This is a real story taken from Violeta Villaroman-Bautista, "Spirituality and Resilience in Disaster Situations: Sources of Life and Strength in Critical Times," in *Walking with God: Christian Spirituality in the Asian Context*, eds. Charles R. Ringma and Karen Hollenbeck-Wuest (Manila: Asian Theological Seminary and OMF Literature, 2014), 172.

As a result, he felt *tampo* ("hurt") with God, and showed his feelings in his opening cry, "My God, my God why have you forsaken me?" The words of the lament in Psalm 22 can be understood as expressions of his *pagtatampo*. The psalmist did not contain his feelings of hurt within him, but expressed them to God. It is not wrong to have *pagtatampo* with God. Even Jesus uttered the prayer found in Psalm 22:1 when he cried out on the cross, "My God, my God, why have you forsaken me?" (Matt 27:46).[2]

It is important that we do not bury our feelings of *pagtatampo* within us (*huwag kikimkimin*). If we do, they will turn into *sama ng loob* ("bad feelings within"), which in turn lead to bitterness (*hinanakit*), hatred (*galit*), and wrath (*poot*). That is why it is important that we process our feelings

There is a Filipino saying, "*Ang nagsasabi ng tapat, nagsasama ng malu-wat*" ("Honesty about what one feels makes a relationship last"). The reason why the psalmist was able to move on to praise was because he dealt with his *pagtatampo sa Diyos* ("feelings of hurt against God").

---

2. Jesus' cry on the cross can be understood as expressing his feelings of *pagtatampo* to his Father. The Scriptures tell us that Jesus is also human, just like us.

PSALM 23

After the stormy lament (in the first half of Psalm 22) and the overwhelming praise that followed it (in the second half of Psalm 22), Psalm 23 is a most welcome and needed addition. Those who put the Psalter together have rightly placed this psalm in its present position. The soul can only sustain so much agony. Overly long dark nights may annihilate it.

In Psalm 23 consolation follows desolation. To the cry of abandonment ("My God, my God, why have you abandoned me?"; 22:1) comes the experience of divine presence: "for you are with me" (23:4). From the season of disorientation we move to the season of new orientation.[1]

It is important, however, to remember that one does not move to a new orientation without going through the disorientation. We have a psalm of confidence because the psalmist has learned to face his doubts and fears. We are able to step into the serene space that Psalm 23 provides because we have been through the stormy seas that is Psalm 22. Even in Psalm 23 some darkness remains, or at least the memory of it (v. 4). The difference here is that the perspective has changed. It is no longer the "worm" that speaks (22:6) but the confident warrior honored by God before his enemies (23:5). The psalmist is no longer a "lost sheep," but a sheep that has regained its strength – thanks to the care of the shepherd. The shepherd has been with the psalmist through the "valley of the shadow of death" and so he can now confidently say: "I will fear no evil" (v. 4, ESV).

God is presented in Psalm 23 as a shepherd (vv. 1–4) and a host (v. 5). The psalm is structured around these two images. There is also a noticeable shift from third person address ("he") in verses 1–3 to a second person ("you") in verses 4–5, before a return to the third person address in the last verse. The change to "you" signals intensification and a sense of directness and intimacy.

23:1–4 "THE LORD IS MY SHEPHERD"

The psalm begins with the famous statement, "The Lord is my shepherd" (v. 1). The image of a "shepherd" is a common metaphor in the ancient Near East and in the Bible. In the OT it is used to refer to leaders or kings (see 2 Sam 5:2). The title is also used to refer to God. For instance, Jacob refers to

---

1. Walter Brueggemann develops the concept of the "seasons of orientation, disorientation, and new orientation" in his book, *The Message of the Psalms.*

God as the one "who has been my shepherd all my life" (Gen 48:15). In the NT, Jesus also used the title, calling himself "the good shepherd." In contrast to those who take advantage of the sheep and have no care for them, Jesus "lays down his life for the sheep" (John 10:11).

One cannot exhaust the richness of the metaphor of the shepherd. Here are some reflections:

1. The provisions of the Lord are rich. In Psalm 23, the image of the shepherd depicts God as a provider, giver of rest, sustainer, and protector. That is why the psalmist can declare, "I lack nothing" (v. 1; 34:10). God's provisions are described as "green pastures" and "quiet waters" (v. 2). The former reminds us of the tree "planted by streams of water" in Psalm 1:3. The latter speaks of calmness and security. It is hard for a sheep to drink water when the current is strong, for it could be swept away.

2. The emphasis is on what the Lord does for us, not on what we do for ourselves. It is the Lord who "makes me lie down in green pastures" and who "leads me beside quiet waters" (v. 2), It is he who "refreshes my soul" and who "guides me along the right paths" (v. 3).

3. The last line – "he guides me along the right paths" (v. 3) – teaches us of the purpose of restoration and rest. It is so that we may continue in our journey with God along the path he has laid down for us. God restores our soul so we can walk in obedience and righteousness (see also 17:5). When our strength is gone, our vision is blurred and we cannot see the path before us, God allows us to get some rest and be renewed so that we are strengthened to continue in the path of righteousness. Rest is not given for its own sake. Rather, it is given "for his name's sake" (v. 3b). Even the disciples had to go down from the Mount of Transfiguration (Matt 17:1-9).

4. The "right paths" (Ps 23:3) does not mean the journey will be smooth, with roads all paved and straight. As Jesus tells us, the road that leads to life is narrow and hard (Matt 7:13–14). So the psalmist also finds himself walking in the "valley of the shadow of death" (v. 4, ESV). Intriguingly, when the psalmist talks about the safe and quiet places, God is said to be the one who "leads."

Twice the word "lead" is mentioned (vv. 2–3).[2] The psalmist does not say the Lord leads towards the "valley of the shadow of death." Yet interestingly, it is when he talks about that dark valley that the language of the psalm becomes more intense and intimate. There is a shift from the third person to the second person. In the previous verses God is simply described. Here in verse 4 he is directly addressed. It is in the dark valley where God's presence is most deeply recognized: "for *you* are with me" (v. 4). God is certainly with us in our high points. But he is especially felt in our deepest and lowest moments. He is with us as we struggle in our fight for justice. He is with us in our struggles with sin and temptation. He is never away, for he promised, "Never will I leave you; never will I forsake you" (Heb 13:5). We experience the comfort of his protection: "Your rod and your staff, they comfort me" (Ps 23:4; see also 1 Pet 4–5).[3]

23:4–5 GOD AS A GENEROUS HOST

Verse 5 maintains the second person address with its intimacy and intensity. This is because "my enemies" are mentioned in this verse. The book of Psalms is consistent: the righteous person will always be opposed, pursued, and attacked (see for example, Ps 3:1–2). Those who walk in the "right paths" will have enemies.

The encouraging thing is that God does not leave his servant alone. The image is extraordinary. A host prepares a feast for his guest in the presence of his enemies. A feast is a time of celebration, a time when people are relaxed. The host even pours perfumed oil on his guest's head and offers him a "large cup of wine that satisfies."[4] How is this possible when there are enemies around? Only God can make this possible. With God it is possible to sleep even in the midst of the battle (3:5); so also one can celebrate in the midst of opposition.

The psalmist's experiences mean he can look forward to a life filled with "goodness": "Surely goodness and love will follow me all the days of my life."

---

2. Two different Hebrew verbs were used but their meaning is similar – *nahal* and *nakha*. Both means "to lead."
3. Believers are protected by the "power of God."
4. Goldingay, *Psalms*, 352.

The verb translated as "follow" (*radaf*) is used elsewhere to speak of enemies pursuing the psalmist (see 7:1; 31:5). But here, instead of enemies it is "goodness and love" that pursue him. This, he claims, will be his lot, not only throughout his life but always: "And I will dwell in the house of the LORD forever."

The image of a generous host resonates with the traditional Filipino trait of hospitality. We are known for welcoming visitors into our homes. One can drop by anytime and will always be sure of a welcome. Those visiting during lunch or dinner will be invited to share in the meal. No one will be left alone and hungry. Indeed, one of the "punishments" that can be given to a Filipino is to be left alone. We have a saying, "*iba ang may pinagsamahan*" ("it's a different thing when you have been together").

But because of poverty, our people know more about the "valley of the shadow of death" than the "green pastures" and "still waters." How then can our people appreciate the message of Psalm 23? How can we experience God as our shepherd in our poverty? We need to go back to the image of the host. When we share the little we have with others, God becomes present in our midst.

PSALM 24

Psalm 24 is similar to Psalm 15. In both, a question is posed about who may be allowed to enter God's holy place (15:1; 24:3). The question is followed by a list describing the character of worshipers (15:2–5ab; 24:4) and a note on the blessing received by those whose lives exhibit these characteristics (15:5c; 24:5). The list of characteristics of worshipers is shorter in Psalm 24, but it is supplemented by a focus on who this Lord is who is worshiped. In this way Psalm 24 adds an important dimension to the idea of entrance into God's holy presence – the focus is on whom we worship. He is the creator God to whom "the earth" and "all that is in it" belong (vv. 1–2) and the "King of glory" (vv. 7–10). The structure of the psalm makes this clear:

> Who God is (vv. 1–2);
>> Who the worshipers are (vv. 3–6);
> Who God is (vv. 7–10).

The structure highlights the connection between the kind of God that is worshiped and the kind of life the worshipers live.[1] "Who God is" forms the foundation for "who the worshipers are." Interestingly, in the psalm the interrogative "who?" is repeated four times – twice in reference to who the worshipers are (v. 3) and twice in reference to God (vv. 8, 10).

The character of this God is also brought into focus by the interplay between the universal and the local, between the whole earth (vv. 1–2) and the sanctuary (v. 3). The God of the whole earth has chosen a particular place for his presence to dwell, but the interplay indicates that he is not just a God of the Israelites. He is the God of all the peoples of the world. "The opening assertion of his universal sovereignty as the Creator of the world offers a fitting caution not to suppose that because he has chosen one city for his special dwelling place, his Presence and activity are limited to it."[2]

24:1–2 "THE EARTH IS THE LORD'S, AND EVERYTHING IN IT"

Instead of beginning with the question, "Who may dwell in your sacred tent?" as in Psalm 15, Psalm 24 starts with a focus on *who* the Lord is. In Psalm 15 the question of who will be worthy to dwell in God's holy hill is

---

1. See also Craig C. Broyles, *Psalms* (Peabody, Mass.: Hendrickson, 1999), 128: "A god may be known by the kind of worshipers he/she desires."
2. Kirkpatrick, *The Book of Psalms*, 127.

directed to the Lord, signaling it is the Lord who determines who may be allowed access to the holy place (see comment in Psalm 15 above). Psalm 24 develops this by highlighting who this God is who is worshiped.

There is a change of image here from that of a shepherd and host in Psalm 23 to the creator God (24:1). God is the rightful owner of everything because it is he who "founded it on the seas and established it on the waters" (v. 2). The ancient Near East language of the water and the seas being hostile forces forms the background to this verse. But the emphasis is on God's sovereignty.[3]

24:3–6 "WHO MAY ASCEND THE MOUNTAIN OF THE LORD?"

The focus on God as Creator (vv. 1–2) brings greater weight to the question posed in verse 3. The people are not just being asked about entrance to an ordinary place; the place is "the mountain of the LORD," the owner of the whole earth. One would therefore expect higher standards for entrance into such a place.[4]

The description of the place as "holy" (v. 3) provides a hint about the requirements for entry. What matters is not one's educational achievements or standing in society, or whether one is rich or poor. The emphasis falls on one's character – the godliness of one's life. The parallel Psalm 15 and the psalms in between all bring out the importance of righteousness. Grogan sees Psalm 24 as forming an inclusio with Psalm 15, with the psalms in between focusing on "godliness commended in these two psalms."[5]

There are four specific qualifications (v. 4). The first two are parallel – "clean hands" and "pure hearts," representing the external and the internal elements of a person's life. The two go together. We would say of a person who is innocent: "there is no blood on his hands; his conscience is clear." The description, "do not swear deceitfully," is a further elaboration of the first two.

The third requirement, "who do not lift up their souls to what is false" (v. 4, ESV), is significant. The word "lift up" comes from the Hebrew word *nasa*, a word that is repeated six times in this psalm (vv. 4, 5, 7 [2x], 9 [2x]). It reappears in Psalm 25:1, linking the two psalms together. The expression to "lift up one's soul" means "to direct the mind towards (25:1); to set the heart

---

3. Mays, *Psalms*, 120.
4. Ibid., 85: "There are hints in the Old Testament and from other religions of the period that lists of qualifications for entering sanctuaries were used (Deut 23:1–8; 2 Chron 23:19)."
5. Grogan, *Psalms*, 76.

upon (Deut 24:15), to desire (Hos 4:8)."[6] The object of the desire which the psalm prohibits is "what is false." The word used can refer to false gods (see the translation in the NIV – "idol") or to anything that is unreal. Those who will be allowed access to the hill of the Lord are those who do not set their hearts on things that are false. We set our hearts on things that are false whenever we try to put our trust in the things that are temporal – our jobs, abilities, material wealth, etc. These are all illusions, part of the web of lies that the world around us has been trying to feed into our minds.

Instead of lifting our soul to what is false, we are to live righteously. Those who do, according to verse 5, "will receive (*nasa*) blessings from the LORD." The psalmist deliberately repeats the word *nasa* ("lift up"/"receive") to establish a link with the previous verse. Blessings do not come from what is false but from the Lord. They are given to those who live godly lives. Verse 6 describes them as "the generation of those who seek . . . your face, God of Jacob."[7] Seeking the face of the Lord is closely linked to having "clean hands and pure hearts." Instead of seeking after false gods or illusions, we are being called upon to seek the face of the Lord (see Pss 25:1 and 27:4).

24:7–10 "LIFT UP YOUR HEADS, YOU GATES!"

The last section of the psalm begins with the word *nasa* ("lift up"). This verb was used earlier with reference to the lifting up of one's soul (v. 4). Here the object of the verb is an inanimate object: the gates, which are commanded to "lift up their heads." This is obviously not meant to be taken literally. Some scholars in the past have linked these words to some event when the ark was first brought to Jerusalem during the time of David. But there is no certainty that this is the background to the words.

The "heads" of the gates, the "ancient doors," are commanded to be lifted up so that "the King of glory may come in" (v. 7). Earlier we read of the worshipers ascending the holy hill and considered who they were. They were said to be those "who do not lift up their souls to what is false." By commanding the ancient doors to be lifted up so that the King may enter, the worshipers are reminded that they should be lifting up their souls to the Lord so that he

---

6. Kirkpatrick, *The Book of Psalms*, 129.
7. In the Hebrew version of the Jewish Old Testament known as the Masoretic Text , v. 6b has "your face, O Jacob." But the the ancient Greek translation of the Old Testament, known as the Septuagint (LXX) has, "the face of the God of Jacob." The majority of modern versions follow the LXX reading.

may enter (see also Rev 3:20). The emphasis is similar to the first section. The gates had to be prepared or made "worthy" for the King of glory to come in.

In the same way that it was earlier asked, "Who shall ascend into the hill of the LORD?" here the question is asked: "Who is this King of glory?" (vv. 8, 10). He is described as "strong and mighty" (v. 8) and the "LORD of hosts" (v. 10, ESV). The word "hosts" usually referred to armies, but came to be associated also with the heavenly host.[8]

---

8. Delitzsch, *Psalms*, 339.

ENTRANCE LITURGY AND THE *KATIPUNAN* OATH

During the Philippine Revolution in the 1890s, the Filipinos formed a group called *Katipunan* (Solidarity) which eventually defeated the Spaniards. Those wishing to become members of this group (*katipunero*) were expected to be examples of humility, patience, righteousness, and hope. As part of the initiation process, the new members had to recite the following oath, which is similar in form and content to what we find in Psalms 15 and 24:

> (Leader): Who is this who has never been initiated who wants to take part in the works of the temple?
>
> (Answer): One who wants light and who wants to be the Son of the People.
>
> (Leader): Profane man, think well whether you are able to fulfill all of these obligations. If at this very hour the society demands your life and your body, are you able to give them? The sound of the bells which you have just heard, what does it mean?
>
> It means you are quitting your former life, as the man in his last agony is quitting his, and your anguish is the sign of your separation from your past life. At the same time it is the sign of your entrance into the society where you will see the true light.[1]

Both this liturgy and those of Psalms 15 and 24 contain requirements for those entering the movement/temple. The qualifications call for the utmost commitment. In the case of the *Katipuneros* the call is for a willingness to lay down one's life for the country. In Psalm 24 the call is to live a life of righteousness. The Katipunan oath seeks to bring change in society. To some extent, we may say the same thing of Psalm 24: those who may stand in God's holy place are those who effect change in their society by virtue of having a "pure heart." Intimacy with God ought to bring about change in society.

---

1. Taken from Reynaldo Clemeña Ileto, *Pasyon and Revolution: Popular Movements in the Philippines, 1840–1910* (Quezon City, Philippines: Ateneo de Manila University Press, 1979), 93; f. n. 28 says: "Katipunan oath and form of initiation, English translation in PIR-SD55 and Taylor, *Philippines Insurrection*, vol. 1, 219. Original Tagalog, not found."

PSALM 25

The previous psalm (Ps 24) describes the kind of people who will be allowed to enter God's holy place. Among others, they are those "who do not lift up their souls to what is false" (24:4, ESV). As explained above, "what is false" may also be translated as "idols." It refers to anything apart from God that we put our trust in. The psalm views all such things as mere illusions. A question that is left unanswered is, "To whom shall we lift up our soul?" Psalm 25 may be read as a response to this question.

Instead of lifting up our souls "to what is false," Psalm 25 exhorts us to lift them up to the Lord: "To you, O LORD, I lift up my soul" (25:1, ESV). We are not to place our hope in riches or money, positions of honor or glory, but in the Lord. In the OT, people who were praying often had their hands outstretched and lifted up to God. "The metaphor portrays prayer as an act in which individuals hold their conscious identity, their life, in hands stretched out to God as a way of saying that their life depends completely and only on the help of God."[1] So to lift up one's soul to the Lord is the same as saying, "O my God, in you I trust" (v. 2) or "I take refuge in you" (v. 20). It is equivalent to the Apostle Paul's statement: "For to me to live is Christ" (Phil 1:21).

One does not easily make such a commitment. It requires knowing God, for it is only those who know their God who are able to trust in him (Ps 9:10). And so the psalmist prays, "show me your ways" (25:4). This also explains the Apostle Paul's desire "to know Christ" (Phil 3:10–11). The more we know the Lord, the more we learn to love him, serve him, trust in him.

Interestingly, Psalm 25 talks a lot about knowing. According to Mays, it uses "virtually every available verb in the vocabulary of instruction."[2] Even the form in which the psalm was composed reflects an emphasis on teaching, for the psalm is an acrostic, with each verse beginning with the next letter of the Hebrew alphabet. This structure made the psalm easier to memorize. But the kind of learning and knowing referred to here is not mere intellectual knowledge, though that is part of it. Rather, the nature of the knowing in Psalm 25 is primarily experiential (see vv. 4–5 below).

Psalm 25 also resembles a lament. It is similar to Psalm 119 in this respect. The latter focuses on the law of the Lord and on instruction, but it too

---

1. Mays, *Psalms*, 124.
2. Ibid., 125.

is composed using the lament form.[3] The combination of instruction and lament tells us that learning occurs in the context of suffering. Often it is only when we are in the depths of despair that we learn to cry, "To you, O LORD, I lift up my soul."

25:1–3 "TO YOU, O LORD, I LIFT UP MY SOUL"

As mentioned above, to "lift up one's soul" means to put one's trust in God alone. The theme of trusting in God binds the whole psalm together. It is mentioned here at the beginning (vv. 1–2) and towards the end (v. 20). The expression of trust at the beginning occurs in the context of conflict: "do not let . . . my enemies triumph over me" (v. 2). The prayer is uttered in the midst of a difficult situation. This is important, for it is easy to say, "I trust in God" when we are okay. But when life hangs in the balance, when so many things are at stake, to say "I trust in you" requires more faith. The psalmist is confronted with a situation in which he may lose face (be shamed) – a serious thing in shame cultures like that which existed in Israel and still exist in many parts of Asia. That is why the psalmist prays, "Do not let me be put to shame" (v. 2).

Shame cultures have a strong sense of community, which is why the psalmist includes in his prayer not only himself but also "all those who hope in you" (v. 3). This is the literal translation of the first line of verse 3. He prays that they too may not be put to shame. Like trusting, shame is an important element in this psalm. It is also mentioned at the end, along with taking refuge in the Lord (v. 20).

Learning to trust in God requires knowing God. Knowing God is the foundation for trust in him. The next verses explore this theme.

25:4–10 "TEACH ME YOUR WAYS"

Knowing God involves more than just knowing things *about* him. It involves experiencing his "ways." The word "way" (*derek*) is a key word in the psalm, occurring six times, sometimes as a verb and sometimes as a noun (vv. 4, 5, 8, 9 [2x], 12). In verse 4 it occurs as the very first word in the Hebrew. Literally, the Hebrew reads, "Your ways, O LORD, teach me." It occurs at the beginning

---

3. William Michael Soll, *Psalm 119: Matrix, Form, and Setting* (Washington, DC: Catholic Biblical Association of America, 1991), argues that Psalm 119 is a lament.

for emphasis as well as to correspond to the fourth letter of the Hebrew alphabet, *dalet* (letter "d").

Interestingly, in the next verse, the psalmist employs the verbal form of the word "way" (*darak*), again as the very first word. The verb is translated "lead" but it also means, "make/let [me] walk."[4] The psalmist is not asking God just to teach him about his ways; he actually wants to walk in them! The metaphor "way," common in the Psalms, invites readers not only to interpret the way but actually to walk in it. The following comment by Alejo, though not directly referring to Psalm 25, is very relevant: "*Parang sinasabi: 'Ako ang landas, subalit huwag mo lamang akong tingnan kundi tawiran mo ako patungo sa tinutudla ko, at hayaan mong ihatid kita roon'*"[5] (It's as if the road is saying, "Here I am, but do not just look at me, rather walk over me towards the direction I am pointing, and let me bring you there"). The same thing applies to knowing God.

We belong to a time when there is an explosion of knowledge. There is more information today about anything and everything than at any time in history. But the question is, do we really "know"? Pope Francis, in his message to Filipino young people, captured it well when he said:

> There is a real danger of living in a way that we accumulate information. We have so much information but maybe we don't know what to do with that information. So we run the risk of becoming museums of young people who have everything but not knowing what to do with it. We don't need young museums but we do need holy young people.[6]

What we need is knowledge that is experiential and relational. To know about the way is one thing. To actually walk on it is another. But to know apart from a relationship with God is cruelty. As J. I. Packer puts it: "Knowing about God is crucially important for the living of our lives. As it would be cruel to an Amazonian tribesman to fly him to London, put him down without explanation in Trafalgar Square and leave him . . . so we are cruel to ourselves if we try to live in this world without knowing about the God whose world it is and who runs it.[7] Psalm 25 invites us to put our trust in God. But

---

4. The verb is in the Hiphil form.
5. Albert E. Alejo, *Tao po! Tuloy!* (Quezon City, Philippines: Ateneo de Manila University, 1990), 68.
6. Pope Francis' homily at the University of Santo Tomas, January 18, 2015.
7. J. I. Packer, *Knowing God* (Downers Grove, Ill.: InterVarsity Press, 1973), 24.

to be able to do so requires growth in knowing God. This knowing involves in its most intimate form the friendship of God. For real knowledge flows from relationship.

As human beings, our way of knowing is more experiential than cognitive. The focus is not on ideas but on experience. This is linked to our focus on emotions or feelings rather than on ideas or thoughts. It is not that we don't like truths or principles. It's just that these are linked to all of life, so that we do not know something until we have felt or experienced it. This understanding is very much at home in this psalm.

The word "paths" (*orakh*) (v. 4b), parallel to the word "ways" in verse 4a, also points to an experiential sense of knowing in these verses. The word occurs later in verse 10 (ESV), where the psalmist declares that "All the paths (*orakh*) of the LORD are steadfast love and faithfulness." To learn God's paths is to experience his steadfast love and faithfulness. The last word – "faithfulness" (*emet*) – is the word translated as "truth" in verse 5. Alexander has rightly pointed out that "truth" here should not be understood in terms of doctrine but as "the veracity of God, or the faithful performance of his promises."[8] The "teaching asked for is thus experiential teaching, or the actual experience of God's faithfulness."[9] It is experiential rather than simply intellectual.

25:11–22 "THE FRIENDSHIP OF THE LORD"

The psalmist wants to experience not only God's faithfulness but also God's mercy in view of his sinfulness (vv. 6–11). He pleads to God: "Remember, LORD, your great mercy and love, for they are from of old" (v. 6). He mentions the word "remember" twice in verse 7 to draw a contrast to his sins. The two verses form a chiastic structure:

> Remember your great mercy and love,
>> for they are from of old (v. 6).
>> Do not remember the sins of my youth,
> According to your love remember me (v. 7).

The words "love" and "remember" occur at the beginning and end of verses 6–7. In between, the idea that God's mercy and love which is "from of old" is

---

8. Alexander, *Commentary on Psalms*, 122. He cites the following passages as support: Pss 30:10; 71:22; 91:4.
9. Ibid. Thus, Luther's translation of *emet* as truth in terms of doctrinal truth may be correct as an abstract meaning "but does not do justice to the context in which the word is used" (Ibid., 239).

contrasted with the "sins of my youth." His sins are nothing compared to the mercies of God. Further, in the middle part of the verses the word "remember" appears, but this time with the negation, "do not remember."

The last part of verse 7 is a plea for God not to remember the sins of his youth, "for you, LORD, are good." This forms the transition to the next verse, which begins with the word "good" (*tob*) (v. 8). At the same time it forms a parallel to verse 11, which contains a similar structure[10] and concern for forgiveness of one's sins.

There is a change in verse 8 from prayer (vv. 1–7) to a reflection on the goodness, steadfast love, and faithfulness of the Lord. The reflection extends until verse 15 before the psalm reverts to prayer in verse 16 and following.

God is good, so "he instructs sinners in his way" (v. 8). The words, "way" and "sinners" recall Psalm 1. The difference here is that, unlike in Psalm 1, there is hope for sinners. At the same time the psalmist is aware that the Lord leads those who are "humble" (v. 9), and God's steadfast love and faithfulness are said to be "for those who keep the demands of his covenant" (v. 10). The psalmist is thus caught in the tension between God's goodness and the requirements of righteousness. Even in verse 12, it is those who fear the Lord whom the Lord will guide according to "the ways they should choose" (v. 12). Yet the Lord teaches/instructs both sinners (v. 8) and the righteous (v. 12). Caught between these tensions, the psalmist pleads: "For the sake of you name, LORD, forgive my iniquity though it is great" (v. 11). Verse 11 is the only second person address in verses 8–15. Ultimately, it is those who fear the Lord who will experience God's goodness in terms of prosperity or well-being (v. 13). Most importantly, they will receive the gift of the "friendship of the Lord," which is "for those who fear him" (v. 14).

The "friendship of the Lord" (v. 14, ESV) represents the deepest experience of knowing God (see Gen 18:17). It speaks of intimacy and of the Lord's faithfulness on which we can always depend. That is why the psalmist's eyes are focused on God: "My eyes are ever on the LORD" (Ps 25:15a). He does not mind if there is a snare waiting to trip him up, for "he will release my feet from the snare" (v. 15b). Some are constantly looking down, too careful lest they fall. They forget that the secret of "not falling" is not looking down but looking up . . . to the Lord. The moment Peter took his gaze away from the Lord, he began to sink (Matt 14:28–30).

---

10. "for the sake of your goodness" (*lema'an tubka*) (v. 7) = "for your name's sake" (*lema'an shimka*) (v. 11)

The friendship of the Lord also means companionship. One of the biggest problems in many cities around the world today is loneliness. In spite of the advances in technology, more and more people are isolated from one another. Even in ancient times this was a problem. The psalmist is not ashamed to admit, "I am lonely" (v. 16b). But the friendship of the Lord sustains him. He can always pray, "Turn to me and be gracious to me" (v. 16a). Even when the "troubles of my heart" (v. 17) multiply, the psalmist knows where to turn.

The psalmist cries out to God, "Look on my affliction and my distress and take away all my sins" (v. 18). In verse 19 we are given a glimpse of the cause of his affliction and trouble – his enemies, who are "numerous" and who "fiercely hate me." In verse 20 he prays that God will "guard" and "rescue" him. He again takes up his request at the beginning of the psalm: "do not let me be put to shame, for I take refuge in you."

Verse 21 reminds us that trusting in the Lord includes living rightly before him: "May integrity and uprightness preserve me" (see also Ps 5). The psalm ends by incorporating the whole of "Israel" (v. 22). Earlier, in verse 3 the psalmist included "those who hope in you." So here he prays that God might redeem Israel "from all their troubles" (v. 22).

It is instructive that the psalm ends with the word "troubles."[11] The psalmist acknowledges not only his own troubles but also those of his people. It is often in our troubles that we encounter the Lord and grow deeper in our relationship with him and with our community.

---

11. "Trouble" (*tsarah*) is also the last word in the Hebrew.

PSALM 26

In traditional Asian cultures, Psalm 26 (see also Ps 17) may seem boastful. In the Philippines we do not speak of our good works before others, much less before God! So when we read this psalm, we sometimes find ourselves thinking of the Pharisee who went into the temple, praying, "God, I thank you that I am not like other people: robbers, evildoers, adulterers—or even like this tax collector" (Luke 18:11). In Psalm 26, the psalmist claims he walks in integrity, with a faith that is unwavering (vv. 1, cf. v. 11). Like the "blessed" person in Psalm 1, he declares he does not sit with the wicked (v. 5). While Psalms 15 and 24 talk about the qualifications of those who can ascend the holy hill of the Lord, this psalmist is already in the holy place, walking around God's altar!

We may find it easier to appreciate the sentiments expressed in this psalm if we take note of the psalmist's claim that he is innocent (v. 6). This suggests that he has been falsely accused of wrongdoing and is in a desperate situation with nowhere to go. The OT makes provision for situations like this (1 Kgs 8:31–32; Deut 17:8). We can pray like the psalmist when we do not deserve the accusations being hurled against us. To be righteous in this psalm means to be "'innocent' in the case to be decided."[1]

The prayer also reveals the extent to which a person in such a situation will go to escape the unjust consequence of his trouble. The presence of this psalm in the Psalter shows us the kind of God we have. The psalmist's prayer, "be gracious to me" (v. 11), not only shows that the psalmist is different from the Pharisee who did not ask for mercy; it also reveals the heart of a merciful God.

26:1–3 "VINDICATE ME, LORD"

The psalm begins with two related petitions: "vindicate me" (v. 1a) and "test me" (v. 2). Each is followed by a statement providing the basis for the petition. In the first one the psalmist asserts, "for I have led a blameless life; I have trusted in the Lord and have not faltered" (v. 1b). Notice how one's moral life is connected with the act of trusting in the Lord. Righteous living and faith in God are inseparable (see Pss 4 and 5). The theme of walking in integrity

---

1. Mays, *Psalms*, 129.

(*tom*) and of the certitude that goes with it is repeated in verses 11 and 12. This highlights the psalmist's sense of righteousness.

At the same time we see an emphasis on God's mercy and grace. Immediately following his prayer for God to "Test me . . . and try me, examine my heart and my mind" (v. 2), the psalmist appeals to God's character, not his own: "for I have always been mindful of your unfailing love and have lived in reliance on your faithfulness" (v. 3). Notice the emphasis on "your steadfast love" and "your faithfulness." God's steadfast love is his faithful and loving way of dealing with his people. It is a translation of the Hebrew word *hesed*, which is best translated in Filipino as *kagandahang loob* ("goodness/ kindness of heart").[2] "When used to describe God its emphasis is on God's faithfulness to his covenant with his people, his promise to be their God always, and to protect them and take care of them. It describes his special feeling for his people."[3] The psalmist is always conscious of God's steadfast love. He has "always been mindful" of God's love (v. 3).

The second part of verse 3 can be interpreted as referring to one's own faithfulness or loyalty to God (NRSV: "I walk in faithfulness to you"). The verses that follow (vv. 4–8) support this interpretation, for they all refer to the psalmist's own actions. But in view of the emphasis on God's steadfast love in verse 3a and the appeal to God's mercy at the end (v. 11), it may be better to interpret the statement as referring primarily to God's faithfulness.

God's faithfulness and one's loyalty to God go together. But the former serves as the foundation for the latter. God is faithful so we respond in faithfulness to him. This also explains the emphasis on trusting in the Lord without faltering (v. 1). The psalmist not only knows that God is faithful; he lives by that truth. That is what the word "walk" indicates. That word occurs in verse 1 and is repeated here in verse 3: "I walk in your faithfulness" (ESV). "Walking" here is a figure of speech referring to how we live our lives. So it is not simply a way of thinking but is more experiential (25:5). Walking in faithfulness, then, means experiencing its reality in one's life. The reason the psalmist can live in confidence and trust is because he has experienced and continues to experience God's faithfulness.

---

2. See José M. de Mesa, *Kapag namayani ang kagandahang-loob ng Diyos* (Quezon City, Philippines: Claretian Publications, 1990).
3. Bratcher and Reyburn, *A Translator's Handbook*, 52.

26:4–8 "I DO NOT SIT WITH THE WORTHLESS"

The metaphor of walking began and ended the previous section of the psalm. The same things happens in the next two verses with the metaphor of sitting. Verse 4 begins: "I do not sit with the deceitful" (v. 4a) and verse 5 ends with "refuse to sit with the wicked" (v. 5b). The use of the metaphors of walking and sitting echoes Psalm 1, which speaks of the blessed person as one who "does not walk in step with the wicked . . . or sit in the company of mockers" (1:1).

The language of "sitting" depicts a more permanent condition than walking. One does not only walk around with the wicked; one becomes like them, doing what they do. Thus, the negation is emphatic: "I refuse to sit with the wicked" (Literally, "I do *not* sit"). He actually abhor the company of evildoers (v. 5a).

In verses 5 and 8 we see a contrast between his attitude towards the wicked and his attitude towards God's dwelling place. The former he hates; the latter he loves. Thus he asserts that he is innocent (v. 6a). The fact that he is able not only to "ascend" the holy hill of the Lord (Ps 24:3; cf. 15:1) but also to "go about your altar" (26:6b) points to a life lived in the righteousness that God requires of his worshipers.

Yet in the very next verse, rather than bragging about his acts of righteousness like the Pharisee, the psalmist sings God's praise and tells of "all your wonderful deeds" (v. 7). It's as if he is saying, "It's not really about me, but about you, O Lord. Your works are wonderful." That is why the psalmist loves "the house where you live, the place where your glory dwells" (v. 8). The focus on the place where God dwells and the glory of God recalls Psalm 24 where the words for place and (glory) also occur (24:3 and 7, 9–10, respectively).

26:9–12 "BE GRACIOUS TO ME"

In view of God's steadfast love and the psalmist's response to it, he prays: "Do not take away my soul along with sinners" (v. 9). The word "with" (*'im*) is significant. It was repeated three times in verses 4–5 where the psalmist stressed he did not sit "with" the wicked. So he now prays not to be treated in the way the wicked are treated.

The psalmist describes the wicked as those "in whose hands are wicked schemes, whose right hands are full of bribes" (v. 10). This contrasts with verse 6 where the psalmist claims he has washed his hands in innocence.

Unlike the wicked, the psalmist walks in integrity (v. 11a). But this does not mean he is secure. He still needs to pray: "Be merciful to me" (v. 11b).

In light of his knowledge of God's mercy and grace, the psalmist has certainty: "my feet stand on level ground" (v. 12a). He is confident that he will not be counted in the company of the wicked but will be in the "great congregation" where he will praise the Lord (v. 12b).

We need to be cautious when using this psalm in Asia, just as have to be when we use Psalms 7 and 17, where the psalmist also asserts his own righteousness. On the other hand, once we know something of the background of Psalm 26, we are able to understand why the psalmist speaks as he does. The psalm is written by someone who has been falsely accused. As such it teaches us that it is not wrong to assert our innocence or righteousness in particular situations, such as the one envisaged here. But the assertion of our righteousness has its foundation on God's grace and mercy, the experience of which enables us to confidently stand up for what is true.

PSALM 27

A common teaching is that when we have a strong faith we will always be confident. There will be no room for fear. We will go from victory to victory, from glory to glory. Psalm 27 contains some of the most confident statements in the Psalms:

- "The LORD is my light and my salvation; whom shall I fear?" (v. 1).
- "Though an army besiege me, my heart will not fear" (v. 3).

Yet in this same psalm we also hear the psalmist crying: "Hear, my voice when I call, LORD" (v. 7). What appears strange is that he has just offered sacrifices "with shouts of joy" (v. 6) when he uttered these words. Yet instead of "shouts of joy" we now hear cries for help. And all these in one psalm! The flow of the psalm is also anticlimactic. Rather than the expected movement from lament to thanksgiving, we have the reverse movement from thanksgiving to lament.[1]

What does this tell us? It reminds us that faith has to do with both crying and rejoicing, struggling and trusting. There are times when confidence in God flows along with our tears in the midst of our struggles, not in the quietness of our certainties. Indeed, it is in our troubles that we learn to stand on God's solid rock (see vv. 5b and 11b below). Like David in Psalm 18:29 ("by my God I can leap over a wall") there are times when we feel we can do anything because the Lord is with us. Yet at other times we find ourselves in the darkest pit, feeling like a worm rather than a human being (22:6), crying out, "My God, my God, why have you forsaken me?" (22:1). Like Psalms 18 and 22, the present psalm is attributed to David.

Structurally, what makes Psalm 27 unique is that it appears to be two psalms put together. The overall tone in verses 1–6 differs from that in verses 7–14. The former are full of confidence while the latter are dominated by petitions akin to the lament. Verse 6 marks the usual ending of a psalm of lament, where the psalmist offers a vow of thanksgiving (see Ps 13). In fact, verse 6 consists of sacrifices "with shouts of joy." But in the very next verse, instead of shouts of joy we hear the voice of one calling for mercy and help (v. 7). These words are followed by a series of verses that contrast sharply with the confident tone of the previous section. This shift has led some scholars to view Psalm 27 as a composite.

---

1. For this reverse movement in the Psalms, see Villanueva, *The "Uncertainty of a Hearing."*

Unfortunately, we no longer have access to the history of the composition of Psalm 27. It may well originally have consisted of two psalms. On the other hand, there are similarities between the two sections that suggest they have been deliberately brought together.[2] But whatever the history of the text, we have to deal with the text in its present form.

A more important question is, "Why put the psalm of confidence first (vv. 1–6) before the lament (vv. 7–14) and not the other way around?" The answer, as noted above, is that this brings out the element of tension which forms a part of the life of faith. So the confident declarations of the first section should be read with the cries for help of the second section, and vice versa. The two are to be held together, forming the two sides of our life in God.

27:1–3 UNWAVERING FAITH

In the previous psalm (Ps 26) the psalmist began with an assertion of his unwavering faith (v. 1). The present psalm spells out in more explicit terms the psalmist's confidence in God. He declares, "The LORD is my light and my salvation" (v. 1). This is the only place in the OT where the Lord is referred to as "my light." "Light" speaks of life and vitality.[3] The words "light" and "salvation" are not to be taken as merely abstract concepts. The psalmist can claim their reality in his life because he has experienced God lighting up his path; he can claim that God is his salvation because he has experienced God's deliverance. That is why he can confidently say, "Of whom shall I be afraid?" This is the first of two rhetorical questions in verse 1. Both emphatically express the confidence of the psalmist. God is not only his light and salvation; he is also his "stronghold." This metaphor speaks of protection.

Verses 2–3 identify the situations when the psalmist can say he is not afraid. There is a heightening of opposition as he moves from speaking of

---

2. Similarities between Psalm 27A and Psalm 27B:

Psalm 27A	Psalm 27B
v. 1 – "The LORD . . . my salvation" (*yishi*)	v. 9 – "My God, my salvation" (*yishi*)
v. 2b – "my adversaries (*tsaray*) shall stumble and fall"	v. 12 – "Do not give me to the will of my adversaries" (*tsaray*)
v. 4 – "One thing . . . will I seek" (*baqash*)	v. 8 – "Seek (*baqash*) his face; your face, LORD, do I seek (*baqash*)"
v. 5 – "He will hide (*satar*) me in his shelter (*seter*) in the day of trouble"	v. 9 – " Do not hide (*satar*) your face from me"

3. According to Bratcher and Reyburn, *A Translator's Handbook*, 261.

evildoers assailing him (v. 2), to an army encamped (v. 3a) and finally to a war breaking out against him (v. 3b). In all of these situations, he declares that he will not be afraid; he will be confident.

27:4–6 ONE THING I ASK

There is only one thing he asks: that he may "dwell in the house of the LORD all the days of my life" (v. 4). Earlier, the psalmist expressed how much he loved God's house (26:8). What is it about God's dwelling place that attracts the psalmist? It is the "beauty of the LORD" (v. 4) which he longs to behold. The "beauty of the LORD" speaks of God's *kagandahang loob*[4] – the goodness of his heart and his loving ways with his people. Those who have experienced the spiritual heights of which the psalm speaks know there is no greater joy than being in the presence of the Lord. Even at the height of his spiritual experience Moses was still not satisfied, so he prayed, "Show me your glory" (Exod 33:18).

What draws people to God is not so much his power as his beauty, or maybe a combination of both. The previous verses speak of spectacular things – an army encamped, war breaking loose. Reading verses 4–5 is like stepping into a room where a baby is sweetly sleeping in the arms of her mother. The psalmist feels secure: "he will keep me safe in his dwelling" (v. 5).

Verse 6 marks the climax and conclusion of the first section, with the words, "Then" (literally, "and now"): "Then my head will be exalted above the enemies who surround me." The assurance flows out of the psalmist's intimate fellowship with the Lord. In response the psalmist vows to offer a sacrifice to the Lord with singing and music (v. 6).

27:7–14 "HEAR MY VOICE WHEN I CALL, LORD"

We would expect at this point to hear more songs of praise. The psalm has already reached its peak, and actually it could have ended after verse 6. But the psalm continues – no longer with thanksgiving but with lament. Some scholars treat verses 7–14 separately from the previous verses. But I think it is important to recognize the present form of the text and to try to discern what it is trying to communicate to us rather than ignoring it.

In my view the present arrangement is deliberate. This is not the only place where we have thanksgiving followed by lament. We saw the same

---

4. See comment on Ps 26:3.

arrangement in Psalm 9–10 (see also Ps 40). These psalms show us that we can only appreciate the declarations of the first section when read in the light of the second. The psalmist declared in verse 1 that the Lord was his light. We appreciate "light" more fully when we have gone through darkness. It is through "the valley of the shadow of death" that we hear the confident words of the psalmist: "The LORD is my shepherd." Likewise, it is through the cries of verse 7 that we appreciate the "shouts of joy" of verse 6. It is through the experience of God's absence that we understand intimacy with God.

Earlier (v. 5) the psalmist spoke of seeking (*baqash*) God in his temple, where he experienced God concealing (*satar*) him under the cover of his tent. This speaks of intimacy and protection. In the present section, the psalmist also speaks about seeking God: "My heart says, 'seek (*baqash*) his face!' Your face, LORD, I will seek" (v. 8). But whereas the former section speaks of God "hiding" the psalmist in his protective care (v. 5), here it is God who seems to be hiding: "Do not hide (*satar*) your face from me" (v. 9). God seems to be absent. The psalmist feels abandoned: "Do not reject me or forsake me, God my Savior" (v. 9b). The confident victor is now the needy one. Yet it is precisely at the point of tension between the presence and absence of God that the psalm moves on to a deeper statement of trust in God: "Though my father and mother forsake me, the LORD will receive me" (v. 10).[5]

Earlier, the psalmist declared that although an army or a war might break out against him, he would not be afraid. Now the image is more intimate, speaking of his parents (v. 10). And the confidence is also deeper: it is not the psalmist who is doing the action but the Lord – "the LORD will receive me" (v. 10). The Hebrew word used for "receive" is the word *asap*. In Psalm 26:9 the psalmist prayed, "Do not take away (*asap*) my soul along with sinners." Here in Psalm 27:10, the psalmist is saying God has not swept him away but has taken him in – the Lord is indeed gracious! That is why the psalmist asks God to "Teach me your way, LORD; lead me in a straight path" (v. 11). The words "straight path" speak of an assurance of victory over his enemies (see 26:12). The psalmist wants to experience this for himself, and so he prays that God will allow him to walk on that path. Yet as the last words of verse 11 and the following verse tell us, the way to certainty is through struggles. There are enemies bent on destroying the psalmist (v. 12). Yet he does not

---

5. The Hebrew of v. 10 can be understood as a statement of fact or as presenting a possibility (see NRSV: "If my mother and father forsake me"). The Hebrew word *ki* ("for") could be taken with the previous verse or with the second part of v. 10. If the former, then it serves as a motivation for the petition in v. 9. If the latter, then it shows a shift to a more positive outlook.

give up but tries to have faith that he will see "the goodness of the LORD in the land of the living" (v. 13). To behold the beauty of the Lord (v. 13) also means to experience his goodness in this life. So there is room for hope. That is the focus of the last exhortation: "Wait for the LORD; be strong and take heart and wait for the LORD!" (v. 14).

In Psalm 27 we saw the opposite movement from new orientation to disorientation. We are familiar with this movement. We call this *gulong ng palad* (equivalent to the "wheel of fortune"). Now we may be at the bottom, but tomorrow we may be on top. Or the other way around. Psalm 27 does have a movement. But it is the other way around from thanksgiving to lament (cf. Psalm 9–10), from top to bottom. We may not like this, for it is obviously tragic, and we do not like tragic endings. We want the usual "And they lived happily ever after" type of ending. But what makes the psalms so powerful book is their capacity to embrace all of life, including the not-so-happy ending. This makes the Psalms a hopeful book. That is why even with the movement from thanksgiving to lament in Psalm 27, the psalm nonetheless ends with the exhortation to "wait for the Lord, be strong, and let your heart take courage" (v. 14).

PSALM 28

Psalm 28 contrasts with Psalm 27 in terms of its movement. Whereas Psalm 27 begins with thanksgiving and turns to lament, Psalm 28 moves in the opposite direction from lament (vv. 1–5) to thanksgiving (vv. 6–9). When read together, the two psalms form the following structure:

A Thanksgiving (27:1–6)
　　B Lament (27:7–14)
　　B' Lament (28:1–5)
A' Thanksgiving (28:6–9)

The alternation between lament and thanksgiving in Psalms 27 and 28 depicts the reality of the life of faith. At one moment, we are crying to God for help. The next we are shouting for joy. And just when we think everything is going to be all right, a problem strikes and we are back on our knees.

The structure shown above also highlights the importance of lament. Notice that the lament forms the center of the structure. Without the lament, thanksgiving has no meaning (see topic, "Thanksgiving and Lament", p. 75). This may be the reason why our thanksgiving is sometimes empty – we have neglected lament.

In Psalms 27–28, prayer reaches the heights of praise because it has born been from the very depths of despair. Conversely, the writers can cry out to God in prayers of lament because they know and have experienced the reality of God's power and might in their lives. This explains the emphasis on God as "my rock" in the opening words of Psalm 28: "To you, Lord, I call; you are my Rock, do not turn a deaf ear to me" (v. 1). God is strong, an ever present help in times of trouble (46:1).

Psalm 28 flows from lament to thanksgiving. The lament consists of an urgent cry for help (vv. 1–2), a personal petition (v. 3), and an imprecatory prayer (vv. 4–5). The thanksgiving consists of praise (v. 6) and a declaration of trust (v. 7), which is then extended to the people and the Lord's anointed (v. 8). The psalm ends with a petition on behalf of the people (v. 9). There is thus a movement not only from lament to praise but also from personal petition to communal intercession.

28:1–3 LAMENT: "TO YOU I CALL"

The first words of the psalm remind us that there is always someone we can go to when we are in trouble: "To you, LORD, I call" (v. 1). As in previous psalms, the psalmist is confronted with treacherous people, the type of people who bless you when you are with them but curse you the moment you turn your back (v. 3b). Aware of this, the psalmist cries out to God: "do not turn a deaf ear to me . . . Hear my cry for mercy" (vv. 1–2). Notice the emphasis on hearing and speaking. Although we can always call out to God, there are times when we feel as if he is not listening to us . . . there is no answer. So the psalmist cries for help: "as I call to you for help" (v. 2). In addition, he refers to the way God has helped him in the past by calling God "my rock." The use of this metaphor reminds us of Psalm 27:5 where the psalmist refers to God as the one who "set me high on a rock." To further motivate God to answer him, he presents the scenario that if God does not answer: "I will be like those who go down to the pit" (v. 1). In other words, he will die if God does not answer him.

In prayer we sometimes lift up our hands. The psalmist does the same in verse 2, lifting up his hands "toward your Most Holy Place." The upraised hands speak of surrender and an acknowledgement that one is totally dependent on God.

The psalmist already used a number of "strategies" to persuade God to hear him. Yet we can discern one more. His prayer in verse 3a, "Do not drag me away with the wicked, with those who do evil," looks back to 27:12. He pleads for God's justice that he not be treated like the wicked. Psalms 26, 27, and 28 share the same concern. But they address the issue from different angles. Psalm 26 focuses on the psalmist's assertion of his integrity (vv. 1, 11). Psalm 27 approaches the issue from his experience of God's deliverance (vv. 5–6). Psalm 28 brings the matter to God by praying against the wicked.

28:4–5 LAMENT: IMPRECATORY PRAYER

The psalmist now turns from personal prayer to intercession. But this is a different type of intercession to the one we are familiar with, for verses 4–5 are an imprecatory prayer (for discussion on this prayer, see "The Imprecatory Psalms as *Pagsusumbong sa Diyos*," pp. 274–276). The psalmist prays that God will give the wicked their due: "Repay them . . . for their evil work" (v. 4; cf. 10:15). Four related words are used to speak of the "works/deeds" of the wicked (v. 4): "work" (*poal*), "deeds" (*maalal*), "work" (*maaseh*), and "due reward" (*gemul*). These words highlight the importance of our actions. Everything that we do will have a corresponding consequence. According to the psalmist, these people not only did evil things, they also show "no regard for the deeds of the LORD" and "and what his hands have done" (v. 5a). For this reason he prays that God "repay them for what their hands have done and bring back on them what they deserve" (v. 4b).

Some of us may be uncomfortable praying this kind of prayer. But we can pray this prayer because it is in harmony with what God wants. He is a righteous God and will not allow the guilty to go unpunished. The psalmist declares that the Lord will "tear them down and never build them up again" (v. 5b).

28:6–9 PRAISE: "BLESSED BE THE LORD"

Without any explanation, the psalmist suddenly turns to praise in verse 6: "Praise be the LORD, for he has heard my cry for mercy." He had uttered an imprecatory prayer in the previous verse; now he is praising God! How can you turn from one to the other in just one verse?

A common explanation is that a cultic prophet must have spoken between verses 5 and 6 and assured the one praying that his prayer would be answered. Some such oracle of salvation is assumed to account for the sudden change of mood. But as already noted (see comment in Ps 13:5–6), the problem with this view is that there is nothing in the text itself which supports the occurrence of such an event. It seems more likely that the very act of calling to the Lord, of crying out to him, has caused a change within the person. Or the lamenting person himself may have sensed that God has heard his prayer, and that is why he moves on to praise. In real life, of course, this does not usually happen so quickly. Sometimes the crying and calling out to God may take days, months, or even years. The encouraging thing is that when we call to the Lord, he hears us. God does answer. As the psalmist declares: "He has heard my cry for mercy" (v. 6).[1]

Verse 7a recalls the title used for God in verse 1 ("my rock"), as the psalmist declares that the LORD is his strength and shield. The psalm moves into rejoicing and singing: "with my song I praise him" (v. 7b). In the last two verses, there is a transition from the psalmist to his community. As the psalmist declares, "the LORD is my strength" (v. 7) so he applies the same to his own

---

1. In v. 6, the psalmist repeats a word he used earlier in v. 2: "Hear the voice of my supplication." In Hebrew the words for "hear," "voice," and "my supplication" are the same.

people and to the king: "The LORD is the strength of his people, a fortress of salvation for his anointed one" (v. 8). The psalm closes with a petition for all the people: "Save your people and bless your inheritance; be their shepherd and carry them forever" (v. 9). This reminds us we do not pray alone but are always part of the bigger community. God has been the shepherd for the king (23:1), and the psalmist prays that he will be the same for the people.

Psalm 28 reminds us of the close link between the individual and his or her community in prayer. We do not stand alone when we come before God. We bring our community with us. Even the individual who speaks in the Psalms is not alone. That individual represents the community. Scholars believe that in a number of the psalms, it is the king who is speaking or praying.

In the Philippines, we use the word *bayanihan* when speaking of community. That word arose from the context of barrios (rural villages) where houses used to be made of such light materials that they could be carried from one place to another. So when a family wished to move to a new site, the community would help them carry their house to their new address. Today, we see a similar community spirit at work in other aspects of society.

We can apply the same *bayanihan* spirit in our prayers. Let us remember that we do not only carry our own burdens, we also carry the burdens of others (Gal 6:2). When we carry one another's burdens, our strength becomes the strength of the community. And together the community is able to bear whatever challenges they may be facing.

PSALM 29

The main theme of this psalm is the Lord's awesome power. The key word that holds the whole Psalm 29 together is the word "strength," which occurs at the beginning and end of the psalm (vv. 1, 11). This power is manifested through the "voice" of the Lord. Repeated seven times in Psalm 29, the word "voice" is understood in the psalm as thunder. As modern readers, we may imagine God's power through the image of thunder. As a boy, I remember a feeling of dread whenever I heard rolling thunder. It depicts power like no other. Before such awesome power we are reduced to nothingness. Often the only "voice" heard from us is the cry for help, the "voice" of need. Interestingly, the word "voice" is repeated twice in Psalm 28 (ESV, vv. 2, 6), serving as a link to Psalm 29. The psalmist is contrasting the "voice of the LORD" (29:3) with the "voice of my supplication" (28:2). Without the power of the "voice" of the Lord we are voiceless. The psalmist acknowledges we are but dust (103:14).

The encouraging thing is that even though this God is so powerful, he is good to his people. He hears the "voice" of our supplications (28:6). He gives strength to his people (28:7). The psalmist declares: "The LORD is my strength" (28:7), the "strength of his people" (28:8). When read in the context of Psalm 29, these declarations from the previous psalm find renewed force. Imagine, the God whose voice is able to shake the wilderness and strip the "forest bare" (29:8–9) is our strength!

But we can only experience the strength of the Lord in our lives when we acknowledge our weaknesses, when we say, "Not to us, Lord, not to us, but to your name be the glory" (115:1). This is what ascribing "glory and strength" to the Lord entails. The proper posture before God's awesome power is that of humility . . . of worship.

As observed above, structurally the psalm is held together by the repetition of the word "strength" which occurs at the beginning and end of the psalm, forming an inclusio. After a brief exhortation in verses 1–2, the psalm expounds on the theme of the strength of the Lord manifested in terms of his "voice" (vv. 3–9). The latter forms the main part of the psalm. A concluding statement (v. 10) and petition (v. 11) close it.

29:1–2 ASCRIBE TO THE LORD

The psalm begins with a call to worship. The exhortation, "Ascribe to the LORD," is repeated twice (vv. 1–2). Worshipers are to ascribe to the Lord "glory and strength" (vv. 1, 2). But there is a difference: it is not the congregation gathered in the temple that is being addressed, but the "heavenly beings" (v. 1). The term, "heavenly beings," comes from the Hebrew word which literally means "sons of gods."[1] Scholars have noted the similarity between Psalm 29 and other religious compositions of the surrounding peoples at that time.[2] In such a context, the term "sons of gods" refers to the lesser gods.[3] But while it is possible that the psalm was composed using the language patterns common at that time, the psalm as it now stands does not share the polytheistic view of the surrounding people. The Psalter maintains there is only one God: the LORD. At the same time, the use of contemporary background materials elevates the call to worship to the realm of the heavenly. By doing so, God is all the more exalted. If he is to be worshiped in the realm of the heavenly beings, how much more in the realm of human beings! The passage in Psalm 96:7 applies the call to worship to human beings: "Ascribe to the LORD, all you families of nations."[4]

29:3–9 "THE VOICE OF THE LORD"

In verses 3–9 the psalmist sets out why the Lord ought to be worshiped, by highlighting the awesome power of the "voice" of the LORD. As noted above, in the poetic language of the Psalms the "voice of the LORD" refers to thunder (18:13).[5] The following structure of verse 3 brings out this sense:

The voice of the LORD is over the waters;
  The God of glory thunders;
The LORD thunders over the mighty waters.

Notice that the verb "thunders" forms the central point of the structure, defining for us what the "voice of the LORD" refers to. A similar image is expressed in verse 7: "The voice of the LORD strikes with flashes of lightning." In the last line of verse 3 the "voice of the LORD" is equated with the Lord

---

1. According to Holladay, *The Psalms*, 16, *elim* is a "very old Semitic term for deity, often appearing in compounds with proper names."
2. Cf. Keel, *The Symbolism of the Biblical World*, 212, cites the following Ugaritic text which resembles Psalm 29: "Baal lets his holy voice resound, Baal repeats the utterance of his lips . . . his voice rang out, and the earth trembled."
3. Alter, *The Book of Psalms*, 98–99, regards the term as "the flickering literary afterlife of a polytheistic mythology," which nonetheless may no longer have been held by those who produced the Psalms.
4. Mays, *Psalms*, 136.
5. Bratcher and Reyburn, *A Translator's Handbook*, 276.

himself (cf. vv. 5, 8). There is also a heightening from "waters" to "mighty waters." In ancient Near Eastern mythology "waters" represented the forces of chaos which needed to be defeated. So to declare that the Lord is "over mighty waters" is to proclaim him as victorious.[6] This explains why in the next verse the "voice of the LORD" is proclaimed as "powerful" and "majestic" (v. 4).

In the following verses (vv. 5–6) the psalmist continues to declare the majesty of God's power. Even the famous cedars – those towering trees of Lebanon – bow down, as they are broken by the voice of the Lord. From cedar trees the psalmist turns his attention to the very ground on which the trees are planted: Lebanon. Yet even "the immobile mountains of Lebanon skip like calves frightened at the sound of a voice."[7] Verses 8–9 speak of wilderness, oaks, and forest, which are all shaken and stripped naked before the awesome power of the Lord.

There is a response in verse 9c: "And in his temple all cry, 'Glory!'" With this short sentence we hear a response from the worshipers in the temple. The call to worship addressed to the "heavenly beings" (v. 1) now finds an audience among believers on earth.

29:10–11 "MAY THE LORD GIVE STRENGTH TO HIS PEOPLE!"

We return to the image of waters in verse 10 (cf. v. 3). God is said to be over the waters in verse 3; here he is over the flood: "The LORD sits enthroned over the flood" (v. 10). We may make the same inference as we did with verse 3. God is the one victorious over his enemies. He "sits enthroned as King forever" (v. 10b).

In the light of the preceding declarations, the psalmist humbly prays: "May the LORD give strength to his people! May the LORD bless his people with peace!" (v. 11, ESV). After encountering the Lord who is powerful and majestic, to pray that one be endowed with his strength is to experience power way beyond our own. It means to be strengthened to do more than we can ever think of or imagine by the power of his might (compare Eph 3:20-21). What amazingly great things await those whose strength is the Lord's!

In addition, the prayer asks for peace, which in Hebrew is the famous word *shalom*. *Shalom* is not just about inner peace. It's about security and abundance, or in Filipino, *kasaganaan* ("prosperity").

---

6. Cf. Keel, *Symbolism of the Biblical World*, 212.
7. Craigie, *Psalms 1–50*, 247.

NATURAL PHENOMENA

Psalm 29 is "the only text in the OT in which the glory of the Lord is so extensively and directly said to be manifested in what we moderns call natural phenomena."[1] But what people in the West consider as "natural phenomena" many Asians view as spiritual, closely linked with the divine. In many parts of Asia, nature is directly linked with spirits and the gods. We do not separate the physical and the spiritual. Even trees are inhabited by spirits.

Traditionally, Asians believe that phenomena like tsunamis and storm surges are caused by God. For example, in Indonesia, people offer sacrifices to the gods every time there is a disaster. That is why any response to what we call natural disasters should consider both the traditional Asian view of nature and the teaching of Scriptures.[2] Both affirm the presence of the divine in nature. Psalm 29 does not deny or reject the presence of spirits or other gods. What it adds to the traditional Asian view is its declaration that God is over and above all forces of nature. He is victorious. He reigns even "over the flood" (v. 10).

There is no question that God controls nature. Even the survivors of Typhoon Yolanda (Haiyan) acknowledged God as the Lord "over the flood," as reflected in their prayers and in their responses to the tragedy.[3] They called on God because they believe he is in control. Sadly, many of them lost their loved ones. How we need the strength that God provides especially for those who are suffering as a result of such disasters. May the Lord give strength to our people!

---

1. Mays, *Psalms*, 137.
2. Cf. Bernard Adeney-Risakotta, "Is There a Meaning in Natural Disasters? Constructions of Culture, Religion, and Science," *Exchange* 38, no. 3 (1 January 2009). Adeney-Risakotta sees that "One of the challenges for a theology of natural disaster is to integrate ancient cultural stories, theological reflection and modern scientific understanding in a convincing account of the cosmos" (Ibid., 237).
3. Karl M. Gaspar, *Desperately Seeking God's Saving Action: Yolanda Survivors' Hope Beyond Heartbreaking Lamentations* (Quezon City, Philippines: Institute of Spirituality in Asia, 2014), for some of the prayers and responses of the survivors; see especially pp. 109–116.

PSALM 30

In some of our churches we have what we call "testimony time." These are occasions when members stand up and share what the Lord has done in their lives. Psalm 30 may be likened to a "testimony." Here the psalmist talks about his own experience of extreme difficulty and how the Lord restored him. The difference is that here the testimony is directed more to the Lord than to the congregation. Although the psalmist addresses the congregation in verse 4, he does so only in order to call them to praise the Lord for what the Lord has done. In the rest of the psalm we hear the psalmist addressing God – "*You* lifted me out of the depths" (v. 1), "I called to *you* for help" (v. 2; see also v. 8), "*You* healed me" (v. 2), "*You* turned my wailing into dancing" (v. 11), etc. Indeed, the psalm may be properly called a "prayer testimony." It reminds us that the proper focus of our testimonies is the Lord, not us. In fact, the name of the Lord (*Yahweh*) is mentioned nine times in this short psalm of twelve verses.

But the psalm does more than remind us of the proper focus of our testimonies. From the psalmist's own experience we also learn important lessons about life with God. The psalmist realizes through his difficulties how easy it is to forget the Lord when we already have everything we need. Long ago, Moses warned the Israelites that when they are blessed they should praise the Lord and not forget him (Deut 8:10–18). Unfortunately, as their history showed, they failed. When they had eaten and were satisfied they turned their backs on the Lord (Neh 9:24–37). How easy it is to put our confidence on what we have when life becomes prosperous.

The psalmist admits: "When I felt secure, I said, 'I will never be shaken'" (Ps 30:6). The psalmist forgot that it was all because of the Lord's favor. And so he suffered. But it was also through his experience of suffering that he came to know about the God who answers prayer, delivers his people from their distress, and heals them (the God of reversals.) In fact, had it not been for his difficulty he would not have experienced or learned about God's power to intervene. There would be nothing to share in the first place. In his experience he encountered the God who was merciful, who answered the cry for help of his people.

This is one of the most powerful testimonies of this psalm: God actually does restore people to life. Others after the psalmist have experienced the same thing, as the superscription indicates. The superscription reveals that the psalm was sung during the dedication of the temple. We do not know exactly what event this refers to. It could be to the dedication of the Second Temple. The Talmud[1] refers to this psalm as being used during the time of the restoration of the temple after it was desecrated. In either case, we have here a testimony to the God who can work even in extremely difficult situations, whether they be the restoration of an individual or the restoration of a nation. They all see God and look to him for answers. An individual has experienced this, and others after him – including ourselves – can experience it also.

The structure of the psalm may be outlined as follows:

> Vow of praise for what the Lord has done (vv. 1–3);
> Exhortation to praise the Lord (vv. 4–5);
> Testimony – what the psalmist learned from his experience (vv. 6–7);
> His prayer (vv. 8–10);
> God's transforming grace (vv. 11–12).

30:1–3 "YOU LIFTED ME OUT OF THE DEPTHS"

The psalm is full of images of the underworld – "realm of the dead" (Sheol), the pit (v. 3; v. 9). It talks about having been drawn up (v. 1),[2] of being restored to life from the "realm of the dead" (v. 3). Although the psalmist has not literally experienced death, his experience may be likened to it. Later in the psalm he talks about dying (v. 9) and of the wailing associated with death (v. 11). We do not know exactly what happened to him. But whatever it was, it was an extremely difficult situation. It was out of this that the Lord has "drawn him up" and it explains why he is praising God (v. 1).

30:4–5 "SING PRAISES TO THE LORD"

Turning to the congregation, he exhorts them to "sing praises of the LORD" as well (v. 4). He has survived his enemies (v. 1b) and experienced healing (v. 2b). Viewing his experience from his present situation, he can say that God's "anger lasts only a moment, but his favor lasts a lifetime; weeping may stay for the night, but rejoicing comes in the morning" (v. 5). People who have gone through recovery may identify with the sentiments of the psalm. But

---

1. The Talmud is an important text among the Jews, considered second to the Law of Moses.
2. Alter, *The Book of Psalm*, 102, notes that the verb *daloh* ("to draw up"), "is the one used for drawing water from a well. Death, then, is imagined as a deep pit from which the speaker has been drawn up by God."

the view is different from those who are still in the process of restoration. Certainly, some people who are suffering feel as if it will be forever. So it is important that we do not impose the view in this psalm on all situations, particularly in cases where suffering is at its worst.

30:6–10 THE PSALMIST'S EXPERIENCE

The situation is different with the psalmist. He is already in a place where he can look back to his experience. What comes out of his reflection is the realization of the grave error he had committed. Looking back, he realizes he had been presumptuous: "When I felt secure, I said, 'I will never be shaken'" (v. 6). A prolonged experience of prosperity and security brings with it the temptation to trust in one's own ability rather than in the Lord. In Deuteronomy 8:10–12, Moses warned the people of Israel to be careful lest they forget the Lord. He instructed them to praise the Lord when they had eaten and were satisfied. Praising the Lord is the proper response to prosperity. But this is often not what happens, as the experiences of the Israelites and the psalmist show. There is the tendency to forget the Lord and to boast of one's strength and ability instead.

On reflection, the psalmist realizes that all the abundance he had experienced was because of the Lord's blessing: "LORD, when you favored me, you made my royal mountain stand firm" (v. 7a). Unfortunately he did not acknowledge this before, and thus experienced the opposite of divine favor – "you hid your face" (v. 7b). The hiding of God's face is a "metaphor which portrays the divine reaction to sin" (Deut 31:17–18; 32:20; Isa 8:17; Pss 69:17; 143:7).[3] This explains why he found himself in the depths.

But as all godly people do when they find themselves in trouble, the psalmist called out to God: "To you, LORD, I called" (30:8; see also 28:1). Earlier he had said, "LORD my God, I called to you for help" (Ps 30:2; see also 28:2). We even have a record of his prayer which he uttered during his difficulties (30:9–10). As a way of motivating God to answer him, he tells God that he will no longer be able to give praise once he is dead: "What is gained if I am silenced, if I go down to the pit? Will the dust praise you? Will it proclaim your faithfulness?" (v. 9). This idea is also present in Psalm 6:5 and in the prayer of Hezekiah in Isaiah 38:18. Later the psalmist gives as the reason for God's answer the same concern for praise: "so that my heart may

---

3. Konrad Schaefer, *Psalms* (Collegeville: Liturgical Press, 2001), 75. He provides quite a few passages to support this statement. I have mentioned some of them above.

sing your praises and not be silent" (v. 12). This tells us of the centrality of praise in the life of God's people. In the OT the doctrine of resurrection was not yet developed, in contrast to the NT teaching which assures Christians today that even in death, especially in death, there is praise. In fact there will be eternal praise. What this psalm teaches us is that praise is not only our occupation in eternity; it begins now while we are still living. That is why the psalmist pleads for mercy to the Lord (v. 11).

30:11–12 YOU TURNED MY MOURNING INTO DANCING

The good news is that God does answer prayer. God is the God of great reversals. All through the psalm we see reversals: from weeping to joy (v. 5), from confidence to God's hiding (vv. 6–7), and now from wailing to dancing (v. 11). The Hebrew word for "wailing" (*misped*) is "normally a dirge performed by relatives and friends."[4] Here the psalmist is portrayed as mourning for himself. Such was the depth of his situation. But God has acted and the psalmist can now testify to what God has done. In gratitude he gives praise: "Lord my God, I will praise you forever" (v. 12).

The experience of a pastor who almost lost his life resonates with what the psalmist testifies in Psalm 30. The pastor almost died while lying in the Intensive Care Unit of the hospital. All of her close relatives and family members had already been summoned to pay their last respects. Meanwhile, many friends and people from the church prayed for her at the hospital, and even in their own homes. Thankfully, God gave her recovery, despite many close encounters with death. She testified that God's favor lasted a lifetime (v. 5). Her children experienced joy as God turned mourning into dancing (v. 11). God is indeed alive even when things look so gloomy and dead around us!

There is hope for our dying lives, dying institutions, dying nations. When we come to the Lord humbly and cry out to him he will listen to us. In extreme difficulty, we can experience the God of great reversals. We can talk to God (vv. 1–3), and testify for God (vv. 4–11).

---

4. Ibid., 75.

PSALM 31

One of the important messages which Psalm 31 communicates through its poetic movements is that restoration is a process. The psalmist had just testified of his experience of how God moved in his life (Ps 30). Here, he is crying out to God for help (31:1). It does not mean that when we have experienced God's healing and restoration, everything will necessarily be all right. As Calvin reminds us, "Creatures of such instability, we need to be confirmed again and again."[1] Psalm 31 does move from lament (vv. 1–6) to a vow of thanksgiving (vv. 7–8). This represents the movement towards restoration and healing. But immediately following the thanksgiving, we find the psalmist crying for mercy again as the psalm returns to lament, this time an extended one (vv. 9–18). Then, without any transition, the psalm shifts back to praise in verse 19 and maintains the tone of confidence and praise until verse 22 when it ends with an exhortation for the saints to continue to be strong and take courage (vv. 23–24).

Thus lament moves to praise twice in Psalm 31. In the past this has been interpreted as two separate psalms being joined together. But there is no clear evidence of two separate psalms here, and even if there is we need to look at the present arrangement of the psalm as we now have it. I believe the psalm was put together to communicate an important message – healing and restoration is a process.[2] Even at the end of the psalm one senses a certain suspense . . . the faithful are still waiting.

We may outline the structure of the psalm as follows:

Lament with expression of trust (vv. 1–6);
Vow of thanksgiving (vv. 7–8);
Lament (vv. 9–13);
Expression of trust (vv. 14–15);
Petition (vv. 16–18);
Praise (vv. 19–22);
Exhortation to praise (vv. 23–24).

---

1. Calvin, *Commentary on the Book of Psalms*, 423.
2. For a development of this theme using Psalm 31, see Federico G. Villanueva, "Preaching Lament," in *Reclaiming the Old Testament for Christian Preaching*, eds. Grenville J. Kent et al. (Downers Grove, Ill.: IVP Academic, 2010), 64–84.

31:1–8 "INTO YOUR HANDS I COMMIT MY SPIRIT"

There is a strong emphasis on the theme of trust in the first verses of the psalm. The statement, "In you . . . I have taken refuge" (v. 1), parallels the statement at the end of verse 6: "I trust in the LORD." It is easy to say these words when life is free from troubles. But when we are confronted with enemies who are bent on destroying us – verse 4 talks about "the trap that is set for me" (see also v. 2 and vv. 11–13)[3] – declaring one's trust in the Lord becomes an act of faith. It requires total surrender as depicted in the words of verse 5: "Into your hands I commit my spirit."[4] With this declaration the familiar statement, "In you . . . I have taken refuge" (v. 1), receives an added dimension. The word "hand" is repeated four times in the psalm (vv. 5, 8, 15 [2x]). The psalmist is grateful to the Lord that he has not "given me into the *hands* of the enemy" (v. 8). Later he prays that he be delivered "from the *hands* of my enemies," for he declares, "My times are in your *hand*" (v. 15). The last one is similar to the expression, "Into your hands I commit my spirit." The language of taking refuge in the Lord and having one's life in God's hands basically expresses the same thing – trust in the Lord. But the two images differ in their emphasis. Taking refuge brings out the element of protection, while having one's life in God's hands speaks more of total surrender. The latter is exemplified in Jesus' use of the psalm at the cross (Luke 23:46).

The next verses indicate that the psalmist has received the answer to his plea: "for you saw my affliction and knew the anguish of my soul" (v. 7; cf. Exod 3:7). The mood has changed to rejoicing and exultation, for God has delivered him (v. 8).

31:9–18 "BE GRACIOUS TO ME"

Somewhat unexpectedly, the psalm returns to petition in verse 9. But this is not the first time we have encountered this feature. Psalm 27 contains a similar movement (see esp. vv. 6–7). Instead of going "from glory to glory," Psalm 31 goes from exultation to grieving. "Be merciful to me," the psalmist pleads, "for I am in distress; my eyes grow weak with sorrow, my soul

---

3. There is a sense of urgency in v. 2: "rescue me speedily." The latter verses depict in more detail the dangers confronting the psalmist caused by his enemies.
4. The word *ruakh* refers to the breath of life similar to the word *nefesh* and should not be interpreted in terms of a soul separate from the body (Alter, *The Book of Psalm*, 106).

and body with grief" (v. 9). If earlier the psalmist speaks about God taking care of him in his "affliction" (v. 7); here he finds himself in "distress" (v. 9).[5] Though he had already declared that God has "not given me into the hands of the enemy" (v. 8), yet he needs to pray again, "deliver me from the hands of my enemies" (v. 15). The enemies find fuller elaboration in verses 11–13. They treat the psalmist as an object to be taunted; his friends reject him and even consider him already dead. He likens himself to "broken pottery" (v. 12). Full of dread (v. 13), he feels his "life is consumed by anguish," and his "years by groaning" (v. 10). And yet with the same determination to keep on trusting the Lord, the psalmist declares, "But I trust in you . . . My times are in your hand" (vv. 14–15). Yes, his life may have been spent in anguish and his years in groaning, but every single day of his life, every moment, is in God's hands.

This gives him hope and courage to continue. Thus he prays, "Let your face shine on your servant" (v. 16). Reiterating his earlier prayer (v. 1), he asks that he not be put to shame. Instead, "let the wicked be put to shame" (v. 17). This section ends with a prayer that God might silence the lying lips and those speaking with pride and contempt (v. 18), that words of praise might be heard once again.

31:19–24 BLESSED BE THE LORD

After the silencing of the boastful and the wicked, the psalmist bursts into words of praise: "How abundant are the good things . . . on those who take refuge in you" (v. 19). This brings us back to the beginning of the psalm where the psalmist declared "In you I have taken refuge" (v. 1). In verse 21 the psalmist blesses the Lord for what he has done to him. He mentions a specific situation – "when I was in a city under siege" (v. 21b). In such a situation, he panicked: "I am cut off from your sight" (v. 22a). He felt God was far from him. And yet when he cried for help, the Lord heard his supplications (v. 2).

In verse 23, the psalmist turns from prayer to exhortation, from addressing the Lord (v. 22) to addressing God's "faithful people" (v. 23). This signifies that personal experiences of God is not for the individual alone, but is meant to be shared with others. When the disciples wanted to remain in the Mount of Transfiguration, Jesus told them they should go down. As the

---

5. The word for "distress" in vv. 7 and 9 come from the same root *tsrr*.

psalmist experienced the abundant goodness of the Lord (v. 19), so he wanted others to experience the same. Interestingly, he exhorts the people first to "love the Lord" (v. 23) before encouraging them to trust in him (v. 24). Trust flows out of one's love for God.

PSALM 32

Traditionally, Psalm 32 is one of the seven penitential psalms, along with Psalms 6, 38, 51, 102, 130, and 143. As a penitential prayer, Psalm 32 has two important contributions. First, it affirms the central place of confession in the practice of repentance. Without acknowledgement of one's sins there will be no genuine restoration. Second, it highlights the joy of the forgiven life. Psalm 32 reminds us that our standing before God is central, not our status in life or the abundance of our possessions. The important question is not how much money we have in the bank or how much in demand we are, but whether God is pleased with our lives. It is those whose sins are forgiven who are blessed.

Psalm 32 is similar to Psalm 1 in terms of its emphasis on the blessed life. It opens up with similar words: "Blessed is the one" (32:1; 1:1). From Psalm 1 we learn that it is those who do not follow the ways of the wicked, whose joy comes from knowing the Lord through his law, who are the truly happy people. However, reading Psalm 1 by itself may lead us into thinking that the righteous life is a life of perfection. Psalm 32 clarifies this: the life of the righteous, indeed the blessed life, is not one in which one has never failed or sinned. Rather, it is a forgiven life, a life which knows what it means to receive grace from the Lord after a time of falling. As Kirkpatrick puts it: "The first beatitude of the Psalter is pronounced on an upright life; but since 'there is no man that sinneth not' . . . there is another beatitude reserved for true penitence."[1]

32:1–2 "HAPPY ARE THOSE"

As noted above, the psalm opens in a similar fashion to Psalm 1. But whereas the emphasis in Psalm 1 is on what a righteous person does and does not do, Psalm 32 shifts its focus to God's action. The two passive verbs in verse 1 underline this. The blessed ones are those "whose transgressions are forgiven" and "whose sins are covered" (v. 1). The agent of both verbs is God.[2] The righteous are the recipients of God's forgiving grace. Reading the Psalter in sequence from Psalm 1, we can say that Psalm 32 has gone a long way. Through the many lament psalms that follow Psalm 1 we realize that the ex-

---

1. Kirkpatrick, *The Book of Psalms*, 162.
2. Traditionally in NT scholarship they talk about the "divine passive."

perience of God's "blessing" does not mean a life free from troubles. Rather, God is found in the midst of all the troubles that plague the righteous. It is not "above the storms of life" that we experience God's intervening power but "through" them. Similarly, it is not in a life free from all mistakes and sins that we encounter the God of grace, but in and through the very darkness of our hearts. It is through the darkness that the light of God's mercy shines.

This does not mean, however, that the psalm is lenient on sin. Nor should this lead us to say, as some did during the time of the Apostle Paul, "Shall we go on sinning that grace may increase?" (Rom 6:1). In verse 2 the psalmist makes clear that God does not tolerate evil: The blessed ones are those "in whose spirit is no deceit" (v. 2b). The forgiven ones are those who do not continue to sin (see 1 John 3:6).

32:3–5 "I ACKNOWLEDGED MY SIN TO YOU"

In verse 3 the psalm turns from a general statement to a more personal note. The psalmist shares his own experience of the truth declared in the previous verses. Some scholars are at a loss to figure out the specific genre of Psalm 32. The opening verses resemble a wisdom psalm (vv. 1–2), whereas the present verses come close to a psalm of thanksgiving (vv. 3–5). And the two are interspersed, so that a clear-cut identification of the genre of the psalm may not be possible. The confusion may be because we tend to separate "wisdom" from what is considered "personal." But the two are closely linked. Wisdom flows from one's personal experience (see Ps 34). What the psalmist just said in verses 1–2 comes out of his own experience, which he tries to share later with others (v. 6).

The psalmist has learned his lesson from personal experience. But he has learned it the hard way, for he tried to hide his sins. He was silent for some time (v. 3a). But unconfessed sin is detrimental to one's well-being: "My bones wasted away through my groaning all day long" (v. 3b). As long as he kept his sin within him, he felt God's hand was heavy upon him "day and night" (v. 4a). There was no rest. The word "heavy" is the opposite of the word "forgiven" in verse 1. The latter comes from the Hebrew word *nasa*, a verb which also means "lift" or "carry." As long as we carry our sins by ourselves, God's hand is heavy on us. The psalmist testifies, "My strength was sapped as in the heat of summer" (v. 4b).

Thankfully, the psalmist decided to admit his sin to God. He comes out into the open and no longer hid his sin but acknowledged it before God: "I did not cover up my iniquity" (v. 5a). Like the Prodigal Son he came to his senses: "I said, 'I will confess my transgressions to the LORD'" (v. 5b). The word "confess" (*yadah*) is an important word. The word means "to admit," "to acknowledge." Confession forms the central element of the prayers of confession in the OT (Ezra 9:5–15; Neh 1:5–11; 9:6–37; Dan 9:4–19).[3]

As a result, the Lord forgave his sin (v. 5). The word *nasa* ("forgive") is repeated here from verse 1. No longer is it the experience of heaviness all day but that of being lifted up, of release, indeed of peace with God.

32:6 "LET ALL THE FAITHFUL PRAY TO YOU"

Verse 6 may be interpreted as the psalmist's exhortation to others: "Therefore let all the faithful pray to you" (v. 6a). Reception of grace leads towards reaching out to others, a reflection of the communal nature of the life of faith. It also underlines the communal nature of confession. The confession of sin is shared not only with God but also with the community. At the same time, we may read the verse as more directed to God than to the audience: "Let all the faithful pray *to you*." The second person address, begun in verse 2 and continued to verse 5, is maintained. From this perspective the statement brings out a stronger element of encouragement. The truth is expressed in the form of a prayer. The psalmist is saying that because of his experience he sees it as all the more important that the faithful should come and offer prayer to God.

Who are the faithful? And what prayer is being referred to here?

The word "faithful" (*khasid*) refers to a person who is devout or pious. The word is often used corporately to refer to God's faithful followers. But by using this word in the context of confession of sins, it implies that the "faithful" also commit sin. They are not perfect. The difference is that God is prepared to extend his forgiveness when they come to him. The prayer referred to here, therefore, though it may be understood in general terms, is to be read in connection to confessing one's sins to God. We should not wait before it's too late to come to God. We should pray to him "while he may be found" (v. 6). Otherwise, we may not be able to withstand when the "mighty waters" come. The image of the "mighty waters" may be interpreted in a similar manner as referring to the troubles associated with a life in which sin is hidden rather than acknowledged. The psalmist exhorts the faithful to

---

3. See Villanueva, "Confession of Sins or Petition for Forgiveness?"

come to God "at a time of distress"[4] (i.e. at a time when they are experiencing similar troubles to what he has experienced in verses 3–4).

32:7–8 "YOU ARE MY HIDING PLACE"

The transition from exhortation (v. 6) to personal experience (v. 7) reflects the earlier similar shift in verses 1–2 and verses 3–4. In verse 6 the psalmist talks about the rushing of "mighty waters." He himself had experienced this, but God became his "hiding place" (v. 7). Earlier, he talked about being silent about his sin which by implication means hiding it. But then he decides to confess his sin to God. Thus, he can say, "you are my hiding place." When we do not hide our sins but acknowledge them before God, God becomes our hiding place from the troubles that beset us. What's more, we receive guidance from the Lord.

The psalmist declares in verse 7: "you will protect me from trouble and surround me with songs of deliverance." This assurance comes from the psalmist's reception of the divine promise preserved in a quote in verse 8: "I will instruct you and teach you in the way you should go."[5] In Psalm 1:6 the psalmist declared: "The LORD watches the way of the righteous" (v. 6).[6] In Psalm 32, God's instruction and teaching are his way of taking care of the psalmist. God's way of teaching is intimate: "I will counsel you with my loving eye on you" (32:8b).

32:9–11 EXHORTATION

It is not easy to understand how verse 9 fits in with the previous verse. There is a shift from second person singular address (v. 8) to a second person plural address (v. 9). The former can be taken as God's address to the psalmist; the latter can be viewed as the psalmist's words of exhortation to his audience. The second half of the verse is also difficult to translate.[7] If we take verse

---

4. The next phrase, translated as "at a time of distress" in the NRSV is an attempt to make sense of the Hebrew reading. The ancient Greek translation of the Old Testament, known as the Septuagint has "fit time" – call to him in a fitting time (ESV: "at a time when you may be found").
5. Admittedly, it is not easy to see the connections between vv. 6–9. One of the difficulties is the sudden changes in address, which seem to indicate changes in speaker/s.
6. The contrast between the wicked and the righteous in vv. 10–11 further confirms the link between Psalm 32 and Psalm 1.
7. For a review of various attempts towards making sense of the verse and a proposal for reading the verse, see Giorgio Castellino, "Psalm 32:9," in *VT* 2, no. 1 (1952): 37–42. He proposes

9 as the psalmist's exhortation, then we may see here a contrast between a life properly guided by the Lord (v. 8), and a life which lacks direction or guidance. The latter is likened to that of a horse which needs to be curbed with bit and bridle to stay on course. God's way of guiding is not the controlling type. He sets his eyes on you but does not control you. The hope is that we will not be like the horse that needs "curbing" but that we will have the initiative and willingness to go where God wants us to go.[8]

This means trusting in God's ways and not our own: "the LORD's unfailing love surrounds the one who trusts in him" (v. 10b). By contrast, the wicked suffer many torments. There is thus reason for the righteous to rejoice and shout for joy (v. 11).

---

the following reading for v. 9b: "Be not like horse (or) mule which does not pay heed to bridle and bit. (If it is) approached for curbing, it will not come near thee," 410.
8. In Filipino we use the word *pagkukusa* ("initiative") to express this idea.

CONFESSION AND THE FILIPINO CONCEPT OF SIN

Sin is a serious matter. The prophet Isaiah explains why: "But your iniquities have separated you from your God; your sins have hidden his face from you, so that he will not hear" (Isa 59:2). One of the ways of dealing with sin and restoring our relationship with God is through a prayer of confession, in which one acknowledges that one has done something wrong. That is why there are a number of prayers of confession in the OT (Ezra 9:6–15; Neh 1:5–11; 9:6–37; Dan 9:4–19). There are also seven psalms, known as the penitential psalms, in which the psalmist confesses his sin (Pss 6, 32, 38, 51, 102, 130, and 143).

But in the Philippines, we face the problem that we do not even have a proper word for sin. We use the Tagalog word *kasalanan* when we speak of it, but that word does not capture the seriousness of the biblical concept of sin. *Kasalanan* simply means a "mistake," nothing really serious. Add to this the social dimension of the concept of sin in our culture and you are left with the idea that sin is only serious when it is found out. As we sometimes hear, *Hindi masama ang magnakaw; ang masama yung mahuli ka* ("It's not wrong to steal; what is wrong is to be caught stealing"). So how do we encourage confession of sins in a culture such as ours, which has a very different concept of sin?

Possibly we need to begin by finding a better Tagalog word for sin, one that makes it clear how seriously God sees it. Jose de Mesa has suggested that we should use the word *pandaraya,* which refers to deceiving someone. To say to a Filipino, *"madaya ka"* (you are a cheater) is much harsher than *"nagkasala ka"* (you have sinned).

Second, we need to emphasize the importance of confession of sins, both to God and to others. Sin is first and foremost an affront to God, but it also has social implications. When Cain murdered his brother Abel, God said, "Your brother's blood cries out to me from the ground" (Gen 4:10; see comments in Ps 51:4). Thus sin has both a vertical and horizontal dimension, and we need to acknowledge both. That is why it is not enough just to confess our sins to God; we also need to confess them to people. We need to be able to say, "I have done wrong. This is what I did . . ."

Doing this takes a lot of humility as well as courage, especially in the Philippines and other Asian countries where the concept of shame is strong. We need discernment and sensitivity when we call people to repentance and ask them to confess their sin – and when we confess our own sins.

But one question we do have to answer concerns our loyalty. Are we more afraid of what people say than what God says?

PSALM 33

The forgiven life is a happy life (32:1). Thus, it is fitting that a hymn of praise follows a psalm of penitence.[1] Psalm 33 picks up where Psalm 32 ends which is by calling on the "righteous" and the "upright" to "shout for joy" (32:11). Psalm 33 begins with the same note (vv. 1–3).[2] But it goes beyond this to include a series of motivations for praise. This pattern of call to worship and motivation is repeated in verse 8 and verses 9–11, respectively. In verse 12 the opening beatitude of Psalm 32 reappears. In Psalm 32, the "blessed" are those whose sins are forgiven (32:1). Here, it is the "nation whose God is the Lord" (33:12). The subsequent verses stress this point: It is the nation that trusts God who is saved (vv. 13–19; cf. 2:11). And so the people express their trust in the Lord and pray that he bestow his steadfast love upon them (vv. 20–23).

Structurally, the psalm may be outlined as follows:

Call to praise (vv. 1–3);
Motivation for praise (vv. 4–7);
Exhortation to fear the Lord (v. 8);
Motivation to fear the Lord (vv. 9–19);
The community's declaration of hope in the Lord (vv. 20–22).

33:1–7 "REJOICE IN THE LORD, O YOU RIGHTEOUS"

The Apostle Paul's words in Philippians 4:4, "Rejoice in the Lord always," find its counterpart in Psalm 33:1 – "Rejoice in the Lord, O you righteous" (NRSV). The word "rejoice" here comes from the Hebrew word *rānan* which means to "shout for joy" (see NIV's "Sing joyfully"). In verse 1 the verb is closely connected with the words "in the Lord." A similar point is made at the end of the psalm: "*In him* our hearts rejoice" (v. 21). The focus is not on something one has accomplished or gained, but on the Lord ("in him"). Rejoicing in the Lord flows from one's trust in God (vv. 16–21). So rejoicing leads to praise, for the one who is trusted is great and worthy to be praised. Praising God comes naturally for those who have experienced his deliverance:

---

1. See Schaefer, *Psalms*, 81: "The just and upright are invited to sing 'a new song' . . . which is the appropriate response to God's renewing grace."
2. The connection between the two psalms is further reinforced by the absence of a superscription in Psalm 33. It should be noted though that the LXX contains a superscription.

"It is fitting for the upright to praise him" (v. 1b). Verses 2–3 give us a glimpse of how praise is expressed. It includes singing and the use of instruments. Here we have the first mention of the instruments used in worship (see Ps 150 for a more exhaustive list of instruments). Verse 3 highlights the skillful playing of instruments: "play skillfully."

But more important than the skillful playing of instruments are the lives of the worshipers – those who praise the Lord are the "upright" (v. 1). Praising God and living righteously go together, for "the LORD loves righteousness and justice" (v. 5). Where there are upright people, there will be praise. Why? Because the upright continue to experience the reality of God. That is why they can sing "a new song" (v. 3). Delitzsch defines a "new song" as "one which, in consequence of some new mighty deeds of God, comes from a new impulse of gratitude in the heart"[3] For example, in Psalm 40:3 the psalmist declares that God "put a new song in my mouth" as a result of his experience of deliverance (40:1–2). God is not just someone who had moved in the world "once upon a time." The God who created the world by his powerful word (vv. 6–7) continues to work in the world (vv. 10–12) and in the lives of those who fear him (vv. 18–19).

It is instructive that right after the psalmist exhorted the people to sing a new song, he goes back to the very beginning – to creation (vv. 6–7). Singing a new song does not mean doing away with the old hymns in favor of the latest "praise and worship songs." What makes the song "new" is not primarily the new composition or the new musical arrangement. Rather, it is the new experience of God, who had worked in the beginning. Conversely, composing a "new song" involves the ability to connect one's present experiences with the God who acted in history, and the faith to see our broken world through the eyes of faith: "the earth is full of his unfailing love" (v. 5).

33:8–19 "LET ALL THE EARTH FEAR THE LORD"

The call to worship in verse 8 broadens, as the psalmist exhorts "all the people of the world" to fear the Lord and stand in awe of him. But one also notices a narrowing down from "all the earth" (v. 8) to "the nation whose God is the LORD" (v. 12) to "those who fear him" (v. 18). The call is given to everyone. But there is a recognition that not everyone will respond. Even the nation

---

3. Delitzsch, *Psalms*, 403.

chosen by God had to be narrowed down still further to a group referred to as "those who fear the Lord."

What does it mean to fear the Lord?

In the context of Psalm 33, to fear the Lord means placing all of one's hope and trust in the Lord. It finds expression in a deep acknowledgement that it is only in the Lord that one has hope. One can never be sure of the plans of the nations, no matter how powerful they are. The Lord frustrates the counsel of the nations (v. 10). A king cannot rely on the size of his army, nor a warrior in his "great strength" (v. 16). Even with the most advanced weaponry, no one is assured of victory (v. 17). It is only in the Lord that one can have hope.

That is why the "nation whose God is the LORD is blessed" (v. 12), as well as those who fear the Lord, for "the eyes of the LORD" are on those who fear him (v. 18; cf. 32:8b). The Lord watches over them to deliver them from death and famine (v. 19). The mention of the words "death" and "famine" indicates the extreme difficulty that the righteous go through. They are not exempt from the troubles of life. Yet the encouraging thing is that the eyes of the Lord are upon them (see 1:6).

33:20–22 "MAY YOUR UNFAILING LOVE BE WITH US"

Recognizing the realities that mark the life of faith, the people declare their trust in the Lord. They acknowledge God to be their "help" and their "shield" (v. 20). They express their trust in his "holy name" (v. 21), and pray that the Lord's "unfailing love be with us" (v. 22). To utter this request after having already proclaimed that "the earth is full of his unfailing love" (v. 5) indicates that the earlier verse is more of an expression of faith than a present reality. Such faith is able to see beyond the present moment and situation to the time when God's glory will fill the earth as the waters cover the sea. It points to the prayer that Jesus taught his disciples: "Thy kingdom come."

PRAISE AND WORSHIP IN THE PSALMS

It has been said that there are two kinds of worshipers: the "Joy to the World" type and the "Silent Night" type. The latter like solemnity and silence, with matching candles. The former like it noisy, with worship viewed as celebration. The beauty of the Psalms is that they show that there is a place for both types. For those who prefer silence, there are psalms that emphasize meditation and rest (Pss 1:2; 62:5; 131:2). There is also scope for rejoicing and celebration and using all the musical instruments at our disposal (Ps 150). The orchestra in that psalm contrasts with the sole instrument, the lyre, mentioned in Psalm 33, the first psalm to mention the use of instruments in worship. Thus there is space within the psalms for churches that allow only the piano and for those that use a wider range of instruments.

But worship is not all about instruments or styles of worship. It has to do with all of life. That is why a number of worship psalms are written using an acrostic structure based on the sequence of letters in the Hebrew alphabet (see, for example, Ps 25). The acrostic style of composition conveys a sense of wholeness. Just as the psalm covers the whole alphabet from A to Z, so our worship of God should involve the whole of our being. That is why we offer him the best that we have in worship. We don't just play instruments; we do it "skillfully" (Ps 33:3). Moreover, our singing and playing should reflect the kind of God we worship. He loves order and harmony, and so our instruments should be well tuned.

Right theology is important in worship. Our understanding of who God is and what he has done in relationship to the world and to his people affects how we approach him. For example, God loves righteousness (Ps 33:5) and so we who worship him should strive to be righteous (v. 1).

Our understanding of God is closely linked with our experience of God individually and as a people. In the Philippines, we were under foreign powers for a long time, and so we tend to simply imitate the songs handed down to us by our former colonizers. Most of the songs we sing in worship are foreign songs. The emphasis on consumerism has also let to a tendency for writers to compose only songs that will sell.

Although we say music is universal, each culture has its own unique way of expressing itself through music and song. There is thus a great need for us to express our faith using our own songs, composed from the depths of our experience as a people and influenced by the received tradition of the Holy Scriptures. The challenge to us is to sing a "new song" that reflects our own experience of God and presents the truths revealed in the Bible through the lens of our own people's experience, context, culture, and history.

PSALM 34

In Psalm 33 the psalmist exhorts the people to sing "a new song" to the Lord (33:3). The "new song" implies a continuing experience of God's ever new ways of working in the lives of his people (see comments in Psalm 33). There is a "new song" because there is a new experience of God (e.g. deliverance). Psalm 34 affirms this. The psalmist testifies: "This poor man called, and the LORD heard him" (34:6). And this is not something unique to him (v. 17).

But one does not receive deliverance and answers to prayer for one's own sake. These things ought to lead to praise and ministry to others. So the psalmist calls on others to "glorify the LORD with me" (v. 3). He longs for others to experience for themselves . . . to "taste and see that the LORD is good" (v. 8). For it is only when we have personally experienced God that we can teach others about him. This is the emphasis of the first part of Psalm 34.

Flowing from the emphasis on experiencing God, the second half (vv. 9–22) of the psalm focuses on teaching. This section is like the book of Proverbs with its emphasis on teaching and the theme of the fear of the Lord. Yet the instruction flows out of a real encounter with God. It is only those who have encountered God who are able to teach wisdom.

The contribution of Psalm 34 lies in its bringing together the elements of a personal experience of God: praise and teaching. The Hebrew acrostic which the psalmist used to compose Psalm 34 holds these three elements together.[1] Each verse begins with the corresponding letter of the Hebrew alphabet. This not only aids in the learning-teaching process (e.g. memorization), but also provides the psalmist with a way of deriving "order and meaning out of the fragments and confusion of their everyday experience."[2] This is necessary. For as will be seen below, there is an element of tension in the presentation of the life of the righteous: the righteous are "blessed" (v. 8b) but they also experience many afflictions (v. 19).

The superscription in Psalm 34 contains the following brief historical background: "Of David. When he pretended to be insane before Abimelek, who drove him away, and he left." These words are taken from 1 Samuel 21:13. Superscriptions were not originally part of the Psalms. Confusion might have occurred between Achish (v. 14) and Ahimelech (v. 8), resulting in the present

---

1. Psalm 34 is close to Psalm 25 which is also an acrostic psalm.
2. Anthony R. Ceresko, "The ABCs of Wisdom in Psalm 34," *VT* 35, no. 1 (1985): 102.

reading.[3] Nevertheless, the superscription as a whole fits with the contents of the psalm. The superscription relates how David pretended to be insane just so he could escape from danger.[4] This presents David as one who will do everything, even going to the extent of pretending to be mad, just to escape death. This gives us a picture of the grave danger in which David finds himself – one which finds resonance in the contents of Psalm 34 itself.

34:1–8 "TASTE AND SEE THAT THE LORD IS GOOD"

Psalm 34 may be divided into two parts: verses 1–8 and verses 9–22. Both sections end with the phrase "who take refuge in him" (vv. 8, 22). Like Psalm 33, the opening verses may be seen as a counterpart of the Apostle Paul's words in Philippians 4:4: "Rejoice in the Lord always."[5] The word "always" finds emphasis in Psalm 34:1: "I will extol the LORD *at all times*; his praise will always be on my lips" (v. 1). The word "bless" (*barak*) when applied to the Lord means praising, as the parallel word "praise" (v. 1b) indicates. The words "at all times" need not be taken literally. David is not always praising. In fact, in the very next psalm (Ps 35) we hear him lamenting. Even in Psalm 34 the righteous do get "brokenhearted" and "crushed in spirit" (v. 18). The opening verses reflect what Brueggemann calls the "season of new orientation,"[6] when one experiences a new intervention of God.

Psalm 34 is in the "season of new orientation," as the psalmist relates how he "sought the LORD" (v. 4) and "called" (v. 6) and the Lord answered him and heard him (vv. 4, 6). As with psalms of this type, we are not given the details. But the language depicts a situation of grave danger. The psalmist talks about his "fears" (v. 4b) and "troubles" (v. 6). An "angel of the LORD" is needed to encamp around the righteous (v. 7). But in all of these, the psalmist experienced not only God's deliverance but also God's nearness, as reflected in God's hearing of the psalmist's cry (v. 6; see also v. 18).

Having experienced God's answer, he invites others to join him in praising God. Specifically, he invites the *anawim* – the humble (v. 3), the lowly

---

3. Terrien, *The Psalms*, 304.
4. The word translated "madness" comes from a Hebrew word which is close to the word "taste" (Ps 34:8). Someone might have seen the connection between the two in the process of the development of the psalm which led to the bringing together of the passage in 1 Sam 21:13 and Psalm 34.
5. See Kyle Monroe Yates, *Preaching from the Psalms* (New York: Harper, 1948), 77, who relates vv. 1–2 of this psalm to Phil 4:4.
6. Brueggemann, *The Message of the Psalms*.

people whose hope and trust is in the Lord. It is these whom he invites, for he knows they can identify with what he was experiencing. He is also like them, calling himself "poor" (v. 6). He also knows how much they need God's gracious intervention. So he encourages them to "look" to the Lord (v. 5).

What does it mean to look to the Lord?

What the psalmist did – to seek God and cry out to him (vv. 4, 6) – were ways of "looking" to the Lord. Those who look to the Lord are those who are in desperate situations, like that of the Israelites who were bitten by the snakes in Numbers 21. They knew the only thing that would save them was to look up at the bronze snake Moses made. To look up to the Lord implies a position of vulnerability, of dependence. As Psalm 145:15 says, "The eyes of all look to you, and you give them their food at the proper time." This is the position occupied by the marginalized, the poor and the oppressed. Yet the position of weakness can also be a position of power, for it is in weakness and vulnerability that we become acutely aware of the power and abundant provisions available to those who know how to "look" to the Lord. To look to the Lord is another way of saying to "take refuge in him." It is these people who are "blessed" (v. 8b).

Verse 8 contains another exhortation: "Taste and see that the LORD is good." The words "taste and see" reinforce the importance of experiential knowledge when it comes to knowing God. We do not know God only with our minds. We can "taste and see" how good the Lord is. These words also bring to prominence the use of the different senses in the psalm: taste, sight, and hearing.[7] The senses of sight and hearing are applied to the Lord: "The eyes of the Lord are on the righteous, and his ears are attentive to their cry" (v. 15). Verse 6 also mentions that the Lord "heard" the cry of the psalmist. The use of these different senses points to the importance of experiencing the reality of God.

34:9–22 "I WILL TEACH YOU THE FEAR OF THE LORD"

One of the key words in this psalm is the word *good* (*tob*). It occurs four times in the psalm:

> Taste and see that the LORD is good (*tob*) (v. 8);
> those who seek the LORD lack no good thing (*tob*) (v. 10);
> Whoever of you . . . desires to see many good days (*tob*) (v. 12);

---

7. Schaefer, *Psalms*, 85–86.

Turn from evil, and do good (*tob*) (v. 14).

As we can see, the word *good* is used in different ways to speak of the goodness of the Lord (v. 8), the goodness or blessings that come to those who fear the Lord (vv. 10, 12) and goodness in its moral sense: doing good (v. 14).

The experience of God's goodness ought to lead to a life characterized by fear of the Lord. The psalmist exhorts others to fear the Lord. It is this life, according to him, which has a lot of good in it. The psalmist is certain everyone wants the good life. But there is a prerequisite to the good life. One must fear the Lord. To fear the Lord is to show utmost reverence to him, the kind of reverence that finds expression in a life worthy of the Lord (33:18). It involves the proper use of one's tongue (v. 13), saying "no" to evil, doing that which is good and pursuing *shalom* (v. 14).

However, lest we think the life of the righteous is easy and smooth sailing, the psalmist clarifies that the "good" here does not mean all things will turn out for the good. The point is similar to that made by the Apostle Paul in Romans 8:28 where the good is defined not in terms of the blessings of the good life, although it may include them. Rather, the good is to be understood as that which makes us more Christlike. All things work together for good in the sense that all things – including the bad things – that happen to the faithful bring us closer to our Master.

Verses 15–22 make a similar point to that made in Psalm 1, and more. In Psalm 1:6 the psalmist declares that "the LORD watches over the way of the righteous, but the way of the wicked leads to destruction." Similarly, in Psalm 34, "the eyes of the LORD are on the righteous" (v. 15). But "the face of the LORD is against those who do evil" (v. 16). This does not mean the life of the righteous is trouble-free. They do cry (34:17). They do experience what it means to be "brokenhearted" and "crushed in spirit" (v. 18). They have "many troubles" (v. 19). It almost seems to contradict everything that has just been said about the good life of those who fear the Lord. But the psalmist is careful to note that in all of their troubles, "the LORD is close" (v. 18). The Lord also "rescues them" from their troubles. He protects them, making sure that not one of their bones is broken (v. 20). This verse, along with Exodus 12:46, may have been in the mind of the Evangelist when he wrote John 19:36.[8]

Psalm 34, with its stress on experiential knowledge, will resonate with many Filipinos, for we are a people who learn through the concrete. We find

---

8. Kirkpatrick, *The Book of Psalms*, 175.

it difficult to comprehend what is abstract. So we appreciate the instruction to "taste and see that the Lord is good." After all, we often say when we speak of the good life, *masarap ang buhay* (literally, "life is delicious"). The psalmist is telling people to experience God in their depth of their being, to feel his nearness and his goodness.

Another way to appreciate this instruction is to think of it in terms of our communal life. In much of Asia, we have a communal way of life in which everything in our daily experience is interrelated and inclusive. So Filipinos will invite you, or any stranger who happens to be around when they are eating a meal, to come and share their food. "Have you eaten?" is a common greeting of the Chinese. It is a way of inviting others to join us in joyful celebration of a common meal. Combining this communal attitude and our desire for a concrete experience of God's goodness, we too should want to join the psalmist in calling others to join us in tasting and seeing God's goodness would inspire us to call others to "taste and see" his goodness.

The psalmist's words also challenge us: When was the last time you felt God in your life?

PSALM 35

Psalms 34 and 35 "form a pair."[1] Only these two psalms – in the whole of the Psalter – mention the "angel of the LORD." Two additional repetitions are the words "young lion" (34:10; 35:17) and "all his/my bones" (34:20; 35:10).[2] Yet if it is true that the two psalms form a pair, they are a complicated mix. For the overall mood in the two psalms is contrasted. A deep sense of gratitude flowing out in praise fills Psalm 34. By contrast, a "deep vexation of spirit" dominates Psalm 35.[3] However, in spite of differences in mood, the two psalms complement each other. When we read them together we understand better what the psalmist is talking about when he says "many are the afflictions of the righteous" (34:19, ESV). The words "brokenhearted" and "crushed in spirit" take on actual forms (34:18) in Psalm 35. We realize that the "deliverance celebrated in that psalm (Ps 34) is now seen to be not invariably swift or painless, but subject, if God wills, to agonizing delays."[4]

The very structure of Psalm 35 communicates a process, a sense that dealing with one's afflictions takes time. The psalm contains three movements from lament to an expression of certainty, to a vow of thanksgiving (vv. 1–10, 11–18, 19–28). There is a three-fold movement between the elements of lament and praise which has led some scholars to suggest the psalm was originally three separate compositions, which had been brought together at some point into what we now have as Psalm 35. But there is no evidence to support this theory. It is best to take the psalm as "a literary unit, describing the Psalmist's experience from three different angles."[5]

The psalm may have been used as the prayer of a falsely accused individual.[6] The narrative in 1 Samuel 24:12–15 may provide a possible background for it. Here David confronts Saul for unjustly trying to kill him. But ultimately he leaves the matter to God, the one true and righteous judge. Some parts of Psalm 35 also contain links with Jeremiah (Jer 23:12 with v. 6; Jer

---

1. Delitzsch, *Psalms*, 416; see also Derek Kidner, *Psalms 1–72: An Introduction and Commentary on Books I and II of the Psalms* (Leicester: IVP, 1973), 142, who sees the present arrangement of Psalms 34 and 35 as "well placed."
2. Villanueva, *The "Uncertainty of a Hearing*," 175.
3. Delitzsch, *Psalms,* 416.
4. Kidner, *Psalms 1–72*, 142.
5. A. A. Anderson, *The Book of Psalms*, Vol. 1, NCB (London: Oliphants, 1972), 275.
6. Klaus Seybold, *Die Psalmen*, Vol. I/15, Handbuch zum Alten Testament (Tübingen: J.C.B. Mohr, 1996), 145.

18:20, 22 with v. 12).[7] So overall, we have a psalm that reflects turbulent times in the life of an individual.

35:1–10 SAY TO MY SOUL, "I AM YOUR SALVATION"

As noted above, Psalm 35 consists of three parallel sections. Each consists of lament and a vow of thanksgiving in anticipation of God's deliverance. The lament occupies a major portion of each section (vv. 1–8, 11–17, 19–26), with only one or two verses devoted to the thanksgiving part at the end (vv. 10–11, 18, 27–28). Despite the similarity in the structure of each part, we have to read the psalm consecutively, for there is a discernible progression throughout. There is also a different emphasis in each of the three parts.

The first section begins with a series of petitions directed to God (vv. 1–3). Using military metaphors the psalmist asks God to do something about his enemies. Like a small child who is attacked by a bully and goes to his father to tell him what happened, the psalmist goes to God and asks him to "fight against those who fight against me" (v. 1).[8] Something unjust has been done to the psalmist. The Hebrew word, *khinam* ("without cause"), is repeated twice in verse 7. In the following section it becomes clearer what this means (see vv. 12–16 below). The problem is that the psalmist, like a small child, is unable to defend himself. He is weak (v. 10b). And so he comes to the one who is able to "deliver the weak from those too strong for them" (v. 10a).

He asks that those who seek his life be put to shame (v. 4). Using language drawn from Psalm 1, he prays that they "be like chaff before the wind" (v. 5) and that "their path be dark and slippery" (v. 6) with the angel of the LORD as an active agent. A powerful imprecatory prayer! Calvin comments:

> As the chaff is driven with the wind, so also he desires, that, being disquieted by the secret impulse of the angel of the Lord, they may never have rest. The imprecation which follows is even more dreadful, and it is this: that wherever they go they may meet with darkness and slippery places; and that in their doubt and perplexity the angel of the Lord would pursue them. In short, whatever they devise, and to whatever side they turn, he

---

7. Kirkpatrick, *The Book of Psalms*, 176.
8. The Filipino term for this is *pagsusumbong* ("reporting something to someone").

prays that all their counsels and enterprises may come to a disastrous termination.[9]

How are we to understand this imprecation? The second section may provide some idea as to what led the psalmist to pray in such a manner.

35:11–18 "THEY REPAY ME EVIL FOR GOOD"

Unlike in the first section, there is no imprecatory prayer in the present one. Rather, what we have is a description of the pain the psalmist felt as a result of his experience. We have here an illustration of the word "brokenhearted" and "crushed in spirit" from Psalm 34:18. There is a change of imagery from a military metaphor to a court setting. The psalmist complains that "ruthless witnesses come forward" (35:11). He has been falsely accused. He suffers undeservedly (v. 12). He relates how he was treated badly by those who he considered to be his friends or family (vv. 13–14). He had been there to sympathize with them in their difficult times. But when it was his turn to stumble, they not only left him but they also attacked him (vv. 15–16). No wonder in the very next verse he cries out to God: "How long, Lord, will you look on?" (v. 17). He had already prayed and it seemed the Lord was not doing anything. But as in the first section, the second section ends with a vow of thanksgiving (v. 18; cf. vv. 9–10). He continues to hope in God.

35:19–28 DO NOT LET MY ENEMIES REJOICE OVER ME

Part of his hope lies in his continuing prayer. In the last section, he resumes his imprecatory prayers. One of the key words here is the word "rejoice." This rejoicing, however, is the opposite of the rejoicing talked about in Psalm 33. He prays that God not allow his enemies to rejoice over his downfall (v. 19). Instead, he prays: "May all who gloat over my distress be put to shame and confusion" (v. 26). As in the first section, he gives an explanation for his prayer. His enemies are deceitful people (v. 20), powerful bullies who say, "Aha, Aha, With our own eyes we have seen it" (v. 21; cf. v. 25). But the psalmist asserts, "LORD, you have seen this" (v. 22).[10] And in verse 23 his prayer becomes more intense, as reflected in the personal pronoun used in his address to God: "my God and Lord."

---

9. Calvin, *Commentary on the Book of Psalms*, 578.
10. Here the psalmist repeats the word *raah* ("see") which he used in v. 21.

In contrast to his prayer against those who oppress him, he prays that those who fight for his cause might "shout for joy and gladness" (v. 27). He wishes that they would praise the Lord with him and say, "The LORD be exalted who delights in the well-being of his servant." The outcome of his vindication is not that the psalmist will be praised but that God will be praised. It is a prayer that God might vindicate the psalmist according to "your righteousness" (v. 24). The psalm ends with a vow of praise (v. 28).

The application of this psalm to our own context is similar to some of the points made in Psalms 17. The psalm may be understood from the Filipino concept of *pagsusumbong* (see "The Imprecatory Psalms as *Pagsusumbong sa Diyos*," pp. 274–276). Another feature that will certainly find resonance with our experience is the emphasis on God's concern for his people, as shown in the special attention he gives to our tears. We are one of the most emotional, if not *the* most emotional, peoples in the world. We know how to laugh, and we also know how to cry. Sometimes we do these at the same time. Because of our difficult history of colonization and our present experiences of poverty, we are able to identify more freely with those who cry. And for us to see God as one who understands our pain, who himself has shed tears in Jesus – that is really encouraging. It touches us to our very being.

PSALM 36

In this psalm we see two contrasting themes: the way of the wicked (vv. 1–4) and God's steadfast love (vv. 5–9). These two form the main parts of the psalm, concluded by a petition (vv. 10–12). As can be seen, the two themes are very different. To further complicate the matter, the psalm moves abruptly from a reflection on the wicked to the exuberant praise of God's steadfast love. How is the shift possible? How can one see God's light when it is too dark?[1] On the former question, it should be noted that a sudden shift from one theme to a contrasting one is not uncommon. Observe the shift from imprecatory prayer to praise in Psalm 35:8–10 (see also 28:4–6). We can pose a similar question about the vision expressed in Psalm 33:5b: "The earth is full of his unfailing love." How can we say this when the world is inhabited by wicked people? How can the psalmist suddenly exalt God's steadfast love when he had just talked about the wicked ways of evil people and the potential threats they bring to the psalmist? As an answer, Psalm 36 points to God's house, where God's presence dwells and where God's people are welcomed by the generous host himself – God (vv. 8–9). It is as one goes into the presence of God that one receives a new vision to see the world, including the wicked through the eyes of hope (73:17).

The psalm is attributed to David, who is here described as "the servant of the Lord." Elsewhere this title is applied to David only in Psalm 18.

36:1–4 "THERE IS NO FEAR OF GOD BEFORE THEIR EYES"

The first line of the psalm – "I have a message from God in my heart" – is not easy to translate. The first word in Hebrew is a noun which is commonly used in connection to the Lord – "the oracle of the LORD." Literally, the Hebrew line reads: "utterance of transgression to the wicked in his heart."[2] A common way of making sense of the Hebrew is to read the first word as some form of a verb with "transgression" as the subject. Thus, "transgression speaks to the wicked." Here "transgression" is personified. The second line is quoted by Apostle Paul in Romans 3:18 "There is no fear of God before their eyes." The word "fear" is not the word usually associated with the "fear

---

1. The sudden change and the differing themes have led some scholars to regard the psalm as originally two separate compositions brought together by the psalmist. But the return in v. 11 to the earlier theme negates this view.
2. The MT has "in my heart."

of the LORD" but comes closer to the word "dread." The wicked is not even thinking of a relationship with God; as far as he is concerned he has nothing to fear about God.

From the point of view of the wicked, there is nothing wrong with them. Their darkened vision causes them not to see their iniquity (v. 2). Their words are "wicked and deceitful" and "they fail to act wisely or do good" (v. 3). The latter may signify that they used to be good but at one point they stopped. They have decided to take their stand (*yatsab*): "they commit themselves to a sinful course" (v. 4; cf. 1:1).[3] They have decided to take the road that leads to evil. This shows us that though the road to wickedness is broader, it is one which one deliberately chooses to take. There is no accidental in evil. An indication that one is already steeped in evil is when one thinks of evil even when one is supposed to be resting. The godly devote bedtime to meditation on God and his law (63:6; 119:48) but "even on their beds" the wicked "plot evil" (36:4).

36:5–9 "HOW PRECIOUS IS YOUR STEADFAST LOVE, O GOD!"

The psalm suddenly shifts to a reflection on the steadfast love of the Lord (v. 5). If the contrast in Psalm 1 is between the wicked and the righteous, here it is between the wicked and God's steadfast love.[4] It is easy to see the contrast with the first, but not with the second. It seems as if the psalmist is suddenly transported to the Mount of Transfiguration. In stark contrast to the first section, the psalmist meditates on God's steadfast love, faithfulness and righteousness (vv. 5–6). The psalmist proclaims the height ("heavens," "skies"), the depth ("great deep"), and the breadth ("highest mountains") of the three divine qualities. Among the three, God's steadfast love is central, repeated three times (vv. 5, 7, 10). The psalmist describes it as "precious" (v. 7), for it expresses God's providential care for his creatures, both human beings and animals (v. 6). God's steadfast love finds expression in his faithful protection (v. 7b) and abundant provision for his people (v. 8).

How is the psalmist able to see beyond his earlier vision of the wicked people?

The answer lies in the experience which he speaks about in verse 8. Here God is presented as more than just a protector. He is also a generous host

---

3. The word "way" recalls the way of the wicked in Ps 1:1.
4. Craigie, *Psalms 1–50*, 293.

"who provides royal entertainment for his guests."[5] Verse 8 speaks of the "abundance of your house." The verse can be read at various levels.[6] "The metaphor is derived from the sacrificial meal, in which God receives the worshiper at his table (Lev 7:15; Jer 31:14)."[7] It may refer more broadly to the experience of communion in worship or in prayer. Those reading this verse may use it in the practice of spiritual reading, where one not only reads the text but also experiences it. This is important, for it is what we experience that we bring with us into the world. And it is in the presence of God that we receive a new vision to see the world from the perspective of God's steadfast love.

Where he could easily have turned into a cynic or a hopeless individual, the psalmist turns into a person full of hope because he has been with the Lord. The very first words of verse 9 are crucial: "for with you." It is with the Lord that there is hope, for he is the "fountain of life" (v. 9). All that has life in it finds its source in God.[8] And those who have communion with him receive a new vision: "In your light we see light" (v. 9b).

But a "supreme vision cannot continue more than a moment."[9] One needs to go down the Mount of Transfiguration. The psalmist is aware that even with the fresh vision he has received, his situation remains the same. He prays that God might extend his steadfast love to all "those who know you" (v. 10). And in verse 11 his earlier reflection is back. This time he asks God not to allow the wicked to trample on him and drive him away. At this point we can appreciate that his earlier reflections were not mere ideas. He was in the middle of it all, a potential victim of wicked people who do not fear even God (cf. Psalm 12). But this time his prayer is more hopeful. He sees the wicked lying "fallen – thrown down, unable to rise" (v. 12).[10] The first word in verse 12 in Hebrew is important: "There" (*sham*). It is not clear to what or where this word refers to. But we could understand the word as referring to the place where the psalmist and all who know God find resolution to their troubles – in the presence of God . . . in the house of God (v. 8). "There" God welcomes his people to a great feast to enable them to continue on their journey.

---

5. Kirkpatrick, *The Book of Psalms*, 186.
6. Mays, *Psalms*, 157.
7. Kirkpatrick, *The Book of Psalms*, 186.
8. Mays, *Psalms*, 157.
9. Terrien, *The Psalms*, 316.
10. The verb "thrust down" comes from the same Hebrew word used in Ps 35:5, which the psalmist used to speak of the angel of the Lord pushing his enemies down.

In a broken world it is easy to find ourselves discouraged. Even our great efforts towards social and political change bear meager results, if any. As a result many give up. They become burned out, fall by the wayside and take on new, more manageable pursuits. Even those who are not actively involved in transforming society can become cynical as they see the increasing evil around them. Without hope of ever seeing change, they live their lives like zombies, physically moving but already dead.

The psalm provides an alternative way of seeing things. It is one which is not afraid to look at life and the world as it is, with all its wickedness and brokenness. But it does not stop there. For amidst all the brokenness there is another reality at work – God's *kagandahang loob* ("lovingkindness") continues to fill the earth. It takes the eyes of faith, however, to see this in our world. We need to receive what the psalmist experienced when he said, "in your light we see light."

One model of how to apply this in Asia is Mother Teresa. As one belonging to a faith community, she saw her work among the poorest of the poor as an outflow of her worship. No matter how busy they are in serving others, they have time to pause in order to pray. Without the nourishment that flows from our times spent with God, it is impossible to sustain our activities of transforming society.[11]

11. Melba Padilla Maggay, *Transforming Society* (Quezon City, Philippines: Institute for Studies in Asian Church and Culture, 1996), 132–133.

PSALM 37

The issue of the wickedness of evil people just will not go away. In the previous psalm the psalmist was able to transcend the reality of the ways of the wicked through the contemplation of the steadfast love of the Lord. But the reality of evil persists and many who try to live godly lives in the midst of a sinful world will find it difficult not to get discouraged, enraged, or envious of the wicked themselves. The wicked people are powerful, successful and abundant. By contrast, the godly are suffering, and deprived of the basic necessities of life.

How do we encourage God's faithful to remain faithful in the midst of these realities?

Psalm 37 is one response to this. Here the psalmist takes the position of a teacher. The psalm belongs to the wisdom literature; it is close to the book of Proverbs. The stance is the traditional one – the wicked will one day perish while the righteous will shine. Job as well as the writer of Psalm 73 oppose this view. The righteous also suffer, and terribly at that. And in some cases the wicked do not reap what they sow, at least not in this life. So the teaching in Psalm 37 should not be taken as a general truth, applicable to all situations. It should be read along with Job and Psalm 73. At the same time, the reality of which Psalm 37 speaks stands. God's people throughout history have experienced God's provisions even in the midst of famine. They have felt God upholding them in their most trying times. The promise that God will never forsake us nor leave us remains true.

37:1–9 "DO NOT FRET BECAUSE OF THE WICKED"

The psalm begins with an exhortation not to "fret because of those who are evil" (v. 1a). The verb "fret" is repeated three times in the psalm (vv. 1, 7, 8). The word also means "to become angry." It is not clear where the anger is directed. Is it to the Lord? Is the psalmist addressing people who have become deeply affected and hold a grudge against God because the wicked are prospering while the righteous suffer? In Psalm 73 the psalmist confesses he was on the brink of losing his faith when he saw the wicked successful and well. That psalm has a different approach from Psalm 37. The present psalm advises the righteous to refrain from anger (v. 8). In Psalm 73 it is implied that the honest expression of anger towards God is allowed. So the two should be read together. There are times when what we need is advice such as that found in Psalm 37.

The problem of the wicked prospering and the righteous suffering presents one of the biggest challenges in the life of the godly in Israel, and even today. The corollary to this is the temptation to be envious of the wicked. So the psalmist advises the godly not to be "envious of those who do wrong" (v. 1b). Verse 2 provides the supporting argument: "for like grass they will soon wither" (cf. Isa 40:6). Throughout the psalm the words "they will be destroyed" (literally, "cut off") is repeated in reference to the wicked (vv. 9, 22, 28, 34, 38). This is another way of saying that they will perish (v. 20).

In contrast to the wicked, "those who hope in the LORD will inherit the land" (v. 9b). Inheritance of the land is a key motif in this psalm (vv. 9, 11, 22, 34). This can be interpreted as a promise for the future or as a reference to the present.

In the light of this, the psalmist exhorts the godly to "trust in the LORD, and do good" (v. 3; cf. v. 27). Trusting in God does not mean doing nothing. One has to "do good." Faith in God and godly living go together. Trusting in God finds expression in how we live our lives (see topic on "Split level Christianity," pp. 44–45). Often, because of the hardship of life, some are tempted to be envious of the wicked. This opens the door to actual acts of wickedness, for sin starts from within (Mark 7:1–23; see especially verse 22 which mentions envy as one of the sins one should watch out for).

The antidote to envy is to "delight oneself in the LORD" (v. 4). Psalm 1 speaks of the righteous not walking in the ways of the wicked but instead meditating (*hagah*) on the law of the Lord (v. 2). Similarly, in Psalm 37 the righteous meditates (*hagah*) on wisdom (v. 30) and the "law of their God is in their heart" (v. 31). "Delighting in the Lord" means delighting in his Word. Psalm 37:4 is the OT counterpart of Jesus' command in Matthew 6:33, of seeking first the kingdom of God and his righteousness. As we do, the desires of our heart become in tune with what God desires. This explains the second part of Psalm 37:4: "and he will give you the desires of your heart." Some people read verse 4 in such a way that the focus is "the desires of their heart." Therefore, they try to delight in the Lord, so that they will get what they want. How easy it is to turn a verse in the Bible into one for personal interests!

The rest of verses 5–9 militates against this. The exhortations, "Commit your way to the LORD" (v. 5) and "Be still before the LORD and wait patiently for him" (v. 7) put the emphasis on what God wants rather than on what we want (cf. Prov 3:5–6). Those who put their trust in the Lord will not only receive the promise of inheritance of the land (vv. 3, 9); the godly will one day be vindicated. And this will come as clearly as the light of the noonday sun (v. 6).

37:10–40 "WAIT FOR THE LORD"

In the previous section all the main themes of the psalm have already been laid down. Most of the following verses basically reiterate the same points. The purpose is to further strengthen the arguments which the psalmist has made. He does this first by describing the wicked on the one hand and the righteous on the other. The former's success and all their glory are here only for a moment: "A little while, and the wicked will be no more" (v. 10; see also vv. 20, 35–36). The "meek," on the other hand, "will inherit the land" (v. 11); they are here to stay.

The psalmist does not minimize the threats and acts of oppression which the wicked try to inflict on the godly. The former "plot against the righteous" (v. 12). They are bent on destroying the righteous (vv. 14, 32). But the Lord "knows their day is coming" (v. 13). Their days are counted. And God knows when their last day comes.

By contrast, the Lord "knows the days of the blameless" (v. 18, NRSV). The word "know" reflects intimacy which includes concern and care as well as protection and provision. The enemy is powerful (v. 14), but God is there to frustrate their plans (v. 15). The idea of divine retribution is not some kind of an automatic system working apart from God. God is actively involved. He "upholds the righteous" (v. 17b, 24). He takes care of their needs, for he knows they have little. Yet the "little that the righteous person have" is "better than the wealth of many wicked" (v. 16). This can be seen in how the wicked and the righteous approach the issue of possessions. The "wicked borrow and do not repay, but the righteous give generously" (v. 21; cf. v. 26). Even in times of famine, "they will enjoy plenty" (v. 19). The righteous are never forsaken. The psalmist affirms this, based on his personal experience: "I was young and now I am old, yet I have never seen the righteous forsaken or their children begging bread" (v. 25).

The psalmist assures the godly that God will not abandon them (v. 28, 33). So he exhorts them again to "turn from evil, and do good" (v. 27). Envying and getting enraged because of the wicked lead the godly to evil (v. 8b) and make them evil as well. This probably explains why he is admonishing them to "turn from evil." Instead, they should continue to "hope in the

LORD" (v. 34) and to take refuge in him, for the Lord saves those who "take refuge in him" (v. 40).

What will the words, "Those who hope in the LORD will inherit the land," mean for those who do not have land?

The words, "Those who hope in the LORD will inherit the land" will find hopeful listeners among our people. For many years our colonizers took our lands from us. Even after the colonizers had left, the rich continued to grab the lands from the peasants. Land is a burning issue on which the lives of many of our people depend.[1] Many people who live in Manila are called "squatters." They do not have the money to rent a house, let alone buy one. So they build temporary structures on abandoned lots, or even under bridges. When will they ever get a land of their own? It is very easy to promise them that one day they will have a mansion in heaven. Unfortunately, many of them cannot appreciate that because of extreme poverty. Salvation is not only spiritual but also physical and material. Salvation for them means *ginhawa*[2] – the equivalent of *shalom* in our context.

Jesus alludes to the concept of land in his Sermon on the Mount (Matt 5:5). Land need not be restricted to the "land of Israel," or be interpreted metaphorically. Material and spiritual gifts are from the Lord. The meek are those who wait for the Lord (vv. 9, 11, 34). The concept of land has both spiritual and physical meaning. Whether here on earth or in life afterwards, we have the assurance that God will grant the "land" to those who wait upon him and live according to the values of the Kingdom.

---

1. Noriel C. Capulong, "Land, Power and People's Rights in the Old Testament: From a Filipino Theological Perspective," *East Asia Journal of Theology* 2 (1984).
2. Jose De Mesa proposed this idea.

PSALM 38

Psalm 38 is one of the seven psalms traditionally known as psalms of penitence (see Ps 32 above). Delitzsch proposes we read Psalm 38 along with three other psalms of penitence in the following chronological order: Psalms 6, 38, 51, and 32. He views these psalms as David's prayers resulting from his sin in relation to Bathsheba.[1] Although there is no proof that these four psalms originally existed in that order, I think this proposal is a helpful way of relating to them. We can see some progression in these psalms. For instance, in Psalm 38 iniquity is "confessed" (v. 18) but there is no explicit admission that the sin is committed against God. This is found in Psalm 51 (see v. 4). However, Psalm 51 does not contain an assurance of forgiveness. One has to go to Psalm 32:5 to find that.

More generally, Psalm 38 is known as the prayer of a sick person.[2] In the OT, sickness is closely connected to sin and this is the underlying theology behind Psalm 38. This is not the only view in the OT or the whole Bible, as can be seen in the book of Job and the story of the man born blind in John 9. Nevertheless, it is the dominant view. At the same time, it should be noted that the person whose voice we hear in Psalm 38 does not belong to those of the wicked. He is one who pursues what is good (v. 20). He does not fight back but remains silent in the face of attacks from the enemy (vv. 13–14). He leaves his case with God (v. 15).

Psalm 38 shows that even the godly fall into sin (see Ps 32). But they do not stay there. The righteous can't live with their sinful situation; they are "troubled" by it (38:18b). So they confess it (v. 18a). In contrast, the wicked are not disturbed by their evil actions; they even plot evil on their beds (36:4). That is the difference between the wicked and the righteous when they fall into sin.

In Psalm 38 we find the words of Psalm 37:24 beautifully illustrated: "Though he stumbles, he does not fall down, for the LORD gives him support" (NJPS).[3] The righteous may be knocked down, but not knocked out. The very presence of Psalm 38 itself proves this point. The psalmist is obviously down. He is struggling. And yet the psalmist "continues to pray despite his despair

---

1. Delitzsch, *Psalms*, 20.
2. Schaefer, *Psalms*, 95; Mays, *Psalms*, 162–163.
3. The ending of Psalms 37 and 38 are very similar – the words for "help" (*'zr*) and "salvation" (*yeshuah*) occur in 37:40 and 38:22.

. . . And the very act of praying, in the context of perpetual sickness, reveals a deep-seated belief in God, beyond logic and beyond the evidence of the present circumstances."[4] Though God's hand may be "heavy" (v. 2), the fact that the psalmist is able to pray shows that God is sustaining him. Psalm 38 points to the God who upholds godly people who fall.

The superscription contains the words "for the memorial offering"[5] (ESV). The background for this is what is called the *azkara*, the portion of the meal offering which is burned.[6] This is where the word "memorial offering" comes from. The offering serves as a remembrance for the one who made the offering. The title occurs only here and in Psalm 70, a psalm whose last verse is similar to the ending of Psalm 38.

Structurally, the psalm may be divided into three sections, each of which begins with a petition: verses 1–8, 9–14 and 15–22. The psalm begins and ends with a direct petition. But most of the verses are devoted to descriptions of the psalmist's suffering and agony.

38:1–8 "THERE IS NO SOUNDNESS IN MY FLESH"

Psalm 38 is commonly read as a psalm for a sick person. Though the language of the psalm can be taken figuratively, it is more likely that the psalmist is suffering from some kind of illness. Twice he complains, "There is no health in my body" (vv. 3, 7). He speaks of "wounds" which "fester and are loathsome" (v. 5), of his "back filled with searing pain" (v. 7). He is continually in pain (v. 17).

As a psalm for a sick person, Psalm 38 is holistic in its presentation.[7] First, there is the spiritual dimension where sickness is viewed in relation to God. A common view in the OT is that sickness is a result of sin. So when a person is sick, one's natural inclination is to think he or she has committed a sin. Though it is not always the case (e.g. Job), sin is viewed as one of the causes of sickness (Jas 5:16). Second, there is the physical aspect of sickness as reflected in the descriptions above. Third, the psychological dimension is explored. Sickness affects not only the physical but also the mental and

---

4. Craigie, *Psalms 1–50*, 305.
5. The ancient Greek translation of the Old Testament, known as the Septuagint has "for remembrance concerning the Sabbath day."
6. Kirkpatrick, *The Book of Psalms*, 198.
7. Cf. Mays, *Psalms*, 162–163.

emotional aspects of a person. The psalmist openly acknowledges: "I am bowed down" (v. 6) and "I am feeble and utterly crushed" (v. 8).[8]

The psalmist is not only open about what he feels about his condition; he is also honest with God. He acknowledges that his condition is "because of"[9] his sin (v. 3b) and "because of" his foolishness (v. 5b). At the same time he also knows it is "because of" God's "wrath" (v. 3a). Three words are used to describe what the psalmist thinks about God's feeling towards the psalmist: indignation, anger and wrath (vv. 1, 3). Though he believes he deserves his situation, the psalmist nonetheless tells God that his condition is a bit too much. The indignation/anger/wrath is too much to bear. He feels God's hand pressing him down (v. 2b). The previous psalm speaks of the sword of the wicked entering their own hearts as part of God's punishment (37:15). Here, "your arrows have pierced me" (38:2a). Both the wicked and the godly who have sinned are treated in a similar way. The psalmist can only plead for mercy and pray not to be treated in anger.

38:9–14 "MY SIGHING IS NOT HIDDEN FROM YOU"

He could not even ask directly for God to heal him. All he could utter is the following prayer, "All my longings lie open before you, Lord; my sighing is not hidden from you" (v. 9). Maybe he experiences *hiya* ("a feeling of shame") before God which prevents him from asking God directly. The "longing" and the "sighing" are parallel. What he desires is expressed through his sighing. There are times when the pain is just too much and we can hardly utter a prayer. I remember visiting a very sick church member in the hospital. She was in so much pain that she could barely speak. She told me that many times she could not pray because of the pain. Reflecting on this later, I realized that the pain and the sighing that went with it were already prayers.

In verse 10, the psalmist feels he's having palpitations. Life is ebbing away as the very "light has gone from my eyes." In the next verse we understand why. His friends, those who were closest to him, have all left him (v. 11). We have mentioned some of the different aspects of sickness above. We may add here the social dimension. This is probably one of the hardest, especially in a culture that highly values community. To be left alone by those you love is

---

8. Both sentences use the expression, *ad meod* ("to an overwhelming degree" Holladay, *The Psalms*, 265) to speak of an overwhelming experience.
9. The word "because of" from the Hebrew *miffene* is repeated 3x (vv. 3 [2x], 5).

like being left for dead. There is no one to defend you against your enemies. The psalmist's enemies quickly took advantage of his condition (v. 12).

How does the psalmist respond? He does not utter a word in his defense (vv. 13–14). He becomes like a deaf mute, "whose mouth can offer no reply" (v. 14). In silence and humility he bears his enemies' treachery (v. 12). And he turns to the Lord.

38:15–22 "IT IS FOR YOU, O LORD, THAT I WAIT"

The progression of how the psalmist addresses God is interesting. In verse 1, he calls him "Lord" (the Hebrew name for God – *Yahweh*). Then in verse 9, he calls him "Lord" (*adonay*). In verse 15, he repeats the title "Lord" (*Yahweh*), and adds "my God" (cf. v. 21). There is a movement towards intimacy. Sickness has a way of bringing people closer to God.

It also has a way of strengthening one's faith and trust in God, as one realizes that God is the only one who can be truly relied upon. Faith and trust in God becomes more evident in the midst of the threats of the enemies, whose triumph appears already certain (v. 16) and who, unlike the psalmist, are mighty (v. 19).[10] The psalmist feels he is about to fall (v. 17). And so he prays, "do not let them gloat or exalt themselves over me" (v. 16), and finally confesses his sins (v. 18; cf. 32:5). But unlike in Psalm 32, there is no explicit resolution. Realizing that his strength has already failed (*azab*) him (v. 10), and that his companions have distanced themselves (*rāḥoq*) from him (v. 11), he prays: "Do not forsake (*azab*) me . . . do not be far (*rakhoq*) from me, my God" (v. 21). The psalm ends with a sense of urgency and without clear resolution: "Come quickly to help me, my Lord and my Savior" (v. 22).[11]

As a psalm for the sick, Psalm 38 is an important psalm for our time. There is an increasing realization in recent years that sickness or illness is more than just about the physical. It involves the emotional, psychological, social, and spiritual. Especially in a society that highly values community and which remains very religious, the social and spiritual aspects become primary. The belief that sickness is due to one's sin persists among our people even today. As such, Psalm 38 provides a guide in presenting a holistic view of sickness. In addition to providing a broader perspective to sickness, Psalm

---

10. One possible reading of v. 19 in Hebrew is "my enemies are healthy and strong," following the MT (*hayyim*). But many follow the proposal to read *khayyim* as *khinnam* ("without cause").
11. D. Erbele-Küster, *Lesen als Akt der Betens,* vol. 87, WMANT (Neukirchen-Vluyn: Neukirchener, 2001), 157, calls Psalm 38, "the open petition structure."

38 also teaches the importance of expressing pain, weakness, the fear of abandonment and all the emotions we feel when we are sick but often try to hide for fear of being rejected. The good news is that we can be honest with God about what we are going through and be assured he is listening. The presence of Psalm 38 is a testimony to this. The fact that Psalm 38 became part of the liturgy in the temple also means that this psalm was used in the congregation. It is okay to admit we are down when we are sick.

PSALM 39

In their present arrangement, Psalms 38 and 39 represent a moving away from the views of Psalm 37. If Psalm 37 is the one psalm that represents the traditional view – the belief which says that the wicked will perish but the righteous will be blessed – then Psalm 39 represents the extreme end of that tradition. Psalm 37 declares that the wicked will be destroyed ("cut off") but the righteous will "inherit the land" (v. 9). Psalm 38 in this case serves as a transition, for here the godly is sick and dying – the opposite of the expectation in Psalm 37 – but at least the psalmist's faith remains unflinching. He remains quiet and does not seek to defend himself before his enemies. Instead, he leaves the matter to God.

With Psalm 39, it is the opposite. Though at first the psalmist tries to be silent, the more he tries, the more he struggles. So he decides to speak out. His words reflect a melancholic intensity. His problem does not concern the issue of why the wicked prosper. Nor does he struggle with sickness. His problem is existential in nature, with the transitory nature of human existence and the feeling that life is not just short, it is simply nothing before God. Though there is a glimmer of hope in the middle of the psalm, the overall tone is one of darkness. Indeed, the psalm ends with one of the most disturbing words in the Psalter – get lost God![1]

How are we to read this psalm?

One common tendency is to try to sanitize the disturbing language of the psalm by explaining away the negative elements in it. The alternative is to read the psalm as a negative psalm, expressing a sense of hopelessness. In the case of the latter, if the psalm is disturbing, it is because it is meant to disturb. The very structure of the psalm reflects this purpose. The psalm has a triadic structure, which, according to Alter, is "a formal expression of a powerful psychological tension. Whereas the dyadic line encourages balance and symmetry, the addition of a third verset is often used to introduce an element of surprise or to destabilize what has gone before it."[2] [For an example of a triadic structure, see v. 12 below]. The psalm is disturbing because the

---

1. J. Clinton McCann, Jr., "Get lost, God! A sermon on Psalm 39," *Journal for Preachers* 31, no. 4 (2008): 21–23.
2. Alter, *The Book of Psalms*, 137.

common expectation is not met. Erbele-Küster calls this psalm an "unheard prayer/petition."[3]

For those looking for some kind of hope in the psalm, it is found in the way the psalm is composed – the psalm is a reflection on life in general, composed as a prayer. Herein lies its hope. No matter how dark and hopeless or melancholic the viewpoint of the psalm may be, it remains a prayer. This tells us that even the contradictions and hopelessness have a place in the presence of God. And the presence of a psalm like this testifies to the God who has to do not only with the positive in life but also with all those things we consider negative. As Exum puts it: "the Bible's uncompromising portrayal of reality as embracing dissolution and despair as well as resolution and repair is the source of its extraordinary narrative range and power. Any less expansive, multifaceted and honest representation of accumulated experience and wisdom would be inadequate and inauthentic."[4]

39:1–3 "I WILL PUT A MUZZLE ON MY MOUTH"

The first three verses are enveloped by the word "tongue" (vv. 1, 3). The psalmist resolves to guard his "ways" that he might not sin with his tongue. It's not clear what sin is being referred to here. In the next line the psalmist employs the metaphor of a muzzle as a means of control to make sure he does not make a slip with his tongue while in the presence of the wicked. But even with this detail, the nature of the specific sin remains ambiguous. Maybe this has to do with the concern not to say anything against God which might lead others to doubt or question God. But as will be seen below, the psalmist says things to God which can easily be viewed as offending to God.

The psalmist was successful at first. He was able to hold his peace (v. 2). But as in the case of Jeremiah, the more he becomes quiet the more he is disturbed. It becomes like fire within him which he cannot contain. He has no choice but to break his earlier resolve to be silent. The remaining verses of the psalm represent the content of his words.

The psalmist addresses his words to God in the form of a prayer, not to the wicked people. This is important. He does not speak to the wicked, nor to the righteous people who may be among his audience. Instead, he utters a prayer. However, the prayer is not the common type of prayer that we have

---

3. Dorothea Erbele-Küster, *Lesen Als Akt Der Betens*, 155.
4. Cheryl J. Exum, *Tragedy and Biblical Narrative: Arrows of the Almighty* (Cambridge: Cambridge University Press, 1992), 152.

known in the preceding psalms. It is closest to a prayer of lament, specifically the type of lament which is directed to God, known as complaint against God. One example is the famous line in Psalm 22:1, "My God, my God, why have you forsaken me?" The difference is that unlike in Psalm 22 which moves on to praise, there is no resolution here. Like Psalm 88, Psalm 39 ends in darkness. Moreover, unlike the other types of lament whose subjects are the enemies or personal suffering (e.g. sickness), the concern in Psalm 39 is existential. It has to do with the question of the transitory nature of human existence and the deep conviction that everything is *hebel* ("breath"), without substance or meaning.[5]

39:4–6 "LET ME KNOW MY END"

The psalmist prays: "Show me, Lord, my life's end" (v. 4). By itself this can be taken to mean, let me die. But the last line of verse 4 indicates that this is a request to make him realize "how fleeting my life is." The psalmist's own reflections in the next two verses show his prayer has been answered. He realizes that "everyone is but a breath" (v. 5). Though "a man seems to stand firm and tall, he is mere breath."[6] People may make a noise for a while and "heap up" for themselves but they do not know what others will do with what they have acquired when they have gone (Luke 12:15–21).

At the same time, the verses above betray a feeling that the psalmist takes issue with the way life has been designed by God. He complains to God: "You have made my days a mere handbreadth; the span of my years is as nothing before you" (v. 5). This statement "amounts to an assault against the divine attitude vis-à-vis human beings."[7]

39:7–11 "MY HOPE IS IN YOU"

But what makes the psalmist different from people who have no faith in God is that even though he may hurl invectives at God, he never lets go of God (22:1).[8] Thus in the next verse, the psalmist declares, "My hope is in you"

---

5. For a discussion of the meaning of the word *hebel*, see Michael V. Fox, *A Time to Tear Down and a Time to Build Up: A Rereading of Ecclesiastes*, 10, 28–31.
6. Alter, *The Book of Psalms*, 138.
7. Terrien, *The Psalms*, 332.
8. Though the psalmist cries out, "Why have you forsaken me?" in Psalm 22, he continues to call him "my God."

(v. 7).[9] This statement stands in the middle of the psalm, which further adds to its importance. It is like the famous passage in the middle of the book of Lamentations: 3:22–23. This verse stands in the midst of the laments over the suffering because of the destruction of Jerusalem.

The statement of hope leads to a prayer of deliverance from transgressions and from the "scorn of fools" (v. 8). Earlier, the presence of the wicked around him makes him silent. So here, mention of the "fool" creates the same reaction. The psalmist is silent (vv. 2, 9). But his silence here is for a different reason. He acknowledges that whatever has befallen him is the work of God himself (v. 9b). His resolve to be silent, therefore, is a sign of submission.

But as with his first resolve, he again fails to become silent. He complains that he is "overcome by the blow of your hand" (v. 10; cf. 38:2). He feels that the way God disciplines his people is too harsh: "you consume their wealth like a moth" (v. 11). Outside of the covenant relationship we might regard this as out of place and irreverent. But the psalmist can speak like this to God because of his intimacy with him, as seen in the next verse.

39:12–13 "HEAR MY PRAYER, O LORD"

Employing a triadic structure, the psalmist prays (v. 12):

Hear my prayer, O LORD,
Listen to my cry for help;
Do not be deaf to my weeping.

In this kind of construction the third line stands out. The first two lines are clearly parallel. But the third line is different. With the first two lines you can hear a sound – the prayer and cry are audible – but tears do not have a sound in them (see last line). They are a powerful expression of what is within a person's heart. Kirkpatrick mentions that in Rabbinic tradition, "there are three kinds of supplication, each superior to the other; prayer, crying, and tears. Prayer is made in silence, crying with a loud voice, but tears surpass all."[10] The Rabbinic saying goes like this: "There is no door through which tears do not pass," and "The gates of tears are never locked."[11]

The motivation for this petition is given in verse 12c: "I dwell with you as a foreigner, a stranger, as all my ancestors were." The view by ancient Hebrews

---

9. Verse 7 is introduced by the climactic transition, *weattah* ("and now").
10. Kirkpatrick, *The Book of Psalms*, 206–207.
11. Ibid., 207.

is that they were resident aliens, mere sojourners in the land owned by God (Lev 25:23; cf. Gen 23:4). Later on the Israelites took possession of the land. But the psalmist does not identify with those who have taken possession of the land. Psalm 37 emphasizes that the righteous will inherit the land. How the sentiment in Psalm 39 differs! Here the psalmist is not even thinking of possessing the land. He is merely a resident alien. But on the basis of God's command to show compassion to resident aliens, he humbly comes to God and prays that God might pay attention to his tears.

The last verse is difficult to take. In many of the lament psalms, God's presence is sought, and his absence is lamented. There is joy in his presence. But here the psalmist asks God to "look away from me" (v. 13). How should we understand this verse? One way to explain this verse is through the Filipino concept of *pagtatampo*.

Psalm 39 may be understood from the Filipino concept of *pagtatampo*. *Pagtatampo* is an indirect way of expressing one's feelings of hurt against someone who is close to you.[12] An important component of *pagtatampo* is the need to be alone (*mapag-isa*) as an expression of the feelings of hurt. Feelings of *pagtatampo* (hurt) against God may arise from tragic experiences. (For more discussion, see topic on "Lament as *Pagtatampo sa Diyos*," pp. 137–138).

The importance of Psalm 39 lies in the fact that God allowed these words to be preserved even though they are disturbing and shocking. It points to the God who not only understands the struggles of his creatures but allows them to express their frustrations, sense of hopelessness, questions, and even their feelings of *pagtatampo* (hurt). There is room in the presence of God for these experiences. Psalm 39 is much needed today, when there is only room for the positive, where questions and struggles are often stifled or silenced for fear of disturbing somebody else's faith. We would rather keep the peace than be honest about what we truly feel or see. We forget that faith is strengthened through doubt.[13]

---

12. Melba Padilla Maggay, *Pahiwatig: Kagawiang Pangkomunikasyon ng Filipino*, 138.
13. See Robert Davidson, *The Courage to Doubt*.

PSALM 40

Psalm 40 may be seen as providing some answer to Psalm 39. In the latter, the psalmist prayed, "listen to my cry for help (*shavah*)" (39:12). The answer is given in Psalm 40:1, as the psalmist declares: "I waited patiently for the LORD . . . and heard my cry (*shavah*)." The verb, "wait" (*qavah*), which occurs at the center of the previous psalm, also features prominently in Psalm 40 (39:7; 40:1).

But the element of tension at the end of Psalm 39 persists even with the answer in Psalm 40. For even though Psalm 40 begins with thanksgiving, it nevertheless ends with lament. The psalm consists of two main parts: thanksgiving (vv. 1–10) and lament (vv. 11–17). Lament psalms usually begin with complaint and petition and end with some form of resolution (see Pss 3, 13). But like Psalms 9/10 and 27, the present psalm moves the opposite direction, from thanksgiving to lament, thus continuing the tension in the previous psalm.

What makes Psalm 40 unique is that the second half of the psalm actually appears as a separate psalm. Verses 13–17 of Psalm 40 are basically the same as Psalm 70.[1] This is not the first time we have seen a link between Psalm 70 and another psalm. Psalm 38 has the same superscription as Psalm 70. Both psalms also end in a similar way. In the case of Psalm 40 and Psalm 70, there are two possibilities: either the author of Psalm 40 incorporated another psalm, that is, Psalm 70 into his composition, or someone took the second half of Psalm 40 and used it as a separate psalm. Because we have no way of knowing for certain which one borrowed from whom, both are possible. Either way, the element of tension remains. For in the case of the former, why would one place the lament after the thanksgiving instead of the other way around? Here we have a case of deliberate re-ordering of the elements of lament and praise for the purpose of highlighting the elements of ambiguity, question, and tension. If the latter, it is interesting to wonder why one would take the lament part and turn it into a separate lament. We usually take the more positive bits in a song and leave out the more negative ones.

---

1. One of the differences is the use of *elohim* in Psalm 70 instead of *Yahweh* for the name of God. But this is explained as due to the incorporation of Psalm 70 into what is called the elohistic part of the Psalter.

40:1–12 "HE HEARD MY CRY"

The psalmist begins with a testimony of how the Lord answered his cry after he "waited patiently for the LORD" (v. 1a). The images of a "slimy pit" and "mud and mire" (v. 2) depict the psalmist's experience. The readers are invited to ponder upon these images to appreciate what the Lord has done. It is out of these that the Lord drew him up and set his feet "on a rock" (v. 2). But before that, the psalmist had to learn to "wait," which is an expression of one's trust in the Lord, and never easy. For the temptation to put one's trust in people or in other gods is ever present (v 4b).

As a result of what God has done, the psalmist sings a "new song" (v. 3). This arises out of his experience of God. There is a new song because God has acted afresh in the lives of his people (see Ps 33). This also puts the experience of deliverance in proper perspective. The salvation experienced is not for the individual to enjoy but something that should be shared with the community. Thus the shift from "I" to "our" God (v. 3), from the individual to the "many" who will trust in the Lord as a result of what the psalmist experienced and that he shares with them.

In verse 5 the psalmist repeats the word "many," this time as a reference to the many wondrous deeds that the Lord does for his people. He speaks not only of God's deeds but also of his "thoughts toward us" (v. 5, NRSV). How comforting it is to know we are in God's thoughts. He has plans for us. As the psalmist declares, those who trust in the Lord are blessed. Verses 3–5 form the following structure:

"Many (*rab*) will . . . put their trust in him" (v. 3).
"Blessed is the one who trusts in the LORD" (v. 4).
"Many (*rab*), LORD my God, are the wonders you have done" (v. 5).

The title of a hymn aptly summarizes the emphasis of the present verses: "Trust and obey." The emphasis of the preceding verses (vv. 3–5) is on trust while the following verses (vv. 6–8) focus on obedience. In verse 6 we are reminded of the story of Saul's rejection as king because of his decision to offer the sacrifices himself rather than obeying the instructions of the prophet Samuel: "Sacrifice and offering you did not desire" (v. 6). To obey is better than to offer sacrifice. The psalmist acknowledges that it is God who has opened his ear. Literally, the Hebrew reads, "You have dug ears for me" (v. 6). This tells us that the act of obedience is also the work of God. It is God who gives us an open ear, so we can obey. We need this, for we are by nature

217

hard-headed or "stiff-necked." The statement also reminds us of the necessity of pain, through which we learn to obey. For in the end, what God wants is not animal sacrifices but our life (v. 7). What God wants is a heart that prays: "I desire to do your will, my God; your law (*torah*) is within my heart" (v. 8).[2]

Verses 9–10 serve as a transition to the petition in verses 11 and following. The psalmist asserts he has not restrained his lips but has proclaimed before the great assembly what God has done (v. 9). So he prays, "Do not withhold your mercy from me" (v. 11).[3] It is with fervency that he implores God, because at present he finds himself encompassed by "troubles without number" (v. 12).

40:13–17 "COME QUICKLY LORD, TO HELP ME"

Here we see a contrast with the first part of the psalm. If earlier he testified how God had lifted him up from the pit (v. 2), here he finds himself again engulfed by troubles. If formerly he could not count the many blessings God had given, now he cannot count his problems: "troubles without number surround me" (v. 12). As a result he can hardly see: "my sins have overtaken me, and I cannot see" (v. 12). He no longer knows how he'll be able to continue, or what to say next. Thankfully, he finds a prayer of lament.[4] He incorporates Psalm 70 in order to pour out his heart to God.[5]

For further analysis of verses 13–17, see Psalm 70. Psalm 40 adds the verb "be pleased" at the beginning of verse 13. This is probably a creative attempt to relate Psalm 70 with the earlier part of Psalm 40. The verb "be pleased" is similar to the noun "will" (v. 8), a word which is used to refer to that which pleases God. Since the psalmist desires to do what pleases God, he prays that God might "be pleased to save me" (v. 13). In verse 17b there is a significant change with Psalm 70. The latter has "hasten to me, O God." Here we have "the Lord takes thought for me" (40:17, ESV). Again, the change is made to create a link with the first half of the psalm, specifically with verse 5,

---

2. The word *torah* along with the expression "happy are those" (v. 4) further supports the allusion to Psalm 1.

3. The words "restrain" (v. 9) and "withhold" (v. 11) come from the same Hebrew word *kala*. The psalmist repeats the words "steadfast love" and "faithfulness" from v. 10.

4. Weiser, *The Psalms*, 340, explains: "The fact that the worshiper is completely cast down and incapable of seeing things clearly on account of his sins may also explain why he makes use in vv. 13–17 [14–18] of a current liturgical text which appeared to him appropriate to his personal circumstances and suitable for the purpose of working out his supplication in more detail."

5. Another psalm which have also been joined together is Psalm 108 which is made up of Pss 57:8–12 and 60:7–14.

which speaks of God's "thoughts toward us." The psalmist trusts that God is thinking about him. That is why he is able to live with the tension that marks the life of faith. This tension is reflected in the overall structure of the psalm which moves in an unusual way from thanksgiving to lament. The ending of the psalm also stands in tension with the opening words: "You are my God, do not delay" (v. 17). Waiting as an act of trusting God is not easy after all.[6]

The importance of Psalm 40 lies in its realistic portrayal of the life of faith. By juxtaposing thanksgiving and lament, the psalmist reminds us that "human certainty is never absolute and is always open to God's gracious turning presence."[7] There is always uncertainty even in our certainties. Waiting is never easy but involves constant trust in God. Struggles are part of the journey and it is those who continue to put their trust in God, in spite of the many contrary options, who are indeed blessed.

6. Anderson, *The Book of Psalms*, 314–315.
7. Dorothea Erbele-Küster, *Lesen Als Akt Der Betens*, 154, translation mine.

PSALM 41

Canonically, the place of Psalm 41 is significant. It is the last psalm in Book 1.[1] Like the first two psalms (Pss 1:1; 2:12), the last two psalms in Book 1 also contain a beatitude (40:4; 41:1). Psalms 1 and 41 both begin with a beatitude. From Psalms 1 and 2 we learn that it is those who live righteous lives (1:2), delight in God's law (1:2) and take refuge in God (2:12) who are blessed or "happy." The beatitude is usually attributed to those who trust in the Lord (33:12; 34:8; 40:4; 84:12; 146:5). In Psalm 41 the beatitude is attributed for the first time to those who show concern for the poor: "Blessed is the one who considers the poor" (v. 1, ESV).

This addition is important. It reminds us that righteous living and meditation on the law should lead to reaching out to others, especially those who are poor and needy. The Torah itself shows God's concern for the poor (Exod 22:25; 23:3, 6; Lev 14:21; Deut 15:11). Spirituality and moral living are incomplete without a deep concern for the poor which issues in concrete actions towards the alleviation of their poverty. Conversely, the ministry of reaching out to others is not separate from meditation and worship. The former is actually an outflow of the latter. As we remain still in the presence of the Lord, we receive renewed strength and insight to enable us to continue in our ministry to others.

Paradoxically, the beatitude in Psalm 41 is followed by a lament (vv. 4ff.). The beatitude is often used for purposes of instruction. But here it is used to introduce the lament.[2] This reminds us that the blessed life is not a life without challenges. The righteous have many afflictions (34:19). In Psalm 41, the psalmist suffers from illness, falls into sin (41:4), and gets attacked by his enemies (41:5–8). Most painful of all, even his friend turns against him (v. 9). Fortunately, what makes the righteous blessed is not just because they are following God, but because they have someone to go to whenever they are besieged by life's troubles.

The psalm begins with a beatitude (vv. 1–3), followed by lament (vv. 4–12), and ends with a doxology (v. 13).

---

1. Those who put together the Psalter have divided it into five books, modelled on the five books of the Law. See Introduction for further discussion.
2. Mays, *Psalms*, 171.

41:1–3 "BLESSED IS THE ONE WHO CONSIDERS THE POOR"

The opening words of the psalm – "happy are those" – come from the Hebrew word *ashre* which literally means "happiness of." The word introduces a blessing.[3] As such, it reflects what the psalmist considers to be valuable. The beatitude indicates a particular way of viewing life, specifically the things that are important. As mentioned above, the beatitude is associated with righteous living and meditation on God's law. Elsewhere in the Psalter it is linked with the experience of forgiveness (32:1–2), the privilege of living in God's holy place (65:5), reception of divine discipline (94:12), and the blessings of children (127:5).

In Psalm 41, the beatitude is applied to a concern for the poor: "Blessed is the one who considers the poor" (v. 1). The word translated "consider" (*maskil*) is usually used to refer to understanding, but it can also mean "to see or look."[4] This is important, for often when we are confronted with a poor person, or for instance with a beggar who knocks at our door, we do not usually at look them in the eye. It's as if we do not want to see them. But the Lord "sees" them, which means he is deeply concerned for them. That is why those who consider them are blessed indeed. They are promised deliverance" in times of trouble" (v. 1) as well as protection and preservation (v. 2a). When they become sick the Lord is there to sustain them and bring healing (v. 3).

41:4–12 "HAVE MERCY ON ME, LORD"

However, the experience of the psalmist is the opposite of the beatitude. For instead of healing and deliverance there is sickness and oppression from the enemy. The present section is enveloped by the petition, "have mercy on me" (vv. 4, 10). The psalmist finds himself afflicted with sickness, which he acknowledges as due to his sin (v. 4). The common view at that time was that sickness was associated with sin. But the psalmist's suffering is not due to his sin alone. His enemies want to destroy him (v. 5) and use evil means to accomplish their goal. The translation in the NIV is not clear here. Speaking falsely (literally, "empty words") (v. 6) is a "euphemism for sorcery and deeds of witchcraft."[5] And the verb "whisper together" (v. 7) is used elsewhere to refer to "snake charmers (cf. Eccl 10:11; Isa 26:16)."[6] Moreover, in verse 8,

3. Holladay, *The Psalms*, 31.
4. Alter, *The Book of Psalms*, 145.
5. Terrien, *The Psalms*, 345.
6. Ibid.

some kind of curse has been unleashed on him: "An evil spell is cast upon him" (NEB). Interestingly, the NT sees Psalm 41 (v. 9) as fulfilled in the act of Judas (John 13:18). Judas' betrayal of Jesus is narrated in the Gospel of Luke as something that is closely associated with Satan (Luke 22:3) – a time when the "power of darkness" takes over (Luke 22:53).

In a culture where the reality of the existence of the spirit world is acknowledged and assumed, Psalm 41 will prove to be an important psalm. The practice of sorcery and witchcraft persists even today. Psalm 41 provides a window to the spirit world of the psalmist where sorcerers and the practice of inflicting curses on one's enemies are a reality (see v. 6 above). This helps us see the power of God all the more. It is no coincidence that the psalm begins with a note on poverty. The experience of poverty makes one realize one's powerlessness. And therefore access to power, especially spiritual in nature, becomes a matter of life and death. At a time when there were not much medicines available for the various illnesses as they are today, one relies only on supernatural powers. Those who belong to the darkness use this power to inflict. That is why God's people need the protective power of God to deliver them and to assist them in defeating the works of the Enemy.

His situation led the psalmist to pray: "Raise me up, that I may repay them" (v. 10b). Christians will find this prayer disturbing.[7] This contradicts the NT teaching in Romans 12:19, which finds an OT counterpart in Proverbs 20:22: "Do not say, 'I'll pay you back for this wrong!' Wait for the LORD, and he will avenge you." But the difference between these two passages is that in the latter, participation of the individual is implied. In Psalm 41 "the supplicant asks Yahweh to assist him to repay his enemies."[8] Understood within the context of the preceding verses, the prayer asks God to empower him so that he will be able to fight his enemies. This could be understood spiritually, in terms of spiritual warfare.

A number of the lament psalms end with a statement of assurance where the psalmist declares he has received God's answer (see e.g. 6:8–9). The events referred to in verses 11–12 may be understood as having already taken place (see NRSV) or as presently happening (see NIV), or to the future. The Hebrew can be rendered in any of these possibilities. Often in the psalms of lament the actual deliverance has not yet occurred, but a transformation has already taken place within the psalmist as a result of pouring out his heart to God.

---

7. Schaefer calls it an "indecent desire for vengeance," 104.
8. Philip J. Nel, "*slm*," in *NIDOTTE*, 4:130.

The last verse contains a doxology which does not relate to Psalm 41. It serves as the ending of Book 1 of the Psalter. The succeeding "Books" each have their own doxologies, with Psalm 150 functioning as the climax not only of Book 5 but of the whole Psalter.

PSALMS 42–43

We usually associate being close to God with experiences of consolation (e.g. peace and joy). But as St. John of the Cross reminds us in his book, *The Dark Night of the Soul*, when God wants to bring his beloved child into deeper intimacy with him, he brings him into the "dark night."[1] Like a parent trying to train her child to walk, God allows his children to experience dryness and darkness. St. John speaks of two dark nights: the dark night of the senses and the dark night of the spirit. The key words for these two dark nights are "aridity" and "darkness" respectively. The former is represented in Psalm 42–43, with the image of a deer longing for water. The latter is illustrated in Psalm 88, with its emphasis on darkness.[2]

All throughout history God's people have experienced what St. John of the Cross calls "the dark night of the soul."[3] Psalm 42–43 shows that this experience is part of what it means to grow in one's relationship with God. Not every experience of being down is wrong;[4] it could be an indication of a deepening relationship with God. Moreover, Psalm 42–43 provides a model for surviving our own dark nights. Finally the psalm gives us the words of a prayer that we could utter to God when we just cannot find our way.

Psalms 42 and 43, the first two psalms in Book 2 of the Psalter, form one psalm. This can be seen in the occurrence of the same refrain in Psalm 42:5, 11; and 43:5, and the absence of a superscription in Psalm 43.[5]

In the superscription to Psalm 42, the psalms is referred to as a "maskil." A "maskil" is a contemplative poem or a cultic song. The present psalm (as well as Pss 44–49, 84–85, and 87–88) is attributed to the "Sons of Korah."[6] However, the Hebrew preposition translated "of" is ambiguous. It could also mean "to" or "for," among other possibilities (see Introduction). So we do not know whether they are the composers of these psalms. The sentiments

---

1. St. John of the Cross, *Dark Night of the Soul* (Mineola, NY: Dover Publications, 2003).
2. Psalm 88 is probably the darkest psalm; it actually ends with the word darkness in Hebrew.
3. See Bruce A. Demarest, *Seasons of the Soul: Stages of Spiritual Development* (Downers Grove: IVP, 2009), 84–87, for examples of people throughout history who have gone through the dark night of the soul.
4. Some experiences of being down could be an indication of the presence of evil or sin in our lives which we need to deal with.
5. Psalm 43 and 71 are the only two psalms in Book 2 which do not have a superscription.
6. The Sons of Korah were Levites who belonged to a family of singers associated with music in the temple (1 Chr 6:1, 7, 16). They were descended from the tribe of Levi through Kohath (1 Chr 6:22).

expressed (e.g. "Why have you forgotten me?" [42:9; cf. 43:2]) are similar to some of the psalms of lament attributed to David (see Ps 22).

The structure of the psalm is easy to discern. Like a typical modern song, Psalm 42–43 contains a refrain (42:5, 11, and 43:5), each time preceded by a "stanza." There are three stanzas: 42:1-4; 6-10; 43:1-4.

42:1–5 "MY SOUL LONGS FOR YOU, O GOD"

Psalm 42–43 is the only psalm which begins with a comparison or simile.[7] The simile identifies the main theme of the psalm, the psalmists deep longing for God: "As the deer pants for streams of water, so my soul pants for you, my God" (v. 1). He likens his longing for God to a deer searching in vain for water in one of the "dry river beds that flow only in winter."[8] The image is a powerful one. Terrien comments: "Anyone who has heard the bellowing of stags dying of thirst on the hills of Upper Galilee during late summer drought must feel in his instinctual self the haunting force of the poet's imagery."[9]

The psalmist "thirsts for God" (v. 2). But like stags dying of thirst, he cannot find the water he is searching for. Instead of water, all he has is "tears" (v. 3). He longs to go[10] into the place where God dwells. He remembers the times when he used to join the throng that went to the house of God (v. 4). But in contrast with the "shouts of joy and praise" that he heard in those gatherings, he now hears a taunting: "Where is your God?" (v. 3b). As a result, he is "downcast" (v. 5). The emphasis on the first appearance of the refrain falls on this note of the psalmist's depression. "Why, my soul, are you downcast?" he asks. This kind of "soul-talk" is not uncommon in the Psalms (see 103:1; 116:7). He tells himself to hope in God, but in the next verse, he admits: "My soul is downcast within me" (v. 6). The repetition of the word "soul" is significant. The word is mentioned twice earlier (vv. 1, 2) to speak of the psalmist's deep longing for God. But here we see that the soul that deeply longs for God is the soul that is downcast.

---

7. Luis Alonso Schökel, "The Poetic Structure of Psalm 42–43," *JSOT* 1, no. 1 (1976): 5.
8. John Goldingay, *Songs from a Strange Land: Psalms 42–51* (Downers Grove: IVP, 1978), 27.
9. Terrien, *The Psalms*, 351.
10. The word "go" is significant; it identifies what the psalmist longs for—to go to the temple and worship. The word is repeated in 43:4.

42:6–11 "MY SOUL IS DOWNCAST"

The confession, "My soul is downcast" is important. It's as if the psalmist is telling us: "You know what? I tried to encourage myself. But to be honest about it, I'm still down." We again encounter the same courageous and honest confession in the Garden of Gethsemane, where Jesus tells his disciples, "My soul is overwhelmed with sorrow to the point of death" (Matt 26:38). The translation "overwhelmed with sorrow" comes from the same Greek word in the Septuagint translation of Psalm 42:5. Kirkpatrick is of the opinion that the "resemblance of our Lord's words in Gethsemane . . . to the Septuagint's rendering of this verse . . . suggests this Psalm may have been in his mind at the time; the more so as he appears to use the words of verse 6, which the Septuagint renders, *My soul is troubled* . . . in a similar connection upon another occasion (John 12:27)."[11] It is also interesting that Jesus repeats his prayer three times in Gethsemane, in the same way that the psalmist repeats the refrain three times in Psalm 42–43 (42:5, 11; 43:5). Both the prayer and the refrain express struggle and trust in God.[12]

The psalmist is cast down but he does not give up. As he did earlier (v. 4), so he tries to "remember" (v. 6). But he "continues to fluctuate between the hope of being heard and despair at being forgotten."[13] The geographical references in verse 6 may be read literally or figuratively. If the latter, then the emphasis is on the word "from"; the psalmist feels he is far away from the God for whom he longs.

Earlier he expressed his longing for God using the image of a deer thirsty for water. The reference to water at the beginning contrasts with the water in verse 7. Now there is water, but instead of giving life, this water proved to be destructive: "All your waves and breakers have swept over me" (v. 7). This explains the bitter complaint against God in verse 9 and the complaint against the psalmist's enemies in verse 10.

It is not clear how verse 8 fits in. The repetition of the words "day" and "night" creates a contrast with verse 4. The steadfast love of the Lord is present even in his tears and complaints. There is thus a tension between hope

---

11. Kirkpatrick, *The Book of Psalms*, 229–230.

12. "Why are you downcast, O my soul?" (Ps 42:5) is equivalent to "My Father, if it is possible, let this cup pass from me"; and "Hope in God" is similar to "yet not as I will, but as you will" (Matt 26:39).

13. Brevard S. Childs, *Memory and Tradition in Israel* (Naperville, Ill.: A. R. Allenson, 1962), 61.

and despair, but with a swing towards hope even as the psalmist repeats the refrain for the second time.

43:1–5 "I WILL YET PRAISE HIM"

Twice in the previous sections the psalmist complains about his enemies (42:3, 10). Here he prays for vindication as he now identifies his enemies as "an unfaithful nation," "deceitful and wicked" (43:1). Verse 2 is similar to 42:9. With the second petition in verse 3 the psalmist begins to see some light at the end of the tunnel, as he asks God to "send me your light." He repeats his earlier longing to go to the place where God dwells (42:2). But this time the longing is more hopeful. In Psalm 43:4 we understand why the psalmist has such a deep longing for God. He refers to God as "my joy and my delight . . . my God" (v. 4). With this statement comes the third and final repetition of the refrain. Even though the refrain may be the same in each case, we have a reason to agree with the observation that there is a clear progression to a more hopeful outlook at the end.[14]

Among the songs that early European settlers brought to New England (later on America) were their Protestant metrical Psalms. The *Bay Psalm Book* was the first book published in English America. Included in this book of songs were laments, one of which was Psalm 42. The hymn closely resembles what we have in the Psalms. Later on, when hymnody replaced psalmody (the use of Psalms), the element of lament was softened. And in the twentieth century, with the coming of the praise and worship style of singing, the song "As the deer" is disrobed of its lament. The song is still good, but the element of lament is gone. The demise of lament is due in part to the American manifest destiny culture and triumphalistic emphasis. Since the Philippines is largely influenced by America, the trend here is similar. Most of the songs that we sing in our churches are from the West, and some of them we blindly borrow.

The challenge is to create songs that resonate with our own experiences as a people, particularly the lament psalms, of which Psalm 42–43 is a good example. One suggestion is to make use of our *kundiman*. These are songs which are closely linked with experiences of crisis. The most popular of these is *Bayan Ko* (My country), which was composed in 1928 as a protest against colonialism and which has been sung since then whenever our freedom has been threatened.

---

14. Cf. Schökel, "The Poetic Structure of Psalm 42–43," 4–11.

PSALM 44

Psalm 44 is closely linked to Psalm 42–43. One of the key words in the latter is the word "downcast" (*shikh*). This word occurs only five times in the whole Psalter: four times in Psalm 42–43. The only other occurrence of the word is in Psalm 44 (v. 25). Both psalms are attributed to the "Sons of Korah." In Psalm 42–43 the psalmist evinces an intimacy with God, as reflected in his deep longing for him. And he still feels so down. Similarly, the people in Psalm 44 claim they have been faithful to God and yet they are suffering. They feel God has rejected (44:9; cf. 43:2) and forgotten (44:17, 24; cf. 42:9) them. The remembrance of times past only makes the present more painful (42:4, 6). The recollection of God's previous acts of deliverance only creates a contradiction with their present experience (44:1–8 and vv. 9–16).[1] The remarkable thing about these psalms is that the people did not keep within them what they were feeling or thinking, but expressed these things to God. They poured out their hearts to the Lord.

Psalm 44 is the first example in the Psalter of a lament by a community. So we have an individual lament followed by a communal lament at the beginning of Book 1 of the Psalter. A similar movement is found at the end of Book 3 (Pss 88 and 89). We have two psalms of the "dark night" (Pss 42/43 and Ps 88) followed by a communal lament (Pss 44 and 89). We do not lament alone. There is a community that laments with us.[2]

Psalm 44 falls into three main sections. The first part is a review of God's past acts of deliverance (vv. 1–8). This is followed by a lament over God's apparent absence, despite the people's faithfulness to the covenant (vv. 9–22). The final section is a series of petitions (vv. 23–26). (For the superscription, see Psalm 42–43.)

44:1–8 WHAT GOD HAS DONE "IN DAYS LONG AGO"

One of the instructions God gave to the Israelites was to tell their children what he had done for them. Here the people testify that "our ancestors have told us" the things that God has done "in days long ago" (v. 1). Specifically, they recall how God himself had enabled them to possess the land through his own powerful hand ("your hand" [v. 2]; "your right hand" [v. 3]). They

---

1. Cf. Schaefer, *Psalms*, 111.
2. Villanueva, "The Rejoicing Church in a Suffering Asia," 14–24.

acknowledge it was not "by their sword" (v. 3; v. 6: nor "in my bow"),[3] but only through the strength that God gave (v. 5). They acknowledge God as the one who "decrees victories for Jacob" (v. 4).[4] So they express their trust in him (v. 6). They boast not in their own strength but "in God" (v. 8). The first part of the psalm ends with a vow of thanksgiving, in which the people promise to "praise your name forever" (v. 8).

In Psalm 34, the psalmist made a similar declaration when he said, "I will extol the LORD at all times" (34:1). But in the next psalm the psalmist was already lamenting (Ps 35).[5] The transition is even sharper in Psalm 44. For right after the vow of thanksgiving in verse 8, we have a strong lament directed to God.

44:9–22 "YOU HAVE REJECTED US"

It appears the previous recollection is done only in order to draw a strong contrast. The word for "enemy" (v. 7) is repeated in verse 10. But whereas God saved them from their enemies earlier (v. 7), now he has made them retreat from their enemies (v. 10). The God who put to confusion their adversaries (v. 7) has now allowed these to plunder them (v. 10). Earlier God had "planted" them (v. 2), but now he has "scattered" them (v. 11). Indeed, the God who actively worked on their behalf, saving them and enabling them to conquer the land, was now actively working against them. Line after line, from verse 9 until verse 14, the psalmist describes God as working to bring them down. God is the subject of all ten verbs in verses 9–14. So if earlier they had made their boast in the Lord "all day long" (v. 8), now their faces are covered with shame "all day long" (v. 15; v. 22).

The people claim that all of this happened to them even though they had not "forgotten" God (v. 17). The word "forget" is repeated three times in the psalm (vv. 17, 20, 24; cf. 42:9). They are not claiming perfection. Their innocence is in reference to the covenant, specifically with regard to the worship of idols (v. 20). If they have committed such a sin, they reason, "Would not

---

3. There is an alternation here between first person singular and first person plural throughout the psalm (e.g. vv. 5–7 and 14–17). It is possible that an individual who represents the people is speaking throughout the psalm. The division between an "individual" and "communal" lament can be tricky, especially in a culture which is very communal.

4. *tsawah* could be taken either as an imperative as in the MT (ESV, JPS) or a participial phrase as in the the ancient Greek translation of the Old Testament, known as the Septuagint (LXX) (followed by RSV, NIV). It is possible that we have a graphic confusion here with the *mem* from the previous word. So I followed the LXX reading.

5. Both psalms are attributed to David.

God discover it?" (v. 21). God knows "the secrets of the heart" (v. 21). As far as they are concerned, their suffering is because of the Lord: "for your sake we face death all day long" (v. 22). It is not clear what they mean by this. Maybe they refer to the taunting they experience from their enemies as a result of their persistent trust in God (cf. "Where is your God?" from Ps 42:10). This concept of suffering for the sake of the Lord is later developed in the theology of the suffering servant (Isaiah 53), with the concept of suffering for others. In the NT the Apostle Paul would later quote Psalm 44:22 in Romans 8:36.

44:23–25 "RESCUE US BECAUSE OF YOUR UNFAILING LOVE"

The people feel God has forgotten them. They claim to have fulfilled their part of the bargain while God seemed not to be fulfilling his. Presently they are cast down. The same word ("downcast") that was used in Psalm 42–43 to speak of an individual's experience is here applied to the community: "We are *brought down* to the dust" (v. 25). Another word that is repeated from Psalm 42 is "oppression" (44:24; 42:9). They complain: "Why do you . . . forget our misery and oppression?" (44:24).

Like the disciples of Jesus when they tried to wake Jesus up as a great windstorm arose, so the people cry out to God: "Awake, Lord! Why do you sleep?" (v. 23). The request appears to be an irreverent way of approaching God, for God is always actively involved in the lives of his people. He will "neither slumber nor sleep" (Ps 121:4). But in times of great danger, one can understand the urgency of the fearful human. And the fact that this type of praying was allowed to be preserved means that God understands the situation of his people. He also understands the level of their faith in him. Compare this, for example, with the faith of the friends of Daniel who declared they would continue to be faithful to God even if they did not experience deliverance (Dan 3:17–18). But God is gracious enough to allow them to express themselves to him from whatever level of faith they might have. It is thus fitting that the psalm ends with the prayer: "Rescue us because of your unfailing love" (v. 26).

Psalm 44 is a communal lament. As such, we might imagine it would be easy to apply the prayer to our own context since we too are communal. But there are difficulties in applying this prayer. First, the claim that the people had not been false to God's covenant is hard to make. Even if we limited this to Christians, at what point could we say as a community that we had been faithful to the covenant? Second, the language of the prayer is too strong for us. We do not normally approach God in this manner.

Perhaps these two difficulties challenge us to reflect on our view of ourselves in relation to God. Often, because of our colonial experience, we are ashamed to assert ourselves. Even if we have done the right thing, we continue to be apologetic. It is easier for us to say, "We are wrong" than to say "We are right" when it comes to God. But God allows us to express our own point of view. He considers us covenant partners. Jesus calls us his friends, not his slaves. So it's all right to assert what we think is right.

The second difficulty is more challenging in view of the way we view authority. Our high respect for the elderly makes it hard for us to even think of questioning God or addressing him in the way the people did in this psalm. But we could interpret this from our own concept of communicating *puso sa puso* ("heart to heart").

COMMUNAL LAMENT AND THE CHURCH TODAY

There are two types of laments: individual laments and communal laments. In the former it seems that an individual is speaking. Yet things are not as simple as they seem, for it is possible that the person using the word "I" is speaking on behalf of the people, as their representative. The common view is that it is the king who is speaking for them. We also have to remember that incorporating these individual laments into the liturgy made them communal. As Kraus puts it, "There is no private piety in the Psalms."[1] Having said that, it is still possible that some of these individual laments were originally the prayers of actual individuals.

The communal lament, on the other hand, is the prayer of the community as indicated by the use of the first personal pronoun "we" (see Pss 12, 14, 44, 60, 74, 79, 80, 83, 85, 89, and 126). When the community experienced a disaster (e.g. plague or defeat in a battle), they would gather together to lament.

It is important for us to note that community gatherings were not always times of celebration. There were times when the people met to mourn, weep, and lament before God. They had songs of mourning as well as songs of praise. How different that is from the way we worship today. We have forgotten how to mourn together and do not know how to join in communal lament. The following observation was made about a Western church, but it is true of many churches in Asia:

> Something was seriously wrong with our church, and despite the fact that I had been attending there for ten years, I had never noticed it. It seemed that we had no capacity for dealing with sadness. As I reflected on the way in which my church worshipped, its emphasis, its tone, its expectations, its expressed hopes, I suddenly understood clearly that *there was no room in our liturgy and worship for sadness, brokenness, and questioning*. We had much space for love, joy, praise, and supplication, but it seemed that we viewed the acknowledgement of sadness and the tragic brokenness of our world as almost tantamount to faithlessness. As a result, *when tragedy hit . . . we had no idea what to do with it or how to formulate our concerns. Because we had not consistently practiced the art of recognizing, accepting, and expressing sadness, we had not developed the capacity to deal with tragedy . . .* In the face

---

1. Hans-Joachim Kraus, *Worship in Israel,* trans. Geoffrey Buswell (Oxford: Blackwell, 1966), 219.

of evil and suffering, we sang cheerful songs and expressed happy thoughts rather than weeping with the wounded and lamenting with the Sovereign God.[2]

The communal lament is an expression of people's ability to wrestle with the hard questions of life. When suffering strikes, the community finds its strength and solace in its capacity for mourning together. The people try to embrace their sufferings together.

One of the conspicuous differences between the individual lament and the communal lament is the absence of resolution in the latter. Individual laments usually move to praise or some form of resolution; but communal laments do not move to praise. For instance, Psalm 44 begins with thanksgiving but ends with lament. The same thing happens with Psalm 89. Some may view this negatively and question the absence of anything positive. But in my view, this tells us about the community's resilience in the face of tragedy. We are more able to confront our tragic experiences when we are together.

---

2. Swinton, *Raging with Compassion*, 92-93, emphasis mine.

PSALM 45

From the individual lament of Psalms 42–43 and the communal lament of Psalm 44, we turn to a psalm of celebration, a royal wedding psalm. Psalm 45 was written on the occasion of a king's wedding. Whereas in Psalm 43:3 the psalmist prayed that God's light and truth might bring him to God's holy hill (43:3), here the wedding participants are led along as "they enter the palace of the king" (45:15).

The psalm has also been interpreted as symbolically referring to the Messiah. In the *Targum* (the Aramaic translation of the Hebrew Bible), we have the following words for verse 3: "Thy beauty, O King Messiah, is greater than that of the children of men."[1] In the NT the author of the book of Hebrews applies the words of Psalm 45:6–7 to Christ: "your throne, O God, is forever and ever" (Heb 1:8–9). Later interpreters also find a link between the image of the church as the "bride of Christ" and the bride in Psalm 45.[2] The openness of the language of Psalm 45 and the poetry of the psalms in general allow for such reinterpretation.

One of the central messages of the following psalm is that God remains in control even if the foundations of the earth seem to shake (see Ps 46). The present arrangement of Psalm 45 likewise tells us that even amidst the chaos, the tensions and the ambiguities of living, life goes on – (what could be a clearer sign that life is normal than a wedding?) – because God is in control. The psalm also teaches us that there is no division between religious and secular. Even a "secular" event like a wedding is included in the Psalms – which are mostly prayers – to show that everything in life is ruled by God.[3] Although Psalm 45 praises an earthly king, in the end the glory goes to God, for it is God who blesses the king (v. 2) and anoints him (v. 7).

Structurally, the psalm is divided into two parts: verses 1–9 which center on the king, and verses 10–17 which focus mainly on the bride. The psalm is a continuation of those attributed to the Sons of Korah. The psalm is to be sung "To the tune of 'Lilies'" (see also Pss 69 and 80). Psalm 45 is the only psalm to be designated a "wedding song."

---

1. Delitzsch, *Psalms*, 73.
2. James F. Melvin, "Psalm 44 (45) and Nuptial Spirituality in Juan de Avila's Audi, Filia," in *Psalms in the Early Modern World* (Farnham, UK: Ashgate, 2011), 175–189.
3. As Kirkpatrick, *The Book of Psalms*, 245, writes: "the inclusion of such poems as this and the Song of Songs . . . helps to place the ordinary relations of human life in a truer light as part of the divine order of the world."

45:1–9 THE BLESSINGS OF THE KING

The opening and ending of Psalm 45 give us a glimpse into the world of the scribes. They scribes were the learned people of their time, well-versed in their literature and traditions.[4] On occasions such as royal weddings they would compose and recite poems like the one we find here. The psalmist is a "skillful writer" (v. 1), and the rest of the psalm is a record of his words.

The "skillful writer" has only positive words for the king. He describes him as "most excellent of men" and eloquent[5] (v. 2). But he is careful to note that this is because of God's blessing: "God has blessed you" (v. 2). The king is blessed not because of his handsome looks and eloquence, but because of God's blessings (cf. v. 7).

The king is not only good-looking and eloquent; he is also strong and full of glory and majesty (v. 3). His enemies fall under him (v. 5). And yet this is all for the purpose of upholding "the cause of truth" and defending the "justice" (v. 4). The royal scepter is described as a "scepter of justice" (v. 6). The shift from description in verse 2 to command in verse 3 emphasizes that the king must use the blessings he has received to execute justice and righteousness, especially on behalf of the weak.[6]

The king is addressed as "God" in verse 6, but this does not mean he is a god. The scribe is simply following the pattern of royal literature at that time. We can make this assertion because in the very next verse the psalmist reminds the king that he is still under God: "therefore, God, your God, has set you above your companions" (v. 7). The king remains a recipient not only of the blessings of "looks" and eloquence but also of his kingship. So the title "God" in reference to the king is about the divine origin of his kingship.

The next two verses (vv. 8–9) introduce the royal entourage and the bride.

45:10–17 THE BRIDE AND THE WEDDING

The psalmist begins his address to the bride with a solemn call, almost reminiscent of the *shema*, only the words are addressed to a lady (v. 10). He refers to the king as the bride's "lord" to whom she must bow down (v. 11). His mention of the people of Tyre (v. 12) indicates that the bride comes from a foreign land. The bride's attire is described in all its magnificence (vv. 13–14).

---

4. Mays, *Psalms*, 181.
5. This is the meaning of the words "grace is poured upon your lips."
6. Cf. the French Common Language Version (FRCL) reading of v. 4b: "in defense of the poor and of justice."

We are given a glimpse of the royal wedding procession (vv. 14–15) before the psalmist ends with words of blessing and praise for the king (vv. 16–17).

In a culture that traditionally puts high value on marriage, the image of the church as the bride of Christ is a fitting model. As Christ loved the church, so husbands should love their wives. Marriage remains the most intimate relationship possible between a man and a woman. There is no dichotomy between the spiritual and the physical in the biblical view of marriage or of a wedding. Everything ought to be done before the presence of the Lord. Let the church prepare herself as the joyful bride of Christ.

PSALM 46

Psalm 46 speaks a lot about the quaking of the foundations: mountains shake (v. 2), waters roar and foam (v. 3), even the "nations are in uproar" (v. 6). The same word (*mot*) is used to speak about the shaking of the mountains and of the tottering of the nations. Then between these two "shakings," the word is used with a negation: "it shall *not* be moved" (v. 5). Here the "it" referred to is the "city of God." Psalm 46 is the first psalm to talk about Zion, the city of God (see also Pss 48, 76).

The shaking of the foundations of the earth need not be taken as referring to literal earthquakes, volcanic eruptions or tsunamis. Such events are vivid in our memories, and the psalmist too may have experienced or heard of these natural phenomena. But his primary purpose is not to teach about them but to bring out an important message: even when our world crumbles, it's not the end of the world, for God is with us.

46:1–7 "GOD IS OUR REFUGE AND STRENGTH"

The psalm begins with an affirmation of trust (v. 1). God is described as "our refuge and strength." The word "refuge" recalls the famous statement: "Blessed are all who take refuge in him" (2:12; 5:11; 34:8). "Strength" is a characteristic of the Lord, for he is powerful (see Ps 29). But the emphasis on community in this psalm is also worth noting: "God is *our* refuge and strength." Throughout the psalm, the first person plural is used. We are strong not only because God is with us but also because we are together as a community. These words of confidence in verse 1 are picked up in the refrain in verses 7 and 11.

The expression of the people's confidence in God is made against a backdrop of extreme trouble. In verse 1 the people speak of God being a "an ever-present help in trouble." Here trouble is portrayed through powerful images of disturbances in nature (vv. 2–3). The reader is to imagine the quaking of the earth, the shaking of the mountains, and the roaring and foaming of the sea. Those of us who have experienced storm surges or watched them on TV can feel the force of this psalm which depicts titanic violence and disturbance. Yet even in such a situation, the people can assert, "we will not fear" (v. 2). For God is not only their refuge; he is in their midst (v. 5).

Amidst all the shaking and roaring, "a river" flows into the city of God peacefully and undisturbed. This image stands in stark contrast to the previous one. We are suddenly transported to a quiet place, away from the danger and disturbances depicted in verses 2–3.

As with the preceding verses, we need not read verses 4–5 literally. There is no river that runs into the city of Jerusalem. The psalmist is using ancient Near Eastern motifs to speak about the centrality of the place where God dwells.[1] In the midst of all the turmoil and troubles of life, God remains in control. There is always help available. The word "help," used earlier as a noun (v. 1b), occurs here as a verb: "God will help her at break of day" (v. 5b). The psalmist is referring here to the city of God. This city "shall not fall" (literally, "be moved") (v. 5a) because God is in her midst.

This contrasts the shaking of the natural phenomena earlier and the shaking of the kingdoms (v. 6). Not only are the foundations of the earth in danger of falling down; even the nations of the world are also being shaken: "the kingdoms fall" (v. 6). But in the middle of all this, the people will not fear because "the LORD Almighty is with us" (v. 7).

46:8–11 "BE STILL AND KNOW THAT I AM GOD!"

At verse 8, the structure of the psalm changes. Previously, it was simply descriptive, but verses 8 and 10 are addressed to the hearers. In the latter half of verse 10, we hear God himself speak in the first person, using the word "I". In this section of the psalm, only verses 9 and 11 are descriptive.

The psalmist invites his audience to "Come and see what the LORD has done" (v. 8). These "works" are both the activities of nature described earlier (vv. 2–3) and those of the nations (v. 9). God's works are described as "desolations" (v. 8b). This fits in with the "vast sweeps of destruction that visit the inhabited earth, whether through natural events or military ones."[2] But God is not only in the business of destroying. "He also exercises the power to end the era of violence and bring peace to humankind."[3] In all of these things God is actively involved. He is in control. That is why the proper response is to "be still and know that I am God" (v. 10). Etymologically, the verb "be

---

1. Mays, *Psalms*, 185, notes: "The image 'comes from the symbolic language used in the ancient Near East to imagine and speak about the dwelling place of the gods. A stream was said to issue from the cosmic mountain where this dwelling was; it was a symbol that interpreted the mountain as center of the universe and source of life (Gen 2:10–14; Ezek 47:1–12; Joel 3:18; Rev 22:1–2).'"
2. Alter, *The Book of Psalms*, 164.
3. Ibid.

still" means "to relax one's grip on something."[4] Often, in our desire to maintain order in our life and in our world, we are afraid of loosening our grip for fear life will fall apart. But God invites us to let go and let God.

Verse 10 is significant. God does not speak often in the Psalms. Many of the psalms are addressed to God. So to hear God himself speaking is important. It is his way of assuring us that he is with us in the midst of all our troubles.

It is normal to express confidence when things are running smoothly. But when there are uncertainties and troubles, it becomes a challenge. Yet such is the nature of faith in God. Confidence in God is experienced and expressed in the midst of life's troubles, when our world is crumbling down, when our marriages are in trouble, when our families and society in general are breaking down. The words, "Be still, and know that I am God" are not given in a time of tranquility and order. God speaks in the midst of our troubles.

---

4. Ibid.

PSALM 47

Psalm 47 belongs to a group of psalms known as "enthronement psalms" that celebrate the kingship of Yahweh (Pss 47, 93, 96, 97, 98, 99). See the "Royal Psalms," pp. 34–35. They have as their background the events surrounding the coronation of an earthly king. In the OT, clapping, shouting, and the sounding of trumpets (47:1, 5) are all associated with the coronation of a king.[1] Psalm 47 celebrates not just an ordinary king, but the "great king over all the earth" (v. 2). The emphasis on "all the earth" recalls Psalm 46:10. The similarities between these two psalms suggest that Psalm 47 may be a sequel to Psalm 46. Among the links between the two psalms are the ancient name "Most High" (*elyon*) (46:4; 47:2), "nations" (*goyim*) (46:10; 47:8), and Jacob (46:7, 11).[2] But it is the exaltation of God in all the earth that is central in Psalm 47. The message is clear: Yahweh is not just king over the children of Abraham; he is also the king over all the peoples of the earth. Indeed, the emphasis on both the national and universal kingship of Yahweh is the important contribution of this psalm.[3]

In terms of its genre, Psalm 47, being an "enthronement psalm," is a sub-category of the hymn. Two of the characteristics which Psalm 47 shares with the hymn are the "call to praise" and the supporting motivations. The two "calls to praise" mark the division of the psalm (vv. 1 and 6).

47:1–5 "CLAP YOUR HANDS, ALL YOU PEOPLES"

In the Hebrew text the opening verse begins with the words "All the peoples." These are exhorted to "clap your hands" (v. 1). The audience is not the community of Israel; the whole earth is being summoned. Verse 2 combines the covenant name for God – "LORD" (Yahweh) – and an emphasis on the universality of his rule as "great King over all the earth." The combination introduces the dual emphases of the psalm: the kingship of Yahweh over Israel and the universal rule of God. The former is the subject of the verses immediately following.

---

1. "Clapping" (2 Kgs 11:12), "shout" (1 Sam 10:24), "sounding of trumpet" (2 Sam 15:10).
2. Schaefer notes that the title "Most High" and Jacob also occur in consecutive psalms elsewhere (118, f.n. 4 and 5).
3. James Muilenburg, "Psalm 47," *JBL* 63, no. 3 (1944): 254, remarks: "Indeed, it is this combination of national feeling and sentiment, and the universal perspectives in the poem that make it so striking."

God's kingship over Israel was established when he defeated the enemies of Israel, giving them the land he promised (vv. 3–4). It was God who
chose their inheritance for them. The word "inheritance" (v. 4a) refers to the
land of Canaan. The words "pride of Jacob" in the next line (v. 4b) parallel
the "inheritance." We may interpret "Jacob" here as a reference not to the
patriarch but to the chosen people. The word "pride" in turn, refers to the
Promised Land.

With God's kingship established through his acts described in verses 3–4,
he is now hailed as the king. The "shouts" and the "sounding of trumpets"
(v. 5) are associated with the coronation of a king.[4] God is said to have "ascended" (v. 5). This word comes from the Hebrew verb *alah* ("to go up" or
"ascend"), an important word in the psalm. It will reappear at the end of the
psalm to speak of God's exaltation. Here (v. 5) the Lord is exalted as the king
of Israel. In the next section the emphasis shifts to God's universal reign.

47:6–9 "SING PRAISES TO GOD, SING PRAISES"

There is a sense of excitement in verse 6. The call to "sing praises" is repeated
five times in verses 6–7. This reflects the high point of the Lord's exaltation as
king (v. 5). Coronations of kings are often associated with great celebrations.
How much more the "coronation" of God as king not only of the people of
Israel but also of the whole earth! Notice the change from "our King" (v. 6)
to God as "King of all the earth" (v. 7). The latter recalls Psalm 46:10. The
sovereign God who is at work in nature and among the nations is the king.
Earlier, in verse 2, the Lord is described as "awesome." In Hebrew the word
literally means "terrible" (*nora*). This recalls the shaking of the foundations
(46:2–3), which is seen to be part of God's works of "desolation" (46:8). God
is not only sovereign over nature and nations (see Ps 46); he is also "the king
over the nations" (47:8). The words, "God sits on his holy throne," represent
the climax of the liturgical "enthronement" of the Lord.

As is common in ancient times, the rulers of other peoples come and pay
homage to the new king. So here we find the "nobles of the nations" gathering (v. 9). But what is extraordinary is that here we have peoples outside
the covenant community being referred to as those gathering "as the people

---

4. The blowing of the trumpet is also a cultic act (Lev 23:23–25; 25:9), so we have here a
liturgical piece as well.

of the God of Abraham" (v. 9).[5] Muilenburg comments: "There is no passage of more genuine universalism in the whole of the OT."[6] The mention of Abraham recalls the covenant in Genesis 12 where God told Abraham that "all peoples on earth will be blessed through you." Psalm 47 sees the fulfillment of this promise.

Another word that finds allusion to Abraham is the word "shields" (v. 9b; see Gen 15:1). As God told Abraham, "I am your shield," so here the psalmist declares "the shields of the earth belong to God" (v. 9, NRSV). By extension we may interpret the word "shields" to refer to the rulers of the earth (see translation in the NIV: "kings of the earth") or to the "guardians of the earth" (NJPS). This interpretation provides the basis for the earlier statement. It is proper that the "nobles of the nations" who represent the peoples of the world should be gathered up as the people of the God of Abraham because they belong to him.

The last line is almost unexpected, but its appearance is significant: "He is greatly exalted" (v. 9c). The Hebrew word "exalted" is repeated, but this time with the adverb "greatly" (literally, "very"). Earlier, God was exalted as the king of the people of Israel (v. 5). Here God is exalted as king over all the peoples of the earth. It is no accident that the word of exaltation is uttered after the inclusion of the peoples outside the community of Israel. When this happens God really is "greatly exalted."

Some of us who do not belong to the community of Israel may feel God is playing favorites. Why choose only one people? Why Israel? Psalm 47 is a powerful reminder of God's purpose in choosing Israel – it is in order that through her all the families of the earth might be blessed (Gen 12:1–3). The God who revealed himself to the people of Israel in the OT is also at work among us who are Gentiles: "The nobles of the nations assemble as the people of the God of Abraham" (Ps 47:9). This verse looks forward to the day when nations from all tribe and nation will gather together before the King of kings and the Lord of lords.

---

5. There is a textual issue with v. 9. In the Masoretic Text, the Hebrew literally reads as in the above (NRSV). But in the Septuagint, the reading is "The princes/rulers of the peoples are assembled *with* the God of Abraham." The difference is the word "people" and "with" which in Hebrew have the same consonants – *'m*. This may have led to the miscopying of the Hebrew. Here I have adopted the text represented in the MT.

6. Muilenburg, "Psalm 47," 237.

PSALM 48

The previous psalm ended with a note on the universality of God's reign as king. With Psalm 48 we are back to the local and the particular. Here the focus is on Zion. Zion is used synonymously with the city of Jerusalem. But it is also distinguished from it as the location where God dwells. In Zion, the people have experienced the reality of God's presence, not only in terms of the spiritual but also in terms of protection and deliverance from their enemies (48:4–7; cf. 46:4–5). If you ask them how they know God is real, they can actually point to a particular place. For us Christians, we also believe God is real because God at one point in history chose to come down and become a human being. The incarnation is the ultimate expression of Zion. In Jesus Christ, God not only dwelt in a particular place to be close to us; he actually came down to be with us! Later, Jesus established his church, so that in this body of believers he will be present through his Holy Spirit. The church, then, is for us Christians what Zion was to the Jewish people.[1]

48:1–8 MOUNT ZION AS THE PLACE WHERE GOD DWELLS

The previous psalm ended with the words, "He is greatly exalted" (47:9). Psalm 48 begins similarly: God is "most worthy of praise" (v. 1).[2] But whereas the note on the former is on the universality of God's reign, the emphasis here is on the particular place where the king of all the earth has chosen to manifest himself. God is to be praised "in the city of our God." Specifically, the reference is to "Mount Zion" (v. 2), the place where people believed God dwelt.

In ancient times, people believed gods lived in the mountains. The Canaanites, in particular, believed their god Baal lived on a mountain called "Zaphon." The reference to Mount Zaphon in verse 2 shows that the psalmist is making use of a common belief among the surrounding peoples but at the same time is applying it to Yahweh. In effect, he is saying that the real mountain of God is Zion. The employment of this concept is an assertion of

---

1. Cf. Cyril Okorocha and Francis Foulkes, "Psalms," in *Africa Bible Commentary*, ed. Tokunboh Adeyemo (Nairobi, Kenya; Grand Rapids: WordAlive Publishers; Zondervan, 2006), 652.
2. Both verses use the word *meod* ("very").

"Yahweh's superiority over all other gods and places him in the position of authority in the ancient Near East."[3]

On Mount Zion stands the temple. In this place the people have experienced the reality of God's presence: "God is in her citadels" (v. 3). There are places like this elsewhere in the OT where one is aware of a presence that transcends the natural world, where heaven meets earth (Gen 28:11–19) and where one has to take off one's shoes because one is standing on holy ground (Exod 3:1–6).

How did the people know God was in Mount Zion? Because they saw how God supernaturally defeated their enemies who attacked them in this place. As soon as their enemies saw it, they "were astounded" (48:5). The defeat of their enemies is likened to the "ships of Tarshish shattered by an east wind" (v. 7). Only God could send a strong wind to defeat their enemies. The people affirm they have "heard" and "seen" what God did (v. 8). Notice that the word "saw" (*raah*) is repeated in verses 5 and 8. It is different when we have actually seen it (see 1 John 1:1–3).

48:9–14 "WE MEDITATE ON YOUR UNFAILING LOVE"

In verse 9 the people meditate or reflect on what God has done (v. 9a). They see God's actions as his "unfailing love." The next line brings us back to the temple. They make their meditation "within your temple" (v. 9b). Sacred places offer the much needed space for quiet meditation and reflection. Oh, how much we need them, especially in the overly-crowded and noisy places where we live! This probably explains the importance of mountains.

At the same time, we are reminded of the need to come down from the mountain. Meditation is not done for its own sake. It is done in order that our vision might be broadened. So in the next verse, corresponding to the words "within your temple," the psalmist declares that God's praise "reaches to the ends of the earth" (v. 10). What God has done for us, what we have seen and heard, is not for us alone to enjoy and to keep. It is meant to be shared. So in the final verses, as the psalmist exhorts the people to walk again on Zion, going around it and even counting its towers (vv. 12–13); he tells them they are to do these things "that you may tell of them to the next generation. For this God is our God for ever and ever" (vv. 13b–14a). We are not to read the actions ("walk," "go around," etc.) literally. They are an invitation

---

3. S. L. Klouda, "Zion," in *Dictionary of the Old Testament: Wisdom, Poetry, and Writings*, eds. Tremper Longman III and Peter Enns (Downers Grove: IVP, 2008), 937.

to behold God's actions, to experience them, to ponder upon them and to reflect on them so we can share with others what he has done.

One potential application of Psalm 48 for Christians is the reflection on the church as the place where God's presence dwells. The church as the body of Christ bears witness that God's Spirit indwells the church as a community and each individual believer. We need to be careful, however, that we do not spiritualize our application too much. Although it is true that the church is indwelt by the Holy Spirit, we remain physical beings, longing for visible places where we can meet God. Especially in many parts of Asia, where even today mountains are believed to be the abode of spirit beings or deities, the theology of Psalm 48 will find a place. Of course, we need to be careful we do not overly identify a place with the divine. But because Christianity has become so spiritualized and "disembodied," we need to explore ways of doing theology which incorporate local concepts of holy places. The author of Psalm 48 has paved the way by "contextualizing" the concept of Zion to the surrounding peoples' concept of a holy mountain.

PSALM 49

This psalm reminds us of the story of the rich fool in the Gospel of Luke, who had so much harvest he no longer had any place to put them. So he said to himself: "What shall I do? I have no place to store my crops.' Then he said, 'This is what I'll do. I will tear down my barns and build bigger ones, and there I will store my surplus grain.' And I'll say to myself, 'You have plenty of grain laid up for many years. Take life easy; eat, drink and be merry.' But God said to him, 'You fool! This very night your life will be demanded from you. Then who will get what you have prepared for yourself?'" (Luke 12:16–20).

Psalm 49 is similar to Psalms 37 and 73. These three psalms tackle the issue of the wealth and riches of wicked people. But the responses differ. Psalm 37 finds assurance in the belief that the wicked will perish but the righteous will "inherit the land." In Psalm 73 the psalmist struggles at first, almost losing his faith when he sees the wicked prospering and living a life of ease, or so it seems – until he enters the sanctuary of God where he understands their final destiny (73:17).

The response in Psalm 49 is more general: rich people, like everyone else, will die. No matter how much money they have in the bank, they all end up in the same place where everyone goes – to the grave. As the psalmist declares, "Truly, no ransom avails for one's life, there is no price one can give to God for it" (v. 7). Death is the great equalizer. The psalm serves as a background to the words of Jesus in the Gospels:[1] "What good is it for someone to gain the whole world, yet forfeit their soul? Or what can anyone give in exchange for their soul?" (Mark 8:36–37).

49:1–4 "HEAR THIS, ALL YOU PEOPLE"

Psalm 49 is the last of the psalms (Pss 42–49) attributed to the Korahites in Book 2 of the Psalter. As we have seen, the subjects as well as the genres have been varied, from a royal wedding psalm (Ps 45) to an individual lament (Pss 42–43) and a communal lament (44), and now to a wisdom psalm. The Korahites must have had at their disposal a wide collection of songs.

Structurally, the psalm consists of a refrain which occurs in two places (vv. 12, 20). In Hebrew there is a slight change in the second refrain (see below). The refrain is preceded by an introduction in which the psalmist calls on "all

---

1. Mays, *Psalms*, 191.

you peoples" as he speaks "wisdom" (vv. 1–4). The Hebrew text is obscure at certain places (esp. v. 14), but the overall sense is clear enough. The presence of words like "wisdom," "proverb," and "riddle" point to the close association of this psalm to what is called Wisdom literature (e.g. Proverbs, Ecclesiastes).

As noted above, the overall message of the psalm is that all end up in the same place, rich and poor alike. The opening words of the psalm signal that it is for a general audience (v. 1). But in particular, he addresses the "rich and poor," "both low and high." Why include the poor? Because they too struggle with the issue of riches. It's not only the rich people who are tempted to rely on their own resources; poor people, too, can live their lives with no other consuming passion than to be like their rich neighbors. The poor and those who do not have much wealth may also feel threatened when confronted by people who boast of nothing but their riches.

49:5–12 "WHY SHOULD I FEAR WHEN EVIL DAYS COME?"

In response to the anxiety caused by riches or the lack of it, the psalmist strongly retorts: "Why should I fear when evil days come?" (v. 5). The word for "evil" is often translated as "trouble." The next line provides a hint as to the nature of his trouble, when the psalmist refers to "wicked deceivers" (v. 5b). These people "trust in their wealth" and "boast of their great riches" (v. 6). It is these people who are giving him trouble. And yet he confidently declares he will not be afraid of them. Why?

It is because, though they are rich, they can never escape the reality that they too will die. No amount of money can pay for a life: "There is no price one can give to God for it" (v. 7b, NRSV). All must go to the grave (v. 9). Even wisdom cannot save a person (v. 10). Like fools, wise people go to the grave. The very thing the rich are boasting about – the abundance of their wealth – will be left to others. They cannot take it with them (v. 10). Though they have owned lands and have their names engraved on memorials, their graves will be their homes (v. 11).

In our country where ninety percent of the wealth is owned by less than ten percent of the population, it is so easy to be envious of those who are rich. But the psalm reminds us we are all equal. We will all die one day, rich and poor alike. As for the rich, the psalm is a warning to not rely on their wealth. For as Jesus said, "What good will it be for someone to gain the whole world, yet forfeit their soul? Or what can anyone give in exchange for their soul?" (Matt 16:26). The important question is not how much we have, for we can take nothing with us when we die, but "are we rich toward God?" (see Luke 12:21; Ps 49:15). As the refrain declares, "People, despite their wealth, do not endure" (v. 12a). No one should put their trust in what they have. For "like the beasts" everyone will perish (v. 12b).

49:13–20 "GOD WILL REDEEM ME FROM THE REALM OF THE DEAD"

Earlier (v. 10), the psalmist had mentioned wise people, whom he acknowledges will also suffer the same fate. Now he zeroes in on "those who trust in themselves" and talks about their end (vv. 13–14). They are referred to as "fools." The "fools" in the book of Proverbs are those who do not fear the Lord. The language of verse 14 is one of judgment and punishment: "They are like sheep and are destined to die; death will be their shepherd." It is the opposite of Psalm 23 which speaks of the Lord as "my shepherd." Here "death" is personified as the "shepherd." The rest of verse 14 is not clear in the Hebrew, but this portion of verse 14 literally reads, "death shepherds them."

In contrast to that, and without any transition or explanation, the psalmist proclaims: "But God will redeem me from the realm of the dead; he will surely take me to himself" (v. 15). This is another way of saying, "The Lord is my shepherd." The mention of death as a shepherd in the preceding verse contrasts that in Psalm 23. God is our shepherd. He will not allow us to remain in the grave forever. It is not clear what specifically the psalmist is referring to here. Is he talking about resurrection from the dead? The doctrine of resurrection had not yet developed in the OT. Or is he referring to an experience similar to that of Enoch and Elijah (Gen 5:24; 2 Kgs 2:11)?[2] We have no way of knowing. Probably we have here an early glimpse of the doctrine of the afterlife (cf. 1:5). If it is, then the possible allusion to Psalm 23 is significant. It is in the context of a close relationship with God that the doorway to the afterlife is discovered.[3]

In v. 16, the psalmist goes back to his earlier assertion: "Why should I fear?" (v. 5). But this time he turns to his audience and exhorts them to not be afraid "when others grow rich" (v. 16). The following verse basically repeats the same points above. The rich will not "take" anything with them (v. 17). The word "take" (*laqakh*) comes from the same verb used in verse 15b when

---

2. The same verb, "receive" (*laqakh*), is used in Genesis 5:24.
3. Cf. Psalm 73. It is when the psalmist entered into God's holy presence that he received the answer to his deepest questions.

the psalmist declares God will "take" (*laqakh*) him. If the repetition is deliberate, the point being made is that unlike in the case of the psalmist, there will be no one to receive these people when they die. Even though they may be successful and happy during their lifetime, the same fate awaits them: like their ancestors they will go to the grave where they will never again see the light (v. 19).

The psalm ends with a refrain which differs slightly from the earlier one. The difference is with the verb: "endure" (v. 12) and "understand" (v. 20).[4] Assuming this is the correct reading, the point is somber. Even with all the explanations above, mortals still do not understand. On our own we cannot grasp the reality that we will all die.

The psalmist started by making a promise that he would solve a riddle (v. 4). What is the riddle? The riddle could be the problem of the common fate of everyone, including the wise – death. The solution? This is not clear, maybe even to the psalmist himself. He can only turn to God for the answer (v. 15).

---

4. This is the reading in the MT. In the ancient Greek translation of the Old Testament, known as the Septuagint, the verb is "understand" in both refrains.

PSALM 50

Worship, acts of service, and everything we do in the church and in the name of God can become mere formalities, rituals detached from the heart. When that happens, all our actions become empty trivialities, and the object of God's rebuke. For God cannot be bought by our expensive offerings and sacrificial acts. He does not need any of these; he is the owner of everything. What he desires is a grateful heart, out of which all our offerings, acts of service and sacrifices become a response of worship. He does not want hypocrites who go to church, praising God with their mouths but whose hearts are far from him. From Psalm 50 we know our heart is far from God when we do not treat our neighbors with love, but instead rob, slander, and violate them. We can never separate our worship of God from our dealings with others (see Pss 15 and 24). This is the message of Psalm 50.

Following a series of seven psalms from the Korahites (42–49), counting Psalms 42–43 as one psalm), we have the first of twelve psalms attributed to Asaph. The other Asaph psalms are in Book 2 (Pss 73–83). Asaph is one of the three worship leaders in the temple, along with Heman and Ethan (1 Chr 15:17). These three were sacred singers who played the cymbals (1 Chr 15:19; cf. Ezra 3:10).

Although Psalm 50 is separated from the other psalms which bear the name of Asaph, it is properly placed here because the call "Listen, my people" (v. 7) fits in with the previous psalm's "Hear this, all you peoples" (49:1).[1] But as we can see, the audience differs in the two psalms. If the previous psalm is addressed to all the peoples of the world, Psalm 50 is addressed to the people of God. It is an "in-house" psalm. The speakers differ as well. Unlike Psalm 49 and many other psalms, God himself is the one who speaks in Psalm 50.

Structurally, the psalm begins with an extended introduction to the speech of God (vv. 1–6). The main body of the psalm contains the speech of God to his people (vv. 7–23). The speech is divided into two sections: verses 7–15 and verses 16–23. These are addressed, respectively, to the covenant people in general and to the disobedient in their midst.

---

1. Delitzsch, *Psalms*, 122.

50:1–6 GOD SUMMONS THE HEAVENS AND THE EARTH

Verses 1–6 introduce the speaker: God. He is described as the God of the heavens and the one who made a covenant with his people. He summons the earth (v. 1) and the heavens (v. 4). There is no doubt about it. The one who is about to speak is our God "who is in heaven." But as in the Lord's Prayer, this God is also "our Father." He is close to his people. He "shines forth" from Zion (v. 2) and has made a covenant with his people (v. 5).

It is to his covenant people that he wishes to speak. But his approach at the beginning is terrifying. He is described as coming with a "fire that devours," surrounded by a mighty tempest (v. 3). God is obviously angry. He comes to judge (v. 4).

50:7–15 "LISTEN, MY PEOPLE"

Although God comes in order to judge, judgment is too strong a word to describe what God is doing here. Reproof or discipline would be a better word. God's approach is made on the basis of his relationship to his people and theirs to him. The people call him "our God" (v. 3); God calls them "my people" (v. 7). He introduces himself as follows: "I am God, your God" (v. 7) – the counterpart of the famous, "I am the LORD, your God" from Exodus.

The word "rebuke" actually shows up twice in the psalm (vv. 8, 21, ESV). God is no longer silent (v. 3). He now rebukes his people (v. 8). Why? The people may have felt God was angry with them because they failed to offer him enough animal sacrifices. The objection here is directed "to the pagan idea that the deity actually needs the nurture provided through the animals offered up on the altar."[2] In some Asian cultures, it is believed that God needs to be appeased or fed with animal sacrifices. This is not explicit in the psalm. But God's response seems to address this issue. God had to tell them he was not rebuking them because of a lack of "sacrifices" (v. 8a). In fact, they were in ample supply: "your burnt offerings, which are ever before me" (v. 8b). God does not need these, for he owns everything (vv. 10–11), and he makes it clear that he does not feed on the flesh of animals. This is the point of the rhetorical questions in verse 13.

The reason he rebukes them is that they have forgotten the most important aspect of offering sacrifices: relationship. We offer sacrifices because we are grateful to God or want to mend our relationship with him. The psalm

---

2. Alter, *The Book of Psalms*, 177.

emphasizes the former. God seeks a sacrifice of thanksgiving (v. 14). This does not mean God is *kulang sa pansin* ("lacking in attention"). God is not "like a vain woman wanting compliments, or a vain author presenting his new books to people who had never met or heard of him."[3] Rather, God "wanted thanksgiving, for that in turn emerged from human lives full of joy; it was the joyful lives of the covenant members, expressed so vividly in the sacrifices and words of the ceremony, which fulfilled in God the richness of relationship which he had given to his people."[4] Thanksgiving removes the attention from ourselves and directs it to God where all the glory is due (v. 14).

50:16–23 LISTEN, YOU WHO FORGET GOD

The first rebuke had to do with the people's behavior in relation to God. The second rebuke is directed to the people's behavior towards their neighbors. The two are directly related. When our relationship with God is not right, our relationship with others falters also. And when our attitude to others is not right, our worship is no longer acceptable to God. For those who come to his holy hill must deal justly and righteously with others (see Ps 15). That is why God rebukes the hypocrites who recite his statutes but do not apply them in their lives (v. 16). Instead, they commit adultery, rob others (v. 17), and slander them (vv. 19–20). These three remind us of the Ten Commandments. But the verses here are not meant to provide an exhaustive list. They are simply illustrative.

The point is clear. It is these two – the offering of sacrifices which does not flow out of a grateful relationship with God and the subsequent violation of others – that cause God to rebuke his people. God is not addressing two groups in this psalm, though it may appear that way because in verse 5 he refers to his "consecrated people" and in verse 16, he addresses the "wicked." The accusation that "you . . . cast my words behind you" (v. 17) is used elsewhere in the covenant people's own confession of their sins (Neh 9:26). And the word "rebuke" is applied to both the "faithful ones" (v. 8) and the "wicked" (v. 21).

The Lord expects his children to be salt and light wherever they may be. But as it happens, many who call themselves Christians are actually "nominal" Christians. They may attend church or go to mass, but their lives remain unchanged by the teachings they hear Sunday after Sunday. They offer

3. C. S. Lewis, *Reflections on the Psalms*, 79.
4. Craigie, *Psalms 1–50*, 367.

prayers and sacrifices, but like the people in Psalm 50, they have forgotten it's all about right relationship with God and neighbor. As the summary of the Ten Commandments put it: "Love the Lord your God with all your heart, and with all your soul, and with all your mind" and "Love your neighbor as yourself" (Matt 22:37, 39).

In the end God gives a warning and opens up an invitation. Life and death is before them. If they forget God, they will be destroyed (v. 22). But if they offer thanksgiving and live the right way, they will be saved (v. 23). Thanksgiving and right living represent the two responses to God's two rebukes above. But the psalm does not end in a rebuke. "The last phrase, 'the salvation of God,' shows how the divine word, even when it accuses and convicts of sins, is a grace."[5]

---

5. Schaefer, *Psalms*, 128.

PSALM 51

The NT instructs us to confess our sins with the promise that if we do, the Lord will "forgive us our sins and cleanse us from all unrighteousness" (1 John 1:9). But what does it mean to "confess our sins"? The passage in 1 John and other passages in the NT (see e.g. Jas 5:16) do not elaborate on this. It is here where we see the importance of the book of Psalms and Psalm 51 in particular. For as the church father Athanasius wrote: "It is the Psalms that show you how to set about repenting and with what words your penitence may be expressed."[1] Psalm 51 provides us with a model of a prayer of confession.

This psalm reminds us that confession is part of the whole process of restoration, of returning (*shub*) to God (51:12, 13). Confession should not be seen in isolation but as part of the whole journey of returning to God. And in this journey we are not alone. God brings other people to help us on our way back to God. Without someone like Nathan, who took the risk of confronting a king about his sin,[2] David might not have been able to return to God (see the "Significance of the Superscriptions," pp. 258–259). Accountability and community form part of the whole process of restoration. At the same time, had David not humbled himself, restoration would not have been possible. The whole prayer reminds us of the importance of humility.

Confession is first of all an acknowledgement of our sin (v. 3). It is telling God we were wrong and he is right (v. 4b).[3] There is nothing in us that would make us worthy of God's forgiveness (v. 5). We can only appeal to his "unfailing love" (v. 1).

The good news is that even before we confess our sin, God has already started the process of restoration. In the previous psalm, we heard God rebuking his people (50:8, 21) in the same way that God rebuked David through the prophet Nathan (2 Sam 12:7–12). At the end of Psalm 50 God gave them the assurance that "those who go the right way" would be shown the salvation of God (50:23). Canonically, Psalm 51 may be seen as the response to God's rebuke and invitation in Psalm 50. The two psalms show some close links

---

1. "The Letter of Athanasius, Our Holy Father, Archbishop of Alexandria, To Marcellinus, On The Interpretation of the Psalms." Online: http://www.athanasius.com/psalms/aletterm.htm (accessed 9 May 2013).
2. The superscription reads: "A psalm of David, when the prophet Nathan came to him, after he had gone in to Bathsheba."
3. The confession, "you are justified (*tsdq*)" (v. 4), occurs in the other penitential prayers in the OT (see also Neh 9:33; Dan 9:14).

(see below). A reading of these two psalms together shows us that the reason we can make confession is that God first made the way. As Christians, we encounter the ultimate manifestation of this truth in Christ.

51:1–7 "HAVE MERCY ON ME, O GOD"

The psalm consists of three movements. The first is the plea for mercy in view of the acknowledged seriousness of sin (vv. 1–7). The second is the prayer for restoration (vv. 8–12). Here the psalmist anticipates the joy that comes from a restored relationship with God. The third is the movement outward, the result of restoration (vv. 13–19). The psalmist is no longer looking inward, into his heart, but is already looking forward to sharing with others what God has done in his life (v. 13), declaring God's praise (v. 15), and wishing for the restoration of the walls of Jerusalem (v. 18).

The central feature of the prayer of confession is the acknowledgement of sin (see comments in Ps 32:3–5). We learn from Psalm 32 that hiding our sins causes much suffering. The very structure of our being disintegrates, and God's hand becomes heavy on us (32:3–4). That is why the psalmist confesses his sin before God (32:5). The opening verses of Psalm 51 reflect the same attitude towards sin. David views sin as something that is serious. This is reflected in the words he used to refer to sin. Unlike in our context (Filipino) where there is no word for sin that is original to us, Psalm 51 uses a number of different words for sin. In verses 1–5 alone David employs four different words for sin: "transgressions" (vv. 1, 3), "iniquity" (vv. 2), "sin" (vv. 2, 3, 4, 5), and "evil" (v. 4). David feels so unclean that he cries out for mercy (v. 1) and begs God to wash him "thoroughly" (v. 2; cf. v. 7). Deeply aware of the presence of sin in his life, he confesses: "I know my transgressions . . . my sin is always before me" (v. 3). He acknowledges that the consequences of his sin are justified: "you are right in your verdict and justified when you judge" (v. 4b). This reveals the depth of his admission of his sin.

David declares, "Against you, you only, have I sinned" (v. 4a). This does not mean he is denying any wrongdoing committed against other people. Certainly, in the case of David, he had violated Bathsheba, her husband and her family, not to mention the trust of his people. We are to understand this verse in the light of the broader system of dealing with sin in the OT as well as the teaching in the NT. In the Pentateuch, for instance, those who have committed sin are required to pay the necessary penalty (see e.g. Lev 6:1–5). The Gospels instruct us to reconcile first with those who have wronged us before we offer our gifts to God (see Matt 5:23–34; cf. Jas 5:16).

Confession includes both the horizontal and the vertical dimension. The latter is the focus of Psalm 51. David knows that his relationship with God forms the foundation for his other relationships. That is why he seeks to deal with this. He acknowledges that sin has taken root in his being. Even from his mother's womb, he admits he was already a sinner: "I was sinful at birth, sinful from the time my mother conceived me" (v. 5). We are not to develop the whole doctrine of original sin from this one verse. What we have here is a literary device called hyperbole, an exaggeration for effect. At the same time, the verse does emphasize the depth to which sin has taken hold of his life. His inner being is dominated by it. The problem of sin lies deep within. And that is where God wants to start: "You desired faithfulness even in the womb" (v. 6).

51:8–12 "RESTORE TO ME THE JOY OF YOUR SALVATION"

One can sense a movement here towards a more hopeful note. This section is enveloped by the word for "joy":

> "Let me hear joy and gladness" (v. 8);
> "Restore to me the joy of your salvation" (v. 12).

Joy is like a magnetic field that pulls David back to God. Those who have experienced the joy that comes from an intimate relationship with God know there is nothing in the world that comes close to it. But David knows there is a big problem – his sin. So he begs God to "hide your face from my sins" (v. 9). The Hebrew word for "face" (*paneh*) is repeated in verse 11: "Do not cast me from your presence" (literally, "face" [*paneh*]). David wants God to ignore his sin without rejecting him. The problem is that his sin is within him; he is enmeshed in it, conceived in it from his mother's womb.

Faced with this dilemma, he utters an extraordinary request: "Create in me a clean heart, O God" (v. 10). The word "create" (*barah*) is the same word used in Genesis 1 to speak of the creation of heaven and earth. In Genesis 1 the word for "spirit" (*ruakh*) is mentioned (Gen 1:2), a word which features prominently in Psalm 51. The word "spirit" appears four times in this psalm (vv. 10, 11, 12, 17). David feels it would take a whole creative work of God, analogous to what God did in the beginning, for him to change. As God breathed the breath of life which gave life to man (Gen 2:7), so David prays that God "renew a steadfast spirit within me" (v. 10).

David knows only God can change the inner being through his Spirit. The "Holy Spirit" (v. 11) is mentioned only twice in the OT: here in Psalm

51:11 and in Isaiah 63:10. In the OT, we do not have a developed doctrine of the Holy Spirit as we do in the NT. What we have here are glimpses of the work of the Spirit who is the main agent for the spiritual rebirth (John 3).

51:13–19 "MY MOUTH WILL DECLARE YOUR PRAISE"

Confession brings restoration. Restoration in turn leads to reaching out to others. David prays that as a result of God's work within him, he will "teach transgressors your ways" (v. 13a). Earlier, he referred to himself as a "sinner" (v. 5); now he wants to be an instrument in bringing "sinners" back to God (v. 13). At the same time he is also aware of the continuing reality of sin in his life. So he prays that God deliver him from "bloodshed" (v. 14), another word for sin in the OT. He knows it is only as God opens up his lips that he will be able to "declare your praise" (v. 15). This recalls the "sacrifice of thanksgiving" which God was seeking from his people in Psalm 50:14. All the while the people thought their animal sacrifices, the externalities of worship, were what mattered. They forgot that God was looking primarily for their hearts. So he rejected their sacrifices (50:8–13). The psalmist reinforces this point here: "You do not delight in sacrifice, or I would bring it; you do not take pleasure in burnt offerings" (51:16). It is not animal sacrifice that God seeks, but a "broken spirit, a broken and contrite heart" (v. 17).

Psalm 51 also abounds in the use of qualifiers or adjectives to describe nouns that in normal situations may stand alone: "pure heart" (v. 10), "steadfast spirit" (v. 10), "willing spirit" (v. 12), "broken spirit" (v. 17), "broken and contrite heart" (v. 17), and "sacrifices of the righteous" (v. 19). This signifies the need for radical change, for genuineness, for something that goes deeper than the surface, deep into one's heart and being. The prerequisite to a "sacrifice of thanksgiving" is a "broken and contrite heart." For without the restoration of relationship with God through confession, there can be no proper thanksgiving.

The restoration of the heart extends to the restoration of the nation. The psalmist prays that like the mending of a broken heart, God would "build up the walls of Jerusalem" (v. 18; cf. Neh 1:3).[4] But for that to happen, indeed for any restoration to take place whether individual or communal, the heart has to be restored first to God.

---

4. There is a connection here with the prayer of confession in Neh 1:5–11. In the preceding context (Neh 1:3), the broken "walls of Jerusalem" form the background for the prayer.

THE SIGNIFICANCE OF THE SUPERSCRIPTIONS

A number of the psalms have superscriptions, that is, brief notes before the first verse of a psalm. Many of these superscriptions contain some information about the person who either composed the psalm or to whom the psalm is attributed (because the Hebrew preposition translated "of" in phrases like "a psalm of David" can also be translated as "for," we cannot insist that the person whose name appears in the superscription is the composer of the psalm).

The superscriptions were probably added to each psalm by those who compiled the book of Psalms after the time of the exile and they give us a valuable insight into how they interpreted the psalms. It seems that when they were doing this, they saw in the life of David something of the reality expressed in many of the psalms. This is also a striking example of the value of narrative. Regardless of whether David actually wrote all the psalms explicitly associated with incidents in his life (Pss 3, 7, 18, 34, 51, 52, 54, 56, 57, 59, 60, 63, 142) it is clear that in the story of the life of David, the community which gathered the psalms together saw their own experience.

It is also striking that most of these thirteen psalms are associated with the difficult moments in David's life. The only one to speak about David's victories is Psalm 18. For the rest, they deal with situations like his son Absalom's rebellion against his father (Ps 13). The superscription to Psalm 51 links it to David's darkest moments in the pit of adultery. Why is there such a focus on the negative parts of David's life rather than on the positive ones? The answer seems to be that these events are the ones that relate to the experiences of the community. The fact that these people appropriated the psalms and applied them to their own lives is also an invitation for us to do the same.

Psalm 51 is an example of a psalm that most likely came from David, but in its present form it has clearly been used by others. We can see this in verse 18, in particular, where there is a prayer for the rebuilding of the walls of Jerusalem. Those walls were destroyed centuries after David's time. Why would this prayer be added to David's psalm? The superscription helps us to answer that question. This psalm is linked to the occasion "when the prophet Nathan came to him after David had committed adultery with Bathsheba." The whole psalm is thus presented as a prayer in response to the words of rebuke by Nathan. Those who compiled the book of Psalms saw this psalm as a response to God's rebuke to his people in Psalm 50 and as an expression of a deep sense of sinfulness that leads to repentance and confession.

We do not often pay much attention to the superscriptions in the Psalms. But in the case of Psalm 51 the little detail that the prophet Nathan was sent by God to rebuke David, provides us with a way of incorporating our very own values of communal life into our reading of this text. It shows us the importance of accountability in the whole process of restoration. Confession should not be seen in isolation but should be understood within the whole process of restoration where the individual stands with the community. The exhortation of the writer of the book of Hebrews speaks powerfully in this context: "And let us consider how to provoke one another to love and good deeds" (Heb 10:24).

The verb translated "provoke" is interesting. It is used positively to mean "motivate" or "encourage." Negatively, it has the sense of "provocation," "sharp argument." Sometimes helping someone stay on the right path requires the act of "provoking" or "rebuking." This is not an easy task, but it is one that God uses to bring his people back to him. For those of us who place a high value on community and relationship, this will prove to be a challenge. We would rather keep something within us than lose the relationship. But if we truly care for our brother or sister and if we want to follow the Lord, we will find ways of helping our brother or sister to get back on the road that leads to righteousness.

PSALM 52

The psalm reminds us of the word of the Lord given through the prophet Jeremiah: "Let not the wise boast of their wisdom or the strong boast of their strength or the rich boast of their riches, but let the one who boasts boast about this: that they have the understanding to know me, that I am the LORD, who exercises kindness, justice and righteousness on earth, for in these I delight," declares the LORD (Jer 9:23–24). Four words from this Jeremiah passage appear in Psalm 52: "boast" (Ps 52:1), "mighty" (vv. 1, 7), "wealth" (v. 7), and "unfailing love" (vv. 1, 8). The psalm serves as a warning against those who boast of their strength and their riches instead of the steadfast love of the Lord. In graphic words the psalmist declares the fate that awaits those who act in this way (v. 5).

The superscription attributes the psalm to David. The psalm is one of the few psalms which contain a brief historical background (see "The Significance of the Superscription," pp. 258–259). The construction of the superscription is similar to Psalm 51. Both employ the verb "to go/come" twice. The background refers to the event narrated in 1 Samuel 22:6–19. King Saul had been trying to find David in order to kill him, but had been unsuccessful. He had become angry with his people for their failure to track David down. Then the Edomite Doeg came and told Saul: "David has gone to the house of Ahimelek." Saul immediately went to Ahimelech's place and ordered his men to kill David's supporters. His men were not willing to kill the priests. But Doeg was. He killed eighty-five priests, along with their families.

Structurally, the psalm may be divided into three sections: a description of the "mighty hero" (vv. 1–4), the judgment of the "mighty one" (vv. 5–7), and an expression of confidence and vow of thanksgiving (vv. 8–9).

52:1–4 "WHY DO YOU BOAST OF EVIL, YOU MIGHTY HERO?"

A major part of the psalm consists of words of denunciation addressed to a particular person. This person is described as a "mighty hero" (v. 1; cf. v. 7), one who practices "deceit" (v. 2) and loves "every harmful word" (literally, "deceitful tongue") (v. 4). The first comes from a word which means "warrior" or "strong man." But here it is used derisively. This person may be mighty and strong but since he uses his abilities and talents to destroy, he will also be destroyed. This "mighty hero" "plots destruction" (v. 2). The "tongue" and actions related to it (e.g. lying, "words that devour") (vv. 2–4) represent a literary device known as synecdoche in which the whole is substituted for the part (see Ps 12). So the image depicted is of someone who is dangerous and bent on destruction.

52:5–7 "GOD WILL BREAK YOU DOWN"

The image presented in the preceding verses might have led the editors of the Psalter to link the psalm to Doeg. By doing so, they have supplied what was lacking in the narratives in 1 Samuel. In 1 Samuel 22, there is nothing about the punishment or even condemnation of Doeg for the grievous act he did. Psalm 52 fills in the gap.[1] The wicked will surely be punished. As we say in Filipino, *May araw ka rin* ("There is a day [of reckoning] for you"). That is the point of the next verse: "God will bring you down to everlasting ruin: He will snatch you up and pluck you from your tent; he will uproot you from the land of the living" (v. 5).

In this single verse, four verbs are used to portray God's judgment. The word translated "bring you down" also means "pull you down." The person referred to in verse 1 might be "mighty" but God will certainly bring him down. In the midst of his rest, God will drag him out, leaving him dead, like a plant uprooted. Then the righteous will see that God is a God of vengeance. He does not allow evil to reign forever (v. 6). The righteous will see that the one called "mighty" (v. 1) is now fallen. The one who trusted in abundant riches has actually "trusted in his great wealth" (v. 7b). The NIV translates the last word as "wealth," following the Syriac. But the Hebrew uses the word "destruction" which should be preferred. The word "destruction" looks back to verse 2. The "mighty one" who plotted destruction thought that by trusting in his riches, he was secure. But the parallel line in verse 7 pronounces the opposite. As Proverbs 14:12 declares: "There is a way that appears to be right, but in the end it leads to death." They who dug the pit have themselves fallen into it.

52:8–9 "I TRUST IN GOD'S UNFAILING LOVE"

In verse 8, the psalmist draws a contrast between those who take refuge in their riches (v. 7) and those who trust in God's unfailing love." The word for "unfailing love" occurs earlier in verse 1b: "The steadfast love of God endures

---

1. Vivian L. Johnson, *David in Distress: His Portrait through the Historical Psalm* (New York: T&T Clark, 2009), 66–67.

all the day" (ESV). This translation is a close rendering of the Hebrew, which the NIV has unfortunately not followed probably because it does not seem to make sense. But the use of "unfailing love" in verse 1 is deliberate. It draws a contrast with verse 8. God's unfailing love is available to everyone, even to the boastful. The difference is that the boastful does not acknowledge it, while the righteous put their trust in it. Those who put their trust in God's steadfast love are likened to an "olive tree flourishing in the house of God" (v. 8). Unlike the destructive person who is uprooted, they are ever fresh, like the tree that is planted by the streams of water (Ps 1). Further, unlike the "mighty hero" who is dragged away from his "tent" (v. 5), those who trust in God's unfailing love are established; they are planted in the "house of God" (v. 8). This leads the psalmist to offer a vow of thanksgiving that he will proclaim in the presence of God's people because of what God has done: "I will always praise you in the presence of your faithful people. And I will hope in your name for your name is good" (v. 9).

The word translated "praise" ("I will praise you") in verse 9 comes from the Hebrew word which actually means "wait." Even with the expression of confidence at the end of the psalm, one still waits for the actualization of the promised destruction of the wicked. We live in the tension between the "already" and the "not yet." And it is only through the eyes of faith that we can continue our journey along the path of righteousness. This side of eternity we still see the "mighty ones" prospering, growing bigger. It seems like they are the "green olive trees" and not the uprooted ones. The temptation to be envious or fearful of the powerful ones in our midst is strong. But the challenge is to trust in God's steadfast love, knowing that in the future they will have their "day." In the meantime, we are called upon to wait upon the Lord, remembering that vengeance belongs to him (Rom 12:9).

PSALM 53

Psalms 53 and 14 are two versions of the same poem, with a few differences. One is the presence of some additions in the superscription of Psalm 53, which adds "according to mahalath. A Maskil" to the one we have in Psalm 14. Another is the change of the name for God from "Yahweh" to "God," a practice that is evident in Psalms 42–83. These are known as the "Elohistic Psalms." The more obvious difference is in verse 5, which elaborates on the terror that will come upon evildoers: "There they shall be in great terror, in terror such as has not been. For God will scatter the bones of the ungodly" (v. 5, NRSV; cf. 14:5–6). The scattering of the "bones of the ungodly" is not in Psalm 14. On the other hand, the statement about the Lord's protection of the poor (14:6) is lacking in Psalm 53.

The presence of these two psalms gives us a glimpse of the development of the Psalter. It is possible that these two versions were part of two originally separate collections before they were brought together in the Psalter. Another possibility is that the editor/s of the Psalter might have deliberately used an existing psalm (Ps 14) because of its similarity with Psalms 52 and 54. Psalm 53 continues on the theme of divine vengeance. This explains the change in Psalm 53:5. In its present position, Psalm 53 also provides a background for Psalm 54:3 (see below). This practice of re-using a psalm is not unique (cf. Ps 40:13–17 and Ps 70).

In its present context therefore, Psalm 53 may be read along with Psalm 52. The superscription in Psalm 52 talks about Doeg who, according to the account in 1 Samuel 22, had murdered eighty-five priests. The description in 53:4 brings out the feeling of dread coming out of that act: "Do all these evildoers know nothing? They devour my people as though eating bread?" The "fools" in Psalm 53 is parallel to the "mighty hero" in Psalm 52. They too will be punished. The addition in verse 5 concerning the scattering of the "bones of the ungodly" which is not in the parallel psalm (Ps 14) might have been added here as the psalm is reapplied within the context of Psalms 52–54. This shows us that though God is a merciful God (Ps 51), he is also a God who destroys the wicked. "It is a fearful thing to fall into the hands of the living God!" (Heb 10:31).

(For specific comments to Psalm 53, see Psalm 14)

PSALM 54

In one of the prayer rallies leading to national elections in the Philippines, one of the bishops shouted, *"Ibagsak mo sila!"* ("Topple them down!"). He was referring to corrupt candidates. Is it okay to pray this kind of prayer? Psalm 54 has a similar request: "In your faithfulness destroy them" (v. 5b). In Psalm 52:5 God is presented as one who pulls people down from their lofty places. Before dismissing these kinds of prayers as unbecoming of Christians, we should first understand the context out of which they arise and the theology behind the prayers. First of all, these people whom the psalmist is praying against are "arrogant" and "ruthless;" they have no fear of God (54:3). They are the "fools" who say, "there is no God" (53:1). Second, those uttering these prayers to God believe he is a just and righteous judge. So instead of taking vengeance themselves, they come to God who will repay evil to their enemies (54:5).[1] Third, these prayers arise out of extremely difficult situations and one should not readily apply them to all situations (see topic on Imprecatory Psalms as *Pagsusumbong sa Diyos* on pp. 274–276).

This is the third psalm since Psalm 51 to give brief historical background in its superscription (see topic on The Significance of the Superscriptions on pp. 258–259). Psalm 54 has affinities with Psalm 52 in that both psalms talk about people who utter words that have deadly consequences. In Psalm 52, Doeg the Edomite gave information to Saul which led to the murder of priests and their families. Here the words of the Ziphites almost led to David being killed (see 1 Sam 23:19–24:1). There are also similarities in the wordings of the two psalms (52:9b; 54:6b).

Psalm 54 follows the typical structure of the individual lament (cf. Psalm 13). It contains a petition (54:1–2), complaint (v. 3), expression of trust (vv. 4–5), and vow of thanksgiving (vv. 6–7).

54:1–3 PETITION AND COMPLAINT

The psalmist asks God to "save me . . . by your name" (v. 1a). The word "name" occurs twice in the psalm, first in the petition (v. 1), and then in the thanksgiving (v. 6). "Name" as used in the Bible and in this psalm, goes beyond just the identification of a person; in this case, God. God's name refers

---

1. Villanueva, *It's OK To Be NOT OK.*

to his character and power. In verse 1, the word "your name" is parallel to "your might."

The psalmist acknowledges his need of God (v. 2) in view of his situation. He complains that there are dangerous individuals who are bent on destroying him. He describes these people as "arrogant,"[2] "ruthless people," who have no "regard for God" (v. 3). The previous psalm mentions the "fools" who say in their hearts, "There is no God." It's not that these people are atheists as we know them today. It's more likely that they believe in God but do not recognize his power. In this sense they are worse than the atheists (see comment in Psalm 14). The psalm expresses the same wish expressed in the Lord's Prayer: that God manifest his power so that people would revere his name (Matt 6:9).

54:4–5 EXPRESSION OF TRUST

As in typical psalms of individual lament, we find a "sudden change of mood" in verse 4: "Surely God is my help; the Lord is the one who sustains me." From the petition, the psalmist declares his confidence in God. The reason the psalmist comes to God is because on his own he cannot defend himself. But God is his "help" and the one who upholds his life (v. 4). Confident that God will repay my enemies for their evil (v. 5a), he prays: "in your faithfulness, destroy them" (v. 5b). There is a change between the two lines in verse 5. The first line is in the third person form of address while the second line is in the second person. The latter is a direct petition; the former is the theological basis for the petition. The psalmist prays in the way he does because of his belief in God's justice. The punishment is part of the working out of the faithfulness of God, who does not withhold his hand from destroying the wicked to preserve the weak who depend on him.

"In your faithfulness, destroy them" (54:5). We do not usually pray this kind of prayer. Even when our leaders are corrupt, we continue to pray that God will bless them. But I think we have it wrong if we only view God as capable of blessing but not of punishing. God is a God of love but he is also a righteous judge, who will not allow the guilty to go unpunished. Those who put their hope on the faithfulness of God are encouraged to expect retribution on those who do evil: "He will repay my enemies for their evil" (v. 5a, NRSV). We can be assured of this because it is part of God's faithfulness. In

---

2. In the Hebrew version of the Jewish Old Testament known as the Masoretic Text (MT), the word is "strangers" (cf. ESV).

saying this, however, we do not mean to sow seeds of hatred nor deny mercy and forgiveness even for the evildoer. But there are people who are simply "ruthless," arrogant, who do not have any regard for God (v. 3). It is to this kind of people that we may utter the prayer above. Not to do so may mean we do not understand or feel the suffering of those who continue to cry out for vindication as a result of the cruelty of the wicked, or worse, we simply do not care.

54:6–7 VOW OF THANKSGIVING

Flowing from his newly gained confidence in God, the psalmist vows to offer a "freewill offering" (v. 6). There are many kinds of offering in the OT (see Leviticus 1–7). "Freewill offering" is the kind of offering that people make to express thanksgiving to God. To appreciate this, one has to go back to Psalm 50. There God rebuked his people for focusing on the externalities of worship (vv. 8–13); they had forgotten that what mattered most was not their animal sacrifices but their relationship with him, expressed in thanksgiving (v. 14). He tells them to "call on me in the day of trouble (*marah*); I will deliver you, and you will honor me" (50:15). In Psalm 54 the psalmist did just that. He called on the Lord in his time of trouble (vv. 1–2), as a result of which the Lord delivered him: "for you have delivered me from all my troubles (*marah*)" (v. 7). This is why he is now offering a sacrifice to the Lord. The fact that God has delivered him further confirms that it is okay to pray that God put an end to the wicked.

PSALM 55

"Cast your cares on the LORD, and he will sustain you" (55:22). These words are familiar to Christians because of 1 Peter 5:7, which echoes the passage in Psalm 55. Here we see how the Psalms often complement teachings in the NT. For example, in 1 John 1:9 we are instructed to confess our sins to God. As we have seen above, Psalm 51 provides a model of a prayer of confession. Similarly, Psalm 55 complements 1 Peter 5:7, showing us what it means to cast our burden on the Lord.

To cast our cares on the Lord means to become open to him about what we are going through and what we feel. Because of his situation (v. 3), the psalmist is afraid. Yet the good thing is that he is not afraid to admit his fear (vv. 4–5). It's okay to admit to God that we are afraid. In the longest prayer recorded in the book of Genesis, Jacob also admits he is afraid: "Save me, I pray, from the hand of my brother Esau, for I am afraid he will come and attack me, and also the mothers with their" (Gen 32:11). Psalm 55 is attributed to David. Yet we see that even the macho man David admits he is trembling with fear: "Fear and trembling have beset me" (v. 5). The psalmist is also open to God about his feelings of hatred for his enemies and for his close friend (vv. 9–15). In this psalm we find some of the most shocking prayers in the Bible (see v. 15 below).

Structurally, Psalm 55 may be divided into three sections. The first is the plea that God pay attention to him because of his situation and his feelings about it (vv. 1–8). This is followed by a description of his situation (vv. 9–15). This section is enveloped by two imprecatory prayers (vv. 9, 15). The last section is the psalmist's extended declaration of his confidence in God in the midst of his situation. This section begins and ends with an expression of trust (vv. 16, 24c).

55:1–8 "I AM TROUBLED IN MY COMPLAINT"

The psalm begins with a typical plea for God to hear the psalmist (vv. 1–2; see also 5:1; 54:2). The difference here is that the psalmist adds: "My thoughts trouble me" (v. 2). Literally, the Hebrew may be read, "I am troubled in my complaint" (v. 2). When we are full of trouble and there is just too much, we can't help but complain. The word "complaint" reappears later (v. 17).[1]

---

1. Here the verbal form of the word is used.

We sometimes think it is wrong to complain. Certainly, there are occasions when complaining is wrong, as we see in the book of Numbers. But the "complaint" here is different. It is being honest to God about what one is feeling or experiencing. In the next verses we hear the psalmist's grievances,

He complains "because of what my enemy is saying" (v. 3). His enemies make life really hard for him (v. 3). Sometimes we are placed in situations where we wish we could just banish or evaporate right away. The psalmist feels the same. He is so afraid (vv. 4–5) he wished he were somewhere else. He wished he were like a bird so he could fly away to a far place (vv. 6–7), away "from the tempest and storm" (v. 8).

55:9–15 "I SEE VIOLENCE AND STRIFE IN THE CITY"

But often God does not answer our prayer for escape so that we may experience his grace in and through the storm. The psalmist must have wished the words of the contemporary song entitled, "Still," were possible for him: "I will soar with you above the storm." But in order to "soar" above his situation, he has to go through it. The good thing is that he knows he does not need to go through it alone. He asks God to go with him through the storm.

In verses 10–15, the psalmist describes his situation using the image of a city in which every corner, wall, center – indeed every available space – is occupied by evil: "Day and night they prowl about on its walls; malice and abuse are within it. Destructive forces are at work in the city; threats and lies never leave its streets" (vv. 10–11). The psalmist employs seven words to describe this evil in their midst: violence, strife, malice, abuse, destructive forces, threats, and lies (see vv. 9-10). It's as if the psalmist goes through the city as it were, actually walks through it, and lives there. In order to conquer a city, one has to go through it. In order to overcome one's fear, one has to face it.

But he has yet to face his biggest fear. In verses 12–14, he tries to grapple with the deeper cause of his misfortune: his own close friend has turned against him. It is hard enough when you are dealing with enemies, but it's harder still when your own friend becomes your enemy. "If an enemy were insulting me, I could endure it . . . But it is you . . . my close friend, with whom I once enjoyed sweet fellowship at the house of God" (vv. 12–14).

We may read the verses above as the psalmist's way of confronting his fears. He does this by giving a name to his troubles. First he describes the city where evil dwells. Instead of denying the evil, he acknowledges it. Second, he expresses his painful experience with his close friend, thus giving a name to his experience. But beyond the naming of his situation, he cries out to God for help. He utters two imprecatory prayers. He prays that God would judge his enemies: "Lord, confuse the wicked, confound their words" (Ps 55:9). The language recalls God's judgment over Babel in Genesis 11. So in Psalm 55:9 the psalmist is praying that God judge the wicked. The second prayer is more shocking: "Let death take my enemies by surprise, let them go down alive to the realm of the dead" (v. 15). We have a softer version of this in Filipino: *Tamaan sana sila ng kidlat* ("May they be struck by lightning"). Our Filipino ancestors would say, "May the crocodiles devour you if you do not tell the truth and fulfil your promise!"[2]

How are we to take such prayers in Psalm 55? They are also present in other psalms (see "The Imprecatory Psalms," pp. 274–276). One way of reading these prayers is by understanding them in the light of the psalmist's situation and in accord with our belief in God's justice. God is righteous and he will not tolerate evil. The psalmist asks God to judge and destroy them "for evil finds lodging among them" (v. 15b). Moreover, these people "do not change, and do not fear God" (v. 19, ESV). They are "the bloodthirsty and deceitful" (v. 23).

The good news is that God understands what we are going through. He knows our pain and allows us to express what we feel. This is better than covering up what we are actually feeling or thinking. Some are tempted to "sanitize" these verses. But God allowed them to be preserved in sacred Scriptures as a witness to the kind of God we have – a righteous, loving God, whom we can trust.

55:16–24 "BUT I WILL TRUST IN YOU"

In the preceding section the psalmist uttered a lament and an imprecatory prayer. But as with typical psalms of lament, the psalm turns to expression of confidence: "But as for me, I call to God, and the LORD saves me" (v. 16; cf. Ps 13:5). He now looks at the past and testifies how he cried out to God "evening, morning, and noon" (v. 17). In Psalm 30, night time is associated with weeping but morning is for rejoicing (v. 5b). But in Psalm 55, even morning is characterized by lament (cf. 5:1-3). The encouraging thing is that there is always someone to whom we can cry out to, whatever time of the day or night. The psalmist utters his "complaint and moan" and God hears his voice

---

2. Antonio de Morga, *Historical Events of the Philippine Islands: Published in Mexico in 1609* (Manila: José Rizal National Centennial Commission, 1962), 292.

(55:17, ESV). We may read the previous section as his complaint (vv. 9–15). Some Christians are against complaining against God and rightly so; there is complaining which are unworthy of the Lord. But not all complaining is wrong. In Psalm 55, rather than being scolded for complaining, God actually "hears" the voice of the psalmist (v. 17).[3] He feels God is on his side; God is on the side of the weak. His enemies are "many" (v. 18), but God is there to save him. Earlier he felt afraid and wanted to escape. There is no indication that his situation has changed. But something has happened within him. He has started to see his situation through the eyes of faith: "God, who is enthroned from old will hear them and humble them" (v. 19). The vision of God seated on his throne is another way of saying God is in control.

That is what happens when we confront our fears and pour out our hearts before God. Our vision is transformed so that we can see things from God's perspective and not just from our own. That is why the psalmist can express his confidence and trust in God (vv. 16, 23) as well as exhort others to "cast [their] burden on the LORD" (v. 22).

How do we apply this psalm to our situation? Traditionally, our ancestors know God as *Bathala*. He is believed to be a powerful God, distant, and people fear him. This image of *Bathala* is actually similar to the depiction of God in the Bible. The God of the Bible is also distant (he is the "God of heaven"). He is "great and awesome" (Neh 1:5). The word translated as "awesome" is from the word which means "terrible." Yet this powerful God who is seated on the heavenly throne is also close to us. We can actually come to him and tell him our troubles. When we cast our cares upon him, "he will sustain" us (55:22). This is because he cares for us: "Cast all your anxiety on him, because he cares for you" (1 Pet 5:7). He understands us. We can be honest to him about what we feel. Jesus shares the same view of God when he taught his disciples to pray, "Our Father, who art in heaven." God is in heaven, but he is also our Father.

---

3. The verb tense of the Hebrew verbs in these verses is in the imperfect, which can be translated as present tense or future tense. The ESV and NRSV opted for the latter. For the former, see NIV.

PSALM 56

Psalm 56 continues the theme of the previous psalm, which ends with the words, "But I will trust in you" (55:23c). In Psalm 56, the psalmist is confronted by his many enemies (vv. 1-2). It's as if the whole world has turned its back on him (cf. 62:3). He has nowhere to turn but to God. And so to God he comes, pouring out his heart to him. He perseveres in his trust in the Lord (56:3) even though "all day long" (vv. 1, 2, 5) his enemies trample on him. For he knows God cares for him. In one of the most moving phrases in the Psalms, the psalmist says to the Lord: "Record my misery; list my tears on your scroll – are they not in your record?" (v. 8; cf. 55:22). This reminds us of the words of Jesus in Matthew 10:30–31: "And even the hairs of your head are all numbered. So don't be afraid." God knows us through and through. He feels every pain, fear, and sorrow we go through. He even has a special place for our tears.

In the previous psalm, the psalmist wished he had wings like a dove so he could fly to a faraway place (55:6–7). Interestingly, the superscription in Psalm 56 reads: "For the director of music. To the tune of 'A Dove on Distant oaks.'" Those who placed Psalm 56 here, following Psalm 55, did a good job.[1] The superscription orients the reader to the overall tone of the psalm. David found himself in grave danger. Having been rejected by King Saul, he was forced to live outside of Judah where he hoped he could hide. But trouble awaited him there too. The superscription in Psalm 34 reveals that David had to feign madness just to escape danger. Here, the superscription further informs us that "the Philistines seized him in Gath." David is always finding himself in trouble (see Ps 57).

Psalm 56 has two refrains (vv. 4, 10–11). Each is preceded by the psalmist's laments. One can see some progression in the laments as well as in the refrains (see below). The psalm ends with a vow of thanksgiving (vv. 12–13).

56:1–4 "I AM AFRAID; I PUT MY TRUST IN YOU"

What the psalmist does in Psalm 56 is best described by what we call in Filipino *pagsusumbong* (literally, "reporting/telling"). Normally when a child is bullied by a stronger enemy, he goes to his parents and reports what has been done to him. But the word "report" does not capture the concept of

---

1. Cf. Delitzsch, *Psalms*, 166.

pagsusumbong well. For the word also reflects a sense of trust in the one to whom the incident is being reported. There is also a sense of vulnerability which causes one to ask for help (for the concept of *pagsusumbong*, see topic above, "The Imprecatory Psalms as *Pagsusumbong sa Diyos*," pp. 274–276).

Here the psalmist asks for mercy (v. 1) in view of his many enemies (v. 2). The incident is not just a one-time event, but an ongoing one. The word for "all day" is repeated three times in the psalm (vv. 1, 2, 5). The verb "press/pursue" (*shaaf*) occurs twice (vv. 1, 2). The situation intensifies from verse 1 to verse 2. In verse 1b, the psalmist complains that "my enemies are in hot pursuit." But in verse 2b, "many are attacking me." And so the psalmist is afraid.

The translation of verse 3 is "when I am afraid, I put my trust in you." But literally, the Hebrew of verse 3a simply reads: "by day I am afraid." I think we should maintain the literal translation of verse 3a, for it is parallel to verse 3b. Together the two lines should read: "by day I am afraid//I will trust in you." The second line does not have the adversative "but," as in "but I will trust in you." The two lines are simply juxtaposed; the two realities side by side: fear and trust. We understand what it means to trust God when we are afraid. It is when fear is acknowledged in the face of trust in God that the former is overcome. We see this in the refrain: "In God, whose word I praise, in God I trust and am not afraid; what can mortals do to me? (v. 4).

56:5–11 "PUT MY TEARS IN YOUR BOTTLE"

After the refrain, the lament resumes and intensifies. The psalmist complains that his enemies seek to "twist my words" (v. 5). In the previous verse, the psalmist declares he trusts in God, "whose word I praise" (v. 4). Here, the psalmist contrasts God's "word" which is trustworthy with his "words" which his enemies see as a means of taking further advantage of him. They devise strategies to destroy him (v. 5b), watching his every "step" (v. 6). In verse 7 he utters an imprecatory prayer. The first line is difficult to translate,[2] but the second is clear. He prays that "in your anger, God, bring the nations down" (v. 7b.) For comments on this kind of prayer, see 52:5 and 54:5b and the topic on "The Imprecatory Psalms as *Pagsusumbong sa Diyos*," pp. 274–276.

---

2. Literally, the Hebrew reads, "On account of [their] iniquity deliver them" (v. 7a), which does not make sense in the context of the psalm. So others translate a different verb, using "repay" instead of "deliver" (see NRSV). Another alternative is to read the verse as a question, "Will you save them on account of their evil?" (Bratcher and Reyburn, *A Translator's Handbook*, 505).

While some of us may be shocked by this kind of prayer, the psalmist does not feel embarrassed to utter it. God accepts his complaints (cf. 55:2, 17). Rather than rejecting him, God shows deep concern for him. God has keeps a record of his "misery." The Hebrew for the word "misery" occurs only here in the OT. It is also translated as "wanderings" or "tossings" (ESV, NRSV). The difficulties David experienced in all his wanderings come to mind. God knows all the troubles he has been through. As OT scholar Delitzsch writes: "He whose all-seeing eye follows him into every secret hiding-place of the desert and of the rocks, counts [his steps] . . . He knows how long David has already been driven hither and thither without any settled home."[3] God knows the journey has not been easy. Many times David found himself in tears. And so he prays, "list my tears on your scroll" (v. 8b). Obviously, he is not talking about a literal scroll. But the image shows how much God values every human experience, including the most important ones – those which cause our tears. One day, the book of Revelation tells us, Jesus will wipe away every tear from our eyes (Rev 21:4). That is at the end. Meanwhile, we will have to accept that there will be tears along the way. The encouraging thing is that God even keeps a record of them. No tear is meaningless.

This gives the psalmist the assurance that "God is for me" (v. 9b). So he is confident God will grant him victory over his enemies (v. 9a). Here there is a change to a more confident note. The refrain (vv. 10–11) further reinforces this certainty. There is an additional line here: "in the LORD, whose word I praise" (v. 10b). In this particular part of the Psalter, known as the "elohistic psalms" (Pss 42–83) because of the dominance of the name "God" (*elohim*) rather than the name "Yahweh," the occurrence of this additional line is significant. It brings out the element of intimacy.

56:12–13 VOW OF THANKSGIVING

The psalmist offers a vow of thanksgiving (v. 12). Earlier, in Psalm 50:14, God told his people he preferred a thanksgiving offering. He challenged them to call on him "in the day of trouble" and he would deliver them (50:15). Here the psalmist has experienced just that: "For you have delivered me from death" (56:13).

---

3. Delitzsch, *Psalms*, 170.

THE IMPRECATORY PSALMS AS
PAGSUSUMBONG SA DIYOS
(TELLING GOD ABOUT THE WRONG DONE TO US)

Many of the psalms are prayers uttered to God. The imprecatory psalm is also a prayer. It is comparable to what is called intercessory prayer – prayer on behalf of others. The difference is that the imprecatory psalm is a prayer against someone or a particular group of people. An imprecatory prayer is a petition to God that something bad or evil will happen to our enemies who are viewed as wicked. It is similar to what we know as curse, though not exactly the same. When we wish that someone will be hit by a thunderbolt (*tamaan sana siya ng kidlat*) we are close to what is called imprecatory prayer. The difference is that this prayer is directed to God. It is not simply wishing that something bad will happen to a person; it is asking God to do this action.

The following are examples of imprecatory prayers:

- "Break the arm of the wicked man; call the evildoer to account for his wickedness that would not otherwise be found out" (10:15)

- "Rise up, LORD, confront them, bring them down; with your sword rescue me from the wicked" (17:13)

- "May those who seek my life be disgraced and put to shame; may those who plot my ruin be turned back in dismay" (35:4)

- "Let death take my enemies by surprise; let them go down alive to the realm of the dead, for evil finds lodging among them" (55:15)

- "May they be blotted out of the book of life and not be listed with the righteous" (69:28)

- "Daughter Babylon, doomed to destruction, happy is the one who repays you according to what you have done to us. Happy is the one who seizes your infants and dashes them against the rocks" (137:8–9)

How should we understand these prayers as Christians? How should we pray them? Or should we pray them at all?

Because of the harsh and violent content of these prayers, some have regarded them as unchristian. They believe the people praying them are sinning. In some lectionaries, some of the words of the imprecatory psalms were deleted. But before we judge these prayers as sinful or evil, we should remember that these psalms have been preserved in the Holy Scriptures. There must be a reason why God has allowed them to be part of our Bible.

All of us will agree that it is better to ask God to punish the wicked than to do it yourself. Those praying the imprecatory prayers are not taking the law into their own hands. Rather, they are bringing the matter to God, who is the righteous judge. They are being honest to God about what they truly feel. They are real. One of the problems we have today is that we have become too nice. I remember one time saying that I was really annoyed by something that happened in a church where I was the pastor. One of the church leaders was shocked that pastors get annoyed!

As followers of Jesus we are commanded to love even our enemies. But we know for a fact that this is far from easy. Some deny that they are angry and claim that they simply forgive those who have done them wrong. But there is also something wrong with forgiving too soon. Without properly dealing with our anger, the emotion can be suppressed. We may think we have forgiven someone when all we have done is deny our anger. Because of the desire to move on, we can rush into the process and in the end find ourselves even angrier than before.

The imprecatory psalms allow us to be human, to admit that we are angry. This is a humbling experience. It is not easy to admit to the Lord that actually we do not love our enemies but instead wish them destroyed. But that is better than denying it, for the Lord knows our heart anyway. So why deny the truth?

The imprecatory prayers should be understood within the context of the justice of God. They are expressions of hope in the God who is utterly just and righteous. We long for justice, but we know that many times justice is denied to those who most need it. Human justice is very imperfect. In many parts of Asia, victims do not have the power or the means to secure even a hearing. The imprecatory prayers in this case become like the *pagsusumbong* (reporting or telling) of a little child to his father or authority figure of the wrong done to him by someone stronger and powerful than him.

The imprecatory psalms can best be understood within our context through the concept of *pagsusumbong*. The word does not have an exact equivalent in English. But in Filipino this concept suggests a person of vulnerability going to a person with authority to "report" and make an appeal over what is perceived to be an unjust act. But you do not just make *sumbong* to anyone, only to people you trust (e.g. your own father). You make *sumbong* because you believe this person has your best interests at heart. You also trust this authority figure as one who is powerful enough to redress the injustice. Viewed this way, the imprecatory prayers become expressions of trust in God our Father who is not only powerful but is just and loving. It brings comfort to those who are weak and oppressed, who have no one else to go to but God. It also serves as a strong warning for the oppressors. There is a God who fights for the right of the weak. The Filipino concept of *pagsusumbong* fits in well with the imprecatory prayers because often the victim is the vulnerable one who goes to a figure of authority whom he trusts and reports what is done to him in order that authority figure will address the matter. The people praying the imprecatory psalms have nowhere else to go to but to God, whom they trust as their deliverer and Lord.

The imprecatory prayers form an important part of the life of the worshipping community. These psalms:

> uncover the mechanisms of violence as actions and strategies emanating from concrete human beings and institutions . . . These psalms can and will make obvious the web of violence presented, especially for the weak, the suffering, and those under attack . . . With their concrete expressions of fear and pain, they bring that pain to the center of ordinary religious and social life. They are the expression of that sensitivity to suffering that is constitutive for biblical piety, and for any way of life that is shaped by the Bible.[1]

When issues of justice are no longer mentioned in the prayers of God's people, they cease to be an issue of prime importance and gets pushed aside, and neglected. To cry out once more before God that something is not right falls in line with the justice of God, who will one day come to judge the living and the dead.

---

1. Zenger, *A God of Vengeance? Understanding the Psalms of Divine Wrath*, 74–75.

PSALM 57

David is presented in this psalm as one who is always on the run. Psalm 57 is one of the thirteen psalms[1] whose superscriptions contain a brief historical background (see "The Significance of the Superscriptions," pp. 258–259). It is close to Psalm 3. In both psalms David is in flight. The phrase "when he fled" occurs in the superscription of both psalms. David was fleeing from his son Absalom in Psalm 3, and here in Psalm 57, from Saul. In Psalm 57, he finds himself in a cave. It is interesting that in almost all of the superscriptions with historical backgrounds, David is presented as someone who is in trouble. He is not the David who is up there, seated on his throne, victorious, in control. Rather, he is the David down below, afraid, yet trusting in God, encountering danger each step of the way. As Brevard Childs puts it:

> the incidents chosen as evoking the psalms were not royal occasions or representative of the kingly office. Rather, David is pictured simply as a man, indeed chosen by God for the sake of Israel, but who displays all strengths and weaknesses of all human beings. He emerges as a person who experiences the full range of human emotions from fear and despair to courage and love, from complaint and plea to praise and thanksgiving . . .[2]

This is probably why the Psalms have so much depth; they arose out of difficult situations. The helpful thing about these psalms, and Psalm 57, in particular, is that they show us the way forward. In the superscription, we find David in the cave. By the time we finish the psalm, we are already with him in the "heavens," praising God. He has moved from lament to praise. The psalm shows us how he moved from one to the other.

Psalm 57 is similar to Psalm 56. The opening words are identical: "Have mercy on me." The verb "pursue" recurs here (56:1, 2; 57:3). Both contain a refrain (56:4, 10–11; 57:5, 11). The way in which the refrain is used is similar to the refrain in Psalm 42:5; 43:5. Though the words are identical, the sense of the refrain changes as the psalm progresses.

---

1. Psalms 3, 7, 18, 34, 51, 52, 54, 56, 57, 59, 60, 63, and 142.
2. Childs, *Introduction to the Old Testament*, 521.

57:1–6 "HAVE MERCY ON ME, O GOD, HAVE MERCY ON ME"

Psalm 57 employs the typical language of the lament. But we should not think that just because they are "typical," there is no more uniqueness about them. As in most cases, closer attention to the details yields something unique in a particular psalm. As readers, we have to pay close attention to the way the psalms are formulated, for it is easy to miss important elements when the words are familiar.

The opening words of Psalm 57 is an example. Verse 1 employs stock language in the Psalms (e.g. the language of "taking refuge"; see 7:1; 16:1). Even the first words of the psalm are like those of the previous psalm: "Have mercy on me" (cf. 56:1).[3] But Psalm 57 goes beyond this by repeating the petition twice: "Have mercy on me, my God, have mercy on me" (57:1). This adds an element of urgency to the prayer and indicates a deep sense of need. When we are confronted with simple problems or needs, we often pray as usual. But when we are faced with extremely difficult situations, our prayers become more intense. We may find ourselves prostrating before God.

As indicated in the superscription, David is on the run, hiding in a cave. There may have been many situations like this in the past. But this one seems to be different. The psalmist uses the word "disaster" (v. 2). Literally, the Hebrew word means "destructions" (*huwot*). The psalmist is confronted not with a simple "storm" but with "destroying storms" (v. 2, NRSV; the Hebrew is in the plural form). This may be compared to occasions in the life of believers when the attack from the evil one is fiercer. The Apostle Paul talks about the "evil day" (Eph 6:13). As believers we are all in a spiritual battle. But there are days when the onslaught is heavier.

The situation envisaged in Psalm 57 is similar. This explains the intensity of the prayer. The good news is that in situations like these, we can always find a safe haven in the LORD: "I will take refuge in the shadow of your wings" (v. 1b). Taking refuge in the Lord primarily involves prayer. The psalmist cries out to God. He refers to God as "Most High" (v. 2) and in the next line we have an ellipsis; the words "I cry out to God" are dropped in order to elaborate more on the character of God. He is "Most High" but he is also one "who fulfills his purpose for me" (v. 2b, ESV). This great God who is in heaven is also with us in our troubles (see Ps 55). He especially sends forth from heaven his "love and his faithfulness" (57:3, 10).

---

3. The words are exactly the same in Hebrew, though in some translations they differ slightly (e.g. NRSV).

In verse 4, the metaphor changes from that of "destroying storms" to "lions . . . ravenous beasts." Here the psalmist further employs metaphors in order to give a name to his situation. One does not move right away into resolution; one has to confront his/her situation. Thus, after the psalmist has pleaded for mercy and taken refuge in God, he now tries to "name" his situation. The psalmist finds himself among devouring lions (v. 4; cf. 22:12–13). The image depicts extreme danger, creating fear on the part of the psalmist. These enemies are set on destroying him. In verse 6a, they set a trap for him. As a result, his soul is "bowed down" (v. 6a).

Yet between the two verses depicting his trouble (vv. 4, 6), we find the refrain (v. 5). The structure of verses 4–6 focuses on the prayer expressed in the refrain:

"I am in the midst lions" (v. 4);
"Be exalted, O God, above the heavens" (v. 5);
"They spread a net for my feet" (v. 6a).

The psalmist asks God that in the midst of his situation, God would be exalted. The prayer is similar to the Lord's Prayer – "Hallowed be thy name" – a petition that God would move in such a way that people would honor his holy name.

God answers the prayer of the psalmist. There is a sudden change of events in verse 6b: "They dug a pit in my path, but they have fallen into it themselves." This explains the change of mood in the next section.

57:7–11 "MY HEART, O GOD, IS STEADFAST, MY HEART IS STEADFAST"

Interestingly, as the prayer of lament is repeated twice, so the declaration of trust is also repeated:

"Be merciful to me, O God, be merciful to me" (v. 1);
"My heart is steadfast, O God, my heart is steadfast" (v. 7).

The repetition in verse 7 confirms that the repetition in verse 1 is not accidental. The poet has deliberately repeated the words to draw a connection between the two verses. There is a noticeable change between verses 1 and 7 from weakness to strength, from praise to lament. What brought about the change?

The previous verses give us the answer. The change involved a process. First, the psalmist acknowledged his need for God's mercy (v. 1a). Though this is something that should not be taken literally, we can say that because he cried for God's mercy twice, he is now able to declare his confidence in God twice also. Had he not cried for mercy he would not be uttering the words of confidence. Second, he took refuge in God (v. 1b). This involves praying to God and crying out to him (v. 2). Third, he took the courage to "name" his situation (vv. 4, 6).

As a result, a change has transpired within him. There is nothing in the text to show any change in his situation. But as the psalmist goes through the whole process just described, his inner situation changes. If earlier he is lamenting; now he is already singing (v. 8). He makes a vow to give thanks to the Lord (v. 9), and not just before God's people, but before "the nations." And in the final refrain, echoes of "the heavens" explode the limits of the cave, as the psalmist reflects on the greatness of God's steadfast love and his faithfulness: "For great is your love, reaching to the heavens; your faithfulness reaches to the skies" (v. 10). The psalmist no longer sees himself constrained by his situation but is already praising God, exalting him, "above the heavens" (v. 11).

We are used to pleading for mercy, so we won't have problems with the opening verses of Psalm 57. We also long for restoration, so the overall movement from lament to praise in this psalm is something we would readily embrace. The question is, are we prepared to go through the process? Our problem is that we want restoration but we are unwilling to face our problems. A common advice given to people with problems is: *Tawanan mo ang iyong problema* ("*Laugh at your problem*"). While our happy outlook on life has enabled us to cope with our problems, we are not good at confronting our issues. We lack that resolve for change. Often, once the emotional fervor has subsided, our determination likewise diminishes. The challenge of Psalm 57 is for us to face our issues, confront them, and "name" them in the presence of God through prayer. In the process we will encounter the God who is not only with us in our heights but also in our depths. Like a good physician, God allows us to go through a painful operation so that true healing will take place. May God enable us by his grace!

PSALM 58

Beware, corrupt judges: There is a God in heaven who is watching you. The supreme Judge will see to it that you will be judged for your actions. The poor and the vulnerable will be avenged. This is the message of this psalm. The main theme is expressed in its opening and closing verses. In verse 1 the corrupt judges are addressed: "Do you judge people with equity?" In the closing verse, the psalmist expresses certainty that there is indeed a "God who judges on earth" (v. 11). The psalm is meant to instill fear among corrupt judges and leaders. There is a God who is running this world. At the same time, the psalm gives hope to the victims of injustice, and encourages us "to pray and work passionately for justice and fairness in God's world."[1]

Though the overall sense is understandable, the Hebrew of this psalm is difficult. In some places we can only guess at the correct meaning of the words (e.g. v. 9).[2] But the overall structure is discernible. The psalm may be divided into three sections: a description of corrupt judges and leaders (vv. 1–5), an imprecatory prayer against the wicked leaders (vv. 6–9), and an expression of confidence in God's justice (vv. 10–11).

58:1–5 THE CORRUPT JUDGES AND LEADERS

The psalm begins with a question addressed to the "rulers" (v. 1a). The word translated "rulers" comes from a Hebrew word that literally means "silence" or "muteness" (*elem*). But this does not seem to make sense in the context of verse 1. So it has been proposed that the word should be *elim* ("gods") rather than *elem* ("muteness"). Here, however, the word "gods" does not refer to the deities in the ancient Near East but to rulers, who were thought to be representatives of the gods. Specifically, these rulers were the people who had been given the responsibility of administering justice – the judges. Verse 1b is addressed to them. The whole question has a ring of doubt in it: "Do you judge people with equity?"

The answer is a resounding "no." These rulers who are supposed to dispense truth and righteousness actually "devise injustice" and practice "violence" (v. 2). The psalmist paints a dark picture of them. In their "hearts" (v. 2a) – the core of their being – they are wicked. The NT teaches that all

---

1. Okorocha and Foulkes, "Psalms," 662.
2. The NIV has a note saying that the "meaning of the Hebrew for this verse is uncertain."

kinds of evil intentions come from the heart (Mark 7:21–23). These leaders are steeped in evil.

The psalmist employs hyperbole (exaggeration) as a literary device to drive home his point. Using language found in the prayer of confession (51:5), the psalmist describes these people as wicked "from birth," speaking lies "from the womb" (58:3). They are as dangerous, as venomous serpents (v. 4a).

It is not clear exactly what the psalmist means when he compares them to a "cobra that has stopped its ear" in verse 4b. Probably he is referring to the hard-heartedness of wicked judges who ignore the pleas of the poor.[3] They appear to be listening, as snakes do when they sway in response to a snake charmer's flute. But they are not really listening (v. 5). It is not in their nature to do so.

58:6–9 "BREAK THE TEETH IN THEIR MOUTHS, O GOD"

When innocent victims – the vulnerable and the poor – cry out for help, those in positions of authority must listen. If they don't, weak and innocent victims will cry out to the supreme Judge. And when they do, God will surely heed their cry (Exod 2:23). The imprecatory prayer in Psalm 58:6–9 represents the cry of the victims of injustice and their defenders. The people ask God to "break the teeth" of the wicked (v. 6; cf. 3:7). They wish their enemies would vanish "like water that flows away" (v. 7). They pray they will be like "the snail that dissolves into slime" (v. 8a, ESV). In many places in Asia, justice may be likened to the snail; it moves very, very slowly! In the Philippines, justice is often called "just-*tiis*" ("suffering").

These imprecatory prayers come from those who are suffering because they have neither the means nor the influence even to secure a fair trial. They come from those who fight for justice on behalf of the vulnerable and the weak. Read in this way, the imprecatory prayers become a means of *pagsusumbong sa Diyos* ("telling God"). (See the topic on "The Imprecatory Psalms as *Pagsusumbong sa Diyos*," pp. 274–276). These verses (58:6–9) are not meant to incite the victims to violence. Rather, they provide hope for the weak and vulnerable. They assure them they have someone they can go to when the powerful and the mighty in the world have turned their backs on them. They can go to God and pour out their hearts. Through the words of the psalm, it

---

3. Alter, *The Book of Psalms*, 202.

is hoped that they will find release so that they do not need to take revenge on their own. Vengeance belongs to the Lord.

58:10–11 "SURELY THERE IS A GOD WHO JUDGES ON EARTH"

The psalmist is certain the "righteous will be glad when they are avenged" (v. 10a). The next line contains disturbing words: "when they dip their feet in the blood of the wicked" (v. 10b). We are not to take these words as a license for inflicting violence. Nor should we try to sanitize the language of the psalm. The language is meant to graphically depict the end of those who themselves perpetuate violence (v. 2b). God is a righteous judge but he is also a terrible one (Heb 10:31).

We live in a time when there is so much injustice, inequality, unfairness. Corruption is high, and present in all levels and sectors of society, including the religious. It seems as if there is no fear of God among many of our leaders and our people. These people commit violence and all kinds of evil and yet they remain unpunished. We sometimes wonder whether there is a God in the world. Psalm 58 is a bold declaration that there is a God who judges the world. It challenges the victims to place their hope not in human judges but in God. It encourages those who work towards social justice to keep on doing their good work, knowing there is a God who sees what they are doing (Gal 6:9). They are never alone. If we fight for justice, God is on our side.

The psalm ends in a note of hope. The hope is that as a result of what God will do, people will say that the righteous will indeed be rewarded and that "surely there is a God who judges on earth" (v. 11).

PSALM 59

The main theme of Psalm 59 is "protection amidst danger." The superscription tells us David was faced with grave danger. Unlike in the other superscriptions, Psalm 59 is explicit in saying that Saul was seeking to "kill him" (cf. Psalm 57). The brief historical background points to the narrative in 1 Samuel 19:8 and following. There Saul sent men to the house of David in order to kill him. The reference to the passage in 1 Samuel makes the danger more vivid. Confronted with such a situation, what did he do? He took refuge in God, who became his "fortress" (vv. 9, 17). Like David, God can also become our refuge and strength. As with most of the Psalms, we can use the words of Psalm 59 to pour out our heart to God when we are faced with danger.

Structurally, the psalm may be outlined as follows:

Petition	(vv. 1–2)	
Motivating statements	(vv. 3–4a)	
Imprecation	(vv. 4b–5)	
Refrain		(v. 6)
Complaint	(v. 7)	
Confidence: "but you"	(v. 8)	
Confidence: "O my strength"	(v. 9–10)	
Imprecation	(vv. 11–13)	
Refrain		(v. 14)
Complaint	(v. 15)	
Confidence: "but I"	(v. 16)	
Confidence: "O my strength"	(v. 17)	

As we can see in the outline above, the psalm contains a refrain which occurs twice (vv. 6, 14). Each of the two refrains is followed by a series of verses that are parallel to each other (e.g. vv. 9 and 17).

59:1–10 "DELIVER ME FROM MY ENEMIES, O GOD"

The psalm begins with a series of petitions which reflect the situation envisaged in the superscription. David finds himself in grave trouble. And he comes to God, pleading for deliverance (vv. 1–2). The petition is followed by motivating statements. Those who are seeking his life are "fierce" (v. 3). He reasons that he has done nothing wrong (v. 4a). With urgency he prays: "Arise to help me; look on my plight!" (v. 4b).

Up to this point it is easy to connect the psalm with the superscription. The next petition is broader. The psalmist asks that God "punish all the nations" (v. 5). Suddenly, we are transported to a different time, probably when David was already king. Or maybe, another king is being referred to.[1] As with many of these psalms, it is difficult to identify one specific setting. It is possible that the psalm was originally composed by David, but was later used by other individuals or the community for other occasions (cf. 51:18–19). That is the beauty of the Psalms. Because they have been used by other individuals and communities, we are encouraged to use them also.

The refrain depicts an image of savagery, with the enemies being likened to dangerous hungry dogs (v. 6). Dogs were viewed very negatively in ancient times. Here they go about howling and "prowling about the city" (cf. 55:9–11). From their mouths come "swords" (59:7) – a "metaphor for cruel and malicious speech."[2] They are boastful. They think they can do anything they please (v. 7c).

But immediately in the next verse, we find a response from God. God laughs at them (v. 8; cf. 2:4). The scene quickly shifts from the streets of the city to the heavens, where God looks at these people with derision. The change encourages the psalmist to look to God, whence his strength comes. He refers to God as "my strength" and "fortress" (v. 9). He is confident God will grant him victory (v. 10).

59:11–13 IMPRECATIONS

Earlier in verse 5, the psalmist uttered an imprecatory prayer for "all the nations." Here he specifically prays for those who attack him (vv. 11–13). The petition in verse 11 is strange: "Do not kill them . . . or my people may forget." Probably the sense is that the psalmist is asking for a slow punishment so that it will hurt more. He prays that God might bring them down (v. 11b) and "consume them in wrath" (v. 13). The prayers here are similar to the imprecatory prayers in Psalm 58. The difference is that here they are more specific. The psalmist asks that God destroy his enemies so that "it will be

---

1. Cf. Kirkpatrick, *The Book of Psalms*, 332.
2. Bratcher and Reyburn, *A Translator's Handbook*, 524.

known to the ends of the earth that God rules over Jacob" (v. 13). The scope of the prayer in Psalm 58 is broader (see v. 11).[3]

The second appearance of the refrain (v. 14) is followed by a pattern similar to the above. But there is a movement in verse 16. The dogs come back every "evening," but the psalmist vows he will sing of God's steadfast love in the "morning." In the narrative in 1 Samuel 19:8 and following, David manages to escape during the night through the intervention of his wife Michal. "Weeping may stay for the night, but rejoicing comes in the morning" (30:5b). The psalmist ends with a declaration of God as his "strength" and his "fortress" (v. 17; cf. v. 9).

Psalm 59 uses language that some may find offensive. It contains imprecatory prayers. These are prayers that God will do bad things to other people, usually wicked enemies. One way to approach these types of prayer is by trying to understand them from the concept of *pagsusumbong sa Diyos* (For a discussion on imprecatory prayers, see "The Imprecatory Psalms," pp. 274–276). These prayers look to God in the hope that justice will prevail. Rather, than taking the 'law' into his own hands and inflicting punishment on the wicked, the psalmist puts his trust in God, the supreme judge. It is certainly better to pray that God destroy the wicked rather than do it yourself.

---

3. For a similar movement from universal to local (Israel), see Ps 47:9 and Ps 48, respectively.

PSALM 60

Psalm 60 is a communal lament, similar to Psalm 44 and Psalm 12. The people feel that God has rejected them, complaining that God no longer goes out with their armies (60:1, 10; cf. 44:9). But as they pour out their laments to God, a response comes. The middle portion represents God's answer (60:6–8). It is given in the form of a divine oracle. Often in the lament psalms, we find a sudden change of mood from lament to an expression of trust which then leads to thanksgiving or praise. One wonders what has caused the change. The most common explanation given by scholars is that in between the lament and vow of thanksgiving, a word from God is given. This in turn would bring encouragement to the person lamenting. How we wish that in our prayers we would hear God directly speaking to us! We could not ask for more.

And yet, as in Psalm 12, the lament resumes after the report of God's response (60:10; see comment on Ps 12:8). This reminds us that even after receiving God's answer, an element of tension remains. We continue to live by faith even when we have already received the answer. For often, the situation remains the same, and it is only through the eye of faith that we are able to continue holding on to God's promise. The people in Psalm 60 continue to come to God in the midst of the tension between God's answer and the present reality, because of their deep acknowledgement that help comes from God alone: "human help is worthless" (v. 11b).

The outline of Psalm 60 may be described as follows. The psalm begins with lament (vv. 1–4) followed by a petition (v. 5). A divine oracle is given in response to the lament (vv. 6–8). We would expect that this would lead right away to praise or to a change in the mood of the psalm. But lament lingers (vv. 9–10). This indicates that the present situation of the people remains unchanged. Despite this, however, the people continue to cling to God, seeking his help (v. 11). Only then does the psalm shift to a confident declaration of trust in God (v. 12). The psalm ends on a positive note. Here Psalm 60 differs from Psalm 12. The latter ends with the element of tension unresolved (see comment in Psalm 12).

60:1–5 "O GOD, YOU HAVE REJECTED US"

To some extent, the overall movement of the psalm reflects the tension between the superscription and the content of the psalm itself. The superscription provides some historical background related to the wars of David: "A Miktam of David . . . when he fought Aram Naharaim and with Aram Zobah, and when Joab returned and struck down twelve thousand Edomites in the Valley of Salt" (cf. 2 Sam 8:3–8; 10:6–18; 1 Chr 18:3–11; 19:16–19). Unlike in the previous superscriptions with background (e.g. Pss 57, 59), David here is already king. Yet it is interesting that he is presented as still struggling. Nonetheless, the overall emphasis of the superscription is on victory. Under the leadership of Joab, the commander of the army, twelve thousand Edomites were killed in the Valley of Salt.[1] Though this victory is attributed to Joab in the superscription, credit is still due to David, being the king (cf. 2 Sam 8:13).[2] So the overall tone of the superscription is triumphant.

This contrasts with the content of the prayer. The psalm begins with a powerful lament by the people: "You have rejected us, God" (v. 1a). The word "rejected" reappears later in verse 10 (cf. 44:9). In contrast to the victories of David, the people complain: You "no longer go out with our armies" (60:10), which they suppose is because God is angry with them (v. 1b). The psalm does not explain why God is angry. Nor is there any confession of sins. This issue is left hanging, unlike in Psalm 44 where the people assert they have done nothing wrong (44:17–19).

They attribute their defeat or lack of victory to God, who is said to have "broken our defenses" (v. 1, ESV). Their defeat is described in seismic terms. The earth quakes, torn open (v. 2). They themselves are staggering like drunkards (v. 3). And God has caused them to retreat (v. 4). It is not clear what verse 4 means. Ironically, the setting up of a banner is a signal for victory. But here the banner is used for the purpose of retreating. The people see defeat where victory was once found.

The disaster had shaken the very foundation of their existence, but not the foundation of their faith. They believe that the same God who has caused all of their sufferings (v. 3a: "You have shown your people desperate times") is also the one who is able to bring healing. They pray, "now restore us!" (v. 1) and ask that God "mend its [their land] fractures" (v. 2). The word translated "mend" comes from the Hebrew word which also means "heal" (*rafa*). Once more they ask that God grant them victory "with your right hand" (v. 5). The

---

1. The Valley of Salt is in the south of the Dead Sea.
2. The same thing can be said with the account in 1 Chr 8:12, which attributes the victory to Abishai. The difference in the number of those who were killed – 12,000 in the superscription and 18,000 in 2 Sam 8:13 and 1 Chr 18:12 – is probably due to a textual error (Kirkpatrick, *The Book of Psalms*, 338).

psalmist describes the people as "those who fear you" (v. 4) and "those you love" (v. 5).

60:6–8 DIVINE ORACLE

The psalm does not provide the details of how the people received the answer from God. What we have here is some kind of report of what God has "spoken in his sanctuary" (v. 6), also known as "divine oracle." Verses 5–12 appear also in Psalm 108:6–13.

The lament of the people centers on military concerns. In the divine oracle, God is presented as a victorious "warrior distributing booty."[3] Several names of regions/tribes/nations are mentioned. Shechem and the Vale of Succoth represent the regions west and east of Jordan, respectively. Both Gilead and Manasseh are associated with the region east of Jordan, while Ephraim and Judah represent the tribes who are west of Jordan. In effect, God is saying, "I am in control; I own all of these."

Ephraim and Judah are specially mentioned: the former as God's helmet and the latter as God's scepter. These two correspond to positions of power and honor, Manasseh to military leadership and Judah to sovereign rule.

The last three names refer to three nations outside Israel (v. 8). Moab is described as God's washbasin, possibly a derogatory term, signifying a menial role assigned to Moab. Or it may simply refer to the area where the place is located near the Dead Sea. The statement "on Edom I toss my sandal" (v. 8) has been interpreted based on two passages: Deuteronomy 25:9–10 and Ruth 4:7. The statement may be a reference to slavery or ownership. The third nation is Philistia, over which shouts of victory are heard.

60:9–12 RETURN TO LAMENT AND DECLARATION OF TRUST

Overall, the divine oracle is making the point that God is powerful. He owns all these lands. The enemies of the people are all under his power. These encouraging words ought to lead to praise. However, instead of a vow of thanksgiving, we have lament. The lament at the beginning of the psalm returns. The psalmist repeats the word he used earlier, "rejected" (v. 10; cf. v. 1).

The representative of the people, probably the king, asks: "Who will bring me to the fortified city?" (v. 9) He is asking who will grant them victory. They

---

3. Schaefer, *Psalms*, 147.

believe it should be God. But they ask: "Is it not you, God, you who have now rejected us?" (v. 10).

While some may be shocked at the audacity with which these people approach God through their laments, we may also appreciate them for their honesty and openness with God. Their lament should not be interpreted as weak faith. On the contrary, theirs is a bold faith, because they are able to confront the realities of the situation without letting go of their faith in God. They do not lament and give up on God. They continue to cling to him. Although they feel God has abandoned them, they continue to pray to him, for they know help comes from him alone (v. 11). As Westermann writes: "In the complaint against God, the sufferers cling to the one who causes suffering, as God is the only one who can turn aside their suffering."[4] The last verse of the psalm shows us that it is when we have poured out our heart to God, becoming honest with him about what they really feel, that we are able to move to a more hopeful outlook: "With God we will gain the victory, and he will trample down our enemies" (v. 12).

Like the Israelites, we have been through difficult times. Our history is replete with stories of oppression, abuse, and domination by foreign powers. We can identify with the words of the people in Psalm 60:3, as we have been through some really hard times too. And yet our sufferings, like theirs, have taught us that real help comes only from the Lord. Without denying the destructive effects of our experiences, we can say that our hardships have taught us to depend more on God.

The challenge for us in the appropriation of this psalm lies in their almost irreverent way of approaching or questioning God. But we should understand this within the context of a covenant in which God and his people are partners. God does not look at us as his slaves. Jesus calls his disciples, and that includes all those who follow him: "friends." Without being irreverent, we can be open with God as God's people. God does not expect us to be like robots who only follow their makers' programming. God desires to deal with human beings who can honestly tell him how much it hurts sometimes. It is such people who can also truly love him and experience intimacy with him.

---

4. Claus Westermann, "The Complaint against God," in *God in the Fray: A Tribute to Walter Brueggemann*, eds. Tod Linafelt and Timothy K. Beal (Minneapolis: Fortress, 1998), 238.

PSALM 61

In this prayer attributed to David, we get one of the most helpful images of prayer and praying: "Lead me to the rock that is higher than I" (v. 2). The prayer recalls the times in the life of David when he had been confronted with situations and enemies, bigger and more powerful than himself. The image of a big rock captures it well. It reminds us of Goliath and of David's days as a fugitive. These are some of David's big rocks, figuratively and literally speaking. David had always been on the run when King Saul was around. And most likely he encountered those big rocks which he desperately needed to scale in order to survive. But it was also through "rocks that are higher than him" that David learned to trust in God, the Rock of Ages.

Like David we also have our "rocks," situations in our life which go beyond what we are able to handle. Rather than seeing these as hindrances, let us view them as challenges and opportunities to learn to trust God more. They are opportunities for us to grow further, to move on. The tendency, when we are confronted with a big rock, is just to stop, sit where we are and not continue. But the big rock before us is actually an invitation to grow not only in faith but also in humility. There will always be a rock that is higher than us. We need God's help. It takes humility and trust in God to admit we cannot do it by ourselves. And that is one of the things Psalm 61 is trying to teach us.

Psalm 61 may be outlined as follows:

- Petition: "hear my cry" (vv. 1–4);
- Response: "you have heard" (vv. 5–7);
- Vow of praise (v. 8).

61:1–4 "HEAR MY CRY"

The first word in the psalm, "hear" (*shamah*), is a structural marker. It is repeated in verse 5 ("you have heard" *shamah*) to indicate the movement in the psalm from lament to praise. The psalm begins with a situation of lament. The psalmist pleads for God to hear his "cry":

> "Hear my cry, O God;
> listen to my prayer" (v. 1).

As can be seen, there is a parallelism in verse 1, with the word "cry" parallel to "prayer." This reminds us that there are times when our prayer is simply crying. We feel so far from God. This is what the psalmist felt when he uttered these words: "From the ends of the earth I call to you" (v. 2). According to Weiser, the prayer reflects the suffering of a man who "has lost courage, so that God and the help he can give rise up before his eyes like a towering rock which he cannot scale. It is in such a mood, such a feeling of being separated from God by an unbridgeable gulf, that causes him to picture himself at the other 'end of the earth' and to cry out from its depths (cf. 130:1; 135:6f.)."[1] His heart is "faint" (v. 2b).

But it is his realization that he is weak that causes him to come to the one who can enable him to scale the "towering rock" before him. In our weakness God's power is made manifest. The prayer, "Lead me to the rock that is higher than I" is an acknowledgement of our limitations and at the same time a recognition of the power of God. The following is a good rewording of the prayer: "Lead me to a rock that is too high for me to reach by my own unaided effort."[2]

It is interesting that the image used to refer to God remains close to the image of the rock, "for you have been a refuge, a strong tower" (v. 3). Those who trust in God not only overcome the big rock that is before them; they are brought even higher. They find in God the very security and safety they are looking for. But there is even more; the more they experience God, the more they are drawn to him, so that they long to be in his presence. In verse 4 the psalmist asks that he might be allowed to "dwell in your tent forever" (see also Psalm 15). Earlier, we had a hard time hearing the psalmist because he is so far away, at the "ends of the earth" (v. 2). Now he is so close, at the very center of the universe. The interplay between distance and nearness is remarkable. It's when we feel so far from God that we're closest. It's when we feel so vulnerable that we are at our best, secure in the "shelter of your wings" (v. 4b).

61:5–8 "YOU HAVE HEARD MY VOWS"

There is a transition in verse 5 from the prayer to an assurance that the prayer has been heard. Here we understand the earlier prayer as part of the psalmist's vows. Encouraged by God's answer, the psalmist goes on to utter some more requests (vv. 6–7). This pattern of answered prayer turning into more petitions is not unique here (see 27:6–7; 31:7–10). The petitions pertain to the king. Specifically, the first request is that his life will be prolonged. There

---

1. Weiser, *The Psalms*, 443.
2. Kirkpatrick, *The Book of Psalms*, 345.

is a progression in the two colons (v. 6) from the king's "days" to his "years." The second request is that the king "be enthroned in God's presence forever" (v. 7). "Forever" does not literally mean "eternity." He is asking that there will always be someone to rule in his line. What is more significant is the qualification, "in God's presence." This reflects the longing for intimacy expressed earlier in verse 4a. God's steadfast love and faithfulness will be his guardian.

The petitions offered on behalf of the king shows that probably the prayer is a royal psalm and that the prayer is uttered by the king himself. It is not uncommon to find third person requests in the midst of prayers in the first person style (e.g. 28:8; 63:11).[3]

In the end, answered petitions and prayers should lead to thanksgiving. Even vows that have been answered lead to more offerings of the same (v. 8).

---

3. Mays, *Psalms*, 215.

JOY AND SORROW AND THE
HEBREW WORD *RINNAH*

Psalm 61 begins with the words, "Hear my cry." There are times when all we can do is cry, especially when we encounter rocks that are higher than we are. But it is interesting that the word translated as "cry" in Psalm 61:1 is the same Hebrew word, *rinnah*, translated as "shout for joy" in Psalms 42:4; 47:1 and 105:43. The same wellspring from which our joys overflow is the place where our sorrows and tears come from. As Kahlil Gibran beautifully puts it:[1]

Your joy is your sorrow unmasked.
And the selfsame well from which your laughter
rises was oftentimes filled with your tears.

And how else can it be?
The deeper that sorrow carves into your being,
the more joy you can contain.
Is not the cup that holds your wine the very
cup that was burned in the potter's oven?
And is not the lute that soothes your spirit,
the very wood that was hollowed with knives?
When you are joyous, look deep into your heart
and you shall find it is only that which
has given you sorrow that is giving you joy.
When you are sorrowful look again in your heart,
and you shall see that in truth you are weeping
for that which has been your delight.

Some of you say, "Joy is greater than sorrow,"
And others say, "Nay sorrow is the greater.
But I say unto you, they are inseparable.
Together they come, and when one sits alone
with you at your board,
remember that the other is asleep upon your bed.
Verily you are suspended like scales
between your sorrow and your joy.
Only when you are empty are you at standstill and balanced.
When the treasure-keeper lifts you
to weigh his gold and his silver,
needs must your joy or your sorrow rise or fall.

---

1. Kahlil Gibran, *The Prophet* (New York: Knopf, 1952), 36–37.

PSALM 62

One of the central messages of this psalm can be summed up in the words of St. Augustine: "our hearts are restless until they rest in you". The psalmist declares: "Truly my soul finds rest in God" (v. 1). The word "truly" (also be translated "alone"), is repeated six times in the psalm (vv. 1, 2, 4, 5, 6, 9) to emphasize this point.[1] Where other psalms simply proclaim God as "my rock" (18:2, 46; 28:1; 144:1), Psalm 62 asserts that God is "truly my rock" (v. 2). God and God alone; there is no other.

But what do we mean by rest? Rest does not mean the absence of trouble or problems. The psalmist is in the midst of trouble (see vv. 2–3) when he makes that declaration in verse 1. He is like the Apostle Paul who penned the famous Philippians 4:4 while in prison: "Rejoice in the Lord always. I will say it again: Rejoice!" We do not wait for the perfect situation, when all our problems are already sorted out and there are no more loose ends. Rather, rest is the confidence that we have somebody bigger taking care of us. This "somebody" is not our boss in the office, our church, or even our loved ones. It is God, our rock and our salvation (Ps 62:2, 6–7).

The psalm contains a refrain (vv. 1, 5), with minor variations. This serves as a structural marker. The first section is a declaration of one's dependence on God as reflected in one's experience of rest (vv. 1–4). The second section is a further assertion, a continued holding on to the declaration made earlier (vv. 5–7). In the third section, the psalmist turns to address his audience, urging them to pour out their hearts to God (vv. 8–10). Finally, the psalmist shares his personal encounter with God and gives his concluding reflection (vv. 11–12).

62:1–4 "MY SOUL FINDS REST IN GOD ALONE"

The superscription contains the words "For Jeduthun," found also in Psalms 39 and 77. Probably, the name refers to the Jeduthun who was one of David's chief musicians, mentioned in 1 Chronicles 16:41. Others think the word means "confession."

The first two verses are statements of trust in God. The psalmist asserts it is only in God that his soul finds rest. As mentioned above, the word "truly/

---

1. Unfortunately, this emphasis is often lost in translation. But see Alter, *The Book of Psalms*, 213–214.

alone" is a key word in the psalm. It highlights the psalmist's complete trust in God apart from any other. In Hebrew, verse 1a is a clause without a verb. Literally, it reads: "In God alone my soul [finds] rest." You just have to supply the verb. It is similar to Psalm 1:2a. Both passages stress learning to rest in the presence of God.

The reason the psalmist is able to rest in God is that he feels secure in him. God to him is "my rock and my salvation" and "my fortress" (v. 2). These ascriptions occur elsewhere in the psalm. It is the emphasis on God "alone" that makes Psalm 62 unique. Verse 2 ends with a strong assertion of confidence in God: "I will never be shaken." Note the word "never."

We would understand perfectly the declarations made above if they were made in times of serenity or quiet, when things were pretty much in control. But such is not the case here! The psalmist describes his situation in verse 3: "How long will you assault me? Would all of you throw me down—this leaning wall, this tottering fence?" He has been under attack for some time now ("how long"). While he proclaims that God "alone" is his rock, yet he feels so alone. The word "me" stands in opposition to "all of you" (v. 3). It's me against the world! His enemies are bent on toppling him. Their primary strategy is falsehood. They bless with their mouths, but "in their hearts they curse" (v. 4).

62:5–7 "FIND REST, O MY SOUL, IN GOD ALONE"

The refrain in verse 5 is similar to verse 1. However, there are significant differences. The first is that instead of "salvation" (v. 1), we have "hope" in verse 5. In verse 2, we find the word "never" making the assertion stronger: "I shall *never* be shaken." Verse 6 is identical to verse 2 with the exception of the missing "never." Most significantly, the word translated as "rest" in verse 1 reappears in verse 5. The difference is that in verse 1 the word "rest" is a noun while in verse 5, it occurs as a verb in the form of an imperative (command):

> v. 1: my soul finds rest in God
> v. 5: my soul, find rest in God

The change is a slight one and can easily be missed. In verse 1 the psalmist describes his experience of rest while in verse 5 he is commanding himself to "find rest in God. Unfortunately, other versions (e.g. NRSV) translates verses 1 and 5 in the same way.[2] But in the Hebrew the word in verse 5 is a verb, which

---

2. But see the translation of Alter, *The Book of Psalms*, 213–214.

is also reflected in the Greek translation of the Hebrew (Septuagint). This has significant implications to the meaning of the psalm. As Long reminds us concerning poetry in the Bible: "Poetry stretches the ordinary uses of words, and places them into unfamiliar relationships with each other, thereby cutting fresh paths across the well-worn grooves of everyday language. Poems change what we think and feel not by piling up facts we did not know or by persuading us through arguments, but by making finely tuned adjustments at deep and critical places in our imaginations."[3]

By making "finely tuned adjustments" from a noun to a verb the sense of the word "rest" changes. Earlier, the psalmist affirms he finds rest in God. Here, he has to command himself to "find rest in God."[4] Some might wonder: We thought he was already rested! Why does he need to enjoin himself to find rest? The change reminds us that rest is never complete. This side of eternity, perfect rest is not our portion. Rest is a process of continually learning to trust in God. As Augustine prays in his Confessions, "My desire was not to be more certain of you but to be more stable in you."[5]

This explains why in the next two verses the psalmist has to pile up one attribute of God upon another (vv. 6–7). Maybe, it is his way of mustering all the assurance from God that he knows of to encourage himself. It is not uncommon in the Psalms to talk to one's soul (e.g. 103:1–2; 116:7).

62:8–10 "POUR OUT YOUR HEART BEFORE HIM"

There is another shift here, as the psalmist turns to his audience to address them. The shift from the psalmist's description of his experience (v. 1) to exhortation (v. 8) reminds us that our experience of rest is not for us to savor and enjoy on our own. The lessons we learn are meant to be shared with others.

As the psalmist has learned to continually trust God, he exhorts others to do the same. The phrase "at all times" (v. 8) is important. We do not trust God only when we feel okay. We trust him in all our situations. The word "all" is also linked to the next exhortation to "pour out your hearts before him" (v. 8b). This can be applied to confession and repentance (32:3–5). In 1 Samuel 7:6 the confession of sin is accompanied by the pouring out of

---

3. Thomas G. Long, *Preaching and the Literary Forms of the Bible* (Philadelphia: Fortress, 1989), 45.
4. Verse 1 is in the indicative, while v. 5 is in imperative mood.
5. St. Augustine, *Confessions* (Oxford; New York: Oxford University Press, 1991).

water. For those who are suffering, this means crying out to him, becoming honest about what we feel (see e.g. Hannah in 1 Sam 1:15). The many lament psalms are examples of this (see Pss 22, 60). Here, what the psalmist has just done in the preceding verses is his way of pouring out his heart (62:3–5).[6]

The last occurrence of the word "truly/alone" appears at the beginning of verse 9. The way in which the word has been used in the psalm is instructive. It is used primarily as an affirmation of trust in God (vv. 1, 2, 5, 6); it is also a characterization of the psalmist's enemies whose only desire is to bring him down (vv. 3–4); and here it is a sober reminder of the ephemeral nature of human existence. Life is fleeting. Literally, verse 9 reads "only breath – humankind."[7] Even the things people desperately want to acquire, like riches, are not able to add any value to life (v. 10). Only a life that finds its truest value and worth in God is worth living.

The reason the psalmist is able to teach others is because he himself has learned what it means to have rest. Ultimately, the psalmist acknowledges that rest flows from one's own encounter with God: "One thing God has spoken, two things I have heard: "Power belongs to you, God, and with you, Lord, is unfailing love" (vv. 11–12a). We do not exactly know what the psalmist means here by God speaking one thing and him hearing twice. What is clear is that the psalmist has "heard" what God has spoken. Not only does he know about the power and the steadfast love of God, but he has also experienced it himself.

No matter how hard we try to recite all the attributes of God mentioned in this psalm, it is still different to actually experience them. Calvin refers to the two things revealed to the psalmist – God's power and mercy – as "the two wings wherewith we fly upwards to heaven; the two pillars on which we rest."[8] Psalm 62 ends with a note on God's just recompense for each person's action (v. 12b). But it is not clear how this relates to the rest of the psalm.

---

6. We have to remember that everything in this psalm is uttered in the presence of God, and thus form part of a prayer. Thus, the complaint in vv. 3–4 is also being made before God.
7. Alter, *The Book of Psalms*, 215.
8. Calvin, *Commentary on the Book of Psalms*, 2:431.

FINDING REST IN THE LORD

Real rest can only be found in God. This peace is not a one-time experience; it is a process of moving from our restlessness to God's embrace. The first step towards experiencing this rest is learning to practice the important discipline of silence or solitude. In fact the Hebrew word translated as "rest" in Psalm 62 also means "silence."

The story is told of a very busy man who came to see a spiritual director in order to ask him for advice on how he could experience peace. The old man took out a basin with water in it. He then dropped a rock into the basin. "What do you see?" the old man asked. "It's not clear; I can't see clearly," answered the man. "That is what happens when we are so busy," explained the spiritual director. There has to be a time to stop, to be quiet, and wait until the "ripples" settle down. One of the challenges we have today is the problem of noise. We need to carve extended periods of time for the practice of the discipline of solitude.

Second, we need to confront the noises within us. One of the things we will realize the moment we practice silence is how much noise there is not only outside but also within us – noises and voices that call for our attention. We tend to try and escape this noise by making themselves busy. But the psalm teaches us a better way, and that is to "pour out our hearts to God" (62:8). The many psalms of lament show us how often the people of God were confronted with troubles and how they poured out their hearts to God. As they did so, they received the grace to confront their fears and embrace their sorrows and pain. We too can experience this grace when we confront our own issues in the presence of the Lord.

Finally, as we pour out our hearts to the Lord, we experience a release and receive the peace that comes from an encounter with God. This peace comes as a result of our efforts to come to that place of solitude. Yet it is also a gift, for without the breaking in of God's presence, we will never experience true rest.

This peace is not for us alone, but is meant to be shared with others. The shift to exhortation in Psalm 62 shows us that when we experience God's rest, other people are also able to find rest in our presence.

PSALM 63

The Psalter, according to James Kugel, is the "spiritual text *par excellence*."[1] No other book in the Bible "seems to summon up the concerns of the spirituality in the biblical period more than the book of Psalms. Its prayers and songs of praise have long served as a model and focus of the spiritual concerns of later ages."[2] In Psalm 63 we find some of the expressions of biblical spirituality. At its center lies the longing for intimacy with God, which may be likened to marriage. Indeed, Psalm 63 uses language which reflects intimacy in marriage (see below). But as in marriage, one does not become intimate with God overnight. We begin with an encounter with the divine (62:11–12) so that God becomes not just the God of our forefathers but "my God" (63:1). This journey then leads to ever growing longing for God. This longing is likened to being in a "dry and parched land where there is no water" (v. 1). This is similar to Psalm 42 which likens longing for God with that of a deer desperately looking for streams. Both psalms show that spirituality includes times of desolation. But it does not stay there. The earnest desire for God will be satisfied (63:5) and there will surely be times of consolation. Praise, rejoicing and exultation of God fill this psalm.

The superscription relates the time when David finds himself in the desert (see 1 Sam 23:14; 24:2). These were difficult moments in David's life. King Saul wanted him killed. So he ran for his life and for some time the desert became his home. Interestingly, those who placed the superscription saw in David's desert experiences, precious lessons in spirituality which resonate with the prayer in Psalm 63. Our context and environment matter a lot in spirituality. Those living in places where the weather is just perfect like in San Diego, California, might not appreciate or find it difficult to identify with what the psalmist is saying in this psalm.

Structurally, the major part of the psalm pertains to the expression of the psalmist's spirituality (vv. 1–8). The rest of the psalm relates to the enemies of the psalmist and his victory over them (vv. 9–11). The mention of the king in the last verse brings Psalm 63 into the category of the royal psalms (cf. 61:6).

---

1. James L. Kugel, "Topics in the History of the Spirituality of the Psalms," 113.
2. Ibid.

63:1–8 THE PURSUIT OF GOD

The psalmist deeply longs for God. Verses 1–2 resemble Psalm 42. The verb "to thirst" occurs in both psalms (v. 1; 42:2). In Psalm 42 the psalmist likens his longing for God to that of a deer searching for water. But instead of finding water, all he has are tears. Here the psalmist portrays his longing for God to that of being in a desert, thirsty but without water. As a result, his body faints. The psalmist is using figurative language to communicate his spiritual experience. He longs for intimacy with God. That he is already close to God is reflected in his statement, "You God, are my God" (63:1) But as reflected in here and in Psalm 42, one mark of a growing intimacy with God is the experience of dryness. One senses an absence so deep, it's dark. And yet it is in the very same place of darkness that we experience God's presence in a deeper way.

Those who have a growing relationship with God do not seem to have enough; they long for more. We see this in the life of Moses. In spite of the great things God has done in and through him, he still wants God to show him his "glory" (Exod 33:18). More than the mighty acts of God, he longs for intimacy. Here, the psalmist's desperate longing for God causes him to seek God in his sanctuary. And there, like Moses, he beholds God's "power and glory" (v. 2).

So overwhelming was the experience of divine encounter that the psalmist declares, "your love is better than life" (Ps 63:3; cf. Phil 1:21). There is no greater joy than being in the presence of God. Verses 2–3 recall the preceding psalm which also mentions God's power and steadfast love (62:11–12). Yet what draws the psalmist close to God is the fact that even though this God is powerful and strong, he is also good. He has experienced God's power and glory, but it is God's steadfast love that lingers long after the encounter. He remembers his experience of God like that of a wandering beggar welcomed into a home with delicious food (v. 5). He will never forget such hospitality.

The psalmist is ever full of praise (vv. 3b, 4, 5b). He meditates on God. The psalmist speaks elsewhere of meditating on God's law (Pss 1, 119). But here, the psalmist "meditates on you" (v. 6, ESV). One of the themes of his meditation centers on God's goodness and how God has delivered him (v. 7). His meditation brings rejoicing. The image in verse 7b is interesting: "I sing in the shadow of your wings." Normally, "the shadow of your wings" is associated with experiences of danger or trouble (e.g. 57:1). Words of petition and lament are often heard "under God's wings." But here, it's the sound of singing and praising that we hear! It is all right for those who take refuge in

God in their times of trouble to stay on in "overtime." Incidentally, the first part of the psalm ends with the psalmist continually clinging to God: "I cling to you" (v. 8). This statement speaks of an intimacy comparable to marriage. The word "cling" (*dabaq*) is the same word as that used to describe the first wedding in the Bible (Gen 2:24). God's response to the psalmist's clinging is to uphold him with his right hand (63:8b).

63:9–11 THE PURSUIT OF THE KING'S ENEMIES

Without any transition the psalm turns to the topic of enemies who are in pursuit of the psalmist (vv. 10–11). Suddenly we are transported back to the messiness of life. Spirituality is always like that. Once we experience the Mount of Transfiguration we need to come down and return to our normal life. The good news is that we do not encounter God only in the sanctuary. He is also with us in the ordinariness of life. Because God's "right hand upholds [him]" (v. 8), the psalmist can experience victory over his enemies (vv. 9–10).

Also without transition, the king is mentioned in verse 11. Probably, it is the king who is praying all through the psalm. If we may relate this to the life of David, it is in the desert – while he was hiding and running for his life – that he experiences God. The note on the king's rejoicing is a fitting response. The meaning of the statement, "all who swear by him shall exult" is ambiguous. It is not clear who is the referent of the pronoun "him," the king or God. It is not easy to see the connection of the last line to the preceding one and to the rest of the psalm (compare the ending of Ps 62).

Psalm 63 will be significant in many parts of Asia where spirituality is the way of life. The world's major religions were born here. Meditation is practiced in many religions. What is unique about Psalm 63 is its theology. God is viewed as powerful, but he can also be intimate with us. God is strong, but he is also good. He owns everything, yet he is a generous host. The psalm reminds us that at the heart of biblical spirituality is relationship. Unfortunately, spirituality in some Christian circles is defined in terms of doing, of performing for God, doing acts of service for him. But any service that does not flow from one's intimacy with God will be an anomaly. For God longs to be with us, before he wants us to do something for him. One of the primary reasons why Jesus chose his apostles was so that they might be with him (Mark 3:14). It was only afterwards that Jesus talked about his sending of them.

PSALM 64

Psalm 64 reminds us that those who want to live godly lives will be perse-cuted (vv. 3–6; cf. 2 Tim 3:12). There will be no shortage of people who will oppose them, plot against them and seek to destroy them through lies and deception. How do we respond in situations like these?

What we will appreciate about Psalm 64 is that it is realistic in its re-sponse. It encourages rejoicing even in opposition (v. 10), but it also expresses complaint (v. 1). It is interesting that the words "complaint" and "rejoice" envelop this psalm. Early on in the Psalter, the psalmist had voiced his com-plaint: "Many are rising against me" (3:1). The word "complaint" is not used in Psalm 3 but it occurs here (64:1). There are times when the righteous will need to pour out their complaints to God. Even those who wait for God's justice at the end of time do this according to Revelation 6:9–10.[1] God does understand when we can no longer carry on, when life has become unbear-able and when we just need to express what's in our hearts. The human heart and mind may be deep (64:6c) but God is perfectly aware of its pains and joys, wishes, and frustrations. The good news is that we can pour out our hearts to God. This is one way of taking refuge in him (62:8).

While the psalmist is expressing his complaint to God, he does not lose hope in God's justice. He is confident God will "repay all according to their work" (62:12; 64:7). So even in the midst of opposition, the psalmist is able to declare: "the righteous will rejoice in the LORD" (v. 10).

The psalm is attributed to David. It is similar to the other psalms of lament. It consists of: petition and lament (vv. 1–6), a declaration of confi-dence (vv. 7–9), and exhortation (v. 10).

64:1–6 "HEAR ME, MY GOD, AS I VOICE MY COMPLAINT"

The psalmist pours out his complaint to God: "Hear me, my God, as I voice my complaint" (v. 1). Some of the complaints in the Bible are unacceptable to God (e.g. the Israelites' murmurings in the wilderness). But the honest pouring out of the heart which arises out of one's intimate relationship with God is welcomed by him (see 55:2, 17).

God understands the situation of the psalmist who expresses how fearful he is "from the threat of the enemy" (64:1b; cf. 55:2–4). He describes his

---

1. The "how long?" prayer of Rev 6:9–10 is similar to the lament in Ps 13:1–2.

enemies in words reminiscent of Psalm 11:2: "the wicked bend the bow, they have fitted their arrow to the string, to shoot in the dark at the upright in heart" (cf. 64:3–4). As in Psalm 11, the arrows are aimed at the "upright in heart" (64:10).

The enemies use the power of the tongue to destroy the righteous: they are described as those who "sharpen their tongues like swords and aim cruel words like deadly arrows" (v. 3). They work in dark places, where they cannot be seen (v. 4). And so the psalmist prays: "hide me from the conspiracy of the wicked" (v. 2). Wicked people are determined. "They encourage each other in evil plans" (v. 5). Here we see the persistence of evil. Those who are under its power work hard to accomplish their destructive schemes. They are committed (see comment in 36:3–4). They have no fear of God, as reflected in the certainty with which they see their plans (64:6; cf. 59:7 – "Who can hear us?"). They think they can never be caught because of their well-planned schemes (v. 6). There is an admission that indeed the human heart and mind is deep (v. 6c). No one can fathom its innermost thoughts except God.

64:7–9 "GOD WILL SHOOT HIS ARROW AT THEM"

But God knows; he hears and he sees (see 10:13–14). The psalmist looks to God in the hope that he will do something about the situation. There is a direct correlation between God's response and the actions of the wicked. As the wicked shoots at the blameless (v. 3) so God will do the same against them: "God will shoot them with his arrow" (v. 7). In accordance to the swiftness with which the wicked have shot their arrows to the righteous, so they will "suddenly be struck down" (v. 7). The very instrument they used to destroy (their tongues) will be their downfall: "He will turn their own tongues against them" (v. 8).[2] Lies and deception always have a way of turning against those who use them.

The result of God's action will lead others to fear the Lord (v. 9; cf. 58:11). It will lead to God's praise as people talk about it and ponder on it (v. 9). On the part of the righteous, it should bring joy to their hearts and encourage them to continue to "take refuge in him" (64:10). The last line is a call for the "upright in heart" to glory in the Lord. The description "upright

---

2. In Hebrew, the sense of v. 8a is not clear. Literally, it reads, "They make him stumble, upon them, their tongue." It seems to be saying that their own words which they have used to destroy others have turned its head against them.

in heart" is a reminder to the faithful to keep their lives pure, for it is so easy in the midst of pressures, to be tempted to give up and commit sin.

Of all the sins in the Ten Commandments, it is the sin associated with the use of the tongue that is most prominent in the Psalms.[3] This poses a great challenge for us. One of the challenges in our culture is how to keep a balance between maintaining our relationship with others and doing the right thing. Many times in our desire to keep our relationship, we do not tell them the truth for fear of hurting them. It's hard for us to be open about what we think is right when it will mean losing our face. We would rather talk to others about the problem. This sometimes leads to gossip. Even within religious groups this is true. Pope Francis, in his Christmas message to the Curia, named fifteen sins. One of them he calls the "terrorism of gossip." This is "the sickness of cowardly people who, not having the courage to speak directly, talk behind people's backs." The Apostle James has warned us of the danger of the tongue (James 3). Psalm 64 adds a warning that those who use their tongue as arrows to shoot at others will themselves suffer the same consequence: "God will shoot them with his arrows" (v. 7).

---

3. Wenham, "The Ethics of the Psalms," 186.

PSALM 65

In our churches today, "singing" and "shouting for joy"[1] are associated with our worship to God (Pss 96:2; 98:1; 47:1; 66:1). But in Psalm 65, it is not only God's people who offer praise to God (v. 5). Even meadows and valleys "shout for joy and sing" (v. 13). The earth itself praises God. God's people and all of creation worship God in response to his bountiful mercy and goodness. Indeed, God is good to all (145:9–10). As God hears the prayers of his people (65:2), forgives their sins (v. 3), and satisfies them with his goodness (v. 4); so he also visits the earth (v. 9), blesses it (v. 10), and crowns it with his bounty (v. 11). As people testify about God's goodness (vv. 1–4), creation does the same (vv. 9–13).[2] Psalm 65 tells us we are not alone in praising God. The earth as God's creation also sings to God.

Unfortunately, we stifle creation's praise through our failure to care for the earth.[3] In our treatment of the earth as an object to be used and manipulated rather than cared for, we silence its praise. Psalm 65 shows us that God is good to the earth and we ought to be good to it also.

Psalm 65 consists of three sections: God's goodness to his people (vv. 1–4); God's awesome power displayed (vv. 5–8); God's goodness to the earth (vv. 9–13).[4]

65:1–4 "TO YOU, SILENCE IS PRAISE, GOD IN ZION"

The first line of the psalm literally reads, "To you, silence is praise, God in Zion" (v. 1a). This is the reading as reflected in the Hebrew (Masoretic Text). But the Greek translation (Septuagint) of the Hebrew Bible appears to have a slightly different reading of the Hebrew. Instead of "silence," the Septuagint has the word "proper," from the Greek word *prepei* ("to be fitting" or "proper").[5] Most modern versions follow the Septuagint: "Praise is due to

---

1. Some church traditions do not practice "shouting for joy."
2. The psalmist speaks on behalf of the Earth.
3. Howard N. Wallace, "*Jubilate Deo omnis terra*: God and earth in Psalm 65," in *The Earth Story in the Psalms and the Prophets,* ed. Norman C. Habel (Sheffield: Sheffield Academic Press, 2001), 51.
4. In the past, the psalm has been viewed as composite. But see Wallace, "*Jubilate Deo omnis terra*," 55–58.
5. The Masoretic Text has *dûmiyyah* while the Septuagint appears to be reading the word as coming from another root – *dmh*, which means "to be like." This is where they got the sense, "to be right, fitting." But this is a rather forced use of the verb *dmh*.

you, O God" (65:1; NRSV, ESV) But in the Hebrew, it reads, "silence is praise." We are following the Hebrew reading here because it forms an integral part of the psalm and its message.

The word "silence" (*dumiyyah*) occurs earlier in Psalm 62:1. The word also means "silent waiting" or "rest," as reflected in the NIV translation of Psalm 65:1, "Praise awaits you." This rest/silence is the result of one's trust in God. When the soul trusts in God, it finds rest (62:1, 5). Here the word is used in connection with praise, which I think is fitting (65:1). For praise flows from a restful and composed spirit (see 131:1–2). That is why God has to command us "to be still, and know that I am God" (46:10). The idea of silence is linked with the silencing of the roaring of the seas in 65:7. Here God is one "who stilled the roaring of the seas, the roaring of their waves and the turmoil of the nations." It is also in silence that we hear creation's praise. It takes a certain posture – that of a quiet heart – to appreciate what the psalmist sees in verses 9–13 (cf. Ps 19). How can we hear the singing of the valley (v. 13) and sense the joy of the hills (v. 12), if we are so noisy and not rested?

The following verses explain why God is to be praised. First, because he hears our prayer (v. 2, cf. v. 5). God's answer comes in the context of silence. In our silence (v. 1), God hears our prayer (v. 2). To hear also means to answer. God is the answering God. That is why vows are performed (v. 1b) and everyone comes to God (v. 2b).

Second, he is to be praised because he forgives our sins (v. 3). The word used to describe their sins ("when we were overwhelmed with sins") literally means "words (*dabar*) of iniquity." When we are full of words and no longer know what silence means, we are prone to sinning (Jas 3:1–10).

Third, we praise him because he satisfies us with his goodness (v. 4). The words "blessed are those" recall Psalm 1: those who meditate on God's law are "blessed." Here, it is those whom God chooses and brings near to his dwelling place who are happy. In God's presence, "we are filled with the good things of your house" (65:4; see also 36:8; 63:5).

65:5–8 "YOU ARE THE HOPE OF ALL THE ENDS OF THE EARTH"

Though the psalm talks about the chosen people of God (v. 4), it is not limited to them. God is the "hope of all the ends of the earth" (v. 5). The word "ends" is repeated in verse 8 to speak of "those who dwell at the ends of the earth" (ESV). In between, the psalmist presents God as strong and mighty (v.

6), who is in control over nature and nations (v. 7). But though he is powerful, he is not like a tyrant. He brings joy to the lands in the east and the west, "where morning dawns, where evening fades" (v. 8). The reference to the east and the west is a literary device called *merism* by which the whole is represented by its parts. Thus, the reference is to the whole earth. God is powerful, but he is also good.

65:9–13 GOD'S CARE FOR THE EARTH

God's goodness is seen in the way he takes care of the earth. God is presented here as someone who takes time to visit his creation, watering and enriching the land. God makes sure his river is full of water, so that the land is provided with grain. The words, "you provide their grain" (v. 9) refers to the people. God blesses the land so that it will produce grain for the people. But it could also refer to the earth's grain.[6] God makes sure he provides the land with grain.

God is actively involved in caring for the earth. Almost all the verbs in vv. 9-10 refer to God as the acting agent: "You care for the land and water it; you enrich it abundantly . . . you drench its furrows . . . you bless its crops" (vv. 9–10). The last one – "bless" – is often used with reference to God blessing his people. But here it is applied to the earth. As God satisfies his people with good things (v. 4), so he blesses the land with his "bounty" (v. 11). The pastures are fully green (v. 12a). The hills, meadows and valleys are described as a person being clothed – "the hills gird themselves with joy, the meadows clothe themselves with flocks, the valleys deck themselves with grain" (vv. 12-13, ESV). They are never left naked but are clothed by God. In response to all his goodness, the hills, meadows, and valleys "shout for joy and sing" (v. 13).

In Psalm 65 we hear creation praising God. Yet presently, it is not the sound of praise that we hear, but of lament. Our country (Philippines) is one of the countries with the fewest trees in its forests. Because of illegal logging many of our forests have been stripped bare. As a result, we have flash floods that have already killed thousands of people. Creation has its way of getting back at us. Psalm 65 enjoins us to come back to God. All flesh, including all of creation, comes to God. It is in the worship of God that we learn to respect his creation.

6. The Masoretic Notes refer to the Symmachus version which has the third person feminine singular pronoun, which points to the "earth" as its antecedent.

PSALM 66

Psalm 66 combines a hymn of praise (vv. 1–12) and a thanksgiving psalm (vv. 13–20). The former is general and communal while the latter is more personal. But the two are bound together, for what God does for an individual is not for him or her alone; it is meant to be shared with the community. As Von Rad notes: "It is as if the deliverance was vouchsafed to the individual only in order that he should pass it on to the community, as if it belonged not to himself, but to the community."[1]

In the first half of the psalm the psalmist tries to link his experience with the past. God's past acts of deliverance are recalled (vv. 6–7) as a way of declaring that the same God who has acted in the lives of his people continues to do so in the present. We sing a new song unto the Lord (33:3) because God has acted afresh in the lives of his people. That is what the psalmist seeks to demonstrate in the second half of the psalm, as he relates his own experience of deliverance to the people. The psalm can serve as a model for formulating our own "sharing" or "testimonies" in the church.

The psalm is divided into five stanzas, each of which begins with an exhortation to give praise to the Lord: a general call to worship (vv. 1–4); an invitation to "come and see" what God has done (vv. 5–7); a call to bless the Lord for the way he has dealt with his people, testing them and restoring them (vv. 8–12); the psalmist's fulfillment of his vow of thanksgiving (vv. 13–15); his testimony and a final exhortation to praise (vv. 16–20).

66:1–12 HYMN OF PRAISE

Psalm 66 is linked with the previous one. The first word, *rua* ("shout for joy"), occurs at the end of Psalm 65 to speak of creation shouting for joy to the Lord. The word "earth" occurs twice in Psalm 65 as a reference to people as inhabitants of the earth (v. 5) and to earth as representing the rest of God's creation (v. 9). Here earth refers to the former. The psalmist is calling on all people to "shout for joy to God" (66:1). If in the previous psalm, praise is associated with "silence" (65:1), here it is about giving praise in terms of words and singing: "sing the glory of his name . . . Say to God, 'How awesome are your deeds!'" (66:2–3). God's works are described as "awesome" (v.

---

1. Gerhard von Rad, *Old Testament Theology*, 359.

3a). Literally, this word means "terrible," which explains why God's "enemies cringe" (v. 3b).

The word "awesome"/"terrible" also refers to God's marvelous acts (v. 5), such as what he did in Exodus when he parted the sea so that his people could walk on dry ground (v. 6). The psalmist exhorts his audience to "come and see" (v. 5) when he recalls this event. The next exhortation becomes "Bless our God" (v. 8) when he remembers the times God "tested" and "refined" them (v. 10). Those were difficult times (vv. 11–12). Yet God sustained them, not allowing them to perish (v. 9), but bringing them to a "place of abundance"[2] (v. 12c).

66:13–20 THANKSGIVING

This section is similar to Psalm 116. In times of trouble, people in the OT would make a vow to the Lord (66:14; see also Gen 28:20–22). Upon receiving God's answer, they would go to the temple to fulfill their vows (66:13, 15). The vow would consist of sacrificial offerings. In other sacrifices, such as in the whole burnt offering, the entire animal was offered to the Lord. But in thanksgiving offerings, only a portion was offered to God. The rest of the animal was given back to the person who offered the sacrifice. So there would be some kind of feasting to accompany the thanksgiving. In the midst of the celebration, the person who offered the sacrifice would stand in front and share what the Lord had done in his life (vv. 16–17). The testimony follows a simple outline of "I cried and the Lord answered me," which then leads to praise (v. 17). The additional detail is the assertion of the psalmist's innocence (vv. 18–19). The vow becomes null and void if there is sin in the person's life. Our sin is a hindrance preventing God from hearing our prayers (see Isa 59:1–2). In the case of the psalmist, his prayer has been answered, which means he is innocent. So he ends with an exhortation to praise (v. 20).

Traditionally, our closely-knit communities provide a good venue for the expression of praise and thanksgiving. When something happens to an individual the whole community is aware of it and can easily identify with the person. With globalization and the internet, our traditional communities have been transformed. We now have what we call a "global community." But while it is true that it is now easier and quicker to communicate with anyone anywhere in the world, we are actually drifting apart from one another.

---

2. The word in the Hebrew means "saturation." Here we follow the meaning suggested by the Septuagint, "relief, respite."

Individualism has crept in. This is one of the challenges of our communities. Psalm 66 reminds us that we can only have a meaningful engagement with one another if we know our common past and if we are able to somehow connect with the experiences of our forebears. The encouragement is that our God is the same yesterday, today and forever (Heb 13:8). He continues to work even today. Constantly sharing with the community what God has been doing in our lives remains a good practice.

Joseph Shao[3] shares his own experience. On the last day of every year, his father would gather the whole extended family to retell the religious history of the Shao clan, praising God for the awesome deeds he has done for the family. Then all the members of the Shao clan would share with others what God has done for them in their own lives. Now he (Joseph) and his wife continue the spiritual holy moment of praising God for his deeds to their family and personal lives.

When one of the members of our church had a kidney failure, the whole community prayed for her. She underwent a kidney transplant operation. Her daughter donated one of her kidneys so she too underwent an operation. Both operations were successful. After both of them recovered, they prepared lots of food the Filipino way (feast). They invited the whole congregation and we thanked God together for what the Lord has done. What a wonderful time to celebrate God's goodness.

---

3. Contextualization Consultant of this commentary.

PSALM 67

We often pray that God's blessing might be upon us. In our greetings, we say, "God bless." But what does it mean to be blessed by God, and for what purpose? Psalm 67 is a prayer for blessing. Blessing is the central word in the psalm (vv. 1, 6, 7). Blessing involves not just the spiritual, but all of life, the material and the physical included (v. 6). More importantly, the psalm reminds us of the purpose of blessing. We are blessed so that we may declare to others the glory of the Lord. The psalmist declares: "May God . . . bless us . . . so that your way may be known on the earth" (vv. 1–2). Just as in the story of Abraham (Gen 12:1–3), we are not blessed for our own sakes but for the sake of others. Indeed, the vision of the psalm is encompassing (vv. 2–4).

The psalm is not attributed to any particular individual or group. The superscription simply says, "To the leader." It is a "song/psalm" to be sung "with stringed instruments." Structurally, the psalm may be outlined as follows:

Prayer for blessing (vv. 1–2);
Summons to praise (vv. 3–5);
God blesses his people (vv. 6–7).

67:1, 6–7 "MAY GOD BLESS US"

The first verse reminds us of the Aaronic blessing in Numbers 6:24–26: "The LORD bless you and keep you; the LORD make his face shine on you, and be gracious to you; the LORD turn his face toward you and give you peace." Psalm 67 repeats three of the petitions: "bless," "make his face to shine," and "be gracious" (v. 1). But there are two differences here. First, instead of the priest proclaiming the blessing on the people, as in the case of the Aaronic blessing, it's the people themselves who utter the prayer of blessing upon themselves. Is this an indication of the movement towards the democratization of the ministry of prayer? The NT teaches the priesthood of all believers (1 Pet 2:9).

The second difference is that the petitions are fewer in Psalm 67 (only three compared to five) and the order in which they appear is also different. The first petition is "be gracious to us." Probably, the change is deliberate. This petition often occurs in the Psalms in situations of great need. By beginning the psalm with this petition, the people acknowledge their need for God. The third petition is to "make his face to shine upon us" (v. 10). This is a prayer that God bestow his favor upon his people. In between these two is the petition "bless us." The structure of the petition in Psalm 67:1 is as follows:

"be gracious to us"
"bless us"
"make his face to shine upon us"

As can be seen, the petition "bless us" forms the center of the structure. This reflects the focus of the petition "bless us" in the psalm. The word "bless" occurs three times in the psalm (vv. 1, 6, 7). The main concern of the prayer is God's blessing. Blessing is best represented by the word "shalom" or well-being. To be blessed is to experience God's presence, which finds expression in all aspects of life. This includes the blessings of the earth's produce. God's blessing is demonstrated in the earth's yielding of its increase (v. 6a). In Psalm 65 we see God's care and provision to the land. God's blessing of his land in turn is his way of blessing his people. That is why after the psalmist declares God's blessing on the earth, he adds, "God, our God, blesses us" (67:6b).

67:2–5 "THAT YOUR WAY MAY BE KNOWN UPON THE EARTH"

But blessing for what? Why are the people asking God to bless them? Some Christians misinterpret the verse, "Delight yourself in the Lord, and he will give you the desires of your heart" (Ps 37:4, ESV), to mean that if they do delight themselves in the Lord, then blessings will follow. So God's blessings become their motivation for following God. The direction is towards self. Psalm 67 is different. The people ask God to bless them in order that God's way "may be known upon the earth" (v. 2). The direction is towards God's glory. They pray for blessing in order to be a blessing to others. For God's way is to bless those who do not have anything (see 68:5–6; Gen 12:1–3). The blessing is not for "me" and "my family" alone, but for "all nations" (v. 2).

Christians are called upon by the Lord to be the salt and light of the world (Matt 5:13). We are to influence our societies towards transformation and change. In many parts of Asia, Christianity remains the minority. Let us pray that the Lord will bless us so that God's ways may be known among our people. This is my own prayer for my country. Presently, the Philippines is the only Christian nation in Southeast Asia. Though we are poor, yet through the witness of many of our overseas Filipino workers (OFW), the message of the gospel is now being shared in many parts of the world. But how I wish that we could experience the blessings of the Lord in our own country!

Though we are a Christian nation, we are also one of the most corrupt countries in the world. This is one of the reasons why many of our people are poor.

All of us desire that God will bless our nation. How will this take place? There is no easy answer. But the prayer in Psalm 67 gives us some clue: "May God, our God, bless us" (v. 6b, NJPS). The petition "May God bless us" occurs three times in Psalm 67. But it is only in verse 6 that the qualification "our God" is mentioned. We will only experience God's blessing when God becomes our God. Being called a Christian nation does not mean we really are one.

The question is, is God really "our" God? What does it mean for God to be our God? God becomes our God when we experience him in our lives both individually and as a people (Ps 62), when we reflect the character of this God in our daily lives through acts of righteousness (Pss 15, 14), and when we seek to uplift the situation of those whom he loves – the poor (Ps 41), the orphans, widows, and the marginalized (68:5–6).

PSALM 68

This psalm is one of the most difficult psalms to translate from Hebrew, and thus, to understand.[1] There is no clear progression in the whole psalm. Many scholars think that the psalm is a joining together of many other poems. In spite of that, we are still able to get a glimpse at some of its central messages. The psalm is mainly about God's victory over his enemies on behalf of Israel. In fact, the psalm has been used through history, for better or for worse, by those claiming that God is on their side.[2] The psalmist recalls God's previous acts for the people as a way of summoning God to do the same in their present situation. In spite of the triumphant tone of the psalm, it is possible to read the psalm from the perspective of those who are on the bottom rung. There is an emphasis on God's might and power. Yet alongside this, God is presented as one who is compassionate, gentle, and kind. He is "father to the fatherless, a defender of the widows" (v. 5). To those who are languishing, he is the restorer (v. 9). The people see themselves as the "poor" ones (v. 10) whom God cares for. They praise God who "daily bears us up" (v. 19). Even Zion, the chosen abode of God, is presented as lowly compared to other mountains (vv. 15–16). Thus, the psalm serves as an encouragement to those who are vulnerable, weak, and powerless. These can look up to God as their defender and provider.

The psalm is attributed to David (see superscription). But scholars do not agree as to the historical period out of which the psalm arose. As noted above, the psalm appears to be a combination of various parts of poems (e.g. Judges 5). The following outline is only an attempt to make sense of the present shape of the psalm:

- Song of the Ark (vv. 1–3);
- Summons to and motivations for praise (vv. 4–10);
- Historical review: conquest of the land (vv. 11–14);
- The lowliness of Zion as God's chosen abode (vv. 15–18);
- God the defender of the needy and the destroyer of the enemies (vv. 19–23);
- Procession of victory (vv. 24–27);

1. Bratcher and Reyburn, *A Translator's Handbook*, 577.
2. Kirkpatrick, *The Book of Psalms*, 377–388.

- Petition that God perform his powerful acts in their time as he did in the past (vv. 28–31);
- All nations summoned to praise God (vv. 32–35).

68:1–10 "MAY GOD ARISE"

The opening lines are taken from the Song of the Ark: "May God arise, may his enemies be scattered" (Ps 68:1; cf. Num 10:35). The Israelites brought the ark with them whenever they went to battle. Here such a tradition is recalled. The wish/prayer is that their enemies would vanish like smoke while the righteous extolled in jubilation (vv. 2–3). The victory of the righteous leads the psalmist to summon the people to "sing in praise of his name" (v. 4). Borrowing language from ancient Near Eastern mythology, the psalmist describes God as one "who rides on the clouds" (v. 4). This is the same epithet for Baal. But the psalmist is careful to make a distinction between Baal and their God. Thus he continues: "His name is the Lord [Yahweh]" (v. 4c). As a further departure from Baal, the psalmist describes Yahweh as "father to the fatherless, a defender of widows" (v. 5).

This God may be up there in the clouds but he is also down here with the vulnerable. That is the big difference between him and the other gods in the ancient Near East. He "sets the lonely in families" and "leads out the prisoners with singing" (v. 6). But as for the "rebellious," God has no place for them but the "sun-scorched land" (68:6).

Verses 7–10 recall the people's own experience of how the powerful God took care of them. There is the same dual emphasis on God's character as powerful and mighty, and yet kind and caring. God's presence with his people (v. 7) is described in the language of a theophany: "the earth shook" (v. 8; cf. 18:7). God is awesome. But the manifestation of his power is for the purpose of reaching out to the needy. The people see themselves as orphans and widows (v. 5), describing themselves as those who are "poor" (v. 10). Yet in their experience, the powerful God is also the God who restores the languishing: "you refreshed your weary inheritance" (v. 9). He is also the one who provides for the needy: "from your bounty, God, you provided for the poor" (v. 10). And he doesn't just do this occasionally; he does it every day: "Praise be to the Lord . . . who daily bears our burdens" (v. 19). Not only does he carry our burdens, but he also carries us. Fittingly, his actions are described as flowing from his "bounty" (literally, "goodness") (v. 10) and so he is praised.

68:11–18 FROM SINAI TO ZION

In the preceding section (vv. 7–10), the people recall their wilderness experience with God. Here, they review how God enabled them to conquer the Promised Land. It is the Lord who "announces the word" (v. 11). This means God is the one who is in control, who gives the people victory. As a result, their enemies flee (v. 12a). Verse 12b relates that the women divided the spoils. This line is taken from the Song of Deborah (Judges 5). It is unclear to what verse 13 is referring. Is it referring to the spoils? The next verse speaks of snow falling on Zalmon. It is rare to have snow in that part of the world. So this is viewed as part of God's miraculous acts (see "abundant showers" in v. 9).

Bashan is literally referred to as "mountain of God" (v. 15). But most translators understand the word "God" as an adjective, so "majestic mountain." Bashan is situated east side of the Jordan River. But it is only in this psalm where a mountain is mentioned in Bashan. Probably the reference is to Mount Hermon, believed to be the abode of the gods of Canaan. The language is that of poetry, which is full of figurative language. Thus in the next line we hear the "rugged mountain" envying Zion, the mountain that God has chosen as his dwelling place (v. 16). Though not as elevated as other mountains, God has chosen to come to this place. God's journey is "from Sinai into his sanctuary" (v. 17). Verse 18 is also not clear in terms of its meaning: "When you ascended on high, you took many captives; you received gifts from people." The verse is cited in the context of Ephesians 4:7–11.[3]

68:19–23 "GOD WILL SHATTER THE HEADS OF HIS ENEMIES"

God is on the side of the righteous (v. 3) and the vulnerable (vv. 5–6), whom he deals with compassion and kindness. But to his enemies (v. 2) and to the "rebellious" (v. 6), defeat and the experience of lack await them. The psalmist advances this point in verses 19–23 (for v. 19, see above). God is salvation to his people (v. 20). But to his enemies, he is a cruel warrior, shattering their heads (v. 21; see also 137:8–9). The gory depiction of God's action along with the image of its aftermath is appalling: "that your feet may wade in the blood of your foes" (v. 23; cf. 58:10). How can a God who cares for the orphans and widows allow such a thing to happen even to his enemies? How can those

---

3. See W. Hall Harris III, *The Descent of Christ: Ephesians 4:7–11 and Traditional Hebrew Imagery* (Leiden: Brill, 1996).

who see themselves as "poor" (v. 10) become so cruel to their enemies? The psalm does not provide an answer. It just presents the imprecation.[4]

68:24–27 PROCESSION OF VICTORY

The image of the procession in verses 24 and following recalls the Song of the Ark (v. 1). Is this a religious procession, or a march of victory? Both are possible. The procession recalls Psalm 24, where God is described as the "king of glory." Singers, musicians and girls playing tambourines are part of the procession (v. 25). In the midst of the procession, God is praised (v. 26). A partial list of tribes is given (v. 27). The listing alludes to the Song of Deborah (Judges 5). Benjamin is in front because of King Saul, who is from this tribe.

68:28–35 PETITION AND FINAL CALL TO PRAISE

In this section, the purpose of the historical review becomes clear. The people recall what God did in the past as a way of asking God to do the same in their time: "Summon your power, God; show us your strength, our God, as you have done before" (v. 28). The recollection is in itself a prayer. Here the people become explicit about it. In some cultures in Asia, this manner of communication or approach is similar. We are often chided for our tendency to "beat around the bush."[5] But that is just our way of communicating. Our *pasakalye* ("introduction"), which could be long, is in fact already part of the message. Likewise, the preceding verses may be viewed as *pasakalye*, with the main petition given in verses 28–31. The petition is cast in metaphors, with the enemies described as "beast among the reeds," a "herd of bulls" (v. 30). They pray that God would defeat his enemies so that tributes in the form of material gifts might overflow (vv. 29, 31).

The psalm ends with a summons for the kingdoms of the earth to give praise to God. The image of God as one "who rides across the highest heavens" is repeated (vv. 4, 33). God is praised for his power and majesty. In keeping with these attributes; he is also exalted as one who "gives power and strength to his people" (v. 35).

Psalm 68 may not be appreciated because of its language of violence (e.g. v. 23). Especially in many parts of the world where violence is associated

---

4. See C. S. Lewis, *Reflections on the Psalms*, on his view about these kinds of psalms that employ violence as reflected in the imprecatory psalms.
5. See Maggay, *Pahiwatig*.

with religion, it is easy to dismiss this psalm and view it as promoting strife among people of differing beliefs. But there is also something in the psalm which reminds us that our God is a God who cares for the vulnerable and marginalized. He is the "Father to the fatherless, defender of widows" (v. 5). Those who first penned this psalm belong to a people who were once slaves in Egypt. But God took care of them and gave them a land to dwell in. Unfortunately, as their own history tells us, after they had settled in the land that God had given them, they forgot the Lord (Neh 9). It is always an important lesson of history to remember that when a people start to have power, the temptation to dominate others becomes stronger. The psalm reminds us we should not forget where we have come from or where we started. And most importantly, we should never forget that we are blessed by God to bless others (Ps 67). Psalm 68 should not be read in isolation but along with its immediate context and in the wider context of the Bible.

PSALM 69

Psalm 69 contains some of the most moving words of lament. As in most lament psalms, we are not given specific details of the afflictions of the psalmist. But here we see some indication that his suffering is doubly hard. The depictions of his suffering (vv. 1–3) indicate that he has reached a point where he is about to give up. Adding to his agony are those who take advantage of his situation by using it as a means to shame him (vv. 7–12). The psalmist complains: "They persecute those you wound" (v. 26). As we say in Filipino: *Nadapa na nga, tinadyakan pa* ("kicking someone who is already lying down"). The psalmist admits he is not perfect (vv. 5, 26), yet he feels that what he experienced at the hands of his persecutors is way beyond what he deserves.

For those who have experienced something similar, Psalm 69 is a great help. First, it tells us that we are not alone when we go through similar situations. Second, it provides us with words we can utter to God when we just don't know what to say, or when we are unsure whether the words we want to say might be too harsh. Psalm 69 contains some of the most shocking prayers (vv. 27–28). Some may be appalled at these prayers. One way of reading these words is to understand them as honest expressions of a person who has been falsely accused and terribly treated by others. But rather than taking matters into his own hands, the psalmist comes to God, which is the third value of this psalm. It invites us to come to God and pour out to him what is truly in our hearts.

Psalm 69 is similar to Psalm 22. Both psalms are cited in the NT and have been applied to Jesus (e.g. Ps 69:9; John 2:17; Ps 22:1; Matt 27:46). The NT writers saw that the sufferings depicted in these psalms were fulfilled in Jesus. These laments best capture what they saw in Jesus. The fact that the NT uses Psalm 69 tells us that this psalm in its entirety is also for Christians.

The psalm is attributed to David and is presumably to be sung "according to Lilies" – possibly the tune of the psalm (compare superscription in Psalm 45). The psalm is a lament, similar in its structure to Psalm 22. Both contain two main parts: lament (69:1–29; 22:1–21) and a hymn of praise (69:30–36; 22:22–31).[1] The laments in the two psalms are similar in their passion and intensity. Where Psalm 69 differs is in its inclusion of a series of imprecato-

---

1. The hymn of praise in Psalm 22 is almost equal to the lament. In Psalm 69, the lament is much longer than the hymn of praise.

ry prayers (vv. 22–28). The Hebrew word *yasha* ("save/salvation") occurs at the beginning and end of the lament in Psalm 69, forming an inclusio. The lament consists of alternate petitions and depictions of suffering.

69:1–29 LAMENT

In verse 1, the psalmist describes his condition using water imagery. The water has reached up to his neck (v. 1). The word translated "neck" comes from the Hebrew word (*nefesh*) which also means "life." His life is ebbing away. He is overwhelmed. He's trying to feel down below him to see if there is still ground on which his feet can stand, but there is none. He has sunk in "miry depths where there is no foothold" (v. 2). And just about that point, a current sweeps him away (v. 2b).

He has been crying out for help like a person about to drown. But it seems no help is coming. He is weary and his "throat is parched" (v. 3). The word "throat" recalls *nefesh* ("neck") (v. 1), which also means "throat." Even his eyes have grown dim. There is no answer from God (v. 3b).

When a person suffered in those days (e.g. from sickness), people usually thought it was because of a sin he had committed. And if the condition did not get any better but instead grew worse, the belief that the person was indeed very bad became solidified. This then led to taunting and other acts of shaming. This seems to be the background here. For suddenly we find enemies showing up and starting to accuse the psalmist (v. 4). Even worse, his own family has rejected him (v. 8; cf. 55:12–14). The psalmist is left with no one to turn to but God.

And so to God he turns: "You, God, know my folly; my guilt is not hidden from you" (v. 5). This statement could be interpreted either as an assertion of his innocence or as an admission of his guilt. In the light of his later statement (see v. 26), it seems more likely that the psalmist is acknowledging he has done something wrong. What he is lamenting is the absence of answer from God, which then gives more opportunities for his enemies to turn him into an object of scorn (v. 12).

He tries to perform all kinds of piety (fasting, putting on sackcloth [vv. 10–11]). We may understand these as part of his zeal for God's house (v. 9). That is why he says, "I endure scorn for your sake" (v. 7). In spite of all these, there remains no answer.

But the psalmist does not give up. Verse 13 begins with a strong adversative, "But I pray to you." He continues to offer his prayer to God. His prayer focuses on two main concerns. The first is directed to his suffering (vv. 13–18) and the second, to his enemies (vv. 19–28). Earlier, the psalmist described his experience in terms of sinking in deep waters, and being swept away by the flood (vv. 1–2). Here he repeats these words as he prays that God might rescue him from sinking in "deep waters" (v. 14), and asks that the flood might not sweep over him (v. 15). He has earlier described his sufferings using the imagery of deep waters and sinking (vv. 1–2). His petition is enveloped by the mention of God's love (vv. 13, 16). He has been waiting for God (v. 3). Now he prays, "Do not hide your face from your servant" (v. 17a) and "come near" (v. 18a). He cites two motivations: "for I am in trouble" (v. 17b) and "because of my foes" (v. 18b). The mention of the "foes" signals the transition to his second prayer concern.

There is an alternation between an emphasis on "you" (God) and "I" (the psalmist) throughout the lament:

"*You* God, know my folly" (v. 5);
"But *I* pray to you" (v. 13);
"*You* know how I am scorned" (v. 19);
"But as for me, afflicted and in pain" (v. 29).

Earlier, the psalmist asserted that God knows everything that he does (v. 5). Now he asserts, "you know the insults I receive" including all the shame that goes with it (v. 19). By juxtaposing these two statements (vv. 5 and 19), we understand that although the psalmist acknowledges his sin, he feels the consequence has been way too much. The attacks from his enemies (vv. 10–12) and the turning away of his own family (v. 8) have broken his heart and led to despair (v. 20). But he does not stop there. He reports to God (makes *sumbong*) what they have done to him (vv. 20–21).

In view of the fact that his enemies are much stronger and more numerous (v. 4), and in view of what they have done to him, the psalmist utters the following imprecatory prayers. (For discussions on the imprecatory prayers, see "The Imprecatory Psalms," pp. 274–276). The psalmist prays that the safe place of communion (table) be a place of disunity and strife (snare) (v. 22); that as his eyes grow dim waiting for God (v. 3) so the eyes of his enemies might also be darkened (v. 23). He prays that God's anger and wrath might be poured upon them (v. 24) and that there will no longer be people left where they lived (v. 25).

The psalmist provides an explanation: these people trample down those already suffering (v. 26). This verse implies the psalmist accepts his situation as coming from God. The problem is that his enemies were inflicting suffering on him more than God did (see v. 29). And so he continues his imprecatory prayer. He asks that their guilt not be acquitted (v. 27) and that they might "be blotted out of the book of the life" (v. 28). The latter is another way of saying, "let them die." As a way of summing up his prayer against his enemies, the psalmist confesses he is "afflicted and in pain" (v. 29).

69:30–36 PRAISE

Without any transition, the psalm turns from the lament to praise (v. 30; cf. 28:4–6). How can one suddenly turn from uttering imprecatory prayer to praising? How do we explain the sudden transformation from grief to joy? The text does not explain. Scholars often refer to the presence of a prophet who delivers an oracle of salvation from the Lord as an explanation for the sudden change of mood (see Pss 12 and 22). But there is nothing in the text which supports such a theory. Probably, the very act of lamenting brought about an inner transformation. Or the later verses might have been added, after the psalmist has recovered.[2] We do not really know. As it stands, the text is a testimony to the God who answers the prayer of his people.

The psalmist offers a song (v. 30), instead of an ox (v. 31).[3] Instead of an animal sacrifice, the psalmist makes a thanksgiving offering (cf. Ps 50:14). Earlier, the psalmist was anxious that those who hoped in God and sought him might stumble because of his situation (v. 6). Now he can encourage them to "be glad" in God (vv. 32–33). God has drawn close to him and answered his prayer. He calls on heaven and earth, and the seas, to praise God (v. 34). The "seas" alludes to his description of his suffering (vv. 1–2). The last three verses make reference to the rebuilding of Zion and the cities of Judah. Interestingly, he mentions the word "servants" (vv. 35–36). Earlier, he uses the same title to refer to himself (v. 17). This indicates that the lament of the individual was later applied to the experience of the community.

The central experience of the psalmist in Psalm 69 is that of "shame." For us, to experience shame is like experiencing death itself, or even worse. We will do everything just to "save face." Those who have been shamed need to be restored on two levels: vertically with respect to God, and horizontally with respect to the community. The psalm is comforting in its emphasis on coming to God when everyone has turned their back on us. God welcomes

---

2. See Villanueva, The "Uncertainty of a Hearing," 1–28.
3. There is a play on words between "song" (šîr) and "ox" (šôr) (Alter, The Book of Psalms, 240).

those who have been rejected. They can come to him as their father and tell him about what others have done to them. They can express to him their *pag-susumbong* ("telling or reporting to God"). At the same time, it is instructive that the psalm ends with a note on the community (vv. 32–36). We can never live on our own. We need both God and others.

When we find ourselves soul-searching in the midst of shameful experiences, let us call on him to save us (vv. 1–22), commit to him to protect us (vv. 23–29), come before him to praise him (vv. 30–36). Though we sink (v. 2), feel shame (v. 7) and weep (v 10), yet we pray to the God of love (v. 13).

PSALM 70

Psalm 70 also appears in Psalm 40:13–17. For further comments and discussions on Psalm 70, see Psalm 40. Psalm 40 consists of thanksgiving (vv. 1–12) and lament (vv. 13–17). The lament part is basically the same as the one we find in Psalm 70. The result is a composition which brings out the element of tension between lament and thanksgiving. It is possible that the second part of Psalm 40 is reproduced to form what we now know as Psalm 70. The two are identical with minor variations, one of which is the change of the name for God from "Lord" (*Yahweh*) to "God" (*elohîm*). The change is reflective of the characteristics of the whole collection of Psalms 42–83, where the word "God" is the preferred title for God instead of Yahweh ("Lord").

The appearance of Psalm 70 as a separate psalm forms an important contribution to our understanding of the lament psalms. Lament psalms usually contain an element of thanksgiving or praise. Usually, lament moves to some form of resolution or vow of thanksgiving. Occasionally, as in the case of Psalm 40, we have the reverse movement from thanksgiving to lament (e.g. Pss 9–10; Ps 27). So Psalm 70 is unique in that it is "pure" lament (cf. Ps 88). There is no resolution at the end. Indeed, the psalm is left with no answer. As Alter comments on Psalm 70: "In the narrative logic of the poem, the speaker cannot yet confidently place himself in the ranks of those who rejoice because he is, after all, encompassed about by murderous foes. And so at the end he declares that he is poor and needy, and, as at the beginning, invokes God as his aid . . . reminding him that the desperately needed deliverance must come quickly."[1]

PSALM 70 AS A 'PURE' LAMENT

As a "pure" lament, Psalm 70 presents a liberating message. It affirms the fact that there are times when the life of faith consists purely of desolation. We do not have to see ourselves always lacking in faith when we cannot find the answer to our situation right away. The psalm can be our companion as we wait for God. The present canonical arrangement of Psalm 70 shows that eventually lament turns to resolution. Psalm 70 shows links with the preceding and following psalm. Psalms 69 and 70 begin with almost similar terms "save me"

---

1. Robert Alter, "The Poetic and Wisdom Books," in *The Cambridge Companion to Biblical Interpretation*, ed. John Barton (Cambridge: Cambridge University Press, 1998), 232.

(69:1; 70:1). The same invocation is found in Psalm 71:2b. But these three lament psalms, as well as the ones before them, eventually find some kind of resolution in Psalm 72 (see below).

PSALM 70 AND "THE DARK NIGHT OF THE SOUL"

Psalm 70 is like Psalm 88. Both are lament psalms which do not have any resolution in them. There is no movement to praise, only the darkness of lament. We may compare this to what St. John of the Cross calls the "dark night of the soul." When God wants to bring his children to deeper intimacy with him, he often brings them to a place of darkness, where there is no consolation, only desolation. We pray but there is no answer. Psalm 70, by ending without any answer, provides an encouragement for those who go through the dark night. When we are there, it's good to know our experience is not unique. Others have been through the dark night.

Interestingly, the Filipino is known as Juan de la Cruz (John of the Cross). Unlike the American who is called "Uncle Sam," we are known for our suffering (cross). And I think this is not an accident that we are called Juan de la Cruz. As Josefina Constantino remarks:

> If God has truly called out every creature into existence by its name, then, indeed we have been called out as *Juan de la Cruz* . . . And our national vocation, according to our name, is to *become* the full flowering of our being: to become a nation marked by great sanctity of spirit – to achieve the pattern of holiness . . . marked out for us by God.[2]

---

2. Constantino, *The Asian Religious Sensibility*, 401.

PSALM 71

Psalm 71 may be called a "psalm for the elderly." Here we see the realities that elderly people are faced with – feelings of abandonment (vv. 9, 18), loneliness (v. 12) and lack of vitality (v. 20). The psalm reminds us that even in old age, trials and difficulties in life, including experiences of oppositions, continue. How we wish that when we are old, life will be easier, more relaxed, with nothing to do but to wait in great expectation for the day we leave this world. But often such is not the case. Abraham faced his greatest trial when he was already old. There is never a time when we do not need God. We continue to take refuge in him (v. 1) and ask for his help (v. 4). It is in our old age that we need to trust God all the more. The psalm shows us it is people who have learned to trust God in their youth who know how to trust him in their old age (v. 5), when it is most needed. You don't start trusting God when you are already old; you start when you are young, before it's too late.

Psalm 71 does not have a superscription, possibly because it is meant to be a companion to Psalm 70. There are links between the two psalms: "shame" (70:2, 4; 71:1, 13, 24), the petition, "O my God, make haste to help me" (71:12; cf. 70:5).[1]

Structurally, the psalm begins with a typical lament which ends with praise (vv. 1–8). This is followed by another lament, closely connected to the preceding one (vv. 9–18). This section is enveloped by the petition, "Do not cast me away/do not forsake me" (vv. 9, 18). The final section is a declaration of what God has done, culminating in a vow of praise (vv. 19–24).

71:1–8 "IN YOU, LORD, I HAVE TAKEN REFUGE"

If we are correct in our view that this psalm is indeed written by an elderly person, then it is instructive that the psalm is formulated using language typical of other psalms of lament (e.g. 16:1; 18:2). Even in old age, the psalmist continues to take refuge in the Lord (v. 1). He still senses his need for God (v. 2). And more than ever, he needs the strength and security only God can provide (v. 3). This is because the wicked continue to harass him (v. 4). Normally, an old person would no longer have the strength for situations such as these. But he does. And his secret lies in the fact that early in his life he has learned to trust God (vv. 6–7, cf. v. 17). Trusting God is like food;

---

1. Schaefer, *Psalms*, 170.

you do not start eating healthy food when you are already old. It'll be too late by then.

This section started with the psalmist taking "refuge" in God (v. 1); it ends with the psalmist declaring God as his "refuge" (v. 7) and praising him (v. 8).

71:9–18 "DO NOT FORSAKE ME WHEN I AM OLD"

The praise at the end of the previous section returns to lament as the psalmist pleads to God not to "cast me away when I am old" (v. 9). He is surrounded by enemies who want to destroy him (v. 10). They tell him God has forsaken him (v. 11). And so the psalmist calls out to God, "Do not be far from me" (v. 12). Elderly people often feel others have abandoned them. They no longer feel as needed as they used to be; they are no longer "in demand." The experience of the psalmist is even worse; he has enemies who try to bring him down.

Finding himself in such a vulnerable situation, the psalmist is left with nobody but God. And so he turns to God and utters an imprecatory prayer (v. 13, see Ps 58 for discussion on imprecatory prayers). Declarations of hope and praise immediately follow the imprecatory prayer (vv. 14–16; see also 69:28–36). It has been the psalmist's practice to proclaim God's "wondrous deeds" since he was young (v. 17). And now that he is old, he prays that God would not abandon him "till I declare your power to the next generation" (v. 18). Some elderly people spend their time just waiting to die. This psalmist is still busy declaring God's praise!

71:19–24 "I WILL PRAISE YOU FOR YOUR FAITHFULNESS"

God has done great things (v. 19). But the psalmist also admits as he looks back that there have been "troubles, many and bitter" (v. 20; see also 34:19) that have come his way. One of the trials of old age is that you get to witness unfortunate events. But this does not leave him hopeless or cynical. He continues to hope that God "restore my life again" from the "depths of the earth" (v. 20). The "depths of the earth" may be a metaphor of the troubles and trials he has experienced (cf. 61:2 – "from the end of the earth"). He believes God will lift him up again and comfort him (v. 21).

Thus with singing and praise, the psalmist declares: "I will praise you . . . for your faithfulness" (v. 22). Through it all he had experienced God's faithfulness. So he shouts for joy and declares how God has delivered him (vv. 23–24).

Psalm 71 has an important message especially for today, when the number of elderly people is increasing as life expectancy increases. Unfortunately, according to sociologists, "older people have no real place in the modern family."[2] My wife Rosemarie used to work among elderly people in the UK. One day, one of them looked her in the eyes and said: "I can sum up my advice to you in three words: Don't get old." My wife jokingly told her, that was four words, "Do not get old." But Rosemarie felt her loneliness and fear. She saw it in others, too. "Some of them were so depressed that they didn't even want to go out of their room." The sense of loneliness was especially acute during the Christmas season because no one visited them.

It is not only the elderly who feel this way. But regardless of whether you are old or young, there are psalms that show that others can heartily identify with your loneliness and sadness. Listen to the prayer in Psalm 71:9: "Do not cast me away when I am old; do not forsake me when my strength is gone." Psalm 71 is realistic in its portrayal of the elderly and their experiences. The psalmist is not ashamed to admit feelings of abandonment and the struggles associated with old age. But the psalmist goes beyond these to focus on the mission of elderly people, which is to pass on to the next generation what they have experienced in life in general, and especially their experience of God. The younger generation would do well to listen to them.

---

2. Peter L. Berger and Brigitte Berger, *Sociology: A Biographical Approach* (New York: Penguin Books, 1972), 102–103.

PSALM 72

The NT exhorts us to pray "for kings and all those in authority" (1 Tim 2:1–2). But we are not given an example which can inform our praying. Psalm 72 can serve this purpose. This psalm is known as a royal psalm (see "Royal Psalms," pp. 34–35). It may have been used originally on the occasion of the coronation of a king. As a prayer, Psalm 72 reflects the ideals of the godly community. It is not primarily intended to instruct the king, but as is often the case, deep and great theologies or teachings are engraved in prayers.

Psalm 72 sets out the foundation of a king's rule, and any rule which derives its authority from the Scriptures – righteousness and justice (vv. 1–2). The kings or rulers are not there for their own benefit but for others' benefit. They have been placed there for a purpose; and that purpose is so that they can be channels of blessing to the people (v. 17). God has placed the people under them. They do not own them; the people remain and will forever be God's people (v. 2). Many of these people are poor, needy and vulnerable, with no one to defend them (vv. 2, 4, 12–14). They all rely on the king or ruler as God's representative to help and deliver them from their oppressors. It is when kings and rulers care for the poor and needy that they become worthy of honor and glory (v. 12; see also Psalm 41).

In its present arrangement, Psalm 72 is a beacon of hope amidst the suffering of the people. It is preceded by laments. Indeed, "Psalm after Psalm in this book we have heard the cry of the oppressed: here is unfolded to our view the splendid vision of a perfect ruler who shall be the champion of the oppressed, whose glory will be the 'redressing of human wrong.'"[1]

Unfortunately, no king in the Davidic line has lived out the ideals set out in Psalm 72. Kings "tend to be more attracted to majesty than to mercy."[2] But the psalm stands as a hope that one day this king will come. Many Jews see Psalm 72 as a Messianic psalm. Christians see in Jesus the fulfillment of the psalm.

Psalm 72 is attributed to Solomon (cf. Psalm 127). We do not really know whether the psalm was composed by him or not. The Hebrew preposition translated "of" ("Of Solomon") can be translated "to" or "for" and the super-scriptions are later additions (see "The Significance of the Superscriptions,"

---

1. Kirkpatrick, *The Book of Psalms*, 416.
2. James H. Waltner, *Psalms* (Believers Church Bible Commentary. Scottdale PA: Herald Press, 2006), 353.

pp. 258–259). Those who put the superscription here might have seen connections with King Solomon. For example, the mention of "Sheba" (72:10)
recalls the "Queen of Sheba" (1 Kgs 10:10). More significantly, the psalm
reflects the prayer of Solomon for wisdom (1 Kgs 3:3–14).

Verse 1 is the only petition in which God is directly addressed using the
word "your". The rest of the psalm consists mainly of a prayer for the king
(vv. 2–11, 15–17). Verses 12–14 describe the rule of the king for whom the
prayer is being offered. As will be seen below, this section is significant to the
overall message of the psalm.

The psalm ends with a doxology which closes Book 2 (vv. 18–19) and a
note that this psalm is the last of the prayers of David. This final note demonstrates one process that the whole Psalter underwent. We cannot trace with
certainty the exact process of its development. But we have here an indication
that at one point, one of the collections ended with Psalm 72.

72:1–4 PRAYER OF BLESSING FOR THE PEOPLE

The prayer begins with a direct petition that God grant the king "your justice"[3] and "your righteousness" (v. 1). The word "your" indicates that these
two qualities are defined in terms of God's standards. Human justice and
righteousness are often found wanting, but God is the true and righteous
judge. The psalmist prays that the king's rule will be characterized by and
rooted in these two divine qualities: "May he judge your people in righteousness, your afflicted ones with justice" (v. 2). In spite of the emphasis in the
psalm on the greatness of the king's rule, the psalm never loses its vision of a
rule that is characterized by justice and righteousness.

In the same way that righteousness and justice are God's, so also the
people are God's people – "your people" (v. 2). This is a reminder to the
king that he does not own the people. They are God's, and as king he stands
accountable to God. Among the people, the marginalized occupy a central
place. The "people" are composed of different social groups. Yet in the psalm
it is the "afflicted" (vv. 2, 4), the "needy" (vv. 4, 12), those "who have no one
to help" (v. 12), and "the weak" (v. 13) who are given a central focus.

Although the psalm is a prayer for the king, the ultimate focus is not on
him but on the people. The psalm will devote a prayer of blessing specifically to the king (see below). But first and foremost, the prosperity is for "the

---

3. In Hebrew, the word is in the plural form.

people" (v. 3). The word translated as "prosperity" comes from the Hebrew word *shalom*, which means "well-being" – blessings in all aspects of life. In verse 3 *shalom* is parallel to "righteousness" (v. 3b). When a king's rule is done in righteousness, *shalom* follows. The twin of righteousness is justice, which is the focus of the prayer in verse 4.

72:5–17 PRAYER OF BLESSING FOR THE KING

Only after praying for God to bless the people did the psalmist pray for the king to be blessed. The requests are extraordinary. He prays for the king's continuing reign (v. 5)[4] and universal dominion with international recognition (vv. 8–11). He repeats similar requests later (vv. 15–17), with the addition of the blessing of prosperity (v. 16). The latter is similar to the petition in verse 3. As "mountains bring prosperity to the people" (v. 3) so here there is abundance[5] of grain "throughout the land" (v. 16). There is a direct correspondence between the blessings of the people and that of the king. The king is blessed so that he can be a blessing to the people, like the "rain falling on a mown field" (v. 6). He receives all these blessings because he cares for the needy, shows pity on the weak and delivers them from oppression (vv. 12–14). The prayer is that "all nations will be blessed through him" (v. 17). We are reminded here of the Abrahamic covenant (Gen 12:3).

Verses 18–19 do not form a part of the prayer for the king. As noted above, these verses serve as the doxology for the whole of Book 2, which ends with Psalm 72. For verse 20, see above.

Psalm 72 is a psalm which finds relevance to our context. We live in a world where the rich becomes richer and the poor becomes poorer. This is true in my own country, the Philippines. We may trace this to the failure of leaders to execute their God-given responsibility of taking care of the poor and the marginalized. Corruption and injustice characterize their rule, rather than righteousness and justice.

But we should not blame only the leaders; we also have a responsibility. In addition to being good citizens, we are commanded by Scriptures to pray for those in authority (1 Tim 2:1–2). Whatever happens to our leaders has an

---

4. "May he live" in the Hebrew is "may they fear you." But it does not seem to make sense in the present context. So most translations follow the Septuagint. The phrase "while the sun endures and as long as the moon" is another way of saying "forever." The wish is that there will always be someone in the king's line to rule.

5. The word translated as "abundance" occurs only here and the meaning is uncertain. But the context of the verse supports this rendering.

effect on us. We are in the same boat, so to speak. In praying for our leaders, we need to be discerning as well. There are times when we may need to pray that God bring down our leaders, especially when they are corrupt (see Ps 59). Although we are to pray primarily for peace, there are times when we need to pray for a change in leadership, for the sake of the poor and needy. May God's will be done on earth as it is in heaven!

BIBLIOGRAPHY

Abriol, Jose C. "Mga Salmo [Psalms]." In *Ang Banal Na Biblia [The Holy Bible]*. Manila, Philippines: St. Paul Publications, 1967.

Adeney-Risakotta, Bernard. "Is There a Meaning in Natural Disasters? Constructions of Culture, Religion, and Science." *Exchange* 38, no. 3 (2009): 226–243.

Adeyemo, Tokunboh, ed. *Africa Bible Commentary*. Nairobi, Kenya: Word Alive/ Grand Rapids: Zondervan, 2006.

Alejo, Albert E. *Tao po! Tuloy!* Quezon City, Philippines: Ateneo de Manila University, 1990.

Alexander, Joseph A. *Commentary on Psalms*. Grand Rapids: Kregel, 1991.

Alter, Robert. *The Art of Biblical Poetry*. New York: Basic, 1985.

———. "The Poetic and Wisdom Books." In *Cambridge Companion to Biblical Interpretation*. Edited by John Barton. Cambridge, UK: Cambridge University Press, 1998.

———. *The Book of Psalms: A Translation with Commentary*. New York: W. W. Norton, 2007.

Anderson, A. A. *The Book of Psalms*. Vol. 1. NCB. London: Oliphants, 1972.

Baethgen, Friedrich. *Die Psalmen*. HKAT. Göttingen: Vandenhoeck & Ruprecht, 1904.

Bankoff, Greg. *Cultures of Disaster: Society and Natural Hazard in the Philippines*. London and New York: RoutledgeCurzon, 2003.

Bautista, Violeta Villaroman. "Spirituality and Resilience in Disaster Situations: Sources of Life and Strength in Critical Times." In *Walking with God: Christian Spirituality in the Asian Context*, edited by Charles R. Ringma and Karen Hollenbeck-Wuest, 164–183. Manila: Asian Theological Seminary and OMF Literature, 2014.

Begrich, Joachim. "Das Priesterliche Heilsorakel." *ZAW* 52, no. 1 (1934): 81–92.

Beltran, Benigno P. *Faith and Struggle on Smokey Mountain: Hope for a Planet in Peril*. Maryknoll, New York: Orbis, 2013.

Berger Peter L. and Brigitte Berger. *Sociology: A Biographical Approach*. New York: Penguin Books, 1972.

Berlin, Adele. "Introduction to Hebrew Poetry." In *NIB, Vol. 4*. Nashville: Abingdon, 1996.

Bratcher, Robert G., and William D. Reyburn. *A Translator's Handbook on the Book of Psalms*. *Helps for Translators*. New York: United Bible Societies, 1991.

Braude, William G. *The Midrash on Psalms*. New Haven: Yale University Press, 1959.

Brown, Michael. "*ashre*." In *NIDOTTE* I:570–572.

———. "*barak*." In *NIDOTTE* I:757–767.

Broyles, Craig C. *Psalms*. Peabody, Mass: Hendrickson / Carlisle, Cumbria: Paternoster, 1999.

Brueggemann, Walter. *The Message of the Psalms: A Theological Commentary*. Minneapolis: Augsburg, 1984.

———. *Hopeful Imagination: Prophetic Voices in Exile*. Philadelphia: Fortress, 1986.

Brueggemann, Walter, and Patrick D. Miller. *The Psalms and the Life of Faith*. Minneapolis: Fortress, 1995.

Calvin, John. *Commentary on the Book of Psalms*. Translated by James Anderson. Grand Rapids: Eerdmans, 1949.

Capulong, Noriel C. "Land, Power and People's Rights in the Old Testament: From a Filipino Theological Perspective." *East Asia Journal of Theology* 2 (1984): 233–243.

Castellino, Giorgio. "Psalm 32:9." *VT* 2, no. 1 (1952): 37–42.

Caussade, Jean Pierre de. *The Sacrament of the Present Moment*. San Francisco: Harper & Row, 1982.

Ceresko, Anthony R. "The ABCs of Wisdom in Psalm 34." *VT* 35, no. 1 (1985): 99–104.

Childs, Brevard S. *Memory and Tradition in Israel*. Naperville: A. R. Allenson, 1962.

———. *Introduction to the Old Testament as Scripture*. Philadelphia: Fortress, 1979.

Clifford, Richard J. *Psalms 1–72*. Nashville: Abingdon, 2002.

Cole, Robert Alan. "An Integrated Reading of Psalms 1 and 2." *JSOT* 26, no. 4 (2002): 75–88.

Constantino, Josefina D. *The Asian Religious Sensibility and Christian (Carmelite) Spirituality*. Quezon City, Philippines: The University of the Philippines Press, 1983.

Constantino, Renato, and Letizia R. Constantino. *A History of the Philippines: From the Spanish Colonization to the Second World War*. New York: Monthly Review Press, 1975.

Craigie, Peter C. *Psalms 1–50*. Waco: Word Books, 1983.

Davidson, Robert. *The Courage to Doubt: Exploring an Old Testament Theme*. London; Philadelphia: SCM Press; Trinity Press International, 1983.

Davies, William D., and Dale C Allison. *Matthew: A Shorter Commentary*. London; New York: T&T Clark, 2004.

Davis, Ellen F. "Exploding the Limits: Form and Function in Psalm 22." *JSOT* 53 (1992): 93–105.

Day, John. *Psalms*. Sheffield, U. K.: JSOT Press, 1990.

Demarest, Bruce A. *Seasons of the Soul: Stages of Spiritual Development*. Downers Grove: IVP Books, 2009.

Delitzsch, Franz. *Psalms*. In Carl Friedrich Keil and Franz Delitizsch, *Commentary on the Old Testament*. Vol. 5. Grand Rapids: Eerdmans, 1980.

Dumbrell, W. J. "*anah.*" In *NIDOTTE* 3:454–464.

Eaton, John Herbert. "The Psalms and Israelite Worship." In *Tradition and Interpretation*, edited by George W. Anderson, 238–273. Oxford: Oxford University Press, Clarendon Press, 1979.

———. *The Psalms: A Historical and Spiritual Commentary with an Introduction and New Translation.* London; New York: T&T Clark, 2003.

Edwards, Timothy M. *Exegesis in the Targum of the Psalms: The Old, the New, and the Rewritten.* Piscataway: Gorgias Press, 2007.

Erbele-Küster, Dorothea. *Lesen als Akt des Betens: eine Rezeptionsästhetik der Psalmen.* Neukirchen-Vluyn: Neukirchener Verlag, 2001.

Exum, J. Cheryl. *Tragedy and Biblical Narrative: Arrows of the Almighty.* Cambridge: Cambridge University Press, 1992.

Fernandez, Pablo, O. P. *History of the Church in the Philippines, 1521–1898.* Manila, Philippines: National Book Store, 1979.

Fokkelman, Jan P. *Reading Biblical Poetry: An Introductory Guide.* Louisville: Westminster John Knox Press, 2001.

Foskett, Mary F., and Jeffrey Kah-Jin Kuan. *Ways of Being, Ways of Reading: Asian American Biblical Interpretation.* St. Louis: Chalice Press, 2006.

Foster, Richard J. *Celebration of Discipline: The Path to Spiritual Growth.* San Francisco: Harper & Row, 1988.

Fox, Michael V. *A Time to Tear Down and a Time to Build up: A Rereading of Ecclesiastes.* Grand Rapids: Eerdmans, 1999.

Gadamer, Hans-Georg. "Reflections on My Philosophical Journey." In *The Philosophy of Hans-Georg Gadamer,* edited by Lewis Edwin Hahn. Chicago: Open Court, 1997.

Gaspar, Karl M. *Desperately Seeking God's Saving Action: Yolanda Survivors' Hope Beyond Heartbreaking Lamentations.* Quezon City, Philippines: Institute of Spirituality in Asia, 2014.

Gibran, Kahlil. *The Prophet.* New York: Knopf, 1952.

Gillingham, Susan E. *The Poems and Psalms of the Hebrew Bible.* Oxford, UK: Oxford University Press, 1994.

Goldingay, John. *Songs from a Strange Land: Psalms 42–51.* Downers Grove: IVP, 1978.

———. *Psalms,* Vol. 1. Grand Rapids: Baker Academic. 2006.

———. *Psalms,* Vol. 2. Grand Rapids: Baker Academic. 2007.

Grassi, Joseph A. "Child, Children," *ABD* 1: 904–907.

Griffiths, Paul J. *Religious Reading: The Place of Reading in the Practice of Religion.* New York: Oxford University Press, 1999.

Greenberg, Moshe. *Biblical Prose: Prayer as a Window to the Popular Religion of Ancient Israel.* Berkeley: University of California Press, 1983.

Grogan, Geoffrey W. *Psalms.* Grand Rapids: Eerdmans, 2008.

Gunkel, Hermann. *Die Psalmen*. HKAT; Göttingen: Vandenhoeck & Ruprecht, 1926.

———. *The Psalms: A Form-Critical Introduction*. Philadelphia: Fortress, 1967.

Haase, Albert. *Athanasius: The Life of Antony of Egypt*. Downers Grove: IVP, 2012.

Harris, W. Hall, III. *The Descent of Christ: Ephesians 4:7–11 and Traditional Hebrew Imagery*. Leiden: Brill, 1996.

Heiler, Friedrich. *Prayer: A Study in the History and Psychology of Religion*. Edited and translated by Samuel McComb. New York: Oxford University Press, 1932.

Hengstenberg, Ernst W. *Commentary on the Psalms*. 3d ed. Edinburgh: T&T Clark, 1851.

Holladay, William L. *The Psalms through Three Thousand Years: Prayerbook of a Cloud of Witnesses*. Minneapolis: Fortress, 1993.

Holladay, William L., and Ludwig Köhler. *A Concise Hebrew and Aramaic Lexicon of the Old Testament, Based Upon the Lexical Work of Ludwig Koehler and Walter Baumgartner*. Grand Rapids: Eerdmans, 1971.

Hwa, Yung. *Mangoes or Bananas?: The Quest for an Authentic Asian Christian Theology*. Oxford, England; Irving, California: Regnum International, 1997.

Ileto, Reynaldo Clemeña. *Pasyon and Revolution: Popular Movements in the Philippines, 1840–1910*. Quezon City, Philippines: Ateneo de Manila University Press, 1979.

Jenkins, Philip. "Reading the Bible in the Global South." *International Bulletin of Missionary Research* 30, no. 2 (2006): 67–73.

Johnson, Vivian L. *David in Distress: His Portrait through the Historical Psalms*. New York: T&T Clark, 2009.

Johnston, Philip. *Interpreting the Psalms: Issues and Approaches*. Downers Grove: IVP/Leicester, UK: Apollos, 2005.

Keel, Othmar. *The Symbolism of the Biblical World: Ancient Near Eastern Iconography and the Book of Psalms*. Winona Lake: Eisenbrauns, 1997.

Kidner, Derek. *Psalms 1–72: An Introduction and Commentary on Books I and II of the Psalms*. Leicester: IVP, 1973.

Kierkegaard, Søren. *Purity of Heart Is to Will One Thing: Spiritual Preparation for the Office of Confession*. New York: Harper, 1956.

Kirkpatrick, Alexander F. *The Book of Psalms*. Cambridge, UK: University Press, 1895.

Klouda, S. L. "Zion." In *Dictionary of the Old Testament: Wisdom, Poetry, and Writings*, edited by Tremper Longman III and Peter Enns. Downers Grove: IVP, 2008.

Hans-Joachim Kraus. *Worship in Israel: A Cultic History of the Old Testament*. Translated by Geoffrey Buswell. Atlanta: John Knox Press, 1965.

———. *Psalms 1–59: A Commentary*. Minneapolis: Augsburg, 1988.

Kugel, James L. *The Idea of Biblical Poetry: Parallelism and Its History*. New Haven: Yale University Press, 1981.

———. "Topics in the History of the Spirituality of the Psalms." In *Jewish Spirituality: From the Bible through the Middle Ages. Vol. 1*. Edited by Arthur Green. London: SCM Press, 1986.

Lee, Moonjang. "Asian Biblical Interpretation." In *Dictionary for Theological Interpretation of the Bible*, edited by Kevin J. Vanhoozer. Grand Rapids: Baker, 2005.

———. "Asian Theology." In *Global Dictionary of Theology*, edited by William A. Dyrness and Veli-Matti Kärkkäinen. Downers Grove: IVP, 2008.

LeFebvre, Michael. "Torah-Meditation and the Psalms: The Invitation of Psalm 1." In *Interpreting the Psalms: Issues and Approaches*, edited by David Firth and Philip S. Johnston. Downers Grove: IVP, 2005.

Legaspi, Leonardo Z. "Filipino Elements in Spirituality." In *Elements of Filipino Spirituality*. Manila, Philippines: Center for Spirituality-Manila, 2002.

Lewis, C. S. *Reflections on the Psalms*. London: Geoffrey Bles, 1958.

Long, Thomas G. *Preaching and the Literary Forms of the Bible*. Philadelphia: Fortress, 1989.

Lowth, Robert. *Lectures on the Sacred Poetry of the Hebrews*. Translated by G. Gregory. Andover: Crocker & Brewster, 1829.

Lucas, Ernest. *Exploring the Old Testament*. Vol. 3. Downers Grove: IVP, 2003.

Lund, Øystein. "From the Mouth of Babes and Infants You Have Established Strength." *SJOT* 11, no. 1 (1997): 78–99.

Maggay, Melba Padilla. *Transforming Society*. Quezon City, Philippines: Institute for Studies in Asian Church and Culture, 1996.

———.*Pahiwatig: Kagawiang Pangkomunikasyon ng Filipino*. Quezon City, Philippines: Ateneo de Manila University Press, 2002.

Mays, James Luther. *Psalms*. Louisville: John Knox Press, 1994.

———. *Preaching and Teaching the Psalms*. Edited by Patrick D. Miller and Gene M. Tucker. Louisville: Westminster John Knox Press, 2006.

McCann, J. Clinton, Jr. *A Theological Introduction to the Book of Psalms: The Psalms as Torah*. Nashville: Abingdon, 1993.

———. "The Shape and Shaping of the Psalter." *JSOT*. Sheffield, UK: JSOT Press, 1993.

———. "The Book of Psalms." In *NIB, Vol. 4*, edited by Leander E. Keck. Nashville: Abingdon, 1996.

———. "Get Lost, God! A Sermon on Psalm 39," *Journal for Preachers* 31, no. 4 (2008): 21–23.

McNamara, Martin. *Palestinian Judaism and the New Testament*. Dublin: Veritas, 1983.

Medina, Buenaventura S. *The Primal Passion: Tagalog Literature in the Nineteenth Century*. Manila, Philippines: Centro Escolar University, Research and Development Center, 1976.

Melvin, James F. "Psalm 44 (45) and Nuptial Spirituality in Juan de Avila's Audi, Filia." In *Psalms in the Early Modern World*, edited by Linda Phyllis Austern, Kari Boyd McBride, and David Orvis, 175–190. Farnham, England: Ashgate, 2011.

Merton, Thomas. *Bread in the Wilderness*. New York: New Directions Books, 1953.

Mesa, José M. de. *In Solidarity with the Culture: Studies in Theological Re-rooting*. Quezon City, Philippines: Maryhill, 1987.

———. *Kapag Namayani ang Kagandahang-loob ng Diyos*. Quezon City, Philippines: Claretian Publications, 1990.

Miller, Patrick D. "The Beginning of the Psalter." In *The Shape and Shaping of the Psalter*, edited by J. Clinton McCann. Sheffield, UK: JSOT Press, 1993.

Morga, Antonio de. *Historical Events of the Philippine Islands: Published in Mexico in 1609*. Manila: José Rizal National Centennial Commission, 1962.

Muilenburg, James. "Psalm 47." *JBL* 63, no. 3 (1944): 235–256.

Negoiță, A. and H. Ringgren. "*haghah*." In *TDOT* 3:321–324.

———. "Meditation in the OT." In *TDOT* 3:323.

Nel, Philip J. "*šlm*." In *NIDOTTE*, 4:135.

Okorocha, Cyril, and Francis Foulkes. "Psalms." In *ABCS*, edited by Tokunboh Adeyemo. Nairobi, Kenya: Word Alive/Grand Rapids: Zondervan, 2006.

Packer, J. I. *Knowing God*. Downers Grove, Ill.: InterVarsity Press, 1973.

Palugod, Sylvia. *Filipino Religious Consciousness*. Track 2 Report, ISACC Conversion to Protestant Christianity Research, 1999.

Perrine, Laurence. *Sound and Sense: An Introduction to Poetry*. New York: Harcourt Brace Jovanovich, 1977.

Pieris, Aloysius. *An Asian Theology of Liberation*. Maryknoll, New York: Orbis, 1988.

Pilario, Daniel Franklin, ed. "Spirituality and Postmodernity in Asia." In *Spirituality of Authentic Witnesses in Postmodern Asia*. Spirituality Forum and Institute of Spirituality in Asia, Spirituality Forum. Quezon City, Philippines: Institute of Spirituality in Asia, 2007.

Raabe, Paul R. "Deliberate Ambiguity in the Psalter." *JBL* 110, no. 2 (1991): 213–227.

Rad, Gerhard von. *Old Testament Theology. Vol. 1*. Edinburgh and London: Oliver and Boyd, 1962.

Rayan, Samuel. "Reconceiving Theology in the Asian Context." In *Doing Theology in a Divided World, January 5–13, 1983, Geneva, Switzerland*, edited by Virginia Fabella and Sergio Torres. Maryknoll, New York: Orbis, 1985.

Rempola, Leo E. "Kundiman as a Vehicle for Worship, Witness, and Service in the Philippine Context." In *Doing Theology in the Philippines*, edited by John D. Suk. Asian Theological Seminary; OMF Literature, 2005.

Reyburn, William D. *A Translator's Handbook on the Book of Psalms*. New York: UBS, 1991.

Ringma, Charles R. *Hear the Ancient Wisdom*. London: SPCK, 2013.

Ringgren, Helmer. *The Faith of the Psalmists*. London: SCM Press, 1963.

Roberts, Joseph. *Oriental Illustrations of the Sacred Scriptures Collected from the Customs, Manners, Rites, Superstitions, Traditions, Parabolical, Idiomatical, and Proverbial Forms of Speech, Climate, Works of Art, and Literature, of the Hindoos*. 2d ed. London: Printed for Thomas Tegg, 1844.

Ryken, Leland. *Words of Delight: A Literary Introduction to the Bible*. 2d ed. Grand Rapids: Baker, 1992.

Sarna, Nahum M. *Songs of the Heart: An Introduction to the Book of Psalms*. New York: Schocken, 1993.

———. *On the Book of Psalms: Exploring the Prayers of Ancient Israel*. New York: Schocken, 1993.

Schaefer, Konrad. *Psalms*. Collegeville: Liturgical Press, 2001.

Schökel, Luis Alonso. "The Poetic Structure of Psalm 42–43." *JSOT* 1, no. 1 (1976): 4–11.

Scobie, Charles H. H. "Biblical Theology and Preaching." In *Out of Egypt: Biblical Theology and Biblical Interpretation*, edited by Craig G. Bartholomew et al., 448–464. Grand Rapids: Zondervan, 2004.

Seybold, Klaus. *Die Psalmen*. Vol. I/15; Handbuch zum Alten Testament. Tübingen: J. C. B. Mohr (Paul Siebeck), 1996.

Shnider, Steven. "Psalm xviii: Theophany, Epiphany Empowerment." *VT* 56, no. 3 (2006): 386–398.

Soares-Prabhu, George M. "Two Mission Commands : An Interpretation of Matthew 28:16–20 in the Light of a Buddhist Text." *BibInt* 2, no. 3 (1994): 264–282.

Soll, William Michael. *Psalm 119: Matrix, Form, and Setting*. Washington, DC: Catholic Biblical Association of America, 1991.

St. Augustine. *Expositions on the Book of Psalms*. Oxford: John H. Parker, 1847–1857.

———. *Confessions*. Oxford / New York: Oxford University Press, 1991.

St. John of the Cross. *Dark Night of the Soul*. Mineola, New York: Dover Publications, 2003.

Stec, David M. *The Targum of Psalms*. Collegeville: Liturgical, 2004.

Sugirtharajah, R. S. *Asian Biblical Hermeneutics and Postcolonialism: Contesting the Interpretations*. Maryknoll, New York: Orbis, 1998.

————. *The Bible and Asia: From the Pre-Christian Era to the Postcolonial Age.* Cambridge, Mass.: Harvard University Press, 2013.

Terrien, Samuel L. *The Psalms: Strophic Structure and Theological Commentary.* Grand Rapids: Eerdmans, 2003.

Thiselton, Anthony C. *Hermeneutics: An Introduction.* Grand Rapids: Eerdmans, 2009.

Vesco, Jean-Luc. *Le psautier de David: traduit et commenté.* Paris: Cerf, 2006.

Villanueva, Federico G. "Confession of Sins or Petition for Forgiveness: A Comparative Study of the Penitential Prayers in Ezra 9, Nehemiah 1, 9, and Daniel 9." ThM thesis. Asia Graduate School of Theology, Manila, 2002.

————. *The "Uncertainty of a Hearing": A Study of the Sudden Change of Mood in the Psalms of Lament.* Supplement to Vetus Testamentum. Leiden: Brill, 2008.

————. "Preaching Lament." In *Reclaiming the Old Testament for Christian Preaching*, edited by Grenville J. R. Kent et al. Downers Grove: IVP Academic, 2010.

————. *It's OK To Be Not OK: The Message of the Lament Psalms.* Manila, Philippines: OMF Literature, 2012.

————. "Reading the Psalms with Asian Resources." *Journal of Asian Evangelical Theology* 17, no. 1 (2013): 35–50.

————. "The 'Dark Night of the Soul,' the Lament Psalms, and Juan De La Cruz." In *Walking with God: Christian Spirituality in the Asian Context*, edited by Charles Ringma et al. Manila, Philippines: ATS/OMF Literature, 2014.

————. "The Rejoicing Church in a Suffering Asia: Participating in the 'pain of God' through the Lament Psalms." In *What Young Asian Theologians Are Thinking*, edited by Theng Huat Leow. Singapore: Trinity Theological College, 2014.

Wallace, Howard N. "*Jubilate Deo omnis terra*: God and earth in Psalm 65." In *The Earth Story in the Psalms and the Prophets*, edited by Norman C. Habel, 51–64. Sheffield, UK: Sheffield Academic Press, 2001.

————. *Words to God, Word from God: The Psalms in the Prayer and Preaching of the Church.* Burlington: Ashgate, 2004.

Waltner, James H. *Psalms.* Believers Church Bible Commentary. Scottdale PA: Herald Press, 2006.

Weber, Beat. "The 'Uncertainty of a Hearing': A Study of the Sudden Change of Mood in the Psalms of Lament." *Theologische Literaturzeitung* 134, no. 6 (2009): 681–683.

Weiser, Artur. *The Psalms. A Commentary.* Translated by Herbert Hartwell. London: SCM Press, 1962.

Welshman, F. H. "Psalm 91 in Relation to a Malawian Cultural Background." *Journal of Theology for Southern Africa* 8 (1974): 24–30.

Wenham, Gordon J. "The Ethics of the Psalms." In *Interpreting the Psalms: Issues and Approaches*, edited by Philip Johnston and David G. Firth. Downers Grove: IVP Academic, 2005.

———."Prayer and Practice in the Psalms." In *Psalms and Prayers*, edited by Bob Becking and Eric Peels. Leiden: Brill, 2007.

———. *Psalms as Torah: Reading Biblical Song Ethically*. Grand Rapids: Baker Academic, 2012.

———. *The Psalter Reclaimed: Praying and Praising with the Psalms*. Wheaton: Crossway, 2013.

Westermann Claus. "Role of the Lament in the Theology of the Old Testament." *Int* 28, no. 1 (1974): 20–38.

———. *Praise and Lament in the Psalms*. Translated by Keith R. Crim and Richard N. Soulen. Atlanta: John Knox Press, 1981.

———. "The Complaint against God." In *God in the Fray: A Tribute to Walter Brueggemann*, edited by Tod Linafelt and Timothy K. Beal. Minneapolis: Fortress, 1998.

Wilce, James M. *Crying Shame, Metaculture, Modernity, and the Exaggerated Death of Lament*. Oxford: Wiley-Blackwell, 2009.

Wilson, Gerald Henry. *The Editing of the Hebrew Psalter*. Chico, California: Scholars Press, 1985.

Yates, Kyle Monroe. *Preaching from the Psalms*. New York: Harper, 1948.

Yieh, John Y. H. "Chinese Biblical Interpretation: History and Issues." In *Ways of Being, Ways of Reading: Asian American Biblical Interpretation*, edited by Mary F. Foskett and Jeffrey K. Kuan, 17–30. St. Louis: Chalice, 2006.

Zenger, Erich. "Was Wird Anders bei kanonischer Psalmenauslegung." In *Gott, Eine Offenbarung*, edited by Friedrich V. Reiterer. Würzburg: Echter, 1991.

———. *A God of Vengeance? Understanding the Psalms of Divine Wrath*. Louisville: Westminster John Knox Press, 1996.

Zimmerli, Walther. *Old Testament Theology in Outline*. Edinburgh: T&T Clark, 1978.

Asia Theological Association

54 Scout Madriñan St. Quezon City 1103, Philippines
Email: ataasia@gmail.com Telefax: (632) 410 0312

OUR MISSION

The Asia Theological Association (ATA) is a body of theological institutions, committed to evangelical faith and scholarship, networking together to serve the Church in equipping the people of God for the mission of the Lord Jesus Christ.

OUR COMMITMENT

The ATA is committed to serving its members in the development of evangelical, biblical theology by strengthening interaction, enhancing scholarship, promoting academic excellence, fostering spiritual and ministerial formation and mobilizing resources to fulfill God's global mission within diverse Asian cultures.

OUR TASK

Affirming our mission and commitment, ATA seeks to:

- **Strengthen** interaction through inter-institutional fellowship and programs, regional and continental activities, faculty and student exchange programs.
- **Enhance** scholarship through consultations, workshops, seminars, publications, and research fellowships.
- **Promote** academic excellence through accreditation standards, faculty and curriculum development.
- **Foster** spiritual and ministerial formation by providing mentor models, encouraging the development of ministerial skills and a Christian ethos.
- **Mobilize** resources through library development, information technology and infra-structural development.

To learn more about ATA, visit www.ataasia.com   or   Facebook /AsiaTheologicalAssociation